The Softball Coaching Bible

VOLUME II

The Softball Coaching Bible

VOLUME II

National Fastpitch Coaches Association

NATIONAL FASTPITCH
COACHES ASSOCIATION

Project Coordinated by Gayle Blevins
Former Head Coach
University of Iowa

Human Kinetics

Library of Congress Cataloging-in-Publication Data

The softball coaching bible. Volume II / National Fastpitch Coaches Association ; project coordinated by Gayle Blevins, University of Iowa.
     pages cm
1. Softball--Coaching. 2. Softball for children--Coaching. I. National Fastpitch Coaches Association, editor of compilation.
  GV881.4.C6.S65 2014
  796.357'8--dc23

                                        2013017610

ISBN-10: 1-4504-2465-1 (print)
ISBN-13: 978-1-4504-2465-3 (print)

The web addresses cited in this text were current as of September 2013, unless otherwise noted.

Acquisitions Editor: Justin Klug; **Developmental Editor:** Anne Hall; **Assistant Editor:** Tyler M. Wolpert; **Copyeditor:** Bob Replinger; **Permissions Manager:** Martha Gullo; **Graphic Designer:** Nancy Rasmus; **Graphic Artist:** Tara Welsch; **Cover Designer:** Keith Blomberg; **Photograph (cover):** J.P. Wilson/Icon SMI; **Photographs (interior):** © Human Kinetics, unless otherwise noted; **Photo Asset Manager:** Laura Fitch; **Visual Production Assistant:** Joyce Brumfield; **Photo Production Manager:** Jason Allen; **Art Manager:** Kelly Hendren; **Associate Art Manager:** Alan L. Wilborn; **Illustrations:** © Human Kinetics, unless otherwise noted; **Printer:** Sheridan Books

Human Kinetics books are available at special discounts for bulk purchase. Special editions or book excerpts can also be created to specification. For details, contact the Special Sales Manager at Human Kinetics.

Printed in the United States of America   10   9   8   7   6   5   4   3   2   1

The paper in this book is certified under a sustainable forestry program.

Human Kinetics
Website: www.HumanKinetics.com

United States: Human Kinetics
P.O. Box 5076
Champaign, IL 61825-5076
800-747-4457
e-mail: humank@hkusa.com

Canada: Human Kinetics
475 Devonshire Road Unit 100
Windsor, ON N8Y 2L5
800-465-7301 (in Canada only)
e-mail: info@hkcanada.com

Europe: Human Kinetics
107 Bradford Road
Stanningley
Leeds LS28 6AT, United Kingdom
+44 (0) 113 255 5665
e-mail: hk@hkeurope.com

Australia: Human Kinetics
57A Price Avenue
Lower Mitcham, South Australia 5062
08 8372 0999
e-mail: info@hkaustralia.com

New Zealand: Human Kinetics
P.O. Box 80
Torrens Park, South Australia 5062
0800 222 062
e-mail: info@hknewzealand.com

E5677

te·na·cious
/təˈnāSHəs/

1. Not readily letting go of, giving up, or separated from an object that one holds, a position, or a principle: "a tenacious grip."
2. Not easily dispelled or discouraged; persisting in existence or in a course of action: "a tenacious legend."

This single word sums up the life of Elaine Sortino. It does not just sum up her coaching career but her very existence through her lifetime. No obstacle was big enough or difficult enough to stop Elaine from maximizing everything she could get from her players, her staff, or herself. Her last season was her first losing season in 34 years of coaching. But the wins and championships never defined her. They were just fodder for others to talk about. They were only the byproduct of what she loved to do more than anything in her life—be a coach, teacher, and educator. First and foremost, her love of teaching was the driving force behind her success. Teaching each athlete that wore the UMASS uniform through her many years of coaching—teaching each one as though they alone could be the one to make or break the team's ability to succeed and that they were important. The importance of *getting a little better every day* was her mantra to each player whether a starter, All-American, or pinch runner. Each player represented a challenge to Elaine that she relished—make them better softball players, better teammates, and better people.

She never lost sight of the big picture. Many coaches use the excuse of having to win to justify bending the rules or playing in the grey area. Elaine only ever knew that doing the right thing was always the right thing to do. She recruited players who loved the game as much as she did. She was one of the best pitching coaches in the country, and she never pitched a game in her life. She was self-taught. She worked harder than most people and loved every minute of it. The softball world will not be the same without her passion or her courage or her vision. It's lucky for all of us that a small piece of Elaine's heart resides in each former player or assistant coach who had the honor of playing for her or coaching alongside her and will hopefully one day pass on that piece to another little girl who loves the game.

Ruth Crowe

Contents

COACHING PRIORITIES AND PRINCIPLES

1

Sharing the Passion

Patty Gasso

I was sitting at a softball field recently, recruiting and taking in a travel ball game. Truthfully, I was not seeing the best talent, and I was not properly equipped for the cold and wind. It was not one of my best days. I remember asking myself, "Why am I doing this?" The pity party did not last long. I looked around the complex and saw hundreds of kids in uniform, playing in this miserable weather. Their parents were there too, bundled in blankets. I thought, "I have the ability to make one of these kids' dreams come true." That realization was powerful. I could be a major role model and a lasting member in one of those athletes' lives. The responsibility and honor for any coach is huge. So I quickly got over my griping and jumped back into my recruiting skin.

I have been blessed with the opportunity to work for the University of Oklahoma and be surrounded with wonderful coaches, athletes, and administrators. I get to go to work every day and call the softball stadium my office. How awesome! Sometimes I take this privilege for granted, and one thing I have learned as I have matured as a coach is to be thankful and to keep working hard, because the day I sit back and think that I have arrived as a coach, the program will be left in the dust. I know that I am in the right profession when after 30 years of coaching, 18 of those years at the University of Oklahoma, I feel that I have not worked a day in my life. A line from one of Jo Dee Messina's famous songs claims, "It goes so fast, and one day we look back and ask, *Was that my life?*" As I am grinning from ear to ear, the answer is an emphatic, "Yes, softball is my life."

FINDING THE PASSION

The answer to this challenge is easy. You find the passion in your heart. When you do anything with passion and put your heart and soul into it, your experience will be rewarding. Too many coaches and players are involved in this sport for the wrong reasons. This orientation is easy to see. Body language is negative; you can see a lack of effort and a lack of respect. A coach or player led by passion is easy to recognize as well—a team player, energetic, enthusiastic, fun to watch, hardworking, demonstrating a genuine love for the game. Coaches or players with passion can't wait to play or practice, and they are constantly working on ways to get better. They have an endless work ethic at an activity that never feels like work. Passionate people are infectious, and they bring out the best of those around them. Unfortunately, negative team members are just as infectious.

I began my coaching career as a junior varsity basketball coach. I was 19 years old, and some of the players were just 3 years my junior. I knew when I was growing up that I wanted to be a teacher and a coach, and by making that decision early in my life, I could immediately go to work on starting my career. The program I took over had a record of 1-14 the year before my arrival. Now I understand why they would hire a 19-year-old student to take over the program! I was pumped to get the job. I knew it would be a challenge to get those young athletes to believe in a young coach. I went in with high expectations and had a personal goal of getting the team to win at least five games. I would have to get rid of the negative feelings left over from the previous season, and I recognized that my most important job was to create a positive and winning attitude. Confidence and a winning expectation had to come oozing out of me at our first meeting. I set the ground rules and talked about my philosophy of blue-collar work (no one will ever outwork us), of working as a team and respecting each other. They then heard the most important phrase I would ever share, and it is still the focus of my players to this day: We will never quit—ever. It is not an option!

My first coaching season was going pretty well. Halfway through the season we had already won four games. I thought it was cool to dress up as a professional when I was coaching JV basketball, although it was apparent that my peers did not share my thought process!

A situation happened to me on the court that season, now 30 years ago, that I will never forget—one of those life-changing moments. We were in an intense game against our conference rival, and the referee made what I thought was a terrible call. I made it known to the ref that I did not agree with his call, and he made a comment that has never left me. The referee said to me in front of my players, "Coach, relax, this is just a JV girls' basketball game!" Ouch. I voiced my passion that day with the referee, and at 19 years old, in my first season as a head coach, I was thrown out of my first game. I thought, "Maybe I'm not cut out for this coaching thing." But my actions that day confirmed to me that my passion for women's athletics and for my team was needed to get the respect we deserved. I am not proud of my outburst, but I would not have changed a thing. My players learned a lesson that day—that they deserved the same respect given to any male athlete—and they understood that I believed in them enough to fight for them. The team went on a winning streak and finished the season with 10 wins, 1 win away from the conference title. Whether it's a junior varsity girls' basketball game or a collegiate women's softball program, girls and women who put their heart and soul into their sport deserve to be taken seriously and treated with dignity and respect. Our job as coaches is to make sure that happens. Passion is about feeling—and acting on that feeling!

WHY ATHLETES TODAY MAY LOSE PASSION

For those of us who have been coaching for a while now, we would all agree that coaching today's athletes is definitely a challenge. Capturing and keeping their attention is difficult. We are dealing with some stiff competition! Cell phones with texting, Twitter, Facebook, blogging—the list goes on. I have not figured out a way to stop this besides keeping it off the field, out of the locker room, and off the bus. My conclusion is that the youth of today need constant stimulation. If you can't beat 'em, join 'em! I make sure that my practices are active and require the players to move constantly. I come up with new practice plans and drills that are relevant and challenging. I try to break practice into segments so that we have the ability to start over and refocus. My players do not get much out of long, drawn-out practices. Don't get me wrong; sometimes these practices are necessary. But my players work best with constant challenges, and I try to bring that every day.

I am fortunate to have peers who share their ideas and their struggles. Many coaches today are struggling with athletes who do not know how to compete. Young athletes can play up to six games a day! How can we expect them to have passion for six games straight? It's an impossible feat. I need athletes who will put it all on the field every day and not look at the competition as just another game. I have a hard time with that. My plan to combat this problem is to make my fall season a challenging and competitive experience. Each day I challenge my athletes, especially in strength training and conditioning. I believe that to get my athletes to understand how to compete, they have to be pushed not to the wall, but through the wall. They have to be deprogrammed from having the attitude that it doesn't matter to taking extreme pride in their efforts. Athletes have to feel the good and the bad and learn how to fight through the tough times. I think that athletes are too quick to surrender. They don't want to put their heart out there, because if they do and they are not successful, they will feel the hurt, shame, or embarrassment. The greatest coach of all time, John Wooden, said, "For an athlete to function properly, she must be intent. There has to be a definite purpose and goal if you are to progress. If you are not intent about what you are doing, you aren't able to resist the temptation to do something else that might be more fun at the moment."

WHERE DID ALL THE LEADERS GO?

When I was growing up, my back gate opened up into a city park that had four softball diamonds, outdoor basketball courts, swings, monkey bars, rings, slides, and lots of open field. Talk about a kid's heaven on earth! During summers I was at the park from 8:00 a.m. until my mom called me home for dinner (no cell phones back then, just the distinct sound of my mother's voice). All the gang knew to meet up at the park, and we would play all day long. It seemed that I never got tired, never too hot or cold, and I did not want to spend time eating because it would take away from my playtime. It was a blast! I realize now that all those hours of play molded me into the coach I am today. I played everything, from softball to flag football, basketball, dodge ball, capture the flag, kick ball—the list goes on. I found that I had some athletic ability, and because I was one of the more athletic girls out there, my friends depended on me to take charge—to make the teams, establish the rules, and set the boundaries (usually pieces of trash were used as bases). Are leaders born or made? I learned at a young age that my friends counted on me to get the games started at the park each day, and I learned that I really loved being that person. The idea of becoming a high school coach was a dream for me ever since I was young. I definitely had the passion burning in me to make that dream come true.

I am an advocate for making sure that young athletes get proper training. Today there seems to be a coach for everything from pitching, hitting, and defense to fitness and strength, running form, and mental training. If you have a need, someone will be able to give you a lesson for it. Training athletes has become a big business. Multisport athletes are becoming a rarity. The commitment now is to year-round training in one sport. I can understand the decision to focus on one sport, especially if a collegiate future is a possibility.

But with so many adults telling these kids what to do and how to do it, I find that these young athletes have no game savvy! The way they play the game is almost robotic. Not much feeling is involved, and if it is, it's purely about individual performance. What happened to the team players? Where did all the leaders go? What happened to the athlete who is passionate for the game, who is upset after a loss and overjoyed following a win? I think many coaches are searching for this answer.

If you want to find out who the natural leaders are on your team and which ones have the passion to compete, go to practice one day with just one softball. Throw it out on the field, go sit in the bleachers, and be ready to bite your tongue! Have them figure out who plays on what team, how to call balls and strikes, and who makes safe and out calls. You will learn a lot from this experience. You may find out that the athlete who you are ready to name captain is someone the players will not respond to. By becoming a spectator at your own practice, you will witness which athletes compete and have the independence to stand on their own. Then you may see the opposite—athletes who are rebellious, not giving their all, not playing with the passion that we are searching for. Some may be saying, "This is stupid. Why are we doing this?" Pay attention to this attitude because it can destroy your program!

I've had to make some tough decisions in my coaching career, and over a year ago I made one of the toughest of my career. I had too many athletes who did not have the passion and commitment that I believed was needed for us to continue to win championships. I needed to take action. I called each of these athletes into the office and tried to talk them into becoming regular students—no more 6:00 a.m. workouts, hard practices, or aching body parts. Freedom to work and make money, hang out with friends, and have more free time. I made it enticing. The problem was that five of them took me up on the offer! But I appreciated their being honest with their feelings, and we parted ways the right way. Now here was my new problem—no depth. How can we win with 15 players, 3 of whom are pitchers only? You will be amazed what can happen when you get a group of athletes on the field who have the same goals, ambition, and passion to win as a team! I never enjoyed a season more, and I was proud of what that team accomplished.

With a depleted lineup, we went on the road to Arizona, winning the best two out of three super regional and making our way back to the Women's College World Series! Players thanked me at the end of the season for my decision to let go of the players who had lost the passion. In return they wanted to prove to me that they could accomplish anything—and they did. That season was one of the most rewarding of my career, and I will never forget the lesson I learned: I must surround the program with athletes who have a mission and a goal to be national champions, even if it means making tough decisions. Passion is about feeling—and acting on that feeling!

A COACH'S RESPONSIBILITY

I think it is cool to be called Coach Gasso. I take it as a form of respect. I also take it as a great responsibility. I have been called to make a difference in the lives of young people. My job is not only to coach them but also to mentor them and prepare them for real life. Unfortunately, collegiate softball athletes who move on to the NPF (National Professional Fastpitch) league do not make million-dollar contracts (maybe someday!) but barely enough to live on. The lights on the field will eventually go out, and my job is to make sure that my athletes are ready to face the world. Here are a few life skills that I hope I can leave them with.

Confidence and Self-Esteem

Whether it is on the softball field or in life, I want my athletes to exude confidence. The coach's task here is difficult. You may have players who have been pushed so hard by their parents that they think they can't do anything right. Other kids are full of excuses; they have to blame someone else for their shortcomings. They are afraid of failure. Some athletes I have met are fragile and afraid to look me in the eyes. They have weak handshakes. They have horrible body language. How do I combat this? First, I never wear sunglasses. I want the athletes to see my eyes. I believe that the eyes are the window to the soul. I want the players to see what I am feeling, and I will make them look at me whenever we are talking, whether at practice or before or after a game. It is important that we connect, and I can tell a lot about the way an athlete is feeling when I look into her eyes. My goal is to bring out a glowing confidence in every one of my players, both on and off the field. We also talk often about appearance and dressing for success. Whenever we fly, I expect the team members to wear dresses, skirts, or nice slacks. We are travel-ing for a business trip, and I want the team to have that mind-set. I also expect all athletes to attend class in proper attire—no sweat pants, sweat shirts, or practice gear. When they are in the classroom, they are students and should dress like students; when they are on the field, then they can wear practice gear.

For me to have any kind of influence on my players, they must trust me. I work to find time to talk with my athletes, build a relationship, and find out what motivates them in life. I encourage my players to stand up for what they believe in and never quit. It is interesting to see the interactions of the athletes at a big university like the University of Oklahoma, where football is king. The female athletes change when they are around the male athletes, almost as if the male athletes are royalty. I want my players to believe that they are as important as any male athlete on campus and to understand that they work just as hard and deserve the same respect. I want my athletes to fight for themselves and never let anyone mistreat them or disrespect them, whether on the field or in their social life. Getting young females to be full of confidence and self-esteem is not easy, but I have a passion for sending my players out into the real world ready for whatever comes their way.

Ultimately, what I am after is for my athletes to discover a sense of independence. They need to be able to stand on their own two feet. They will never become independent if things are always handed to them or if we as coaches are always there to bail them out. It drives me nuts to watch athletes on the field, especially the pitcher on the mound, who are constantly looking in the dugout for a coach's approval. We need to allow our athletes to make mistakes and let them know that messing up is OK. Mistakes are the greatest learning tool. Athletes need to count on themselves—no lame excuses or blaming others. No crutch! We want them to take accountability for their actions and their lives, and to trust themselves.

Pride

The definition of pride is a "sense of personal dignity." Pride is correlated with confidence and self-esteem, but my push is for athletes to take pride in representing themselves and our university in everything they do. Wearing the Sooner uniform is a privilege, not a right! You reap what you sow; you earn what you get. I invest my time wisely and with my heart. I work hard for it, and it means something to me.

As a coach I understand this saying: "If you don't have the struggles, you won't know the strengths." I have witnessed teams go on major emotional roller coasters. The coaster is going straight down, and it looks as if there is no light at the end of the tunnel. The ride isn't fun! But the trip is necessary to get where you want to go. Many athletes do not want to experience this kind of frustration, pain, and embarrassment, but the mature athlete understands that this experience is part of her development. Sometimes it hurts a lot, but to me, feeling is a lost art! I want my players to have a sick feeling after a loss, because they worked hard and then let someone prevent them from reaching their goal. My trust is that they do not want to experience that sick feeling again. Any time you invest your heart and soul and it doesn't work out the way you want it to, it will hurt, but when it does work, no feeling is sweeter and more rewarding in your pursuit of excellence! Legendary football coach Vince Lombardi once said, "The harder you work, the harder it is to surrender."

These are the sources that drive pride:

- Pure enjoyment and passion for the pursuit
- Desire to feel important and successful
- The quest to fulfill your potential
- Pride in your performance
- Joy or love of ongoing learning and improvement

KEEPING THE PASSION

Maintaining passion is challenging because at times we all experience a sense of burnout. I think that feeling comes with hard work. Having a chance to breathe and gain a renewed spirit and sense of excitement toward your players, your practices, and your season is important. I know that December is an important month for me to unwind from the stress of practice and recruiting. I use the time to become rejuvenated for the team to return in January and get hungry for the start of the season. What can I do about the other 11 months?

Balance

In the book *Life Wisdom From John Wooden*, Coach Wooden wrote, "Don't let making a living prevent you from making a life." One of the greatest gifts we can give our athletes is to demonstrate balance in our lives. We may think what we do is the most important thing in the world and that the softball world cannot exist without us. Get over yourself! I am fortunate to have a husband who reminds me of this every day. At times, I could work until midnight every night because I think that there are not enough hours in the day. I realize now that the same work will be there for me tomorrow.

When I come home from practice or from the office, I need to let go of my job and focus on my job as a wife and mother. I have to be honest and say that I don't always do this. I often find that when I'm at home I am thinking about a new lineup or new drills, about why our practice did not go well, and so on. Getting softball out of my head can be difficult. I found that if I can get home and engage myself with my kids or husband and not talk much about softball, I don't think about it as much. As a wife, mother, and coach, I am pulled in many directions. Many times I have thought that as a mother of two kids I should not be coaching. The time and travel required to do this job successfully is not fair to my kids. But I also know that God led me into this position of coaching at a young age and that my mission is to work with young people and be instrumental in helping change their lives. I had a conversation with my kids when they were young (they are 23 and 17 now) about what I do for a living. I asked them whether they wanted me to stop coaching. They said, "Mom, you wouldn't be who you are if you weren't coaching. You are supposed to be a coach and we love you!" That was all the confirmation I needed, and it helps that they get great seats for all OU football games!

Continue to Learn

I have been coaching long enough now that it is easy to think that I know enough about softball and coaching. But that is not the case, and I am smart enough to know that! I enjoy speaking at coaching clinics, mostly so that I can hear other coaches speak on a variety of subjects. I love to learn about new ways of doing things. I am also interested in sport psychology and finding better ways of communicating with my athletes and coaches. Knowledge is power, and it will keep you ahead of the game. Proverbs 24:5 reads, "A wise man had great power, and a man of knowledge increases strength." If I can increase my strength as a coach through knowledge, I will be passionate about learning!

Love What You Do and Show It

I know I am one of the luckiest and most blessed people on earth because I love what I do and get to do it every day. I hope that my athletes feel this energy from me daily. Don't get me wrong—not every day is full of roses. We will not always be at our best. But remember that we have a huge responsibility to our athletes. They are counting on us to bring discipline, organization, structure, knowledge, and accountability, which all lead to their feeling a sense of security and comfort. Athletes need to master these important qualities so that they can let go of distractions and be at their best.

Finally, just as it is important for our athletes to show their emotions, we as coaches need to share our passion with our athletes. By sharing, I have formed a trusting bond with my athletes. I may feel a little vulnerable at times, but I am real about it and not afraid to show it, good or bad. I am not big on showing affection, but you can be sure that my athletes know how I feel about them. They have my heart, and they know it. I am fully invested with each one of them. I celebrate with them, and I hurt with them. If you ask an athlete who the most influential person is in her life, she is likely to name a coach she has worked with throughout her playing career. I want to be that person! My passion is to change lives first and win championships second. Remember: Passion is about feeling—and acting on that feeling!

FINAL THOUGHTS

The day I start thinking about being tired of volunteering all my time, feeling taken for granted, and feeling unappreciated is the day I need to retire. I am not in it for the praise or notoriety. We put in too many hours, and we are not always paid accordingly. If you want to be monetarily rich, this is not the profession for you! The rewards of coaching are the grin that an athlete gives you when she achieves something she has been working hard for, the hugs you get after a huge victory, the sense of pride you feel watching your team handling adversity and never giving up, the long thank-you letters you receive from your former student-athletes. These are what keep me going. Retired NFL quarterback Kurt Warner states in the book *The Greatest Leader Ever*, "Leading is less difficult when you love what you do."

CHAPTER

2

Defining Expectations

Jeanne Scarpello

In my 13 years as a head coach, I tried to keep things simple. As all programs do, we try our best to surround ourselves with good people, from the people we hire to the athletes we recruit. We try to have high standards not only for our athletes but also for our coaching staff. I believe that success comes from communicating what we expect from all and then consistently holding our team members to those standards. By doing those two things, communicating and holding members accountable, I think that any coach can help set a culture within her or his program. Having a culture at any program means that the team will have a set of shared attitudes, values, goals, and practices that characterizes the organization. When looking at that definition, think about how you want your players to carry themselves at practices, at games, in the classroom, and in everyday life. Through your expectations you can instill in your players some discipline and confidence regarding their attitudes and influence their demeanor, the way they speak, and the way they think.

GOALS VERSUS EXPECTATIONS

Every year most if not all programs set goals that can be controlled as well as some outcome goals that cannot be controlled. Outcome goals are easily measured—you either accomplish them or you don't. For some programs, the goals might be to have a team GPA of 3.3 and win a state championship, a conference championship, or even a national championship. Although you might not achieve some of your goals every year, these goals become your program's mission. Your team's goals become a target to which your team commits its effort. If teams are committed, goals should be a motivator to bring enthusiasm to practices every day. Accomplishing the mission should not be the only gauge of a success, but the mission can help athletes set their sights, their focus, and their direction for the yearlong journey. Your players should feel some excitement when they imagine the possibilities of what they can accomplish together. But for them to achieve their mission or goals, coaches must clearly communicate their daily expectations and continue to hold players accountable throughout the season.

PLAYER EXPECTATIONS

Each year your coaching staff and team leaders need to let the new team members know what you expect in terms of character, practices, games, communication, academics, and so on. Expectations should be realistically attainable and practical. Clearly and frequently stating expectations can reduce the distractions, drama, and setbacks that may occur throughout the year. We want our new players to have confidence, to be problem solvers, and to make smart and mature decisions throughout their collegiate career and later in life. Of course, talent will always help any team succeed, but if coaches can get players to meet their expectations consistently, they have a better shot at a successful season and may contend for a title.

The first item that coaches should try to accomplish to help their players buy into their standards and expectations is to teach them to have pride in the program. Most young women who have played for University of Nebraska Omaha (UNO) know that this is the only place for me. They know this because of how I speak about our program and athletic department. I love the opportunity I have to coach here at UNO, and I try to make that apparent to my players. Take the time to talk about the people who have played for your program, your past championships, and the way in which that was accomplished. If you're a building program, talk about traditions you want to develop, your vision, and how you plan to get there. You want the players to believe in the blueprint and the plans that you will have them follow. Have your players take pride in the program they play for, understand why the standards are set, and be proud of the culture at your school or organization. The players need to understand that they are continuing the culture or, for some, building the culture that will characterize your program. Here are a few simple ideas to build pride in your program: Have players wear their apparel and logo proudly, know their school fight song, know what the mascot is and what it stands for, support other athletic teams in the athletic department, and understand the history that they are representing every day. When we talk about pride, we ask our players to be the standard for our athletic department.

Expectations in Character

I believe that much of the success at our program has come from surrounding ourselves with good people. We try to recruit players who we believe already have admirable character traits. They will make mistakes throughout the course of a year, but if you have a team made up of responsible, caring, trusting, and respectful people, mistakes will occur less frequently. These four traits are important not only during their athletic careers but also later in life.

Respect

Look for players to be respectful. They should treat others as they would like to be treated. A few items that come to mind are being punctual for all meetings, practices, and events; making eye contact when speaking or when being spoken to; being aware of tone when speaking; speaking less and listening more; shaking a hand to introduce themselves; and using the phrases *please* and *thank you* every day. We respect everyone who comes in contact with our team, whether the person is an All-American pitcher, a pinch runner, a secretary, or a trainer. No matter what a person's role may be, we do our best to make that person feel valued.

Trust

Expect that your players will be trustworthy. We trust that coaches and players are doing right by the team and themselves even when no one is looking. Trust can be seen as material, such as working out on their own over a break, doing the correct number of reps in the weight room, running a captain's practice the way that we would expect, going to class even though the professor does not take roll, and going to bed at a decent hour the night before practice or a game. Trust can also be nonmaterial, such as telling the truth when asked a question or keeping it to themselves when told a secret. We don't encourage secrets on our team, but we do expect our players to keep it within our family when we have taken disciplinary action. After trust is broken, it is hard to rebuild. Trust takes time, dedication, and commitment. We ask our players to keep these four points in mind: Do what you say, never lie, volunteer information to prove that you have nothing to hide, and don't omit important details.

I had a player who chose not to attend some of her classes. The professor was not taking roll, so there was no reason to go to class because she assumed that I would not find out. Well, I asked our player whether she was attending her classes. I could tell by the look on her face that she knew she was caught. My trust was broken. We needed to find a way to rebuild the trust. We decided to have her professors sign a sheet every time she was in class. They were not to sign it if our player was a second late to class or left a second early. Every day, she would hand me a sheet with all her professors' signatures on it. If she didn't produce a sheet, she would not practice, which meant that she would not play. Imagine this—our player soon explained to me how much you can learn by going to class. She earned back my trust (after three months of signatures), and now I believe that we have instilled the habit of consistently going to class even though we no longer collect the signatures. Of course, this episode encouraged others to attend classes from that point on.

Responsibility

As coaches, we ask our athletes to be responsible and make smart, mature decisions every day. Obviously, players who are committed and invested in reaching their goals can accomplish this easily. The difference between being responsible and being irresponsible comes down to two things—accountability and adaptability. I have always appreciated a player's telling the staff of a mistake she made before we find out from another player. Our players encourage each other to do so. Players must face up to a mistake, make no excuses, and then learn from it.

After the player takes responsibility for her action, meaning that she engages in some form of correction, our coaching staff holds no grudges, and the player is not allowed to hold any grudges for having to carry out the correction. Depending on the mistake, we communicate to the team the situation and the corrective action. Discussing the mistake made by one person can be a learning experience for all. If you communicate the situation, others may not have to make the same mistake later during the year. This approach keeps the team all moving forward toward accomplishing your goals with as few distractions as possible. We try to get the players to understand that these traits are essential to the success of our team. But should a player continue not to understand the difference between right and wrong and fail to show that she cares for the well-being of the team, we might decide as a coaching staff that the young woman is simply not a good fit for our program. This decision can be the hardest one that a coach may face.

Thoughtfulness

Finally, our players must be caring people; they must care about the team's goals and their teammates rather than their individual goals. Before they make a decision, we want them to ask themselves, "Is this best for the team?" We want to create a family atmosphere. Players who genuinely care for each other on and off the field will create this family atmosphere. They may not always get along, but they must appreciate and respect each other's differences, beliefs, and backgrounds. We hope that our players look after each other and mentor each other in all areas of life. In the end, players won't always remember who hit in the winning run during a game, but the friendships they make will last forever.

Help your players understand your character expectations by discussing throughout the year what these qualities mean to you and what they feel and look like. You can do this by continually showing general concern for your players and support staff by building strong relationships with each of them. We make it a point to give our appreciation to those who have helped our program in big or small ways by offering a thank you, a card, a personal invitation to a game, a T-shirt, or other gesture. Our players see our staff act in this manner, and we make subtle suggestions for the players to do the same. As a staff, we make sure to display positive energy around those we work with and show the love we have for the game and our opportunity to coach at UNO. Your coaching staff can be the best example by showing your players thoughtfulness, respect, trust, and responsibility every day. If you're going to talk the talk, you've got to walk the walk.

Expectations at Practice and Games

I don't think that we demand any more at practice than any other program does. Teams should hustle and work hard to the point that they feel as if they deserve victory. Players can easily control all items that we expect during practices and games. Most items that we expect are based on their approach to the game or practice. This quotation from the book *Practice Perfect Baseball*, edited by Bob Bennett (2009), sums what we as coaches expect:

> Be careful of your thoughts, because they will eventually become your body language.
>
> Be careful of your body language, because it will eventually become your words.
>
> Be careful of your words, because they will eventually become your actions.
>
> Be careful of your actions, because they will eventually become your habits.
>
> Be careful of your habits, because they will eventually become your character.
>
> Be careful of your character, because it will eventually become your destiny.

How they approach the day and its challenges come from their enthusiasm and commitment to be prepared. It all starts by the way we dress: If we look good, we will play good. This expectation is pretty simple. Whether it's practice or a game, our players are dressed in our red and black gear including belts, socks, jerseys, and undershirts. To this day, I have alumni call telling me of the nightmares they had of forgetting their uniforms. Our expectation on apparel must have been clear.

Dedication

Our coaching staff spends a tremendous amount of time planning practice. Our practice plan is posted in the dugout so that the players know what we are aiming to accomplish. Our drills and the equipment needed for each are listed. Our players read the practice plan, organize the equipment for the first drills listed, and have that drill set ready for action. They do this before we do our stretching and warm-up routine. Of course, this required preparation means that the players have to be at practice at least 15 minutes early as well. We want our players to come to practice with a purpose in mind. At times we may have our players write out and hand in what they want to accomplish for the day so that we know they thought about it before they step on the field. Other times I just ask a single player what she is seeking to accomplish at practice. This approach usually prepares all players to have an answer ready. Answers vary from "I want to work on tracking the ball better today" to "I want to work on my first step to the ball."

Every year we face opponents who are stronger, faster, and more talented, but every team has about the same amount of time to spend on the field. How we choose to spend that time is important. Players need to be prepared to be there physically and mentally in each drill. Catchers should always block and frame with proper posture while in the bullpen, outfielders must always show enthusiasm for making diving catches and having no fear of fences, and infielders must always perform disciplined fielding actions. Athletes should walk into practice with no distractions. Athletics allows players to have three hours away from reality—no academic problems, no relationship issues, no stresses. The only thought in their minds should be about improving their game!

Players understand that the game of softball and practices are all about getting lots of repetition! To become consistent, our players know that they will be asked to repeat skills over and over, and to do so with enthusiasm. To get the repetition that we want, we stress the importance of doing a drill with discipline, meaning doing it the right way and in a consistent manner, working on quality not quantity, and then hustling from one drill to the next to allow for more repetitions during that particular drill. We say, "When in doubt, hustle." Our players never finish on an error or a bad hit; they always ask our coaching staff for one more.

Determination

We expect our players to want to be challenged mentally and physically, to see themselves pushed to their limits. As coaches, we are looking for what Southern Mississippi strength coach Paul Jackson calls as little pushback as possible. Pushback shows up in the form of quitting, complaining, whining, pouting, or hanging one's head. Pushback players think that they are already good, don't want to be called out for mistakes, and might choose not to work as hard. We confront any poor body language immediately—one-on-one and in private. I have been known to remove a player from a drill when I see poor body language or hear a negative comment, such as "I can't." Our players must speak with the language of "I will" and "I can." We ask our players to walk tall, to look our staff in the eye when talked to, and to show signs of confidence in our performance. Players need to be open to coaching, to changing, and to growing as players. Again, as a coaching staff, we try to walk the walk here as well. Coaches need to be open and continue to grow with their players.

Teams should be ready to be competitive and play any game or challenge at practice with the mentality to win. Never should players show defeat. No matter what the scoreboard shows, when spectators walk into our game they should never know by our demeanor or effort who is winning or losing. We have adopted the phrase *get big* from Brian Cain's *Toilets, Bricks, Fish Hooks and Pride* (2011). I expect our players never to place any team or player on a pedestal. We play every game with the intentions to win; after all, the game of softball never knows who should win on the field! We ask players to compete bigger than what their stature may be. We have always told our recruits and players that although they may wear a size 6 shoe, if they play with attitude, intensity, and competitive spirit, they will leave a footprint here at UNO bigger than a size 12.

Overall, what most of us find is that the good teams are desperate to get better, the poor teams are not interested, and the average teams are interested but cannot do what it takes on a consistent basis. Consistency in positive thought and actions is key to the success of any athlete and program.

COMMUNICATING OUR EXPECTATIONS

The easiest way for a coach to communicate expectations is to be an example of what is expected from the team. How you treat people in your life, how you prepare for practices, how you carry yourself with confidence, how hard you work and display your passion for the game can all be used as a measuring stick by your athletes. When you communicate, your expectations must be clear and concise. When I know of a minor or major problem, I address it that day. Our players take the same approach when they make a mistake. They communicate, apologize, and have a solution ready for the coaching staff. This approach is what we expect—communicate the problem, hold themselves accountable, and then solve the problem by coming up with a solution.

An example of this occurred when a freshman knew that we were doing grade checks about a month into the semester. This freshman was used to getting As and Bs in high school, but she was receiving a D in her math class. Before I received her grade check, she let me know what her grade was. She went on to say that she had already discussed her situation with the professor, had signed up for a tutor, and had asked her cousin to change her password on Facebook so that she would not waste any more time on that site. I'm sure that I added an hour or two to our freshman's study table requirements as well, but I was thrilled that she took it upon herself to let me know what the situation was early, to come up with a solution, and to hold herself accountable. At the end of the semester, she received a B in her math class.

Timing of Expectation Communications

Your first team meeting is a good time to communicate most if not all expectations. At this time you may want to lay out the areas where you may have expectations, such as character, practice, competition, and academics. We not only discuss these areas with all team members and the coaching staff but also spell them out in our team handbook. At our first team meeting, we discuss this handbook page by page and have the players sign a contract that they understand the material covered. Signing the contract does not mean that players will not make mistakes, but they understand that consequences come with the decisions that they make throughout the year. Should we have any issues of people not meeting the expectations, we talk to the team as a whole or have an individual meeting discussing the change of pace we need and why.

Communicating Expectations Through Mentoring

We continue communicating these expectations through a mentoring program. The purpose of this program is for our players to be accountable not just to the coaches but also to one another. We have found that our mentoring program can do that and build leadership from within. The mentoring program allows our athletes to stay on top of tasks that need to be accomplished, and by relying on our team leaders to communicate these tasks, I free up my time for other duties.

In addition, communication works better when it is coming from team members, not from the coaching staff.

Our mentoring program works like this. We split up our team into three teams of six players each. They are labeled the red, black, and white teams. Each team has mentors, typically seniors and juniors who have been through our program and understand many of our expectations. Each team also has new players who are still learning our system. Each team is required to get 50 points each semester to receive a small reward. The reward is small because our expectations involve items that the players can easily attain and that they should be doing every day. Points are tallied up weekly, and we add or subtract for items that have or have not been accomplished. The scores are posted in the locker room. Nobody likes to see her team coming in last, especially those who believe that they are leaders.

Teams tally up points by accomplishing tasks or goals that we think are important to having a successful program. We listed six areas in which teams could earn points this year:

- **Time-sensitive items**—These were items that needed to be handed in to our coaches or support staff such as monitor and compliance forms, food journals, uniforms to be washed, and so on.

- **Academics**—Grade checks are done throughout the semester. For each grade check that we do, each team member received a certain number of points for every A or B and had points deducted for any Ds or Fs. Final grade points are doubled because they are the most important.

- **Weights**—Our team is tested monthly on their sprint and agility times, vertical jumps, and certain lifts. Teams received points if a member of their team improved on the selected test of the month.

- **Pride**—Teams earned points for attending university events including other athletic events together as a team. Should a team get two or more players from another mentor group to join in attending an outside event, more points are awarded.

- **Full team functions**—Points were accumulated for having team dinners, going bowling, and so on when all members of our entire team were present.

- **Practice effort and performance**—As coaches we chose various days to grade each player's performance and effort. The players were not told that it would be a grading day until the end of the practice. Often they were excited after they were told because they were pleased with the effort that they gave.

- **Community service**—Each team member can earn bonus points for helping out in the community. This area is used throughout the year and when a team is behind on points or when a team member made a mistake. That person could help get a point back by volunteering time back to our community.

Mentoring groups had points subtracted from their totals if a member was responsible for any social misconduct, lack of effort at any practice (not just on our grading day), leaving apparel behind, missing class, missing study hours, being late to practice or a meeting, and so on.

Although we have the team split up in small groups, we stress the importance of all three groups succeeding and reaching their 50 points. If all the groups reach our point total, we are likely improving ourselves as student-athletes, receiving the grades needed to graduate, improving overall team chemistry, and experiencing fewer distractions throughout the year, which is a bonus. We believe that this program allows each player to meet our expectations in the areas of concern. In addition, the program encourages teammates to look out for each other.

Players are also taught that they have a responsibility to the team and that their individual actions will affect our success as a team. We find that the players communicate with each other even more. They remind each other of items that need to be taken care of without the coaches ever having to be involved. Leaders usually emerge in the individual teams, because if someone doesn't, that team will not succeed. We want all three groups to reach the goal, not just one. I have found that the mentoring groups help our seniors or leaders because they have a smaller group to look after and they don't have the option to wait for someone else to step up.

Mentoring Program at Work

One fall a freshman was having a difficult time adjusting to college life. For some reason, the freshman was the only one struggling. After her second issue, I had a discussion with her about whether she was a good fit for our program. Our upperclassmen knew what this meant—the freshman might not be asked to stay on the team. Our seniors asked if they could have a meeting with me to discuss the situation that was developing. I was never more proud. The seniors asked me to give them the opportunity to watch over the freshman to help her make smarter and more mature decisions. The seniors did a great job, because I never had another issue with this player. What we hope for in this program is that the player who once struggled will one day become a mentor to another freshman who may have difficulties making positive decisions.

The mentoring team program has always been a work in progress that we add to each year. It has worked well for us in holding players accountable and developing some leadership in our system. Our expectations are clearly communicated, and players are often reminded of their standards.

EXPECTATIONS FOR COACHES

The expectations that we have for our players need to be matched by what we expect from ourselves. If we ask our players to carry themselves in a certain way, we as a staff need to hold ourselves accountable for acting in the same manner. Our players learn what we expect from them because we show them that we have the same expectations of ourselves. One of the first things that we want our players to know is that we care for them not just as athletes but also as people. Our coaching staff schedules weekly meetings with our athletes to chat and ask about anything other than softball. As coaches we are always working on the finer details of game strategies and practice organization, but we need to find time to understand our players and let them know that we care what is going on in their lives. I believe that the more we show that we care, the more our athletes give on and off the field for our program. Doing this can be as simple as sending a text message to a player to make sure about a test grade that she received or asking about a sibling. Most of our communication is done face to face, but modern players relate to text messages just as well. Find ways that your players will communicate with you. The more time that you can invest in your athletes, the more they will know that you care.

As a coach I value and respect the commitment that our players give to our program. As much time as this job takes to be successful, I know that it takes the same amount of time for them to be successful as players and students. I respect and appreciate their commitment by being on time if not early for our practices and making sure that a lot of planning and thought has gone into each practice plan. We are organized and expend a lot of effort in making sure that we meet our players' goals of becoming the best players they can be. My staff and I show them respect by the way we speak to them at practice and by showing them that we do listen to their concerns or problems. We show our respect for them by the way we speak positively about them during a speaking engagement, in the newspaper, to fans or spectators, and during team functions.

Finally, as coaches we try to earn their trust by the way we communicate to them. I believe in being upfront with our athletes, not sugar coating anything. This way of conversing starts during the recruiting process when we are upfront about our needs and our plans for them as athletes. Whether the conversation is during the recruiting process or while they are playing with us, they may not like what we have to tell them. We are honest with them in our assessment of their skills, their playing time, their role, and the possible need to improve athletically and academically. We keep drama low on the team by a direct communication style. If a player is not accomplishing something that we believe she should, we tell her immediately. I want my players always to know where they stand with our coaching staff. This approach leads to fewer questions and less confusion for our athletes. If for some reason an athlete has a question about a matter, we have an open-door policy whereby our athletes can stop in any time for a discussion. The number one goal of our staff is to make sure that our players know that we have their best interest at heart during these conversations and that we will always make time for each of them. Being upfront, honest, and straight to the point in our communication style has always been our way to take responsibility for our decisions, to earn our players' trust, and to show our players that we respect them.

FINAL THOUGHTS

Defining expectations is much like establishing a coaching philosophy. Many of us have expectations for ourselves that we developed from our experiences, our parents, past coaches, and our mentors today. I have always looked at coaching, whether it is on or off the field, as just placing our team and players in a position to win or succeed. Players will soon form good habits if we make sure to communicate and hold them accountable to what we expect. For some, this job is simple because we look to add players to our roster that have much of what we expect already in them.

But we can teach expectations as well if we have players who want to continue to grow. Of course, our goal is for our players to become the best that they can be as people and as athletes. The longer that your standards, expectations, and culture are in place, the easier the communication piece can be. You will soon find that the mentors who have been developed through their years in your program are doing much of the work of helping your athletes succeed.

3

Establishing a Winning Attitude

Chris Bellotto

Attitude! We all have one, whether a good one or a bad one. How do we develop a good attitude? And more important, especially in athletes, how do we keep a positive or winning attitude when things are not going well? Attitude can be described as a state of mind. Attitude is really a choice of having a winning attitude or a losing attitude. How can coaches ensure that athletes maintain a positive, winning attitude in the toughest of circumstances?

BENEFITS OF A WINNING ATTITUDE

Let's first talk about why a winning attitude is important. From the day we are born, we are influenced by parents, relatives, and friends. Everything we touch, feel, and see is a part of making us who we are. We have all read studies in which two siblings raised in the same environment came out of that familial involvement with far different experiences. Learning how to react positively in the light of bad circumstances is something we all need to learn. And reacting positively inspires those around us.

Having a winning attitude keeps us motivated and keeps us striving to set goals. Winston Churchill once famously said, "Never, never, never, give up." Why do some people never appear to be defeated? What sets them apart from others? The answer is simple. Attitude! If we are what we eat, then we certainly are what we think we are. Surrounding ourselves with positive, like-minded people helps us stay positive in our coaching careers.

What can we do to develop a winning attitude in our players? Let's explore some ideas.

Be an Example

If you want your athletes to have a good attitude, lead by example. If you are passionate about your job, it will show. Remember the saying "Attitudes are contagious—is yours worth catching?"

Have Clearly Defined Goals

Everyone from your staff to your players needs to be on the same page. Goals give us direction and purpose. They should not be so hard that we don't have a chance to attain them, but they should not be so easy that your players get bored and lose focus.

Accentuate the Positive!

When good things happen, let your team know about it. These good things can happen in a game, but they also happen off the field. "Catch them doing good" is one of my favorite sayings. A positive outlook is contagious, and everyone loves being part of a winning team.

Be Committed to Winning

Your players need to have a will to win. But more important, they need to have the daily commitment to do what it takes to prepare for winning.

Practice as if It Is a Game

Many athletes like to think that they can put in a subpar performance in practice and then turn up the knob in games. Perspiration plus preparation equals relaxation. As with preparing for a big test, if your athletes work hard daily, they will be more focused and relaxed because they know that they have put in the time needed to succeed.

Look Ahead, Not Behind

We cannot change the past or what people around us do. We can only control our own actions. Reading positive books and affirmations keeps us thinking about life, work, and relationships positively. By being happy we will do a better job coaching. The one thing that we can control is our attitude. The more positive we are, the more positive people we will attract.

Encourage Self-Evaluation

Have several good friends evaluate you, both on and off the field. Truthfully, this kind of evaluation is hard to do, but if you are willing to listen, evaluation from those close to you provides insight into the most real you. Do you respond well to stressful situations, or do you overreact? Can you see the positive in any situation, or do you find that you need a long time to recover?

Another quote by Winston Churchill states it plainly: "Attitude is a little thing that makes a big difference." No one likes to be around someone who always finds fault with everything. A bad attitude makes it difficult to achieve great things.

KEEP POSITIVE WHILE LOSING

Perhaps the most difficult task a coach faces is helping a team keep a winning attitude during a losing streak. Most teams go through a string of losses at some time. Your team has the talent and even the right attitude, but the results on the field are not showing. As a leader, you need to continue being positive. As a coach, I wear my heart on my sleeve.

When we are not winning, I am not happy and my whole team knows it. But I make it a point to let them know that I am not upset with them, just the outcome. General Dwight Eisenhower said, "I never saw a pessimistic general win a battle." As a leader, you must always have a winning attitude. Keep your team working hard and focus on the positives. Eventually good things will come.

Striving for a winning attitude is imperative, particularly in softball. Seasons are long, and failures can be many. Trying to hit a round ball with a round bat is one of the hardest things to do in sport. Hitting it well can be deemed a failure (a line drive right at someone), while hitting it poorly can be a success (a soft liner off the hands that falls in for a hit). Your ability to continue to try, to not be defeated, and to continue no matter what to give your all is what matters. Positive attitudes don't just happen; you have to make them happen.

How important is a positive attitude? From the website goal-setting-for-success. com comes a favorite story of mine about attitude.

Attitude Is Everything

Jerry was the kind of guy you love to hate. He was always in a good mood and always had something positive to say. When someone would ask him how he was doing, he would reply, "If I were any better, I would be twins!" He was a unique manager because he had several waiters who had followed him around from restaurant to restaurant. The reason the waiters followed Jerry was because of his attitude. He was a natural motivator. If an employee was having a bad day, Jerry was there telling the employee how to look on the positive side of the situation.

Seeing this style really made me curious, so one day I went up to Jerry and asked him, "I don't get it! You can't be a positive person all of the time. How do you do it?" Jerry replied, "Each morning I wake up and say to myself, 'Jerry, you have two choices today. You can choose to be in a good mood, or you can choose to be in a bad mood.' I choose to be in a good mood. Each time something bad happens, I can choose to be a victim or I can choose to learn from it. I choose to learn from it. Every time someone comes to me complaining, I can choose to accept their complaining or I can point out the positive side of life. I choose the positive side of life."

"Yeah, right, it's not that easy," I protested.

(continued)

"Yes, it is," Jerry said. "Life is all about choices. When you cut away all the junk, every situation is a choice. You choose how you react to situations. You choose how people will affect your mood. You choose to be in a good mood or bad mood. The bottom line: It's your choice how you live life."

I reflected on what Jerry said. Soon thereafter, I left the restaurant industry to start my own business. We lost touch, but I often thought about him when I made a choice about life instead of reacting to it. Several years later, I heard that Jerry did something you are never supposed to do in a restaurant business: He left the back door open one morning and was held up at gunpoint by three armed robbers. While he was trying to open the safe, his hand, shaking from nervousness, slipped off the combination. The robbers panicked and shot him.

Luckily, Jerry was found relatively quickly and was rushed to the local trauma center. After 18 hours of surgery and weeks of intensive care, Jerry was released from the hospital with fragments of the bullets still in his body. I saw Jerry about six months after the accident. When I asked him how he was, he replied, "If I were any better, I'd be twins. Wanna see my scars?" I declined to see his wounds but did ask him what had gone through his mind as the robbery took place. "The first thing that went through my mind was that I should have locked the back door," Jerry replied. "Then, as I lay on the floor, I remembered that I had two choices: I could choose to live, or I could choose to die. I chose to live."

"Weren't you scared? Did you lose consciousness?" I asked.

Jerry continued, "The paramedics were great. They kept telling me I was going to be fine. But when they wheeled me into the emergency room and I saw the expressions on the faces of the doctors and nurses, I got really scared. In their eyes, I read, 'He's a dead man.' I knew I needed to take action."

"What did you do?" I asked.

"Well, there was a big, burly nurse shouting questions at me," said Jerry. She asked if I was allergic to anything. "Yes," I replied. The doctors and nurses stopped working as they waited for my reply I took a deep breath and yelled, "Bullets!" Over their laughter, I told them, "I am choosing to live. Operate on me as if I am alive, not dead." Jerry lived, thanks to the skill of his doctors but also because of his amazing attitude. I learned from him that every day we have the choice to live fully. Attitude, after all, is everything.

By Francie Baltazar-Schwartz

Do you want additional examples of people who failed yet kept a positive attitude and went on to succeed?

Bill Gates: Gates didn't seem like a shoe-in for success after dropping out of Harvard and starting a failed first business with Microsoft cofounder Paul Allen called Traf-O-Data. Although this early idea didn't work, Gates' later work did, creating the global empire that is Microsoft.

Walt Disney: Today Disney rakes in billions from merchandise, movies, and theme parks around the world, but Walt Disney himself had a bit of a rough start. He was fired by a newspaper editor because "he lacked imagination and had no good ideas." After that, Disney started a number of businesses that didn't last long and ended with bankruptcy and failure. He kept plugging along, however, and eventually found a recipe for success that worked.

Thomas Edison: In his early years, teachers told Edison he was "too stupid to learn anything." Work was no better, as he was fired from his first two jobs for not being productive enough. Even as an inventor, Edison made a thousand unsuccessful attempts at inventing the light bulb. Of course, all those unsuccessful attempts finally resulted in the design that worked.

Abraham Lincoln: Although he is remembered as one of the greatest leaders of our nation, Lincoln's life wasn't easy. In his youth he went to war a captain and returned a private (if you're not familiar with military ranks, just know that private is as low as it goes.) But Lincoln didn't stop failing there. He started numerous failed businesses and was defeated in numerous runs he made for public office.

Oprah Winfrey: Most people know Oprah as one of the most iconic faces on TV and one of the richest and most successful women in the world. Oprah faced a hard road to get to that position, however, enduring a rough and often abusive childhood as well as numerous career setbacks including being fired from her job as a television reporter because she was "unfit for TV."

On a personal level, I am blessed to have two parents who taught me how to have a winning attitude. I grew up on a ranch with two older sisters and one younger brother. Ranching and farming are hard work but rewarding in many ways. I am forever grateful for lessons my parents taught me and would like to share some of them with you.

My parents taught me about hard work by having me help herd the cattle on weekdays after school and on weekends. I learned a tremendous work ethic from my father, who still gets up at 4:30 a.m. at age 86! I literally did fall off a horse and learned how to get back up, dust myself off, and get back on.

I learned to respect everything and everyone around me—nature, my parents, siblings, and ranch employees. I learned that everyone and everything does have a value, even if I don't always agree with their viewpoints and actions.

I learned that the harder you work, the better the results you will get. At times it may not seem like my hard work pays off, but in the end it always does if I stick with it.

I learned that failing brings out the true character in us all and that even though I hate failing, it has always taught my things about myself that success rarely does.

I learned that although you may be on top of the mountain today, at some time you will find yourself at the bottom of the mountain, so being humble is always the way to be as a coach. Gilbert Keith Chesterton said, "It is always the secure who are humble."

I learned that treating people with respect and showing them that you care is one of the best motivators of all time.

I learned that listening—truly hearing what someone has to say—is more educational than talking because I already know what I know. By listening I learn what others know.

I learned you never stop learning as a coach and that even your players can teach you some things if you allow yourself to be receptive.

I learned that knowing who you are and what you stand for is invaluable. These qualities will be tested repeatedly in coaching, mostly in your darkest hours.

I learned that playing by the rules of the game is more important than winning the game.

Sadly, some in our coaching profession think that they need to cheat to win. This notion is not only untrue but also sets a terrible example for our athletes, who should look to us as role models.

A country song says, "I gotta stand for something or I don't stand for anything." Sometimes doing the right thing as a coach is not easy. Benching your star player in an important conference game for instance. But keeping your moral standards is far more important in the long run.

All these lessons have helped me be a winner in my career, both on and off the field. These tried and true ethics serve as a common thread among successful coaches and those with winning attitudes.

COMBAT LOSING ATTITUDES

So far we have discussed winning attitudes. But what happens when you have players or staff members who have a losing attitude? Bad attitudes can be just as infectious as good attitudes. What strategies can we use to combat bad attitudes?

A famous song from the Broadway musical *The King and I* is "Getting to Know You." Making a real effort to understand others and their backgrounds can be a key to uncovering why they may have a bad attitude. Players may rebel because somehow their self-worth has been eroded. Sitting down with that person and listening to what she has to say can be meaningful to both parties and help you strategize how to deal with the person in the future.

Involve the entire team as much as possible. I have found that if things are not going well in a season, some of the best practices that my teams have don't involve a glove, bat, or ball. Allowing team discussions regarding rules, tactics, or team conflicts are healthy approaches to resolving inner conflicts.

The same can be said for coaching staffs. I like to refer to these as "staff infections." Trust me; these can be as bad as or worse than any team problem. As a head coach, your staff needs to be a direct extension of your moral values, beliefs, and strategies. Your team needs to see your staff as unified and truly caring and believing in each other and each other's talents. Reaching this goal can prove difficult at times. Some assistants find it hard to check their egos at the door. They may undermine your beliefs to players. Having regular meetings with your staff is important in ensuring that you are always on the same page.

Positive Reinforcement

Giving credit to your staff is important. As head coaches, we can never do everything by ourselves. So publicly and privately giving credit for your success to your staff and others is important in keeping your staff a happy working unit. Team-building activities have become popular recently and are a great way to promote unity. These types of activities aim to have every member feel wanted and needed and are a useful way to start a new year. The more a part of the team they all feel, the healthier their attitudes will be. Your team will be happier together, on and off the field.

I like to have a cookout before the start of our season every year. This event allows me to get to know the players better off the field and allows them to know the real me a little better. Your team needs to know you as a person who has interests besides coaching. By letting your hair down, you allow them to see you in a different light and gain a better understanding of you. Other examples would be a pumpkin-carving contest or building a float with your athletes for a Christmas parade. Helping your community through volunteering with organizations like Habitat for Humanity is an excellent way to have your team bond and give back to the community.

Offering incentives for positive actions is another effective way to develop teamwork and discourage bad attitudes. Rewarding your team for achievements like making excellent grades or even demonstrating kindness toward teammates builds and promotes healthy attitudes and becomes contagious among team members. Be an example in your leadership and be ready to respond quickly to a negative situation. One day I walked onto the field for practice and witnessed two of my players in a heated exchange with other teammates around. I quickly put myself between the two of them and told them to follow me silently to my office. When we reached the office I calmly explained that their behavior was not acceptable, that it would not be tolerated, and that they would need to work it out. I then told them to stay in the office and not to come out until they worked through their issues. By having them resolve their problems without my intervention, they had to do their own problem solving and decision making, and the outcome was more powerful. To this day they are friends! Be flexible in your dealings with players. I used to think that it was fair to treat everyone on the team the same way. But this approach is not the best because we all have different personalities and react to situations in different ways.

Look for the Good

Years ago a young lady who had a troubled upbringing played for me. Some of my players said that I treated her differently (I did) and let her get away with things (I didn't; I just bent the rules a little). But ultimately, I saw the best in her and knew that she had worth, not only as a player but also as a person. And you know what? I am proud of the person she has become. She has a beautiful family, is healthy and happy, and is a role model for others today. Sometimes you have to be flexible in your dealings as a coach to allow for all types of people. Find the positives in the negative.

A prominent rabbi named Harold Kushner, author of the book *How Good Do We Have to Be?* says it best: Life is not a spelling bee, where no matter how many words you have gotten right, if you make one mistake you are disqualified. Life is more like a baseball season. Where even the best team loses one-third of its games and even the worst team has its day of brilliance. Our goal is not to go all year without ever losing a game. Our goal is to win more than we lose, and if we can do that consistently enough, then when the end comes, we will have won it all.

FINAL THOUGHTS

In conclusion, the combination of a lot of qualities and actions by yourself and others can develop and maintain winning attitudes. There is no magic formula, no magic road to follow, no surefire way to achieve success. But your actions as a boss, coach, friend, and mentor can go a long way toward helping those around you establish a winning attitude.

4

Playing Hard
and Respecting the Game

George Wares

Respect can be defined in many ways. For this writing I will define it as "the condition of being esteemed or honored." We must respect the game to play it and to have full appreciation for the opportunity. We need to respect all aspects of the game, including our opponents, the umpires, our equipment, our teammates, our coaches, and our fans. And it starts with respect and appreciation for the history of our game.

RESPECT FOR THE HISTORY OF THE GAME

I will not try to go back to the very beginning, which shows softball being invented on Thanksgiving Day in 1887. For this chapter, I start with the law that affected all of us, Title IX., Passed in 1972, Title IX requires gender equity for males and females in every educational program that receives federal funding. This law has had a pronounced influence on the sport of softball by increasing playing and coaching opportunities for young women and growing the sport. When the bill was signed by President Richard Nixon on June 23, 1972, and became a law on July 1, 1972, none of us really knew the effect it would have on young girls and women and their right to play sport at a level equal to that of their male peers. The initial law did not mention sport specifically, and no one thought that the sport component of Title IX would take on a life of its own.

RESPECT FOR PIONEERS IN THE SPORT

I do not think we can coach women today at any level without making it a point to get them to understand the privilege they have as players. This privilege comes from the work of many pioneers in our great sport. I will not try to make a list of those people in this chapter for fear of forgetting some, but all coaches should have their own list to share with their players. This list can be local or national, but the names need to be remembered for what they went through to give opportunities to players today. The foundation of respect for the game must start with respect for its history. Every woman who competes in a state championship, plays for a national championship, or appears on ESPN would not have the opportunity to do so without the hard work and dedication of many in the past. If we as coaches fail to address this with our players, we are neglecting one of our biggest obligations in coaching. The sense of entitlement that some coaches and athletes have today will only get worse if they are not reminded that their rights of today came from the work of others in the past.

RESPECT FOR OUR OPPONENTS

Realistically, without opponents, what do we have? We should not care who our opponent is, just that we have one when we show up at the field. They are the ones who make it a game, who bring us a challenge to compete against. Their pitcher challenges our hitters; their hitters challenge our defense. The better they are, the better we become. Respecting our opponents does not mean that we don't want to beat them. Respecting our opponents does not mean that we don't have rivals we hate to lose against. But we must treat them fairly, compete with them honestly, make all our comments toward them positive, and thank them for giving us someone to compete with. I have believed that whenever we show up at the field, we will be ready to play anyone who is there to compete against us. I hope that whoever that opponent is will play well against us, pushing us to play just a little better. Without quality opponents we have no game.

RESPECT FOR UMPIRES

Why do we need umpires? The simple answer is that we would not be fair in calling a game for ourselves. Imagine that you are coaching third and a close play occurs. You know your runner is out, and you have to make the call. In a perfect world that is the way it would work. But because of our desire to win (sometimes at any cost) many of us would not believe that an opposing coach or player would make that call fairly. Thus we need the men and women in blue. Respecting them does not mean that as coaches we never challenge calls or stand up for our players. What we do is sometimes less important than how we do it. We all have had to deal with bad or questionable calls, and that issue will continue to be a part of our game. But by using derogatory or demeaning language or failing to use a civil tone, we shift the focus of the game to ourselves, which is disrespectful. The umpires for the most part try hard and hustle in an attempt to get the calls right. If this is not the case, you have ways to make sure that those umpires do not work your games. But after the crew assigned to your game shows up, you have an obligation to give them respect for what they do and demonstrate that respect to your players. In return, umpires should respect your players and coaching staff. When we go over the top in arguing a call, who are we really frustrated with or mad at? Is it the umpire who made the call? Perhaps we are frustrated with our players, or maybe we are mad at ourselves and are taking it out on the umpires. Remember, the umpires are present only to help call the game fairly.

Players should never respond negatively to umpires. Throwing equipment after a perceived bad call or making a sarcastic response to a call either verbally or by demeanor has no place in our game. If a player does it once or twice, get her to understand how her action is disrespecting the game. If it continues to happen without consequence, then the coaching staff, not the player, is at fault. I do believe that emotion is and should be part of our game. But we are obligated to demonstrate to our players that negative emotion that disrespects any part of our game or shows up someone else cannot be part of what we are.

RESPECT FOR EQUIPMENT

The equipment we use should be part of us. When we throw a bat or a helmet, we are disrespecting that piece of equipment and thus the game. In today's world, where much is taken for granted, we as coaches have an obligation to teach our players to take care of the equipment we use, whether the school buys it for us, whether we have a sponsor, or whether players buy it themselves. Breaking in a glove properly, putting bats and helmets away, and helping to take care of the field are all examples of small habits that teach valuable lessons. The next time you have a camp or clinic for players, ask them these two questions: "Who bought your equipment? Who paid for you to come to this camp?" The normal response will be mom and dad. When players do not buy their own equipment, they may forget to be grateful to those who do. As coaches, we need to remind them. Having respect for equipment extends to respecting any person who prepares the field for practice and games. How often do you ask your players to thank those people for the work that they do?

RESPECT FOR YOUR COACHING STAFF

Players being respectful of the coaching staff is an obvious expectation, but does it really occur? As a head coach, do you demand that your players listen to the assistants when they speak, make eye contact, and give them the same attention as they do you? This will happen only if you give those on your coaching staff the same respect you ask them to give you. Do you as a coaching staff give the players the respect they deserve? Getting respect is much easier when we give it.

I realize that each of us is different in how we want to be addressed by our players. I am old school; our players address our coaches as *coach*. I especially want this to happen when we have a younger assistant on our staff who is close in age to our players. We do not allow the players to call our coaches by their first names. Having your players call you coach does not guarantee that they will respect you, just as allowing them to call you by your first name does not guarantee that they will not. But by making certain demands and having certain standards, we are more likely to set a tone of respect for the coaching staff.

RESPECT FOR TEAMMATES

This point also seems obvious. But are you sure that all players respect each teammate? As coaches we have a great responsibility and privilege to teach mutual respect. We must get our players to understand that although we can have a few or even many differences, we can still work together to create an environment that will make everyone feel included. This approach will allow us to be more successful on the field. Ultimately, we must make sure that we become a team, not a collection of small groups. I do believe that it is OK to have freshmen carry the equipment or rake the field after practice. At times, however, I think that sophomores, juniors, and seniors should do this. Seniors may take it upon themselves to do these tasks not as chores but as an opportunity to show respect. We should also observe how players treat each other on and off the field. Does our least talented player receive as much respect from our coaching staff as our best player does? If your answer to that question is no, then you cannot expect your players to model respectful behavior. We need to teach our players to display empathy toward each other. What better message can we give the women who play for us?

SELF-RESPECT

This point is listed last, but it is perhaps the most important quality we can help instill in our players. Doing the things mentioned earlier is difficult if players lack self-respect. Self-respect can be defined as "the quality of being worthy of esteem and respect, and having faith in yourself." How much better prepared would our players be for softball games if they had self-respect? Even more important, how much better prepared would our graduating players be for what is ahead of them in life if they had self-respect? This idea is easy to understand but not easy to accomplish. We know that players come to us with a different level of understanding of self-respect. We must develop a relationship of trust with each player that will allow our coaching staff to help all players move forward in this area regardless of where they start.

HOW DO WE DEVELOP RESPECT?

First, we must consider intentional work in these areas to be important. What we choose to do in practice every day, in team meetings, in games, and during the off-season is what our players will think is important to us. Telling our players that they need to respect the game is not enough. We must explain what that means and then model it for them. We cannot say how important this is to our program at the beginning of the season and then never mention it again until the end of our season. We must practice it just as we practice hitting or pitching.

The Culture of Our Program

Every program in the country at every level creates a culture or climate that becomes who they are. We must first decide as a coaching staff what we want our program to represent. What do we want our climate to be? If I ask you and your staff each to write down the top four items that you want in your program, would you have the same four on each list? Would they be in the same order of priority? Try it; you might be surprised at the answers you get. Then include your captains and see how their answers match those of the coaching staff. I would like to think that our seniors, after having played three years for our coaches, would be on the same page in answering this question.

Decide what is important and then let your players know by your actions that you will demand that they try to accomplish what is on your list.

Let's say your list looks something like this:

1. We will win a championship at the highest level.
2. We will become sound in fundamentals and smart in the game of softball.
3. We will develop people who understand the importance of mutual respect.
4. We will develop people who are more prepared for the life after graduation because of increased self-respect.

I offer the preceding list only as an example. I think we can agree that it would be a solid list for any level of play. But what is wrong with the order of the list? I know that many coaching staffs, ours included, have at times put winning a championship at the top of our list, which makes our players think that winning is our number one priority. I would argue that the preceding list is acceptable but should be changed and put in reverse order. Don't take this as meaning that I do not like to win. I believe that winning is important and that teaching our players to win is a valuable lesson. But let's say that you still want winning a state or national championship to be your number one priority. I believe that your team is more likely to accomplish that goal if you place it in the bottom spot instead of the top.

If we leave it at the top, the pressure on our players to win might actually hinder the likelihood of success. What happens if we have a losing streak during the season and confidence decreases? What happens if we have a couple of injuries to key players? What happens if we have some team chemistry issues? All teams go through struggles during a season. Some of these will be small and some not so small. The programs with a solid culture will be more equipped to handle those struggles and continue on a path of success for their season.

Imagine building a house by starting from the top and working down. Obviously, the house would not stand long because it lacks a foundation. The same is true with a softball program. Too many of us try to build the program from the top down instead of patiently developing a solid foundation. After we have established that foundation and all coaches and players are on the same page, then we can handle the adversities that come our way. Let's now look at each of our four components but reverse the order.

Prepare Athletes for Life After Graduation

This task sounds overwhelming, but isn't accomplishing it really why we coach? The work starts during the recruiting process. Aren't we at that point in the process trying to develop a personal relationship with each recruit? Aren't we trying to convince her that we are the best coaching staff for her to play for? And aren't we telling her and her parents that we will take care of her and help her grow as a person? If we say those things, we can't end the process after we gain a commitment, can we? The building of that relationship is a never-ending process, as it is with all relationships. Each of our players will go through substantial changes during her four years at our school. Whether we are talking about 14- to 18-year-old high school students or 18- to 22-year-old college students, many things, both good and bad, will likely happen. The more we can equip them with tools to increase their confidence and self-respect, the more they will be able to enjoy the good things that happen and the better they will be able to handle any negatives that they must go through. We can do this only by getting to know each player individually and understanding that each is unique and will respond to things in her own way.

How do we do this?

Develop a Personal Relationship With Each Player

Get to know each player as a person. The old saying that they do not care what you know until they know that you care is still true. As a staff, show an interest in their academics, their families, and other aspects of their life away from the game. Schedule individual meetings on a somewhat regular basis, and make sure that your players know that they can come and talk to any member of the coaching staff whenever they want to do so. The development of this relationship will increase your athletes' confidence and self-respect.

Set a High Standard of Excellence

Set a standard of excellence that you will not compromise. Our expectation for players is often too low. How often have we praised a player for hustling out a routine fly ball to right? How often have we praised a player for not complaining to an umpire about an obvious bad call? We better serve our athletes by not praising them for behavior that should be a norm of our program. That standard of excellence can carry into off-the-field areas as well. Our players will usually give us what we ask for. If we set the bar low and continually praise mediocrity, then that is probably what we will get. When we as a coaching staff do give compliments, our players know that they are given because they have accomplished something extraordinary.

That approach is a great way to increase self-confidence and self-respect in our players.

FINAL THOUGHTS

I believe that the majority of this discussion of respect is talked about by most, if not all coaches. But just like in any other part of our program, we cannot just talk; we must do. Many teams, and I include the many I have had the privilege to coach, do not reach their highest level because they lack many of the intangibles talked about in this chapter.

I like to use the comparison of building a three-story house. It is obvious that we cannot build the house from top down. Yet, in coaching a particular team or trying to build a program, we often try to work from the top down. We instantly want to teach advanced situations, advanced skills, and we want to play games immediately because we think this is the best way to improve. As long as things are going well, in theory this approach might actually work. What it does in reality, however, is create a false sense of security and confidence. What happens to our team or program, when we have a 4- or 5-game losing streak? What happens if we have a couple of very serious injuries to our key players? What happens if we have some team dynamic issues? What happens during a game when we make a couple of mistakes? What happens in the sport is the same thing that happens to a house that is not built on a sturdy foundation. It crumbles, and we have to start the building all over again. If our program is built upon a foundation of respect, trust, belief, communication, and other strong qualities, we will survive any obstacle that stands in our way.

I know it sounds like a cliché, but a team that is built of players and coaches with a foundation that is firmly sitting in a circle hand in hand and realizes the strength of that circle, will always be stronger than one that does not. This magic of togetherness does not replace fundamental soundness, situational awareness, talent, great coaching, etc. It does, however, add to it. When talent and coaching are equal, the team that understands the need to always respect the game will always come out on top.

Beyond the game and winning championships, this way of playing can become a way of life for our players in the outside world. This goes way beyond softball, and allows your players to have a greater chance of success in the future. It also allows them to be more equipped to handle the obvious failures that life will bring them.

Following this philosophy will give you a greater opportunity for success. It will allow you greater chances of winning conference, state, or national titles. You must always keep your eyes on the prize. When you do that, the important process takes care of itself. By living this philosophy, you are doing what coaching has always been about. You are putting your players in the best position to win. You are also giving them a great understanding that the game is bigger than any of us as individuals.

5

Leading by Example

Kris Herman

In her senior year the captain is only a role player on her team. That's how someone outside the program might look at it. She doesn't play much; she's a pinch runner expected to use her speed to create scoring opportunities for the team. Her game goals usually are to score one run and be ready to do whatever else the team might need on the field. She is not particularly vocal, but she has the complete respect of her teammates. She knows each of them well—this has been her mission for a year—and has worked hard to know and have total confidence in herself. She is confident because she is prepared.

This player is willing to take on the risks of not being always liked by her teammates, of taking heat when things are not going well, of holding *her* team accountable for doing what they said they'd do. In the final 10 games of her career, she plays four different positions in place of injured or younger starting teammates, and does it well and with a purpose. She is a consummate leader and earns the respect—forever—of teammates and coaches alike.

Most coaches have stories of the kid that really gets it. She is able to lead herself and her team in tough times; she is composed and confident on the outside, committed and filled with strong character on the inside. She is committed to the team because she has great relationships with everyone she needs—each of her teammates, her coaches, and the team as a whole. She understands her commitment and leads with her team's values in mind each day.

Most coaches can also count those kids as the minority among team leaders with whom they've worked. We remember them because they made it look easy, but we sometimes forget how much work went into that becoming a leader. We also sometimes neglect to do the work to make ourselves the best example of leadership we can be.

Leadership is a huge and profitable business. At every turn—in books, on television, in staff meetings, at conventions, on the web—people are being encouraged to improve their leadership skills. Leadership studies is an academic major at some of the best colleges in the world, and graduate programs in the field are popping up everywhere. As coaches we emphasize that our players should find ways to be leaders. They should hone their skills in leading on the field and off, find their voice, and find a way to have people follow them. We work to find ways to train our players to become effective leaders as they get to be upperclassmen, to lead by their words and actions, and to do things so that others will want emulate their actions. Coaches are expected to do the same—to be leaders, and especially to lead by example.

Common wisdom supposes that leaders strategize and think big, whereas followers do the work. This hierarchical view is oversimplified and not the way that it works in a strongly led organization. True leadership is much more than top-down direction and implementation of standards and enforcement of rules.

BE CONNECTED TO YOUR PEOPLE AND VALUES

Widely considered the father of the field of leadership studies, historian James MacGregor Burns, in his seminal book *Leadership* (1978), describes leadership as a collective process, a characteristic of the relationship between people rather than a property of individuals themselves. He chose to shift the focus from the personality of a leader to the behaviors of the leader and named this idea transformational leadership.

> I define leadership as leaders inducing followers to act for certain goals that represent the values and motivations—the wants and needs, the aspirations and expectations—of both leaders and followers. And the genius of leadership lies in the manner in which leaders see and act on their own and their follower's values and motivations. (pp. 18–19)

Leadership is not only about taking action but also about developing relationships. Leading requires a set of skills that can be learned or improved, but more important, it requires a set of characteristics. It's about who you are and how you show character and commitment each day in all your actions. It's about how much you care about those around you and how well you get to know them. Becoming a better leader is about personal growth, awareness, and understanding the goals and values of the organization that you represent and the people and processes that make up the team.

Some think that leadership is a given trait rather than a learned trait, but the tenets of commitment, character, communication, and empathy that are crucial to relationships with others and with the organization are things that can be taught, or learned, or both. Coaches have many opportunities to help team members learn to be better leaders. Some, as in direct teaching of leadership skills, are easy to plan, but providing opportunities for players to practice their developing skills, to fail and rebound with improved strategies, requires more creativity. Becoming a good leader takes practice.

Earlier this year a former player asked me to write a recommendation for graduate school. I respected this player as a hard worker, tremendous student, good-but-not-great athlete, and dedicated team member. I had no trouble writing a flattering recommendation, filling in the bubbles, and writing short-paragraph responses. Although I worked hard on the referral, in passing I asked my former player what one instance she would have listed in response to the request: "Talk about the most important piece of constructive criticism you ever gave the candidate, and what her response was." Five years later she said almost verbatim what I had written. Out of the hundreds of interactions we had, this one was clear to us both. It was a small matter—related to the example she had provided to our team—but I had noticed and provided simple feedback that will stick with her forever, not for my words but for the fact that I had made her step up, take a risk, and provide leadership, within her personality even if it was outside her comfort zone, at that moment.

I believe that both the advice as it was given and received years ago and the recall of the event by both of us were memorable because we had a strong player–coach relationship and a shared commitment to each other and to the ethos of our team and program.

FIRST KNOW YOURSELF

As Burns notes, leadership is not about charisma but about working together toward common ends, considering the values of both leaders and followers. The business of forging great relationships in a leadership role requires a coach to take stock of her or his own values and behavior. An organization needs to have a vision, and the leader must know what specific values this vision will suggest.

What is important to you as a coach and to your program? What are your values? Do you know them well yet revisit them? Can you quantify them? If you can articulate these things and get your student leaders to believe and commit to them, then you have a strong foundation and a program that will attract people who believe in similar values and principles and are ready to commit to them.

To develop a vision for the team, program, or organization, you need to know what matters to you as the leader. Self-reflection can be done through professional tools or simply by thinking about your strengths and challenges, about what you like and what you don't like to do. You can do a formal assessment or take other personality tests to learn how you work best, how you communicate, and how others perceive you. Alternatively, you can just make time to create notes about coaching style and personal areas of improvement, study them, and then prepare a well-defined plan about how best to take advantage of your natural style.

Through meaningful self-reflection as well as communication of personal, team, and program values, coaches show their hand about what they think is important to success. From there, everything from recruiting to practice planning becomes an opportunity to advertise those values. Beyond understanding personality or style, the coach should evaluate the methods that are most effective for the team and players. What really moves your team forward? What are the actions, as well as the traits, that lead to success? Getting a group to move from thinking to doing is a key to success as performers.

The traits of being a good listener, being a good communicator, having a positive attitude, having a passion for and understanding of the game, being willing to take risks, being honest and enthusiastic, preparing and planning each day, and working that plan are core values in my coaching. I believe that other things are central to having an outstanding program—including talented and motivated players—but these are the important behaviors I feel most compelled to model. I work on them and try to evaluate myself regularly. I also ask others to help me understand what I'm good at, what's working, and what's not.

EMBODY YOUR VALUES

All interactions create memorable impressions and affect a relationship. Recently, a football coach was asked to curate an art show at the college museum. This coach was willing to leave his comfort zone to work on the project, although it was intimidating. Alone with a mandate to do whatever he liked with a selection of 25 pieces of museum-quality artwork, he created a moving and meaningful exhibit that was critiqued and visited by his entire team as well as many other members of the community. This coach provided an example to his players and many others by stretching to put himself out there and take on the risk of falling short. In this example the coach modeled risk taking, a trait that is crucial for athletes if they are to succeed in competition and one of the most difficult parts of being a captain or student leader.

Coaches must demonstrate the values and behaviors they want from players and from the program. Enthusiasm, passion for the game, a positive can-do attitude, attention to detail, being on time, clarity of communication—all these might be as important to you as they are to me. We also must model some of the most challenging things we ask of our players—risk taking, facing the fear of failure, soliciting feedback, being a good listener, and making changes when needed.

Having a personal network of advisors that will provide feedback is a tremendous asset and an important way to gain self-awareness, which often is a key to improved efficacy as a leader and teacher.

John Wooden had been coaching more than 10 years before he won his first NCAA men's basketball national championship at UCLA. He often gave much credit for the first championship to the fact that assistant coach Jerry Norman challenged his thinking on team defense. Wooden had been opposed to using a full-court zone press for many years but took the input from a talented and persuasive assistant. He allowed himself to take the risk of change, and that year won the first of 10 NCAA titles.

We are always being watched. What we do is constantly being viewed and reviewed on many levels. As the old coaching adage goes, players don't care how much you know until they know how much you care. Regardless of personality, when we have strong personal relationships—coach to player, coach to team, coach to assistants, coach to captain—and when we encourage others to have strong personal relationships, we are empowering leaders and strengthening the teams to which we have committed.

DEVELOP LEADERS ON YOUR TEAM

Helping players and teams to have self-confidence can be a coach's full-time job. For many coaches, that is the ultimate goal. If kids are to improve their leadership skills and become leaders, both player and coach must put forth effort. Coaches need not have close personal relationships with players, even the most important team leaders, in terms of their off-field life. But they must share a commitment to values and norms that are at the core of the program, and working toward this purpose is much easier with good person-to-person connections. This process starts in the recruiting period and continues with consistent communication and shared commitment to the values of the program.

The coach–player relationship serves as a foundation for the work to be done in helping players both to understand the risks of being a team leader and to have the confidence and composure to go along with the nonnegotiable commitment they have to the team and the program. Without the baseline commitment to the other members of the team and to program values, a player cannot be a strong and positive team leader.

The risks for a player in taking a strong leadership role are real, and some players find these easier to take on than others do. The leader will be watched, and teammates and others won't always like decisions. She will have to deal with conflict, she probably will be blamed for some things, and she will need to have some hard conversations. The coach should address those significant risks and help the player–leader prepare by offering practical advice and strategies and by helping the leader understand her own style.

Just as a coach should do, the player should start the process of becoming a good leader through the twin steps of getting to know herself—learning how she reacts to things, knowing what is most important, being able to hold herself accountable, developing confidence through active preparation—and then forming strong and meaningful relationships with everyone on the team.

Student-athletes often think that leadership or captainship comes with the territory of being a veteran player or that they will automatically will be good leaders if they are good players. Coaches have a critical role in helping these players see that being an effective captain requires work. They need to know themselves and the way in which they operate, they need to forge strong relationships with teammates and coaches, and they must completely buy in to the ethos of the team and be able to model those values.

SHARED VALUES

We have a stated vision for our program, a set of values that we hope to embody. Each year, however, we review, refine, discuss, and work together to define our plan—the set of values that we are committed to this year—and then talk about how we will work that plan. This is the core of how we all commit to becoming a team.

Program Values

Fitness and personal preparation

Physical and mental toughness

Loyalty to each other and our team

Direct, honest, and timely communication

Laughter and friendship

Unwavering commitment to our program and our vision. Team first.

Using our central values as a starting point, we discuss, refine, ask questions, dig deeper, determine how to quantify, talk through how we want to display these values (and determine whether these values are indeed what this team thinks is most important), and come up with a set of behaviors that we agree are important to being the team we want to be. We are planning our work by detailing and defining our future critical behaviors.

The entire team should be involved in this process to ensure both understanding and buy-in. Along the way we are helping some kids take the lead and asking all to be good followers.

In our program we ask many questions, and we expect everyone to take part in answering them. Here's a typical progression:

1. What do we want? What are our goals? What does this team want to look like?
2. What will we have to do to achieve these goals?
3. What specifically will we commit to—day-by-day, on the field and off?
4. What we will *always* do (proscribed lifts, be on time, go 100 percent on the bases)?
5. How will we measure the things we say we want to do?
6. How many reps will we do, how much sleep will we get, when will we work out, and so on?
7. What resources do we need in terms of time, equipment, teammates, and so on?
8. Who can help us reach the stated goals?

The questions can seem endless to those who are not used to making commitments. Many people say that they want to do more or try to get there more often next week. Our system demands the identification of specific, measureable steps to take. If we find that after a few measurements the group is not doing what it said it wanted to do to achieve its goals, then we need to adjust either the commitment or the goals themselves. Perhaps, as shown by the measurements, the team really does not want to be what they say they want to be. On the other hand, maybe they can achieve even more given their actual commitments.

Note that the outcome goals are not as important as working on the plan set in motion by the group. While working through this process, the team automatically becomes closer, and individual relationships among players, captain, and coaches are strengthened by the conversation.

A discussion of required inputs and desired outcomes is often held in a conversation in which all players and coaches provide input and make commitments. They do so in full view of others who share the team values. The discussion is a key process piece of team goal development that establishes the what and the why of team values.

Players also complete this process for individual goals. They plan their work in a somewhat public forum (with the input and questioning of at least the coaching staff) and have an opportunity to amend their plans to meet the amount of work they commit to and demonstrate. This process works regardless of skill or level of play. As long as the promises and behaviors match up, success will come. Although doing everything we say we are going to do may not give us everything we want, the beauty of sport is that personal satisfaction likely will result.

As teams go through this process repeatedly, they learn to put stock in the little things. The process offers an opportunity for those in de facto positions of leadership, like captains, to lead by example, but it also offers an opportunity for all team members to present a strong positive example to teammates. A person simply does what she said she was going to do. She shows up. In that way she is presenting an example and is empowered because the process was organically generated—the activities were the idea of the individual and the team, not the coach. It's not easy, but it is quite simple.

RELATIONSHIPS, RULES, AND EXPECTATIONS

Clear communication on team policies makes things simple. We have a typical communication policy in our program: Our "yes, no, or when" policy means that every question gets either an answer or a projected time frame for an answer. No request goes ignored, and thus respect is easily proved. We also have a policy we call "no neutral" that applies on the field but works off it as well. No one is allowed to just be—if you are not giving some energy or input, you are automatically taking some away. Through these behaviors we demonstrate the importance of direct, timely communication and loyalty that are pieces of our program values.

Make sure that team expectations are clear and enforceable, and follow them if they apply to you. Do your meetings and practices start and end on time? If so, then you show respect for players' time. If you have a cell phone policy, then turn yours off during meetings.

It took only one instance when I sent our entire team, minus one, out onto campus in the snow wearing indoor practice gear to retrieve their teammate who had overslept a morning practice to cement in the team's mind that I was serious about being punctual. On the other hand, I know a successful coach whose teams consistently complain that the worst thing about the way the coach runs the program is the fact that the coach is often late for meetings and practices after making being on time a big part of that team's rules.

Some teams have team guidebooks that are dozens of pages long. Others have just one or two central rules that may or may not be written down. The content of team expectations and consequences, defined through the values of the coach and the team, is not the most important thing; the communication of and belief in those standards is what makes them work or not work.

Just as with off-field rules, the critical component in allowing team rules to work on the field is that the de facto leaders—the coaches, captains, seniors, and so on—are committed to them and model them all the time.

LEAD, FOLLOW, OR GET OUT OF THE WAY

Followers are often disparaged, just as leaders are revered. Good followers, however, are crucial to a strong organization. Training people to understand and commit to their roles, to buy into the goals and vision of the program, to believe in the values of the team, is key. To have this happen, all members need to contribute. Each team member should be able to articulate the goals of the team, commit to helping shape the values, and exhibit the necessary behaviors. By encouraging team members to think critically about the norms and be active participants in the team, we create excellent team members, even of those who are not considered leaders.

Having effective followers is one of the critical pieces of having a good team. Too often coaches and other named leaders are content to have yes people—those who do what needs to be done. But because they don't think about the whys of their actions, the foundation of the behaviors, yes people often do not work together as an effective team. Effective followers and effective leaders must be both active participants—that is, doers—and critical thinkers. They must participate in the process of developing team values, vision, and behaviors.

Commitment to the goals and norms of an organization is critical for both leaders and followers; everyone involved needs to know the vision of the group, the values of the project, the mission and purpose of the program. In this regard leaders are not more responsible than those who are following. Strong leaders spend time training others to take the lead at times and know how to follow and when to get out of the way.

Everyone in a truly effective organization must be an active participant and think critically about the nature of the program. People who are true leaders then must learn to be flexible—to take the lead at times and to follow another at other times. A secure leader must not always be a boss; she must be willing to trust the preparation she has done with her players and be willing to give up the traditional leadership role at times to empower others to lead. This opportunity is one of the best gifts a leader can offer to those in her charge.

OUT OF THE OFFICE

I happened to sit next to a coach I didn't know at a clinic and struck up a conversation about hitting mechanics. Our love for the game and for coaching has led to a lifelong friendship and made us both better coaches along the way. I now view this coach, and many others, as an important part of my coaching circle. Mentoring is a crucial component of being a good coach. I spend a lot of time talking to other people, not just coaches, and learning through their experience and example. Allowing mentors to influence me is also central to staying passionate in my job.

Every conversation offers insights and opportunities to improve my coaching and to add to someone else's career and program. I have mentors in and out of my sport, mentor others from afar, and would like to have my own defined coach. Different from teaching and mentoring models, coaching models presume that no matter how well prepared a person is, maintaining a high level of achievement on one's own is difficult. Coaches never finish coaching; they observe, judge, suggest, tweak, work to perfect.

We should all strive to get better, to improve continuously. Sport coaches have traditionally not had their own coaches. Significant benefits can result from having others critique us at practice, in the locker room, in games—the places where we are actually doing the work of developing players and teams—and offer specific suggestions for improvement, as a coach would to a player.

Participation in organizations and activities outside my team is crucial to my efficacy as a coach, and doing these things helps keep me excited about my work. Any campus offers hundreds of opportunities to learn and lead. Serving on committees, going to lectures, and actively participating in community activities or charity programs on and off campus are some ways to show commitment and learn from others. In softball we can be a part of the NFCA, speak at clinics, go to local teams' practices, write articles, and make an active effort to speak to and learn from someone new. Every simple conversation is an opportunity to teach and learn, and we as professionals must find opportunities to interact outside the athletic arena.

FINAL THOUGHTS

We honor the game by passing along our love. We should do our jobs passionately—doing what we say we'll do and loving the people who are on our team. We respect the game by doing all this with professionalism. Showing up to mentor other coaches, being part of clinics and organizations that work to grow and improve the game, dressing and acting professionally, and finding ways to help others are all important ways to lead by example.

Each of us needs to determine what the important standards are for our program or organization, to create a plan around a set of values, to determine how the team should best display and live out those values, and then get to work. Working with our personal and team values in mind and doing so with an air that communicates that we respect the game, ourselves, and our athletes, as well as the process, are important to success.

As a coach, one inherently is a leader in that such a position implies power and being at or near the top of a hierarchy. With this position comes the responsibility of leading people, of managing people and projects, of communicating the mission and direction of a group. By understanding that leading is as much about how you connect, about how you are present and accountable to the core principles and goals of your organization as it is about how you speak or what your macro strategies are, you become better able to lead, to get the organization moving in a particular direction. This point applies to coaches in their day-to-day example and in helping student-athletes be good leaders.

Finding and sharing personal passion in coaching on and off the field is at the crux of our ability to be successful. The primary way of leading in coaching softball is to form great relationships, starting with the love of the game and all aspects of it—the skills, your players, your assistant coaches, all parts of your job in softball. Even if some parts of the job are hard for you to love, such as recruiting, going to staff meetings, whatever might not be exciting, find a way to make them a positive. Set goals and standards, delegate and teach, mentor and be mentored by others in your school or program, and learn from each opportunity.

Being secure in preparation and having a passion to share with others makes being a leader by example natural. Displaying care for the game by sharing knowledge, working to understand all those who work together in an organization (including yourself), and doing so with a professional air is at the heart of leadership.

PART TWO

PROGRAM BUILDING AND MANAGEMENT

6

Building a Successful High School Program

Bob Ligouri

Volumes have been written about special plays, strategies, philosophies, and the training of athletes. Over my 37-year career of coaching at all levels and sports, I believe I have read or watched about all of them. Experience is also a great teacher, and in my case I believe that it has taught me four valuable lessons:

1. There are no magic plays or magic fairy dust to sprinkle on the heads of athletes to ensure success.
2. Regardless of the level, sport, or gender—it is still a players' game.
3. The most successful coaches are excellent teachers who keep the game simple.
4. Athletes perform at their best when the game is fun.

As a long-time coaching survivor, I have learned many lessons the hard way. We have seen successful coaches quickly leave the profession and watched other coaches grow to enjoy tremendous success. The following basic principles are keys for long-term coaching success:

KNOW YOURSELF AS A COACH

Most coaches can easily outline their coaching philosophy, offensive and defensive systems, and late-game strategies. The starting point for coaching success, however, is self-knowledge. What are your strengths as a coach? No coach is strong in every area, and every coach has areas in which he or she excels. The most successful coaches understand their strengths and develop their system to play to those strengths.

What are your weak areas as a coach? These weak areas may be in technical areas of the game, emotional make-up, or communication skills. Again, successful coaches take the time to understand their weak areas and fill in those gaps with others.

All of us know our shortcomings, but many coaches have too large an ego or are unwilling to adapt or change to minimize the gap. A coach may have a shortcoming like one of the following:

- Coach is a control freak and too detail-oriented.
- Coach has poor time management or organizational skills.
- Coach cannot communicate with athletes from lifestyles different from his or hers.
- Coach is too emotional, or perhaps lacks passion for the game.
- Coach is unapproachable by his or her athletes or is too close to them.

The key for the coach is to understand those limitations and build a staff that fills in the weak areas. Two examples for me as a coach illustrate how this approach affects a staff. For one thing, I am highly competitive. I learned that when I speak a great deal to my team before a game, my players tend to tighten up. My adjustment over the years is to limit my pregame talks and allow my staff to do all the prep. I then focus on the game—where I am most effective. I am also big-picture oriented. I have a tendency to not be as involved in the minute details as others, so I need a detail-oriented assistant coach to pick up the key pieces.

KEY CONSIDERATIONS IN BUILDING A STAFF

Putting together a staff is without question a critical element for both short-term and long-term coaching success. The following are key positives that we look for as we build and evaluate a staff.

Loyalty

A disloyal assistant coach can destroy a coaching career and a program. Loyalty is a key consideration that a head coach cannot overlook! An assistant coach must be on the same page as the head coach and buy into the direction of the program. Unrelenting problems can arise within a program if an assistant coach is not loyal to it and the head coach.

Teaching

Assistant coaches must be good teachers. What they know is less important than the effectiveness of their teaching. A head coach can teach an assistant coach a system or drills but probably cannot make an assistant coach a good teacher.

Communication

The assistant coach should have strong communication skills and fit the style of the head coach. The program benefits considerably when the assistant coach is able to complement the skill set of the head coach. The ability to communicate includes listening as well as talking.

Hard Work

The assistant coach should have a strong work ethic. A great staff enables the program to grow and the head coach to build. Exceptional results occur when a group of coaches work well together, have complementary communication styles, and have a drive for success.

Enthusiasm

The assistant coach should love the game. If the assistant coach is doing it for the money, his or her motivation will be obvious to all. Players will notice it, as will parents and other staff members. A genuine love of our game is contagious to all who touch the program.

Several minefields should be avoided if at all possible:

* The assistant who is purely ego driven, who believes that everything is about him or her, not the team
* The assistant who wants to be friends with the players and avoids all confrontations and negatives, leaving those for others on the staff while making himself or herself look good to players, parents, or administrators
* The assistant who does not have a work ethic, who talks the talk but is unwilling to pull his or her share of the workload, who never comes to the field to work when it rains, whose car is the last one into the lot and first one out of the lot on practice nights

MENTORS ARE CRITICAL TO COACHING SUCCESS

In today's coaching environment coaches do not lack for sources of evaluations. Game results, players, parents, administrators, and fans all serve to provide input to coaches. But the best positive tool for a coach to gain insight and self-knowledge is a strong mentor who the coach respects.

As a young coach, I evaluated myself in a simple way—wins and losses. As my career evolved many factors came into play and had a far greater influence than just the Ws and Ls. I have been blessed to have three mentors who frankly saved my coaching career. Whatever success I have had is a direct result of their influence on me. Each brought something different at a different time in my life and was critical to my development as a coach.

Mentor 1: Patience and Maturity

My first mentor was highly successful. He took a competitive, young, impulsive coach and showed me how to channel my work ethic and competitive fire into my career and program. Through him, I learned how to build a program and sustain it without burnout or destroying all who came in contact with me. He showed me the importance of loving the game and transferring that love to the athletes. He taught me the importance of a work ethic. I learned from him that if you wanted success, you had to outwork your opponents. The secret to coaching success, if there was one, was hard work. I also learned that you cannot expect others to work hard for you unless you are at the front of the line, not the rear.

Mentor 2: A Balanced Approach

My second mentor took me as a 24-7 coach and gave me a life off the field. He too was highly successful, and through him I learned the importance of having balance in my life. I learned to balance my competitive fire with family, athletes, and the world around me. I learned how to live a life outside coaching. I learned how to relax, that it was OK to laugh, and, yes, that it was even OK to lose. Without this mentor, I would have flashed and then burned out as a coach. As I look through our coaching world, I see many friends who lost families and other things because they too were 24-7 coaches. When I look closely at those fractured lives, I am truly thankful for my second mentor.

Mentor 3: Paying It Forward

My third mentor had incredible influence on me as a coach and person. He was at the end of his life—a life that included a Hall of Fame coaching career and numerous awards for excellence. He talked of what he believed was truly important as a coach and teacher. He talked of how he hoped that his teaching a game that he loved helped his athletes after they completed their competitive careers. He spoke often about teaching life skills through softball, and he always related our game to the future. My third mentor really helped me evolve as a coach, and since his passing I often reflect on his teachings.

One clear suggestion I can offer about coaching success is to identify and work with positive coaching mentors whenever possible. This approach is helpful not only for the inexperienced coach but also for even the most experienced coach. Working with a mentor is invaluable to a coach who wants to excel in all areas of life.

TEACHING IS PART OF COACHING

There are no magic plays or systems. There are no magic DVDs or books. It is not what you know as a coach that is important; the important point is what you are able to teach your players. Specifically, long-term coaching success usually comes to coaches who do the following:

- Base their practices and organization on basic learning principles.
- Take the time to know each of their player's learning styles and communication keys.
- Use various strategies to present key concepts to their players.
- Stay current with recent teaching methods and innovations.
- Keep it simple!

As a young coach, I had the opportunity to go to dinner with some of the top college coaches in the country. They had taken teams to the NCAAs and produced great athletes. Also at our table were several other young coaches. As the dinner progressed I found it interesting that the people asking the most questions were the most successful coaches and that some doing the most talking were the least successful. Driving back to the hotel after dinner I asked one of the successful coaches why he was so quiet. He said it directly, "It is hard to learn when you are the one doing all of the talking." Lesson learned!

Coaches must apply two additional key principles when teaching a team to be successful. The first is from coaching legend John Wooden: "Do not let what you cannot do interfere with what you can do." Over the years, I have learned how critical this statement is to the learning and achievement of both teams and individuals. As a coach you need to have a clear picture of both the strengths and weaknesses of your team and players. The true measure of a successful coach is the ability to put athletes in situations that play to their strengths and away from their weaknesses. We try to follow a few key points.

We believe in a strong evaluation system and share it with each player on an ongoing basis several times per year (preseason, in-season, and postseason). The evaluation system includes

1. strengths,
2. weaknesses,
3. action plan to improve, and
4. priorities.

How Your Coaches Can Help

We first ask our players to evaluate what they see as their top three strengths and weaknesses and how they think their coaches can help them improve. We then offer the player our coaches' evaluations. As coaches we add two additional key items for each player. We prioritize improvement areas, and we offer each player individualized drill work that she can use to improve each priority area. We conclude our evaluation meeting with two final questions:

1. How do you think our team is getting along?
2. Is there anything that we as coaches can do to help our team improve?

Over the years, we have tried to refine our system and involve our players more in the evaluation process. We believe that this approach has helped.

After the players and coach are all on the same page, we adjust our system to the strength of the team. Each team is different, so we may need to change or tweak the style. One summer our team went 45-3. As a team we hit just five home runs, but we stole 105 bases and five players had at least 10 SBs.

◆ **We adjust our practice schedule according to our players' needs.** We have at least one individual development practice per week when players come to work out and determine themselves the areas in which the coaches can help them improve. This method has proved to be highly effective for us. We also structure our practices to create a proper classroom situation.

◆ **Keep it short.** We believe that we are most effective when we keep practice relatively short, normally 90 to 100 minutes. We are organized and have little or no down time. We come to practice, get to work, and get them out. As a result, many of our players stay for extra work.

◆ **Practice the whole–part–whole method.** For example, when working on a pickoff play, we first show the whole play. Then we work on the individual parts of the play before going back to practice the whole play.

◆ **Explain every drill.** We explain what we are trying to accomplish at the start and model the behavior or technique that we are expecting. We want our players to understand why we are doing the drill and how to execute the drill and skills properly.

◆ **Keep instructions simple.** We keep the process simple with as little clutter as possible in the instructional phase. We focus on specific individualized priorities with each player.

◆ **Learn by doing.** We enable the players to learn by doing and give them enough repetitions to gain proper muscle memory. We have evolved to using practice tapes as a teaching tool, and the method has proved effective.

◆ **Prioritize the practice.** Players should not work at seven or eight techniques at once. Instead, they move forward after first mastering the basic key steps. For example, during our hitting fundamentals breakdown drills, each player has one key skill on which she is to focus. As a coach, I go up to each player and ask her, "What are you working on today?" This approach helps us a great deal in players' skill improvement.

◆ **Provide an environment with a great deal of peer instruction and feedback.** We have accountability partners in many of our workouts and pair up our players in many drills. Each player has an opportunity to help a teammate. We change partners often.

Although we have found that the preceding guidelines are critical to the success of our team, the number one goal for us is to teach the concept of working by emphasizing process over outcomes. (Control the things that you can control!)

An example is what we do with our hitters in game or scrimmage situations. Players, parents, and fans often judge performance on outcomes. That appraisal is often self-defeating and causes problems for the athlete. We focus on the opposite. We chart our hitters on quality swings or quality at bats, not batting average or other standard stats. We tell our players that in a game they may get up to 10 swings. We tell them that at the end of the game we are going to ask them how many of the swings they took were quality swings. They have to tell us. What this approach has shown us over time is that the players become more centered. They play one pitch at a time and one swing at time when they focus on process. In some instances we have a coach chart the quality of swings for a player and then compare our evaluation to her estimates.

Teach Lessons on Losing

As Bobby Knight once said, "In order to win, you must first understand what goes into losing." A mark of great coaches is not just their game knowledge but their ability to teach the game to their athletes. Coaches must teach their athletes how to play the game so that they can maximize their opportunities for success. Here are some basic principles:

- Teach your team first not to beat themselves, to make their opponent beat them. Physical mistakes are a part of the game, but great teams seldom make many mental mistakes.
- Teach your team the roles that each player must willingly accept so that you can use your team most effectively. Players' willingness to accept the correct roles is critical for a team to understand what goes into losing. How many times do you see a singles hitter go to the plate and overswing? How often do you see a slow player try to take an extra base at the wrong time? The list is endless; as coaches we must take the time to teach our players what it is that gives our team the best opportunity for success.

A STRONG MENTAL GAME IS THE KEY TO SUCCESS

I believe that the mental game controls performance so much that it becomes a critical factor for success. We focus on several key areas:

- Team building
- Confidence-building techniques and strategies
- Teaching techniques to handle pressure
- Teaching techniques to handle failure
- Teaching athletes to focus on process, not outcomes
- Developing accountability
- Developing leadership and followership
- Relationship strategies

A coach who does not consider these points in today's competitive environment will ultimately face a team of equal or greater talent who does work on the mental game and will lose.

When both teams are good, toughness wins!

Bobby Knight

As stated earlier, the good team that has a strong tough mental game will usually defeat the good team that lacks a strong mental game. The weak team will blink first. As a coach, you need to take the time to develop a strong mental game

Effective Communication Is Crucial

We believe that communication is at the heart of successful teams and players. We spend a great deal of time on the mental game. The following are some of the key questions that we discuss either individually, in small groups, or as a team:

1. What makes you nervous? How do you perform when you are nervous? How can we help you not be nervous?
2. How do you feel when you make a mistake? What is the most effective way to help you after a mistake? What can a teammate do that helps you the most? What is the worst thing we can do when you make a mistake?
3. What is a good teammate?
4. What is a bad teammate?
5. What is a clique? Do we have them? What can we do as a team to keep cliques from forming?
6. What distracts you in practice or games? What can we do to minimize the distractions?
7. How do you best prepare to play a game?
8. How do you prepare for an at bat? What is your ritual?
9. How do you evaluate yourself?
10. How do you talk to yourself?
11. What does self-confidence mean? How do you think a player can develop confidence?
12. How can you help a teammate develop confidence?
13. What is a leader? What are the key characteristics of a leader?

for each of your players. This difficult task is often neglected. Those who become champions don't ignore the importance of the mental game.

CREATE A CULTURE OF SUCCESS

What is the culture of your team and program? What are its foundations? Over the years I have evolved from using a one-legged stool model based on sound x's and o's to using a model that has three legs of almost equal importance: (1) athletic performance, that is, the x's and o's; (2) academic performance; and (3) community service.

When we first started building our program we were plagued with off-field issues. Although our team records were solid, the experience was not. We decided then that our team culture must change. We have these expectations and beliefs:

1. Always do your best, regardless of what it is that you attempt.
2. Be a positive influence as a teammate, as a student in class, and in the community.
3. Have a great work ethic—you are accountable for yourself!
4. Expect success in all that you do.
5. Find joy and fun in all that you do.

We expect our team culture to create an environment where self-motivation and achievement flourish.

We begin with a key precept that frankly has changed for me over time. We begin with all the players knowing that they have the respect of their coaches. Although earlier in my career one of my favorite phrases was "You must earn my respect," our philosophy has evolved in another direction. Our players have our respect and will keep it unless their actions cause them to lose it. This philosophy has worked well for us. It corresponds to one of Coach John Wooden's basic teachings: "Your players will believe in you when they know you believe in them."

After we have established that basic precept, we find it far easier to provide our players with meaningful evaluations and realistic individualized roadmaps for success.

After we have developed the precept that we are going to develop a culture of success, we believe that it is critical to involve the players directly in this process. The following are examples of two strategies and actions that we follow.

Leadership Council

After we have had several practices and scrimmages at the start of the season, we ask our team to vote for the top four or five girls who they would be comfortable with as a team leadership council. It usually evolves that four to seven players are selected to the council. The leadership council is then charged with developing a team contract. Our leadership council (with input from the other squad members) writes 100 percent of this contract. The contract may differ a little from year to year, but it usually includes expectations in a variety of areas:

1. Practice attendance
2. Social network policies regarding, for example, what goes up on Facebook and what is said on Twitter
3. Academic expectations
4. Drinking, tobacco, and drugs
5. Interaction issues, cliques, conflict resolution, grievance policy
6. Sportsmanship

After the contract is completed, each player signs it, and a copy is given to both the coach and the player.

We have found the contract process to be positive because it establishes the expectations and culture of our team. It is original each year, and each player believes that she has input into the team and its organization. Coaches may be apprehensive about giving up some authority and control, but we have found the opposite to be true. We get much greater buy-in, and players have a sense of ownership of their team.

Team Questionnaire

In addition, we ask the following questions to gather information from our players at the start of the season. We review these with them often, together as a team or in small groups.

1. Why do you play softball?
2. What kind of player do you think you are for your team?
3. What kind of player do you want to be, and how can we best help?
4. What would you like to accomplish in softball?
5. What is possible this year?
6. What do you think is the greatest strength of our team this year?
7. What is your greatest fear for our team this year?
8. How do you want to be remembered?
9. How do you want to be thought of by your teammates?
10. What sacrifices are you willing to make for your team this year?
11. What sacrifices do you expect from your teammates?
12. What do you want from your coaches?

We summarize questions 7, 10, and 11. We then put them all together on an expectations and promise sheet and give to each of the team members. We use our team questionnaire many times during the season and in postseason meetings and evaluations.

We believe that a critical part of developing a culture of success is helping each player develop a strong foundation of confidence. A method that we have used that has been effective is to ask each player to keep a success diary. This diary is simple; we ask the player to keep a daily record of what they do to get better. When we get to a big game or championship game, we urge our players to pull out and read their success diaries. They then realize all the positive things they have done to prepare themselves for the upcoming challenge. This year, our team played for the state championship. I approached a player who was going to play a key role for us in the upcoming game. I asked her, "Are you ready?" She said, "Yep, read my diary last night, Coach!" She played a terrific championship game with total confidence.

> ## East Softball—a Class Act on and off the Field
>
> Teams are often evaluated only by wins and losses, but we expect more from you as an East softball player. Specifically, we expect the following:
>
> - Our team plays with a lot of energy and has fun. When people come to watch us play, I hope they see a team that shows they love to play softball and are having fun doing it.
> - Our team is close. We care about each other.
> - Each girl believes in herself and is willing to do her best, regardless of the results of her efforts.
> - Our team never gives up. We play to the last out in every game.
> - Our team treats our opponents with respect. We never degrade them or gloat. We expect success and will never do anything unsportsmanlike.
> - Each girl on our team takes on the responsibility of being a leader in our community. Remember that you are a role model, on and off the field. You must conduct yourself as if the eyes of all the little girls in our community are watching you. Be a good person, not just a good player.
> - We treat our fans as special. We speak to them first, thank them for their support, and encourage them to come back to see us play.
> - We treat our parents and families with respect. We do not argue or become rude at the field.
> - Smoking, drinking, or drugs will not be tolerated.
>
> In summary, we are not just building a championship team. When people talk about our team, they are going to talk not only about how good we are but also that we are a class act! I hope you are looking forward to the season as much as your coaches are.

Like all coaches, we have developed some things over time that are not negotiable in our program. Many of them came because of coaching mistakes that I made or observed others making. The following is a handout that we give to each player:

Coaches Must Never Forget That Softball Is a Players' Game!

A coach has never hit a home run or struck out a batter. Athletes have their greatest success when they look to the coach to help them reach their goals and dreams. Coaches need to park their egos and become mentors and teachers of the game to their athletes. As coaches we must never forget that the best way to produce true athletic achievement is to make the game fun and enjoyable for the athletes.

FINAL THOUGHTS

The coaching profession is one of the few where a person can have a lasting influence on young people. We have great power—for the good or the bad. As coaches we need to understand the positive effect we can have on the life of a young person. We have great power in being able to tell a young person, "I believe in you!" We must never forget to put our own agenda and ego to the rear and push our young people's to the front. With this approach, the coach will earn the greatest long-term success.

In closing, one of the greatest bits of knowledge I received was from an 88-year-old former coach who was in the Hall of Fame and had won many championships over the years. I asked him what he considered his greatest achievement. I will never forget his answer:

> *I truly believe* that no player ever lost their love of the game of softball while they played for me, and I like to think that I taught many to love our game.

What a wonderful legacy we all would have if each of us could say the same thing!

7

Building a Successful College Program

Karen Weekly

The only place success comes ahead of work is in the dictionary.

Joan Cronan, former women's athletics director at the University of Tennessee

This idea is certainly true when it comes to building a successful college softball program. Planning, dedication, and attention to detail are required to develop the physical and mental attributes necessary for success at the collegiate level. Championship teams are not developed overnight. Champions are forged in fire and molded through a long process. Coaches and athletes alike must be committed to this process and understand that it will take time. As a coach you should develop a plan for your program that takes into account your priorities and values, your vision for the program, the way that you will build a staff, your recruiting strategy, team policies and expectations, community and fan support, goal setting, and program traditions.

PRIORITIES AND VALUES

Your program will reflect who you are as a person and what you stand for. Take time to think about and articulate your priorities and values in life, and the ways in which they influence your program. We have a set of priorities that we communicate during our first conversation with a prospect. These principles may be a turnoff or exactly what the prospect is looking for—either way it's good to know early. Our priorities are the following:

1. Faith
2. Family
3. Academics
4. Attitude
5. Softball

We have maintained those priorities since we began coaching at Pacific Lutheran University, then an NAIA program, in the late 1980s, and we have continued to win at the Division I level using them as our guiding principles. We do not seek to convert our student-athletes to our value system, but we believe they should know who we are when making a decision to spend four or five years of their life in our program.

Faith

Faith reflects the importance of religious beliefs in our personal lives, and we will honor and respect our players' beliefs as well. We do not require anything of our players regarding religious practices, and in fact we rarely mention it. We simply state that we value the place that faith holds in people's lives and will support their spiritual growth in whatever manner they choose.

Family

Family refers to the importance of our families in all that we do, as well as the belief that our team is itself a family system. We remind our players to express appreciation and gratitude for their parents and siblings and the many sacrifices made to help them accomplish their softball goals. When times are toughest, we know that we can rely on our family members. In the same vein, we want our team to appreciate its family attributes. We can laugh, cry, love, argue, celebrate, and commiserate together, just as traditional families do. But no matter what, we always have each other's back.

Academics

Academics reflects the importance that we place on academic success. Our players are in college to be students first. Softball is certainly an important part of their collegiate experience. But softball is a four-year career for most college players, whereas academic achievements will serve them for a lifetime.

Attitude

Attitude reflects our belief that a positive, determined attitude is critically important to achievement in all facets of life. We place it above softball because athletic talent alone will not ensure success. A person must have the right attitude. Attitude refers to many characteristics we deem important in our program, including integrity, perseverance, commitment, loyalty, accountability, and responsibility, among others.

Softball

Softball is at the bottom of the list to reflect the fact that talent by itself, without proper value placed on the other areas, will not be enough. We believe that when a student-athlete maintains these priorities, in the order listed, success on the field naturally follows.

Your set of priorities should fit your beliefs and value system, and by no means are we suggesting that you need to adopt our list to have a successful collegiate program. We do believe, however, that any successful organization must be able to articulate who it is and what is important in the daily pursuit of excellence.

VISION

When we arrived at Tennessee in the fall of 2001, we needed to define our vision for the program and then go about creating a culture that would inform our vision. Developing a vision is like planning a vacation road trip and includes the following questions:

- **Where do you want to go?** This is your destination, or goal.
- **How do you want to get there?** This is your roadmap.
- **What do you want to look like en route?** This is the manner in which you want to travel.

Where did we want to go? We wanted to build a program so that our team could compete for a national championship within five years. How would we get there? We would get there by recruiting great players who were committed to excellence in all phases of their lives, who embraced the goal of blazing a trail and creating a winning tradition at Tennessee. Winning in softball starts in the circle, so we knew we needed to recruit outstanding pitching, build our team up the middle (catcher, shortstop, centerfield), and find a terrific leadoff hitter to spark our offense. What did we want to look like en route? We wanted people to watch us and say

> They give 100 percent; they play with confidence; they are disciplined; they play with class; they work hard; they play with energy; they take pride in their performance; they look like a team; they make the right choices off the field, and they act like winners.

After you establish your vision for building the program, the next step is to make sure that your daily actions reflect that shared vision. Your entire staff and team must buy in to what you are trying to build. Before they jump on board and invest in the program, they must see that the head coach is passionate about and committed to the vision. Everything about your program needs to reflect your vision—practices, staff and team meetings, recruiting materials and interactions, community involvement, facilities, and equipment. Something as seemingly small as the cleanliness of your facilities and equipment speaks volumes about the pride you take in your program. Remember that you don't get a second chance to make a first impression.

BUILDING A STAFF

The most important decisions you will make center on hiring a staff. The people you choose to surround yourself with can make or break the program. This point applies not only to the assistant coaches but also to anyone who has frequent and consistent contact with your team, including athletic trainers, strength coaches, managers, administrative assistants, and so on.

Loyalty Is Essential

Your staff must be loyal to you and share your vision and priorities. Building a successful program is not easy, and you will encounter many obstacles along the way. The obstacles are even greater when you take over a losing program and inherit someone else's recruits versus starting a program from scratch. People don't like change and naturally tend to resist it. Your staff must stand strong with you in the face of the expected resistance. Your staff members should understand that although they may not always agree with your policies and decisions, they must support them 100 percent. Nothing will tear a team apart quicker than assistants who are undermining the head coach and trying to build disruptive allegiances with players. Teamwork and chemistry among the staff are essential and will form the model for teamwork and chemistry among your players.

There Can Only Be One Boss

Leadership and communication are important ingredients in building a staff. First, the entire staff must understand that there can be only one leader. Although the head coach should and will rely on input from the staff, at the end of the day only one person can make the decisions. Not all decisions will be popular. Make sure that your staff understands this principle of leadership and your expectation that they will support your decisions regardless of their personal feelings. Communication is key here. Staff members who believe that they have been heard and that their opinions are valued are more likely to be invested in the process and be supportive of the ultimate decision.

Surround Yourself With Great People

Hire talented coaches who can augment your strengths. Successful leaders surround themselves with good people. Successful leaders are secure and confident in their abilities and are willing to hire people who may have more knowledge in some areas and bring new ideas to the table. Some find it threatening to hire people who will challenge the status quo, but I believe that we experience true growth in any aspect of life only when we are willing to open our minds and expose ourselves to different ideas. Loyalty is paramount here, and a staff that understands the importance of loyalty is able to disagree passionately behind closed doors yet always present a unified and cohesive stance to the team.

Define and Delegate Responsibilities

Delegate and clearly communicate responsibilities among your staff. One of the hardest things for a head coach to do is delegate responsibilities. You likely rose to this position because of your hard work and success as an assistant when you had defined areas of responsibility, or perhaps you were head coach in a smaller program where you did everything yourself. Now you must adjust to leading a staff of capable people. If you want to get the most out of your staff, you must allow them to do the job for which you hired them. Within our coaching staff, areas are clearly defined. One coach handles infield and the short game, another coaches outfield and hitting, and a third coaches the pitchers and catchers. We are readily available to help one another and rely on each other's shared knowledge all the time. But by having clear areas of responsibility, we are each more accountable for the performance outcomes and able to develop strong relationships with the players in our respective areas.

Building your staff also includes addressing and delegating off-field responsibilities. Although these areas are not as noticeable as on-field performance, they are just as important. Depending on the resources available at your institution, separate people and departments may handle strength and conditioning, sports medicine, academic monitoring, nutrition, sport psychology, and so on. Although you may not have day-to-day contact with these people, they need to know and understand your philosophy and share your approach to preparing your athletes for success. They will be meeting with your athletes on a regular basis, so you want your athletes to be getting the same message from these folks as they are from you. I believe a key to our success is the close working relationships that we have with all these areas on our campus and the way in which we support one another in our respective endeavors. In some cases we were included in the hiring process, although in others we were not. In all situations we have had open conversations with each person involved with our team and have outlined our priorities, values, and expectations for those staff members in their dealings with our student-athletes. Your players receive a powerful message when they hear the same goals for success from all facets and layers of your program.

Be Willing to Make Tough Decisions

As the head coach, you must be willing to make the tough decision when your goals are not being met and a staff change becomes necessary. Making such a change is not easy and likely will not happen without considerable thought. If a coach is not loyal, does not share your vision, does not buy into your priorities and values, or is not getting the job done in her or his areas of responsibility, team morale and the ability to enjoy success will be compromised. I encourage you first to counsel the staff member and try to help her or him improve in the problem areas. Document these conversations and outline your concerns and expectations in writing. If the desired changes do not occur, you will have no choice. As difficult as such decisions are, they often result in addition by subtraction, and your team will be better off in the long run.

RECRUITING

"You don't win the Kentucky Derby with a plow horse." I wish I had a nickel for every time I've heard Ralph, my husband and cohead coach, utter that phrase. But the expression is true, and it is one of our guiding principles when it comes to recruiting. Good coaching is certainly a key component of a successful program. But without great players, coaching will only take you so far. You must work tirelessly to find the best players you possibly can who will fit with your program's priorities and your coaching philosophy.

Close the Borders

When we arrived at Tennessee, our first goal in recruiting was to close the borders. We made an effort to keep the best players in Tennessee at home, wearing the orange and competing for their state university. Many athletes in the South grow up with fervent loyalty to the university that bears their state's name. That loyalty translates to tremendous passion and heart on the field. Our players who hail from Tennessee and have loved the university since birth feel a pride unlike any other when they put on the uniform. A colleague of ours said it well: "If they're wearing Tennessee on their chest, I want them to have Tennessee in their heart." Likewise, your local fan base will appreciate cheering for one of their own. Although fans first want a winning team, they love having homegrown talent competing and succeeding in the program.

Keeping in mind the importance of recruiting student-athletes who can compete at your level, you must remember that recruiting locally will not serve you well if the talent pool is not sufficient to meet your competitive needs. First, you need players who will help you win. Second, you can create problems for yourself when you have local players sitting the bench who are disgruntled about their lack of playing time. When recruiting in our state we ask ourselves two questions: (1) Does this player have the ability to be a starter in our program, and (2) if she isn't strong enough to start, does she understand and agree to the limited role for which we need her (pinch runner, bullpen catcher, defensive specialist).

Communication is essential in the latter case. Over the years many in-state players have told us, "I don't care if I play. I just want to be a Lady Volunteer and I will do whatever it takes to be a part of the team." After a year of sitting on the bench, players sometimes forget that they ever spoke those words. We have frank and honest discussions with every player we recruit regarding how we see her fitting into our team. This conversation is especially important with the players who won't see the field as much.

Build Relationships

When building a program from the ground up or resuscitating a losing program, building positive relationships with youth coaches is essential. At this point you won't have a tradition of success to rely on. You will, however, have your vision, goals, values, and priorities, and it's important that you get the message out and communicate clearly and passionately who you are and where you are going. High school and club coaches are the first point of contact with prospects and an important audience to hear your message. Take time to speak to them in person, touch base by phone, and maintain an open line of communication. Be sure to offer your services to the coaches to answer questions, speak at clinics, and share knowledge. Invite them to your practices. The golden rule applies here—treat others the way you would like to be treated.

A story from our coaching career illustrates the importance of relationships and the manner in which you treat people. It relates to the recruitment of Monica Abbott, one of the greatest pitchers in the history of collegiate softball. We began recruiting Monica during our first season at Tennessee. The program had suffered through two losing seasons before our arrival and had reached NCAA postseason play only once in the six years that Tennessee had sponsored the sport of softball. Although our first season was a success in terms of achieving a winning record and getting things headed in the right direction, we didn't qualify for NCAA Regionals and failed to make the Southeastern Conference tournament (the top eight teams qualified). So we didn't have a great softball tradition at Tennessee to sell to recruits. Monica's club coach, Keith Berg, had met Ralph several years earlier when he was coaching a 10-under team. He listened to one of Ralph's sessions at a coach's clinic and waited at the podium to ask Ralph a question following the session. Ralph spent the better part of the next hour talking softball with Keith over lunch. As Keith tells it, "I was so impressed that he was willing to spend time with a 10-under travel ball coach. . . . Most college coaches are in a hurry to get away." Six years later that first impression paid huge dividends when Keith's now 16-under team included the number one pitching prospect in the country. Granted, much more work went into the recruiting process, but I have no doubt that the exchange between Ralph and Keith and the impression it left on Keith opened the door for Monica and her family to listen to our vision for the future of Tennessee softball.

Ralph always makes a point to thank club and high school coaches for the time and effort they spend training young softball players. When he coached in the United States Olympic program, he frequently said that we have the best softball players in the world because we have outstanding and dedicated youth coaches who provide most of the developmental training for young athletes. These coaches don't get paid high salaries, don't have the resources of a collegiate coach, and often have to deal with challenges and obstacles that we never face. I was recently recruiting at a club exposure tournament when a young club coach sought me out. She said, "When I met your husband the other day, he thanked me for what I did. I have had 17 players go to college on scholarships, and he is the first college coach ever to thank *me* for coaching these girls. Please tell him how much that meant to me."

Work Smarter . . . and Harder

On the field we often tell our players to play smarter, not harder. We want them to understand that playing hard won't solve every challenge; sometimes the key is to take a more thoughtful and intelligent approach. In recruiting, working hard is essential. Recruiting is a tireless, never-ending part of your job as a college coach. One of the key reasons for our success at Tennessee is the amount of time we put into recruiting. We work many hours in the summer watching prospects at travel ball tournaments. The fall is more of the same, and we host prospects on the weekends when we stay at home. Rarely do we have a weekend away from softball and recruiting. Recruiting has changed significantly in the past five years, and coaches are now required to recruit at least two or three classes at a time, adding substantial hours to the workload.

Working smarter has played a big part in our success as well. One of the things that you must do in your program is analyze what makes you unique. Assuming that everyone is going to work hard, ask yourself, "What can I do or offer that will set me apart from my competitors?" In our first season at Tennessee, we were able to take advantage of the fact that we didn't advance to the conference tournament to make a statement in recruiting. Our regular season ended the last week of April, and most teams were playing for another one or two weeks. Rather than take an early vacation, I flew to California to watch our top two juniors play their final high school regular-season games. I was the only college coach at either game. The unusually cold weather made for unpleasant viewing, but I made sure to stay the entire game. I even had fans tell me, "Oh, it's nice of you to come, but I'm sure she's going to XYZ University," which was an outstanding academic institution and softball program much closer to home. But our flying across country to watch a single high school game made quite an impression on both young ladies. Both commented that no college coach had ever come to their high school games before, even those within an hour's drive. Both girls ended up signing with Tennessee, and between them, Monica Abbott and Lindsay Schutzler garnered seven All-American awards, three Academic All-American awards, two Academic All-American of the Year awards, one USA Player of the Year award, and numerous other conference and regional accolades. They were instrumental in building Tennessee softball into the program it is today.

Know Your Strengths, Be Yourself, and Recruit Positively

We haven't won every recruiting battle, but over the years we've won more than we've lost. I believe that one of the reasons is that we are confident in our strengths and those of our university and program. We emphasize these aspects in every recruiting conversation we have with coaches, parents, and prospects. What do you have to sell? Make a list of everything you believe is positive about your program, whether it is academic reputation, facilities, climate, winning tradition, fan support, commitment to women's athletics, longevity among coaching staff, graduation rates, strength of your conference, and so on, and make sure that your recruits hear about these things often.

At the same time, every program faces challenging elements in the recruiting landscape. Your opponents may be quick to point out your challenges to recruits, so take the wind out of their sails by addressing them early in the process and showing that you have a plan to deal with them. Perhaps weather prevents you from practicing outside year round, but you have a terrific indoor facility to tout. Speak confidently about yourself and the vision you have for your program. Until you believe in yourself, no one else will. This belief must come through loud and clear in your words and actions.

We make it a point never to engage in negative recruiting. When you talk disparagingly about another program, it reflects a lack of security in what you have to offer. Prospects have commented more than once that they appreciate the fact that we don't recruit negatively. From my experience, it doesn't work with recruits.

Be honest and open about yourself and your expectations for your student-athletes. Any question a parent or prospect has is fair game, and we answer them thoroughly and honestly. We tell our players to do the same thing. A recruiting visit can be full of glitz and glamour, but behind all that is the real day-to-day life of a student-athlete on your campus. The prospect should learn early what that experience will entail rather than be surprised later when it is too late. Neither you nor the athlete will be happy in that case.

TEAM POLICIES AND EXPECTATIONS

Setting your team policies and expectations and communicating them to your staff and players is an important component of building a successful program. We begin the communication during the recruiting process. We want prospects who ultimately choose Tennessee to understand early our expectations for their behavior and performance on the field, in the classroom, and in the community at large. Our first team meeting when the players arrive in the fall centers on the communication of team policies and procedures. We include our upperclassmen in explaining the policies and rationale behind these rules to the freshmen. The new players recognize that the upperclassmen support team policies and will help make sure that they are followed.

As the head coach, you must decide what policies and rules are important to you. You may involve your staff and team leaders in this discussion, or you may find it necessary to set the tone yourself if you are trying to change the culture of a program. When we took over at Tennessee we thought it important to establish our priorities and change the culture to fit our coaching style and personalities. Our approach was, as a matter of necessity, more authoritarian, and we did not include players in discussions about team policies. We understood that those players, none of whom we recruited, had signed to play for another coach who had a different philosophy and had come to Tennessee with different expectations than ours. But we needed to make it clear that we expected them to adhere immediately to our policies and expectations. We left no room for discussion, dissension, or a slow period of transition. If they could not or would not commit to our way of doing things, we supported their decision to leave the program and helped them find a place that better fit their personality and desires.

As the years went by and the culture of our program solidified, we included players in the formulation and adjustment of policies and expectations. You should review your policies on a yearly basis. Some may have outlived their usefulness or necessity. I don't believe in making rules just to have rules. Each policy must have a purpose, one that reflects your priorities and can be clearly understood and followed by your players. We have made changes over the years, in consultation with staff and team captains. We have added, deleted, and sometimes simply changed the wording to enable clearer communication. Players are more likely to adhere to team policies when they feel a sense of ownership. Ownership occurs when they are a part of the policy formulation process. We are pleased and amazed to see the sense of collegiality that develops among current and former players in the program when they know that everyone is representing Tennessee in the same manner and doing things on and off the field the Tennessee way.

Following the team meeting when we review and explain the policies, each team member signs a document stating that she agrees to adhere to the softball program policies and understands the consequences for failure to do so. The following is an example of our team policies at Tennessee:

Lady Vols Softball Pride Policies

1. Respect Policy

I will respect myself. I will respect the people around me (coaches, staff, teammates, administrators, faculty). I will respect the Lady Volunteer tradition. I will respect university and team rules.

2. On-Time Policy

I will be on time for all scheduled events—classes, practice, team meetings, medical appointments, weights, study hall, tutors, and so on.

3. No-Miss and Up-Front Policy

I will attend all classes and sit in one of the front three rows. I will attend all assigned functions such as study hall, practice, tutor sessions, medical appointments, banquets, team meetings, and so on.

4. Academic Policies

I will follow all Thornton Center policies and procedures. I will complete all assigned study hall hours. I understand that I may do no more than two hours of study hall in the computer lab. I understand that I must complete study hall hours by noon on Friday. I will develop good relationships with my professors and maintain frequent communication with them.

5. Effort and Hustle Policy

I will give 100 percent effort in all that I do—classes, practices, games, strength and conditioning workouts, rehab sessions, and so forth. I will hustle on the field at all times. I understand that my effort and commitment are key to my success as a student-athlete and the success of the Lady Volunteer softball team.

6. Dressing Room and Equipment Policies

I will take care of all equipment I am issued as a softball team member. I understand that I am responsible for any losses or damage to equipment. At the end of the season, I will turn in all equipment to the head manager. I will take pride in keeping my locker room neat and clean and will not leave items out.

7. Dress Policy

I will dress like a winner. "You never have a second chance to make a first impression." I realize that the image I project will be a reflection on all of us. Tattoos and body piercing (except ears) are not to be visible during any Lady Vols function including practices, games, meetings, camps, office, travel, and so on.

I will abide by the athletic department policy regarding wearing Adidas products and will follow the Varsity Inn dress code. I will wear assigned game and practice attire as designated by the coaching staff.

8. Alcohol, Drug, and Tobacco Policy

I will not consume alcohol, drugs, tobacco, or any other banned substances during the practice and playing seasons or in the presence of recruits. I will not purchase alcohol, drugs, or tobacco products for, or provide them to, minors.

9. Communication and Follow-Through Policy

I will return all phone calls and answer all e-mails within 24 hours. I will follow through and communicate until an assignment or task is completed ("I left a message," "I called and no one answered," or "I stopped by but they weren't there" is not sufficient).

10. Housing Policy

I understand that I must obtain written permission from the cohead coaches before I enter into an agreement to live off campus. I understand that I must coordinate my selection of roommates, on or off campus, with the cohead coaches before the beginning of the academic year.

I have read and understand the preceding team policies, which I must follow to be eligible to play at Tennessee. I understand that violation of the policies may result in disciplinary action up to and including dismissal from the team and revocation of my scholarship.

_____

Name   Date

Courtesy of the University of Tennessee.

In addition, we have some policies regarding team travel that are worth mentioning. With rare exceptions, we require our players to eat meals together on road trips. We believe that this practice creates a sense of togetherness and camaraderie. Unless we are involved in pregame scouting or preparation activities, coaches are present at team meals as well. We do not allow our players to talk on their cell phones while on the team bus or to have their phones out during meals. We want them to use this time to grow closer in their relationships with one another and enjoy each other as people without outside disruptions. At curfew we collect cell phones and keep them in a staff member's room until breakfast the next morning. This procedure allows our players to get adequate and necessary rest so that they are able to perform to their fullest potential. It is also a courtesy to the roommate who might be kept awake by a teammate talking on her phone into the night. We expect our players to go to sleep at curfew, so they have no reason to have a cell phone after that time. In case of emergency our players' families know that they can always call us if they need to reach their daughter. Our players have come to appreciate and support the policy of having no cell phone after curfew.

COMMUNITY AND FAN SUPPORT

At the earliest opportunity possible, you should make a plan for building support for your program within the community and developing a loyal fan base. Everyone loves to follow a winner, but if you are tasked with building a successful program, chances are that you are starting from scratch or taking over a losing program. We took over a program that had suffered through two consecutive losing seasons and had advanced to postseason play only once in six years. We did a number of things to generate community and fan support.

One of the first things you should do is reach out to the youth softball community. Team and youth discounts are available at all our games. Teams are allowed to participate in "dugout run-out," in which a youth team forms a tunnel for our team to run through during pregame introductions. If teams attend our games, we invite them onto the field afterward to participate in our postgame meeting. Our players are available to sign autographs after every home game. Our team participates in two free clinics each year to help expose inner-city kids to the sport of softball. In addition, we offer free postgame clinics on SEC weekends. These are all great ways to connect with kids and provide positive role models. In turn, the kids want to keep coming back to support our players and team.

We extend an open invitation for softball coaches to attend practice any time, and we make ourselves accessible to them. During our first year at Tennessee, we hosted a free clinic for all high school and youth coaches in East Tennessee. We run several camps and clinics throughout the year to help grow softball in our area.

Another way to generate community support is to volunteer to speak at local Rotary, Kiwanis, and other clubs' lunch meetings. We typically do four or five such speaking engagements each year, and these events provide a great opportunity to sell our passion and program to a wide range of community leaders. Many of these attendees become fans and may even provide significant financial resources for our program needs. People will support something they believe in, and the only way to convince them is to get out in the community and share your vision.

Community service has always been a cornerstone of the Lady Volunteers athletic department. Our players participate in a variety of activities throughout the academic year, including Habitat for Humanity, sponsoring needy children at Christmas, canned food drives, helping with the Juvenile Diabetes Research Foundation gala, spending an hour each week at a local inner-city elementary school mentoring young children, children's reading programs, and the Martin Luther King Day parade, among others. All these programs are terrific ways to give back to the community and form personal relationships with people who inevitably become big supporters of our players.

After you get fans to come to your games, you need to make the experience one that will entice them to keep coming back. We are fortunate to have an outstanding marketing department at Tennessee that does an excellent job of creating a fun, family-oriented game atmosphere. Anything that gets the crowd involved and gives people an opportunity to win a prize is always a big hit. We offer several giveaways at our games, including free pizza to the loudest group, free T-shirts when we hit a home run, trivia contests between innings, and so on. Such events, combined with the excited fast-paced brand of softball that we play, make our games fun for everyone.

GOAL SETTING

Along with creating an overall vision for your program and its future, you should have a goal-setting program that will guide you in the short term. As a staff, we sit down each off-season and evaluate the previous season. What did we do well? What do we need to do better? What new or different dimensions would we like to add to our program? What did we learn from another successful program? We evaluate everything—our statistical outcomes in every phase of the game (pitching, defense, hitting), team chemistry and cohesion, game preparation, practice plans, medical training and injury management, nutrition, strength and conditioning training, teaching methods, player–coach relationships, staff responsibilities, video analysis, and so on. This honest and thorough evaluation provides the feedback we need to drive our goals for the following season. Staff should give one another constructive criticism when warranted. A coach, like any professional, can become complacent or stuck in old methods that may not work as well as they did previously. Like our athletes, we need challenges to help us grow. Exploring new ideas and approaches is not always comfortable, and most of us are not naturally adaptive to change. But I find that the coaches who are most successful over a period of years are the ones who actively pursue excellence and are willing to adapt their methods when necessary while remaining true to their core values and principles.

Plan of Action

Our players also participate in a goal-setting program. As a team, we meet each year to set goals for the season. Each player sets goals as well. We ask them to set three types of individual goals on a monthly basis: (1) softball skills goal, (2) mental game goal, and (3) fitness goal. The plan of action that accompanies the goal is probably more important than the goal itself. Without a specific plan of action, goals become dreams that are never achieved. For example, if a player wants to improve her bunting skills, a plan to "bunt more at practice" is not specific enough and doesn't invite a level of measurement and accountability. An appropriate plan of action and one that would ensure successful achievement of her goal is "bunt 25 balls per day off the pitching machine three days per week."

Make Your Goals Attainable and Measurable

Goals must be specific, measurable, and attainable. If you establish goals that are not attainable, you are setting yourself up for failure and will likely be disappointed early in the season. I remember going into the locker room of a conference opponent several years back. This particular opponent had struggled to finish above .500 most years and had never won a conference championship. The team goals posted in the locker room included the following: win the conference championship, win every conference series, go undefeated at home, and advance to the Women's College World Series. These goals were all unattainable for that team at that point in time. Their first conference series was at home against one of the top teams in the nation, so they were likely to lose any shot at two of those goals early in their season. A team can quickly become deflated if they set goals that are too far out of their reach.

Goals must also be measurable. Players often state a goal in terms of "getting better," but measuring a vague goal like that is difficult. A hitter who wants to improve her batting average, for example, would be better off to have a specific goal to hit .350. Although that goal is certainly measurable and the player can easily judge whether she achieved it, I suggest using a variation that focuses more on the process and things that are within the hitter's control. A hitter can have a great at bat and hit a screaming line drive that goes right to a defensive player for an out. Conversely, the same hitter can have a terrible at bat in which she swings at a bad pitch off balance but bloops a single just over the shortstop's head. The second scenario results in a base hit that helps her reach the .350 batting-average goal. But the process is much better in the first scenario and over time will result in more successful at bats, which will likely lead to a positive outcome. For this reason, we like our players to focus on process-oriented goals rather than outcome-oriented goals. Process-oriented goals are also typically controllable and afford the player an opportunity to achieve the goal more consistently (having a good at bat versus batting .350).

CREATING TRADITIONS

Developing traditions that define your program is essential in building a successful college program. Some of these will naturally evolve over time, whereas others will result from a concerted effort on your part and reflect your values and principles. We have several traditions that are part of the fabric of Lady Volunteers softball. Many of these have been part of our program at every coaching stop, and some are unique to Tennessee. Traditions help to form a bond between players and are a bridge that connects all Lady Volunteers past and present.

A couple of postgame traditions have been part of all our programs. During our team meeting after each game the players "throw bouquets" to one another. Teammates complement each other on a great performance, a well-executed play, an example of great hustle, providing positive leadership or support from the bench, or anything else that contributed to the game that day. Players are empowered by hearing these things from one another rather than just from the coaching staff. These "bouquets" are especially meaningful after a difficult loss or when a player's effort inspired her teammates even if the outcome wasn't in our favor. Our second postgame tradition is to join hands and end every postgame meeting with a team prayer led by a coach or player.

As part of our pregame ritual, the players come together shortly before introductions and say the Lord's Prayer. The players started this tradition early in our tenure at Tennessee. We can't remember how or why it began, but it has remained an important part of their pregame preparation.

Hoosiers Night is a long-standing tradition on all our teams. Every freshmen class comes to the head coach's house to have dinner and watch the movie *Hoosiers* early in their first semester. *Hoosiers* contains several valuable lessons for success in athletics and life and is a powerful teaching tool. After the movie we talk with the freshmen about inspirational parts and the lessons learned from them. The hero in *Hoosiers* is a character named Jimmy Chitwood. Jimmy is the best basketball player at a rural Indiana high school of fewer than 100 students. His team faces a powerful urban school of over 2,000 students in the state high school championship. Despite being huge underdogs, Jimmy's team has a chance to win the game at the end, and Chitwood wants to take the shot that determines their fate. To reflect the importance of wanting to be in a clutch situation and having the confidence to succeed with the game on the line, we award "JC" stickers for the most clutch performances, offensive and defensive, each game, and the players place these stickers on their helmets.

"JC" is part of another tradition in our program. During practices and games, whenever a player receives a compliment from a member of the coaching staff, the player responds by saying, "JC." This response lets the coach know that the player heard and acknowledges a job well done. When a player receives constructive criticism from a coach, she responds by saying, "Magic." In this context, MAGIC is an acronym for "Make A Greater Individual Commitment." By responding in this way, the player is communicating that she heard and understands the criticism and will make an effort to improve. These oral acknowledgements are important pieces of communication in the teaching and learning process.

Many teams have traditions that help to form stronger team bonds, and ours is no different. Each year shortly before the season begins we have Family Night, when each player brings pictures of her family members and tells the rest of the team about her extended family (parents, siblings, grandparents, and so on). This time of sharing can be emotional as players talk about family members who are meaningful and influential in their lives. The activity helps us grow closer to one another and deepens relationships away from the field, all of which assists us in becoming a stronger unit on the field.

A traditional event we did at UT–Chattanooga and recently rekindled at Tennessee is to go on a team retreat. We traveled to a lodge in the Smoky Mountains for a weekend in the fall. Senior captains held a draft and divided the team into four smaller teams of four or five players each. Each team was responsible for preparing and serving a meal for the whole group, and the teams competed against one another throughout the weekend in fun games like egg toss, lip sync competition, team Pictionary, scavenger hunt, foosball, and others. A retreat is a terrific way to appreciate one another's personalities and talents away from the softball field and come together under one roof to enjoy a weekend of fun, food, and fellowship.

FINAL THOUGHTS

Building a successful college program takes time and patience. Like a house, a team must have a strong foundation to withstand the storms that will inevitably occur. Build your foundation on solid principles and values that reflect who you are and what you stand for. In this age of the quick fix, getting caught up in the win-now mentality and compromising yourself can be easy. Remember that you are not building a team that will be a one-hit wonder in the short run; instead, you are seeking to build a program that will enjoy long-standing and consistent success. Take time to make a detailed plan that encompasses everything important in a successful program. Share your plan and vision with everyone involved in your program. Understand that building a program, like anything important in life, will take a tremendous amount of time and work. Then go about it passionately and with great enthusiasm!

8

Selecting and Mentoring Your Staff

Elaine Sortino

Throughout the past three decades as a Division I softball coach, I have had the good fortune to be associated with many fine young women who have aspired to coach our great game. Although constant change has made its mark on many aspects of our sport, the roles that we play in mentoring our assistants remain the same.

This chapter is divided into sections that describe a head coach's most important obligations. Although they are not in any particular rank or order, none of these categories is optional. I would venture to say that all successful coaches will have these on their list in some form.

CREATING A CULTURE OF LOYALTY

We all want loyalty, and I am sure we would find this on the list of every head coach. Although we all expect to have it, loyalty within a coaching staff requires hard work on the part of everyone. Our assistants should know that at all times they can rely on our loyalty toward them.

As we begin to build our relationship with our assistants, their loyalty is most often the first thing we ask for in return. From that point on, the responsibility is ours to make sure that we create an atmosphere in which that loyalty can be nurtured and grown. Loyalty is a two-way street; therefore, we should expect from them only what they consistently receive from us.

It begins with the way the head coach respects, honors, and treats them. Our assistants must know that when issues arise that may concern them, whether with administrators, departmental coaches, coaching peers, team members, parents, or fans, we will always speak about them with high regard. If an issue that concerns them arises with any of these constituencies, they should hear about it from the head coach first whenever possible.

Additionally, the head coach should always show respect and honor toward an assistant in the presence of the team. Head coaches who praise and speak highly of their assistants contribute to the team's level of competency and the program's future success. Players thrive in an atmosphere that is rich with respect and competent coaching.

Any head coach who would publicly reprimand or embarrass an assistant, in any situation, is giving the players permission to do the same. Such an example frees our players to be disrespectful not only to the coaching staff but also to each other.

ENCOURAGING COMMUNICATION

Making the time to talk is one of the most challenging aspects of our profession. We seem to run harder and faster with each season. More often than not, we think that we barely have time to coach our team. Additionally, we operate in a culture that is driven by e-mails and texting! This environment presents one of the most difficult obstacles to our success.

There is no substitute for communication in the form of talking in person. We are most effective when we have the opportunity to look into someone's eyes and have dialogue. If we hide all day behind our e-mails and texts, we will never see how the other person is reacting in a given circumstance. We need to take advantage of every opportunity to deal with each other face to face.

No head coach among us would want to teach or train our players without having the advantage of daily interaction because we learn and understand so much from body language. Yet we often will not sit down and confront tough or uncomfortable situations with our assistants. If an assistant does something contrary to the way we want it done, we need to provide the feedback necessary so that she or he can make adjustments and improve. Issues that are left alone may end up causing many problems down the road.

Through constant communication, especially positive and negative feedback, we can actively process and refine our teaching skills, and communicate our principles to our players with greater consistency and clarity. Most staffs do their best work in this area, but it is all the other stuff that requires more attention.

Taking time to check in on how we are all feeling about what we do every day is important. Through this process our assistants have the chance to learn and understand our core values and the standards we hold for our program. When our daily responsibilities consume us, we are not attentive to taking the time needed to check in with each other. We need to set aside time each day not only to plan practice but also to make sure that everyone is OK!

These daily conversations allow our staff to become more deeply invested in our goals and expectations. We minimize confused messages from the coaching staff to the players, prospects, parents, and fans on everything we are about. We as a staff feel a sense of ownership and sense that we are all in this together.

Encouraging an atmosphere of daily conversation also allows our assistants to be able to disagree, which is vital to the growth of the relationship and helps everyone break out of the box. Although we may be uncomfortable while it is happening, in the end we are all in a better place.

Here is where the greatest leadership originates, because we all have to settle on one course of direction. After we choose a direction or make a decision, the entire coaching staff needs to present a united voice. Anything other than that is unacceptable and will create a chaotic environment for the program.

If we disagree, the head coach must make sure that the decision is clarified. Nothing should be assumed as understood or left to chance. Regardless of the issue, an assistant coach should not have to take the initiative to rectify a situation. All conflict needs to be resolved, and when it can't be, we need to agree to disagree and move on.

A coaching staff should never go to practice or to a game with any sense of anger or frustration with each other. The negative energy produced by this type of situation is unproductive and no use to our players or each other. The bottom line here is that without frequent and constant communication, staying in sync with each other is difficult, and most problems begin at this point. Players have effective radar in these instances, and many other problems can develop for the team.

Establishing Boundaries With Staff

In our coaching staff interactions and relationships, the establishment of boundaries is also important. The more muddled our interactions become in terms of who we are to each other, the more difficult it becomes to address issues. Although familiarity offers comfort in day-to-day operations, it also presents an obstacle when we have to deal with challenging situations.

When head coaches choose to say nothing after observing something they do not like, deterioration of relationships within the coaching staff and between the staff and players will begin immediately. Loyalty means being honest in good times and bad, no matter how hard being truthful might be, and we always need to trust each other. Regardless of the chronological age of staff members, the head coach needs to take care of the situation as soon as it arises. For example, a head coach who observes an assistant coach acting disrespectfully toward an umpire should address the issue privately with the assistant as quickly as possible. The head coach may want the assistant to apologize to the official and then perhaps address the team (who probably observed the behavior) to explain that his or her response was not appropriate. Obviously, the head coach would not expect to see such behavior occur again.

Establishing Boundaries With Players

Although communication within the staff is critical, communication from the coaching staff to the players is equally important. As head coaches, we need to have respectable relationships with all our players, and we must encourage our assistants to have the same. Because of the age proximity between players and assistants, a player is more likely to confide in an assistant coach than in the head coach. This sort of interaction can be helpful for the team and can prevent major setbacks in some cases.

As younger coaches start their careers, they may be drawn into the team's dynamics more as peers than as coaches. In these instances, the head coach needs to provide feedback, direction, and guidance to make sure that the assistants are able to establish themselves as coaches, not teammates. Assistants should be encouraged to build strong, trusting relationships while establishing clear boundaries with the players.

For a number of reasons, assistants often have problems relating to certain players, or particular players have a problem with an assistant coach. Again, our job as head coaches is to step in and help them find common ground. This issue, although difficult, is not up for negotiation, and we need to make sure that mutual respect exists between player and coach. These situations need to be addressed immediately and will often need more than one attempt to resolve.

CLARIFYING STAFF ROLES

Regardless of the number of coaches within a staff, all of them should know and understand their roles. We are crystal clear with our players when it comes to defining playing roles, and we should do the same for our assistants.

Although the task is painstaking and time consuming on the front end, after our staff is organized, accountable, and responsible for defined aspects of the softball program, things certainly run more efficiently and effectively.

In practice and games, head coaches frequently overlook the talent and expertise of their assistant coaches. Although the planning aspect of practices typically falls under the auspices of the head coach, dialogue and discussion should occur about the plan and its implementation. Everyone needs to be on the same page about the practice plan and aware of why it is being done in that fashion.

With regard to games and practices, assistants should be assigned to areas that most accurately match their level of expertise. All positions and aspects of the game should be discussed at daily meetings so that all are familiar with what is going on, regardless of position.

Before the start of each season, the head coach should ask assistants to make a list of the elements within the game that they think will be important to overall success. In daily prepractice meetings, they need to make sure that these parts are being implemented throughout the season. After practice is designed, assistants need to be trusted to implement and execute the plan with the team.

Assistant coaches, particularly younger ones, should receive daily oversight and feedback from the head coach about practice implementation. One of the most important parts of the head coach's teaching and mentoring of staff is observing the execution of practices.

Assistant coaches should always be delegated certain game responsibilities to make the program stronger in competition. More often, these are areas in which they are comfortable and knowledgeable. Assistant coaches are not just drill facilitators, but rather teachers and role models who represent the future of our game.

Professionalism should always be discussed as a staff. The way that we present ourselves in all situations is important. Head coaches should be role models in how they appear at practice, competitive, recruiting, departmental, and formal functions related to our sport. The attire that we wear as a staff should always reflect appropriateness and class. Our body language and personal appearance contribute to the perception of our program by players, parents, and fans.

DELEGATING DUTIES

Behind the scenes, a multitude of program aspects contribute to its success. If assistant coaches are delegated only the lower levels of responsibility, neither they nor the program can develop to the highest potential.

Duties should be clearly assigned throughout the program, and assistants should understand that outcomes and expectations are attached to each. Coaching and administrative assignments should be discussed, defined, and frequently clarified. If shortcomings arise in any assignment area, the head coach needs to assume the oversight and communication necessary to resolve the situation. This responsibility is one of the most challenging jobs for a head coach. A giant leap of faith goes with delegating responsibility and letting assistant have control of a situation.

An approach that can facilitate less obtrusive oversight from the head coach is a weekly check-in time. During this meeting each staff member gives an update on his or her area of concern so that the entire staff is informed about each part of the program. The head coach will have the opportunity to learn what is going on without the assistants feeling that someone is hovering over their shoulders.

We should be willing to delegate responsibilities that will prepare our assistant coaches to become head coaches. We often assign responsibilities that match a person's strength or affinities, but we might consider changing these from year to year to make sure that each assistant receives as much experience as possible within the duties of the program. Budgets, travel, academics, strength and conditioning, media relations, marketing, game management, clinics, and fielding duties, among many others, are all significant parts of the coaching profession that we should address as we mentor and prepare our staffs for the future.

Occasionally, head coaches have given major responsibilities to their assistants and later have identified that as the reason that the program struggled or failed. Training our assistant coaches and allowing them to grow is far different from being lazy and not wanting to do the work. Every duty delegated to an assistant coach is ultimately the responsibility of the head coach if execution falls short.

Regular check-ins with our staff ensures that nothing will be forgotten or left to chance. Checking in also provides the opportunity to rectify any actions that may warrant a change of course or other type of adjustment to meet the goals of the program. As stated earlier, this process takes time, but it provides the best possible opportunity for our staff to reach maximum potential. In the end, a coaching staff will function at a much higher level of efficiency and productivity.

CREATING A CULTURE OF TRUST

As we develop as a staff, our assistant coaches should feel that they are trusted. Trust is not given; it is earned, and winning trust obviously requires time. If we are effectively communicating our thoughts, beliefs, values, and goals on a daily basis, our assistants will likely be aware of these characteristics and incorporate them as their own. Discussions among the coaching staff should be about more than just the technical skills of executing the game. Trust encompasses many aspects within the program.

Head coaches who have done their jobs effectively to this point should have few problems in this regard. Assistant coaches are far more effective when they are confident in what they are speaking about to the players. Having a staff that is empowered to communicate with the players only makes the program better.

After practice has been discussed and planned, assistants must be trusted with implementing things in the way in which they were planned. Again, this comes down to clarity of communication and making sure that staff members are all on the same page. Players will receive more effective training and have greater opportunity to solicit feedback about their game.

In regard to the external view of the program, head coaches need to know and trust that the assistant coaches will carry the message of the program with pride and credibility. As they speak to parents, coaches, and players in the recruiting process, this point is crucial. Most important, however, is the opportunity that head coaches have to foster and improve our sport by mentoring assistants and making sure that they are in the sport for the right reason. If we care about our program, then we certainly must articulate and share its values. Assistant coaches need to be committed to the core values of the program. This is all about sharing what we believe and knowing what we stand for!

SHOWING GRATITUDE

Every day we hit the ground running hard, and many days are filled with crisis management. We are constantly delegating tasks and barking orders about mundane things to our coaching staffs. The more success a program has, the higher the expectation of the head coach seems to be. Each season we are doing more and asking our assistants to do the same.

As we become more harried, we seem to have less time to remember to say, "Thank you!" Nothing validates the hard work we do any better than hearing those two simple words. We all flourish when we know that what we do is appreciated. We must always remember to be grateful for the contributions that our assistant coaches make each day.

In a high-functioning staff, assistant coaches who are capable of reading the head coach's mind may think of tasks or issues before the head coach does and take care them without being asked. This circumstance comes with the familiarity and understanding that can develop over time. Unfortunately, assistant coaches are often taken for granted in such situations. We all need to remember to validate and appreciate the time that our assistants spend doing everything. For example, we may want to give them an unexpected day off. A head coach who likes to cook could give them a home-cooked meal. The head coach who knows what's going on in the assistants' lives could perhaps contribute toward a purchase of something that they are working on buying.

ENCOURAGING STAFF FEEDBACK

The best forum for teaching assistant coaches occurs on a daily basis when all are together as a coaching staff. This opportunity applies not only to the game but also to all the principles and values of the softball program.

Talking shop presents a tremendous opportunity for all of us to share our beliefs, to explain why doing it this way might be better than doing it that way. For those of us who are passionate about teaching, this is the best part of the day. Although we can quickly say why a particular skill should be executed, we should actively encourage our assistants to give their opinions as well. We need to provide a safe environment where all the members of the staff feel respected for their knowledge of the game.

In the case of a younger staff, achieving this type of dialogue will require patience and time as they begin to feel safe about voicing their opinions. We need to continue to stay the course and foster their confidence over time. This type of interaction guards against stagnation and allows assistants to improve their knowledge and understanding of the game, which in turn keeps the program on the cutting edge in terms of development.

We should encourage our assistants to have discussions with their coaching peers as well, because we all become better teachers of the game with this type of dialogue. Head coaches are critical in this atmosphere, and they need to be competent and confident in all areas to mentor their staffs. Coaches who are not secure in their knowledge will not be effective in engaging in any dialogue that might reveal this shortcoming, so they need to be persistent about improving their ability to teach, analyze, and understand the skills and offensive and defensive strategies of the game.

We have discussed why skill and strategy discussions should occur on a daily basis, but it is also important to check in on our thoughts and values regarding other aspects of the program. Head coaches should be diligent about including these aspects in discussion when possible. Assistants will then have the opportunity to discover what is important to the head coach and to develop a better foundation for implementing their own programs in the future.

IMPROVING STAFF RELATIONS

Each year, coaching staffs usually have a series of meetings with their players to check in and see how things are going. An individual meeting should also be offered to assistant coaches. A meeting provides an opportunity for an assistant to grow, to rectify mistakes, and, most important, to feel appreciated. Assistants will be allowed to express what they thought went well, voice their concerns, and discuss their future.

This meeting also provides the head coach with the opportunity to receive feedback on vital issues that can strengthen the coaching staff. Assistants should be asked to speak to their sense of ownership and their level of comfort with offering suggestions. They can assess their areas of responsibility and their effectiveness in managing those assignments. The staff can make sure that there is organization, effective management, interpersonal communication, and a constant increase in their knowledge of the game.

A head coach can be extremely helpful in mentoring an assistant. The head coach can serve as a sounding board to help assistants negotiate their way through difficult coaching challenges, assure them when they lack confidence or direction, and support their aspirations and hopes for the future.

FINAL THOUGHTS

One of the most difficult tasks for me is to sit still and write. The challenge of putting my thoughts on paper in some logical form was difficult for me. But although writing this chapter was not easy for me, I believe that doing it was invaluable. The process of organizing and explaining my coaching ideas will help me be a better coach in the future, and I am sure that my assistant coaching staff will appreciate it as well.

9

Promoting Your Program

Frank Griffin

In 1996 the Stetson fastpitch team played and practiced 6 miles (10 km) from campus at a city ball park. I inherited one set of five-year-old uniforms, 2.3 scholarships, a volunteer assistant coach, and a legally blind outfielder on which to build a program.

Fifteen years later, we play on a $2.5 million state-of the-art playing facility located in the center of the university's residence hall district. We have a fully funded scholarship program, two full-time assistant coaches, and eight sets of uniforms to choose from. Obviously, this didn't occur overnight; it was more of an evolutionary development.

THE APPROACH

Henry Ford said, "If you think you can or you think you can't, you are probably right." And the Stetson fastpitch program adheres to this philosophy. We take a positive approach to the overall development, marketing, and promotion of our program.

The four Ps, or principles, of marketing are useful tools to apply when promoting any product, especially an athletic program.

Product

Fastpitch at its finest is composed of fun, entertaining, and amazing athleticism. Knowing your market constituency is important. Who wants to have fun and be entertained? The answer: families, fans of the sport, and young athletes. Who enjoys the demonstration of top-notch skills and athleticism? Again—families, fastpitch fans, and young players, as well as visiting teams, recruits, and potential donors. Who wouldn't want to see a young woman throw a 60 mph (95 km per hour) fastball?

Price

Price is a key factor for building a fan base. No one wants to be gouged at the concession stand or the souvenir kiosk. Your aim might be to get team memorabilia in the hands of every fan and not let cost become a factor. Sell your T-shirts and ball caps at cost and offer free game programs and team posters at the gate. Although making money is important to a program, making it from marketing tools should not be the priority. I have found that selling a hat at cost is appreciated and often reciprocated with a generous donation. Making friends is also important; after all, enemies don't give you money. A family of four needs to know that they can afford a visit to the ball field and a trip to the concession stand without breaking the bank. Retirees will spend many more days and nights at the ball field if doing so is affordable. Senior discounts, season tickets priced at less than a dollar per game, and family packages will put softball on the list of things to do in any town.

Place

We've come a long way from playing ball at the city park, but it didn't happen overnight. The dream was to have a ballpark that we could be proud of and where a team would feel safe practicing and playing. We also wanted the field to be aesthetically pleasing. After clearing the empty lot and establishing a rough field, it became apparent that I could not coach, recruit, and hold practice while weeding, seeding, and feeding. The university graciously funded the hiring of a field maintenance technician, George Marshall. George understood what I as a coach knew to be crucially important to our program and the programs of visiting teams. Annual tilling and laser grading improved the quality of the playing field and created a level surface free of valleys and hills, thus reducing the potential for broken noses and chipped teeth.

Furthermore, batting cages were a welcome addition to our evolving complex. As any coach will attest, a poorly designed batting cage is a safety hazard. The metal poles supporting the net's cable system must be at a distance sufficient to prevent ball deflection. I have put into place a protective netting system that prevents balls from dropping from the ceiling of the cage. A protective screen was designed and built by DeLand Metal, a local metal fabricator, to protect the pitcher overhead and in front. With these measures, I made sure that my batting cages were effective and safe. Consider also the following features:

- Hitting stations should be distanced from one another and numerous enough to accommodate a team. Backstops should be padded for safety and low to the ground for the fans' viewing pleasure. Brick backstops and other hard surfaces can cause serious injury to players and umpires. We want teams—and umpires—to return.

- A sizable warning track—ours is 12 feet (3.7 m) of crushed red rock—lowers the potential for collision with fencing or poles and reduces the risk of injuries.

- Incorporate your team colors for a cohesive look. This program could be as elaborate as painting the team logo at the sidelines or as simple as hanging a team banner on the ticket booth. You can even paint the trashcans outside the stands to match the team colors.

As previously stated, visiting teams are key targets in our promotions plan. The safety of players and fans is essential to the success of that plan. Safety on and off the field communicates our commitment to our visitors' well-being just as does the number and cleanliness of restrooms and water fountains. Adequate, comfortable seating and shade is also imperative for an enjoyable experience. Trees are attractive on the perimeter of the park, but they are a groundskeeper's nightmare when used as shade for bleacher seating. We have opted for numerous picnic tables and market umbrellas to provide seating, shade, and picnic facilities. The comfort of our field keeps our fans coming back year after year.

Promotions

A key factor in the process of promoting our program is the team itself. Attitude, athleticism, and achievement speak volumes to potential recruits and their families, as well as sponsors, administrators, visiting teams, and fans.

A positive attitude and good sportsmanship leave fans, umpires, and visiting teams with a favorable impression. A few years ago, one of our fans made a rude comment to the umpire for which I apologized, and I promptly addressed the crowd in the stands, "We don't behave that way!" Well, the crowd suddenly became quiet. One fellow raised his hand and said, "It wasn't me, Coach." That fellow was university president Dr. Doug Lee. He was fond of repeating that story every year at the athletic department kickoff as he reminded us that sportsmanship should be stressed as much as academic and athletic success. If your team and your fans know that you appreciate and expect first-class behavior, they will strive to live up to those expectations. Your fans as well as the visiting team will enjoy the positive atmosphere. Prepared and competitive athletes convey a winning attitude, and everybody loves a winner. Stetson University has a long-standing reputation for producing outstanding student-athletes. This year, the Stetson fastpitch team was ranked in the NCAA Division I top 10 GPAs as well as the National Fastpitch Coaches Association's top 10 all-academic teams. Achievement on and off the field establishes our student-athletes among the finest in the nation.

THE SIGNAL

Sending the right signal sets the tone for the overall experience. Whether you have a large, well-equipped facility or are using a public space, keeping the grounds maintained and pristine is important to giving visitors a great first impression. Your field should lack in neither prestige nor class, regardless of size or budget. And visitors see more than just the field. You can enhance the overall experience by keeping any amenities, like the field house, training room, locker room, press box, and concession stand, in top shape, too. These facilities provide a practical and aesthetically pleasing welcome to visiting teams, potential recruits, and visitors to your fastpitch facility. Pride of place should be your calling card.

Another key component to the experience is making your visitors feel welcome. When a recruit visits your complex with her family, give them the tour, which consists of a meet and greet with current players, a walk about campus, a classroom visit, and lunch or dinner at one of your local sponsors. Provide the full-on fastpitch experience to your guests. As a youngster growing up in the South, I was taught early on that you always offer your guests a glass of iced tea and something to eat. The same holds true today. We offer our visitors something to drink and, depending on the season, something fresh from the garden. That's right; part of our landscaping includes fruit and vegetables along with plants native to Florida. Even the dugouts are flanked with upside-down tomato plants. Every year, visiting teams ask about those crazy tomato plants, which have even piqued the curiosity of the local newspaper. One afternoon, a local sportswriter stopped by to check the progress on the field and noticed my tomatoes growing upside down from a five-gallon (20 L) TPS bucket. He asked what TPS stood for. Feeling a little cheeky, I replied, "Tomato plants, stupid." He led the headline with my remark, and we gained four column inches (10 cm) on our program and a photo of the tomato plants.

Many visitors have taken away a jar of pickled green tomatoes or hot peppers, and they've returned the gesture with their own veggies, jams, or jellies. Visiting teams are offered oranges in the dugout. Little brothers and sisters are given an ice pop while they tour the facility. A potential donor should never leave without an autographed ball, ball cap, or T-shirt. You want your visitors to feel welcome and leave with intentions to return.

Make use of all your resources. Does your athletic department have a marketing department? If not, solicit your college of business or local business association for ideas from their marketing majors or employees.

Here are a few of the ideas we like:

- Pocket schedules can be made available at the checkout registers in restaurants and stores.
- Table tents featuring a team picture and schedule can be placed on the tables at our favorite restaurants and sports bars in the community.
- Team posters can be given away at the gate and posted in the windows of stores in town.
- Yard signs on game day attract a great deal of attention.
- Press conferences are a wonderful way to send a positive message—win or lose.
- Selling banner ads or trading them for services establishes a relationship with the community and brings in sponsors.
- Make promotional items easily accessible to your fans. They shouldn't have to make a trip to the bookstore to get a T-shirt. Set up a souvenir kiosk or make items available in the concession.

- Bumper stickers with catchy slogans such as "If it's a pitch, make it fast" and your organization's logo will get the attention of folks all around town. Large plastic drinking cups with the team logo that entitle the bearer to refills for the remainder of the season can be sold. Ball caps should also be available.
- Calendars or calendar posters are also a great promotional tool. The August page could have a photo of the newest players on the team. The calendar could have other photos of the team, including May's graduating seniors. Note your fall schedule of games, alumni game, open practices, barbeques, and booster club meetings.

During the construction of the first phase we had little time to seek out donors. Instead, the donors came to us. Visitors would stop to say hello or see how things were progressing and hand me a check as they left. When the money ran out and the backstops and dugouts had yet to be completed, we had to make a decision. Do I wait it out and hope that the money comes in, or do I keep working and hope that the money comes in? I kept working, from sunup to sundown. During that time, I hired Tracy Rieppenhoff to be my assistant coach. Instead of handing her the key to her office, I handed her a hammer and we kept working. And people kept stopping and asking whether they could help; they would give me a check and come back the following week with a friend who would give me a check. Without sounding egotistical, although I am a coach and it comes with the territory, I believe that folks are attracted to success and want to be a part of it. People were literally stopping by and handing me checks! I attribute this generosity to their inclusion in the process. We gave them tours, discussed the next phase, and solicited their input. With construction nearing completion, it occurred to me that everyone who stopped by wanted to be part of what was happening. We always made time for visitors. So when it came time to pave the sidewalk, we did it with good intentions. We made brick pavers available to donors for a nominal fee, and in no time our seating was fronted by a brick path paved with the good intentions of our Stetson family and friends. Years later, brick donors stop just to look at their names on the bricks or to take a picture of the field. Give your fans an opportunity to be a part of the experience and be sure to express your appreciation for their involvement.

THE WINDUP

Stetson is a small, private university but makes no bones about the importance of education and the cost involved in delivering a quality education. The green light to commence construction was based on one contingency: All construction must be donor funded, and no tuition money would be used. Obviously, the ballpark construction required a chunk of change, so fund-raising became a priority. With the assistance and support of Athletic Director Jeff Altier, President Doug Lee, and Vice President for Development Linda Davis, we raised more than $2 million. On more than one occasion I've asked myself, "How did we do it?" The answer is always the same: "With a little help from our friends." Correction—with a lot of help from a lot of friends. Fund-raising, marketing, and promotions are all about building relationships.

Initially, we focused on phase 1—building the field. After we were informed that restrooms would be necessary to make play a possibility, we developed a few additional phases. While completing the backstops and dugouts, we were visited by the city manager and director of parks and recreation, who were looking for ideas for the new city dugouts. During their visit we learned that portable facilities would allow us to play ball. With that, Stetson University became the proud owner of some first-class port-a-potties!

Involve the Community

The next four phases would require additional friends. Before building a softball field, I was an avid fisherman. Fishing, like golf (which I stink at), is one of those activities that can be used to help develop relationships. Out on the water you want to catch fish, not talk, but when the fish aren't biting the talk turns to softball. Before you know it, you've got a bite! It may seem as though fund-raising takes precedence over marketing and promotions, but they go hand in hand. If your program relies on donor funding, you can't have one without the other. For example, fans like to watch games under the lights from nice seats in front of a state-of-the-art scoreboard. Our lights were donated by friends of Stetson fastpitch. So, I fished and golfed and even learned to smoke. First, I went out and bought a smoker—not just any smoker but a custom-made 250 gallon (1,000 L) propane tank with a fire box on the rear capable of holding 30 Boston butts, which would feed up to 300 friends. That smoker has been the key component of my fund-raising, marketing, and promotions program. Who knew? I have auctioned off Super Bowl parties featuring my now famous butts and beans barbeque with homemade sauce recipe that I will gladly sell to you at a reasonable price. We start the season with a barbeque, and we end it with a barbeque. By the way, the tip jar accepts cash as well as checks. The alumni game is our favorite event. Fans want to see the alumni they have come to love, meet the newest members of the Stetson team, and enjoy a little BBQ. Community events like the Progress Energy game in which we play a group of power company employees with the help of one of our pitcher–catcher combos brings out the locals as well as our steadfast fan base. The fun doesn't stop there. When the game is over we typically feed 400 people and win a new set of fans. Seriously, if you can't play golf, you should get a smoker!

As I've said, I am not a golfer. Yet, year after year, I play fifth to a group of fairly good golfers in the Chipper Jones Celebrity Golf Tournament. Why embarrass myself? Because Chipper Jones is a friend of Stetson University and Stetson fastpitch, and the tournament contributes to a children's charity as well as Stetson University's athletic department. The team I play with would do well to find another player, but they are also friends of Stetson fastpitch and want a chance to bring the trophy back. And we have—twice. Chipper's presence on campus is also a big draw; donors and fans show up to get an autographed baseball and a handshake. If you can't get a smoker, get a celebrity.

Professional marketers know that the customer belongs to them if they can get them in the door three times. I believe this principle also holds true for softball.

Take stock of your surroundings. Does the facility look its best? Are the restrooms plentiful and clean? Does the concession provide quality products at an affordable price? Is the seating comfortable, and does it offer an unobstructed view? Is your announcer positive, professional, and entertaining? Do your guests feel welcome? Are they going to have fun and feel safe in the environment?

Involve the Fans

Invite your fans to become part of your fastpitch family. Host an open house the weekend before your season opener. Invite local organizations like the Rotary Club, Lions Club, and Kiwanis Club; veterans' organizations; 12-and-under teams; Girl Scouts; campus organizations; and the faculty. Give your guests a program and a map of the stations they will visit during the open house. Place team members at each stop to demonstrate the features of that station. Encourage your team members to make it a positive experience for your guests by interacting in a fun, positive manner. I am particularly proud of my players for being gracious with our visitors. They go out of their way to meet and greet our fans, to learn their names, and to give a wave to the stands in an effort to make them feel welcome and part of the Stetson fastpitch family.

Bring them into the club. Your athletic department doesn't have a lock on the booster club. The Diamond Club starts the season with a barbeque and a guest or celebrity speaker. Club members are acknowledged for their contributions and celebrated for any milestones that may have occurred since last season, such as new grandchildren, a 50th birthday, or for bringing in new members. This is also a good time to solicit suggestions from your most loyal supporters. Their input is valuable, and because they love your program, they will be kind.

Get your team involved in the community. It's good PR for the university, and that's good PR for you. Free clinics for kids and talks to local organizations and high school or recreational coaches' associations will draw positive attention to your program. Organize your team to sponsor a cause near and dear to the team. Kennesaw State (Georgia) does a terrific job of this by sponsoring Lexi's Day to draw attention to children with special needs. Before the game, they introduce Lexi and tell the crowd about her life with cerebral palsy. They take a collection to benefit her charity for cerebral palsy and children with special needs. To honor Lexi, the home team wears pink jerseys and the visiting team wears purple jerseys. At Stetson, the baseball team hosts a blood drive to benefit the Red Cross. Our team volunteers their time to support the Lions Club to provide glasses for the visually impaired. By getting involved in your community, you will build interest in what is happening in your program.

The following events have proved to be worthy of a repeat:

- Theme days—Girls Scouts get special seating and an opportunity to sell cookies to the crowd.
- Raffle off seats in the VIP room with a primo view, heating and air conditioning, cushioned seating, and food.

- Greek Day—Recognize sororities and fraternities.
- Brrr, baby, it's cold outside! The start of the season is frequently chilly because spring is yet to arrive. Try a fleece blanket giveaway to 10 lucky ticket holders.
- First pitch—Honor the university's first lady by asking her to throw out the first pitch of the season. Veterans, celebrities, and major donors also get top honors.
- Breast Cancer Awareness Day—Order pink T-shirts for the team and the visiting team.
- Little Hatter Day honors our local 12-and-under fastpitch team with special seating, a walk onto the field as they are announced, and a meet and greet with the team.
- Veteran's Day—Honor local veterans groups by trouping them onto the field. Play the national anthem and invite the high school ROTC to bear the flag.
- Team Up Against Hunger—Host a canned food drive to benefit a local food pantry.

Whether you use auctions, barbeques, in-game promotions, or celebrities, find a way to bring in the fans. Show them a good time, and they'll come back.

THE RELEASE

Computer technology has broadened our release of information through the use of the university's website, GoHatters.com, and social media. We don't sit around anymore waiting for the local newspaper to throw us a bone. You should take charge of the information that your fans and prospective recruits receive; polish it and make it positive. Enlist the talents of a skilled professional. Too much information can be mind numbing. Make it specific and attention getting. The schedule, roster, and team statistics are the essentials. Current team news with live stats, audio, and video stream is a plus. Develop the reader's interest with winning headlines and eye-catching photos—lots of photos. Provide links to camp information, Facebook, Twitter, and YouTube. Update your information regularly; no one wants to see old stats or photographs from last season. I will admit that I am the last person I would hire to build a web page, but I know a good release when I see one, and so do you.

Maximize Technology

The most efficient way to promote your program is through the use of technology. Everyone has access to a computer or smart phone, and nearly everyone is using them. Posting, tweeting, linking, texting, e-mailing, and blogging make communicating 24 hours a day, 7 days a week inexpensive and convenient. We use social media because it is the fastest way to connect with fans, players, and sponsors. The stream of information is available through cell phones, tablets, and computers on a 24-hour basis anywhere in the world. We have linked our Twitter and Facebook accounts to post and tweet the same sentiments. We use these formats to make a positive connection with our fans. Unlike the box score, social media give our team a human side. Stetson sports information liaison for softball Jesse Cazakoff uses Facebook and Twitter to promote upcoming events and as a link to recaps of games on our website. He describes social media as a resource for monitoring the conversation about Stetson fastpitch, particularly on Twitter. Part of that monitoring is rebroadcasting (retweeting) when he comes across something interesting and positive that someone has said about the program, such as "Congrats on winning today. Go Hatters!" According to Mr. Cazakoff, assistant coach J.J. Payette makes Stetson fastpitch the most active on Facebook and Twitter of any of the sports at Stetson.

Making use of technology to promote our program has enabled us to take Stetson fastpitch literally around the world. I am delighted when a prospective recruit connects with us by social media or an online search. We have been able to reach more students and narrow our search with less travel in part because of the use of an athletic recruiting software program. The program allows us to manage our prospects with a customized search featuring online questionnaires to add to our Facebook page or Twitter stream for recruits to use to inquire about our program and update their information. These tools are yet another way in which fans and recruits connect with the program. We strive to make them pop with action shots of the team, images of the facility, and attractive banners.

Never Forget the Personal Touch

Now for the curve ball. Although I am sold on the use of technology, I believe that the personal touch is the most effective way to reach fans and prospective athletes. I don't like voice mail, and I try to avoid using it. Because I am usually away from my office, I forward my desk phone to my cell phone. I also believe that a handwritten note still makes the strongest impression. To personalize your technological approach, use an e-mail list management software program and make weekly or monthly contact in the form of an online newsletter. Items of interest for your newsletter might include a quote from the coach, quotes from fans or recent visitors to your facility, photos of the team, and news related to the team's success, such as "Academic All-American," "Pitched a No-Hitter," and my favorite—"Hatters Win!" Don't forget to add a schedule of events that includes fall practice, team workouts, BBQ fund-raisers, telethon dates, charitable work, and team birthdays. Insert notes of appreciation to sponsors and booster club members for their support. An online newsletter is also a great way to collect information from your fans like birthdays to acknowledge later at games and phone numbers to collect for an autodial system. Many schools currently use an autodial system or text alert to notify students of important information and deadlines. Turn your autodial into a fastpitch connection and send automated calls to inform your fans of game dates and times. Marketing and promotions by written word or personal contact should be about establishing a meaningful and engaging relationship with your fans. From 2008 to 2011, we have seen a 114-percent increase in attendance at home games. The process of promoting our program is evolving. Given our increasing attendance, I believe it is working.

FINAL THOUGHTS

When the day is done, whatever the result on the field, our goal is to make everyone feel a part of the Stetson fastpitch experience.

10

Recruiting the Right Way

Bonnie Tholl

Although the culture and rules in college athletics have changed in the last 100 years, effective recruiting has always separated the most successful programs from the rest. Good recruiting does not always ensure a good team, but a coach's ability to identify and secure the best talent that satisfies program needs gives the best opportunity to win on the field.

The culture of today's college recruiting is different from what it was even 10 years ago. Recruiting practices that were once associated only with big-time revenue sports are now common in college softball. The way in which we identify prospects and communicate with them has changed drastically, causing coaches to restructure their recruiting efforts.

No exact formula will produce great recruiting classes, and the process is school and program specific. In our quest to find and secure top-tier talent, we likely have individual considerations that are specific to the culture of our program and university. Identify your program culture and make that the starting point for determining the type of student-athlete whom you want to pursue. Begin building that brand or identity. Sports have become a huge part of our socialization process. The commercialization of college athletics has a significant emotional bearing on today's young prospect, so creating a brand can help them identify with your school and program.

DETERMINE A PHILOSOPHY

Determining a recruiting philosophy for your program will provide you with a roadmap as a reference for current and future recruiting seasons. Creating a philosophy establishes a solid foundation that will provide consistency in your recruiting efforts. This philosophy will assist in guiding you when you are evaluating prospects on the playing field and in the classroom. Example questions that may stir discussion among your staff when developing a recruiting philosophy may include the following: Will you pursue prospects who are regionally located, or will you recruit on a national scope? Are you dedicated to pursuing prospects who are multipositional? Will you focus on a pitching prospect who can be in your offensive lineup? Do prospects need to have a minimum academic grade point average before you will consider them? These questions may become the structural foundation of your program's recruiting philosophy.

At the University of Michigan our philosophy is tailored toward student-athletes who understand the value of a Michigan degree. We have the greatest success when we identify prospects who are attracted to this type of competitive academic environment and want to compete at the highest level of Division I college softball. Because we have a large alumni base in many regions of the country, we pursue athletes regardless of their geographical location. More important, we try to identify prospects who are not afraid to experience something different for four or five years of their life, considering that the personality of their hometown may not match that of Ann Arbor.

Make a Selling Point

Every school, large or small, urban or rural, has its own distinctive feature. Highlight that feature and make it a selling point that is attractive to the prospect.

Regardless of the philosophy that you and your staff decide on, be sure to make recruiting a priority. The entire staff should agree that recruiting is of great importance because any resistance to this belief will hinder your efforts. Involve all members to some extent. A congruent staff that understands its role in recruiting will assist in making your recruiting efforts more productive. Recruiting needs to be a full team effort.

VALUE OF A RECRUITING COORDINATOR

Let me first speak to the value of establishing a recruiting coordinator on your staff. Having a coach who dedicates the majority of the workday to your recruiting can enhance your efforts. Naming a coordinator negates any uncertainty that can occur when trying to identify, evaluate, or communicate with prospects. The head coach creates the mission of the entire program, and recruiting is one facet. The coordinator should work within the framework of this mission to help realize all your recruiting objectives. Often, the head coach may not serve in this role yet will direct the coordinator about what the goals may be. The coordinator's responsibility is to organize those recruiting thoughts for your program. This organization will come in the form of scheduling off-campus evaluations, researching and communicating with prospects, networking with coaches, and scheduling campus visits for prospects and their families.

Willingness to Invest the Time

Choosing the coach on staff who is the right fit to lead your recruiting efforts requires careful thought. The position requires a tremendous time commitment, and no shortcuts can be used when it comes to deciding on recruits. There is plenty of truth to the saying "Your time is not your own" when referring to work hours. The coordinator needs to be available when recruits can speak with the coach on the telephone after school or practice. Follow-ups by Internet research or communication with a club coach cannot always be completed during traditional work hours, so the coordinator needs to be prepared to sacrifice personal time to advance your program's recruiting. Consider which coach on staff has an established rapport with club team coaches or high school coaches. Examine other program responsibilities to determine which coach has the ability to devote most of the day to the recruitment of prospects.

Choosing a Detail-Oriented Coordinator

A strong work ethic is an obvious requirement, yet because of the volume of recruiting communication today, the staff member who demonstrates a knack for attention to detail may be a natural fit. Whether it's organizing your on-campus visits or evaluating talent off campus, describing the uniqueness of your program to a prospect and her family may pay dividends when a prospect is deciding whether to attend your school. A considerable understanding of what separates your school from your competitors in the recruiting process often requires this attention to small but relevant details.

An example of attention to detail can be simple communication with the prospect's high school or club coach to find out what style of coaching resonates with that prospect. This information can be used as a talking point with the prospect or as a determining factor in whether that prospect will be a good fit in your program. You may even take note of the type of equipment the prospect uses when she competes and incorporate that information into your recruiting conversations. The prospect will be impressed that you pay close attention to specific details.

The coordinator should not be afraid to make tough decision when choosing between prospects. Often times, the head coach seeks the opinion of assistant coaches to make a final recruiting decision. The coordinator should feel empowered in sharing an opinion, having placed significant effort into researching and evaluating the prospect.

After you have chosen a coordinator, make plans to use all coaching staff members and support staff in your recruiting framework. Use your athletic director, admissions officer, strength coach, academic advisor, or anyone else who can assist in providing information to the prospect and her family. Each of these staff members can offer a prospective recruit a different perspective about what her experience can be as a student-athlete at your school. Therefore, the prospect can gain the knowledge needed to make an educated decision, regardless of her list of priorities when choosing a school. Use every resource available that can be relevant to the prospect's recruitment.

CHANGING TIMES

The recruiting landscape has undergone major changes over the past few years, forcing coaches to adjust their philosophy and strategy. Some of the contributing factors include a greater emphasis on sport specialization of student-athletes at a younger age, the trend of early commitments, changes in competitive playing schedules, and the ongoing development of Internet websites that promote the visibility of prospects. Regardless of whether you believe that these factors have had a positive or negative effect on the recruiting process, all have provoked change in the way that coaches recruit.

For example, Michigan softball has historically recruited prospects who have competed in multiple sports at the high school level. Our reputation was such that we recruited athletes who excelled in more than one sport. The opportunity to attract a multisport prospect to Michigan does not present itself as often today. Fewer top-tier athletes are participating in more than one sport because of an expanded playing season that has led to increased sport specialization. We now see fewer college softball prospects competing in other activities at their high schools. Because we can no longer easily achieve our (Michigan) philosophy of assembling a team of well-rounded multisport athletes, we now pursue prospects who have the ability to play multiple positions. We have adapted our strategy to the changing recruiting culture.

Implications of Expanded Playing Seasons

As you will notice, one factor affecting the recruiting process often influences another. The trend of prospective student-athletes committing earlier to schools can be considered a result of expanded playing seasons. The argument is compelling because expanded playing seasons allow college coaches to evaluate younger players more often than they could in the past. One implication of early commitments for you as a college coach may be that you will choose to recruit athletes who play various positions and are not fully developed at one defensive position. Instead of charting a defensive lineup during the recruitment process, a more useful approach may be to consider the prospect's offensive prowess, knowing that her defensive position may change after she arrives on campus.

21st Century Recruiting

The Internet has had a profound effect on our daily lives, from the way that we communicate to the accessibility of information on a number of topics. As we have come to experience, athletics is a huge cyber industry that has reached the softball nation. A multitude of Internet sites promote the visibility of the sport of softball in one way or another. Prospective student-athletes use these sites to promote their talents, a method barely used a decade ago. This information can be useful to you during the recruiting process. You can now become far more familiar with the student-athlete's achievements, playing statistics, families, and outside interests by surfing the web. You can learn all this information without ever having had a conversation with the player's coach or seen her compete on the field. Why is this relevant to your efforts? The answer is that you have a base knowledge and talking points when you do engage in conversation with the prospect or her coach.

WHOM TO RECRUIT

In the summer of 1979 a group of talented amateur hockey players gathered at the Olympic Training Center. From that group of 68, 20 would be chosen to represent the United States on what would become the most celebrated Olympic hockey team in the nation's history. Coach Herb Brooks faced criticism when the posted roster included players considered less physically talented than some who were left off the list. Brooks' sentiment was that his priority was not about getting the best team, but about getting the right team. Coach Brooks had a vision for his hockey team that would come to serve as the guideline in selecting the 1980 U.S. Olympic Team.

The Right Fit

Great value often results from choosing the prospect who is the right fit for your school and program, as opposed to the better talent. After you have determined the type of athlete who fits into your philosophy academically and athletically, examine the other variables that may give you a recruiting and competitive edge. For instance, after you have identified a desired benchmark of talent and found several prospects who possess that level of talent, prioritize the person who has shown greater attentiveness to your school. Cultivate the recruiting atmosphere of wanting those who want you! What you might sacrifice in talent can be made up by attracting a quality prospect who thrives in your system. She may not have been the big-name recruit at your level, but she becomes more valuable in many ways. And she often outperforms the big-name recruit as well.

In the fall of 2005, our staff here at Michigan was pursuing two pitchers who were seniors in high school. One prospect had been competing at the highest level of 18U, attending top tournaments, and attracting interest from traditional top 10 softball programs. The second pitcher had not competed in one inning of gold-level softball up to that point, so she was not a recruiting target for many top programs. The second pitcher had intriguing athletic qualities that our staff did not identify in the first pitcher. The second pitcher was from the state of Michigan, was familiar with our program's history, and grew up wanting to be a Wolverine. Though she was not as developed as the top-level player was, we believed that the second pitcher would become a greater contributor to our program because of her many intangibles. We decided to make the second pitcher our first choice. She was the right fit for our program and ended her Michigan career as a three-time All-American.

Determine whether your prospects' ideals parallel the ideals of your program. Pay attention to the rhetoric of the prospect and those close to her. Does she speak your language in terms of softball ambition, or is she concerned only about securing a scholarship? Unfortunately, the many youth tournaments inadvertently encourage a showcase environment instead of a competitive environment. Remember that you coach your team to reach their potential and win, so build your team with people who desire the same things.

Controlling the Process

You may be highly invested in the pursuit of a particular athlete, but don't allow any prospect to hold your program hostage. Your primary objective is to look out for the welfare of your entire program, which includes dozens of people. The prospect's priority is to satisfy her wants. So although you may allow the prospect a reasonable amount of time to make a thoughtful decision, consider having a deadline so that you can control your own destiny.

Maintaining control of the recruiting process can become difficult. College coaches are confronted with timelines that vary for prospects who are making their college choice. Your top prospect may delay your ability to move on another player. If you decide to wait on that top prospect, you risk losing choices two, three, and four in the meantime. The best approach may be to communicate early in the process that a timeline needs to be met. Your timeline may not offer an adequate amount of time for the prospect, so expect various reactions. Regardless of the reaction, developing a recruiting depth chart is imperative because your top prospect may choose another school or lose interest in your school. A recruiting depth chart is a simple way to project your future team needs with a graph that plots your existing players and prospective players. Post this chart in your office or somewhere that is visible on a daily basis to serve as a reminder of your recruiting needs. Most recruits seriously consider three or four schools, so you should consider the same number to fill that position need.

A colleague of mine compares recruiting to airplane overbooking. Airlines typically oversell seats on a flight to assure a full plane, because some ticketed passengers will be no-shows. To secure greater profit, airlines have passengers readily available to fill their airplanes. If airlines don't exercise this policy, they will be left with fewer clients, which means less profit. Likewise, college coaches should have an extended list of talented players. If your top-tier prospect chooses another school, you will need to have another quality player to pursue.

Short-Term Versus Long-Term Vision

Spend time evaluating your strengths as a team and the areas that will need improvement. Identify your short-term needs. You may have to act on these needs more often. For instance, you may need depth in your catching position because a player has sustained an injury that forces her to switch positions. You may need to investigate the option of a junior college transfer in this scenario. Identify your long-term needs as well and project a player's value to your team performance long term. As much as you would like your entire incoming class to have an immediate impact on your team in the conference and nationally, expect only one or two to make an exceptional transition at your level.

When it comes to prioritizing for the long-term future of our program here at Michigan, we choose pitching, offense, and defense, in that order. We consider it a bonus when we recruit a dual-threat competitor who can contribute as both a pitcher and a hitter. Of the nine All-American pitchers in the program's history, three solely pitched, and the rest contributed as pitcher–hitters. We have benefited greatly in our recruiting efforts by having dual-threat athletes, but if we need to choose one or the other for our program, pitching wins out.

Softball has become a game of offense. Secondary only to strength in pitching is having players who can produce at the plate. Offensive ability should be a huge factor when creating a list of prospects to pursue. These players come in all shapes and sizes. Some run to first base in less than 2.8 seconds and gain their advantage by placing pressure on the infield defense. Others hit the ball with power and pose a huge RBI threat. The common denominator here is that both types of players produce offensively and force pitchers to be at the top of their games to win.

Of course, defensive ability is not to be overlooked, and a championship team needs key people at skilled positions outside the circle. Two position players that should be of the highest importance in your recruiting efforts are your shortstop and your catcher. Shortstops are typically the best athletes on the team. They have the ability to play other positions because of their all-around athleticism. The shortstop position requires nimbleness on the defensive side that many other players do not possess. Catching is a skilled position because the athlete needs experience handling pitchers and must undergo specific physical preparation.

Players Who Know How to Win

Recruit players who are proven winners, who are products of a winning culture. They understand the challenges faced and perseverance needed to win at a high level. Magic dust does not surround proven winners. By becoming accustomed to the difficulties of preparation and the adversity faced in games, they develop a competitive trait. They learn how to win from winning. So take a close look at the history of your prospect's teams, and then determine whether that track record is a standard that you wish to have in your program.

Recruiting the Family

The prospect's family will have a huge influence in decision making, so take time to recruit them as well. In many cases the youth softball experience has become a huge family investment, both emotionally and financially. Playing softball and subsequently choosing a college has become a family endeavor. Getting to know the family's values may help you decide early in your pursuit whether the prospect is someone who will be a good fit for your program. As stated earlier, prospects are making oral commitments to colleges at a younger age than ever before. Pay attention to family involvement, because younger prospects are more likely to rely on the direction of their parents. You will eventually coach the prospect, not the family members, but it will serve you well to know the type of influence your player will receive.

The following list includes the five factors that we have historically relied on to make recruiting decisions at the University of Michigan.

Five Factors When Considering a Student-Athlete for the University of Michigan Softball Program

1. A person who has the athletic ability to compete at the highest level, which means that she offers power, speed, and the versatility to produce offensively and defensively

2. A person who is the right academic fit for Michigan

3. A person with high character who has demonstrated a passion to compete with a diligent work ethic

4. A person who offers outstanding leadership skills on and off the playing field and will keep the mission of the program a top priority

5. A person who understands that Michigan is a special place, has researched our university and program, understands its rich tradition, and wants to be a part of continuing to make it great

WHERE TO RECRUIT

Many of you have had great success in previous years recruiting student-athletes to your school. Whether it was a specific academic curriculum offered, your school's location, or your program's winning record, you provided recruiting information through traditional forms of communication. As coaches, we rely heavily on the printed material produced by the school or our own office to capture the attention of the coveted prospect.

How Does the Prospect See You?

Today's high school students relate to electronic media, where they spend hours perusing social media sites. Changing your strategy to use Twitter, Facebook, and Skype is a necessity. For most of you, rules govern all these avenues of communication, yet creating an environment that prospects relate to will certainly enhance your recruiting. First, become familiar with what forms of communication are permissible, and then become familiar with how these mediums can spark the interest of your prospect. Prospects can learn a great deal about you and your program, and in turn you can learn a great deal about them.

Establish a Geographic Relationship

Coaches are often attached to certain regions of the country that have historically been productive for them. You may attract great interest from prospects who live in those regions, or you may have identified a big talent pool in that area. Regardless of your specific reason, maintaining your visibility in that area from year to year is often helpful. High school and club programs can create a relationship with you because of your visibility, even if you have not initiated formal communication with them. You can also evaluate the level of a program and prospect over a longer period, which can help you make a better decision on the talent. I have found that forming relationships with coaches in specific areas helps to create a recruiting bond. The coaches come to understand the type of student-athlete I frequently pursue, and they often become an extra set of eyes for me. When they encounter a prospect who they believe has the characteristics that I am looking for, they communicate that information to me. I often say that I miss many more athletes than I ever see during the recruiting process. Recognizing that, I need to establish a network of people who have seen these prospects compete.

WHEN TO RECRUIT

I cannot overstate the importance of evaluating a prospect over time. Committing to having a person on your team is a huge investment. Treat it as such, because the time that you spend making an additional trip or two to see her play is insignificant compared with the time you will regret recruiting her if she ends up not filling your program need. Make these multiple evaluations on separate weeks of play so that you can get a true read of her ability. If budgetary constraints prevent you from making numerous trips to see a prospect, find a way to evaluate her at a camp that you may be hosting or working.

Importance of Practice and Game Evaluations

Limiting your evaluation to only a game or only a practice prevents you from obtaining crucial information about the prospect's ability. What you observe a prospect demonstrating during a practice setting is not always what occurs on game day. Make time in your recruiting schedule to watch the prospect in competition to see what that practice swing produces against opposing pitching. Her swing may look great in the batting cage off the tee or front toss, but you need to see what she can produce in a game. Don't be afraid to be result oriented because it may be an indication of how the prospect competes at game time.

Likewise, expand your knowledge of the prospect by observing her in a practice setting. Sometimes a player's athleticism shines in this environment, which may sway your opinion. The number of repetitions that you witness in practice will usually exceed what you will see during a game, so allow yourself the opportunity to evaluate in this setting. Many of the intangibles of a player can further be identified during practice, and this information can be invaluable.

Watch how the prospect conducts herself during warm-ups. You may not have the opportunity to watch an outfielder field the ball and make a throw to the plate during a game, but you will see her perform that skill often during a warm-up routine. Offensively, the prospect swings more during pregame than you will typically see during the game, so take advantage of this chance to evaluate her. Consider warm-ups to be a minipractice during which you can gather information, so arrive at the ball field in time to see this pregame routine.

Notice the Intangibles

Observe the prospect's mannerisms in the dugout when she's not playing defense. Is she engaged in the game or in her teammate's at bat? How the prospect reacts to adversity often reveals itself inside the dugout through either simple body language or the manner in which she communicates with her coaches and teammates. Pay close attention to this behavior, whether you characterize it as positive or negative. This aspect may become another consideration in deciding whether to recruit her or pursue someone else.

Being the first school to recruit a player can be a powerful advantage. As college coaches, we forge relationships with young people who are highly impressionable. Young players remember the first school that shows interest in them, whether it is through a letter received or a game attended. Of course, showing continued interest in the prospect is imperative, but making the first impression in the recruiting process can be valuable. As a coach, you may not always be aware of the chronology of your prospect's recruitment, but recognize the benefits of your early arrival on the recruiting scene.

Campus Visit

A prospect's visit to your campus can be one of the defining moments in the recruiting process. The athlete and her family will undoubtedly evaluate your academic environment, your campus facilities, your team camaraderie, and your coaching style. The campus visit offers an inside view of your program, allowing the prospect to determine whether her future can be at your school. Consider this your time to shine!

The campus visit is revealing of the prospect as well. First, her commitment to spending time on your campus speaks to her interest in your school. The visit also reveals the prospect's personality and character traits, which you have evaluated only from a distance. Commit time in the visit itinerary for one-on-one interaction with the prospect so that you can further assess her individually. Allow your players time to connect with the prospect as well. Your players who understand the mission of your program can be your greatest asset in recruiting. They attract prospects who are the right fit, and they often share their concern if a prospect displays behavior that may be detrimental to your program.

FINAL THOUGHTS

College athletics is a people business, driven by young athletes who have dreams. Understanding the value of appealing to those dreams will benefit you greatly in recruiting. Steve Jobs, cofounder of Apple, was passionate about his company's philosophy of selling dreams, not products, to people. He thought that it was important to connect on a personal level and allow people to imagine improvements to their everyday lives realized through Apple products. As coaches, we have the same opportunity to present possibilities to young athletes who view college softball as an avenue to achieve their dreams.

◆ PART THREE ◆

EFFECTIVE PRACTICE SESSIONS

11

Structuring Indoor and Outdoor Practices

Michelle Venturella

A difference is always apparent between the good teams and the great teams. One of those differences comes when looking at how a team practices and what they accomplish during that time. I can remember as a new head coach being eager to go to practice with my new team and then quickly realizing that it's not as easy as it looks. Great coaches make practice look easy by the way each session flows as well as by the manner in which they help that group of athletes come together a little more each day. We have several challenges when it comes to structuring efficient practices in various situations. For example, teams in some areas of the country have to deal with inclement weather. Others have limited space and time for practice, although the expectations for winning don't seem to change. Some coaches have to deal with not having everyone for the whole practice because of class schedule conflicts, injury, or illness. Regardless of what we are dealing with, we are all expected to find a way to get it done. I will give you several ideas about using what you do have to put the most prepared team possible on the field.

Let's start by working backward and look at what we ultimately want to accomplish during practice, regardless of what level we are coaching. We want our team to be prepared mentally, physically, and emotionally. We need to make sure that everyone understands the long-term goals of the program so that we all know where we're headed. We want the players to be fundamentally sound so that they can keep up with the speed of the game. We want them to have been in as many strategic situations as possible so that they know how to respond without thinking. We need to make sure that our communication is consistent so that everyone is talking the same language. We also want them to be able to handle the game on an emotional level by being able to stay in control. Our players need to be able to trust one another. They need to be accountable for themselves and must learn to deal with conflict. Ultimately, they need to master their minds! Their sense of trust must be tested to make sure that they stay together and do not separate from one another in difficult times. We need to prepare them to feel the confidence they need to compete in any situation. We need to make sure that team chemistry is building, and we want to create situations that allow leaders to emerge. And, of course, all this needs to have an element of fun!

Now we can start to get a sense about what makes good teams great. We have to remember that although we are always trying to create leaders, the coach is the ultimate leader. We need to foster this atmosphere with our teams and get them to come together at the right time. Structuring successful practices is much more than working fundamentals and situations. My goal is to provide a variety of ideas to foster this kind of inclusive approach, whether you are practicing inside or outside, whether you have a big facility or a small one, and whether you have a short preseason or a long one.

THE START OF IT ALL

I did something different this year at our first team meeting. We went over the expectations of the program both on and off the field. We talked about where this team is headed and about what was going to get us to the next level after coming off one of our strongest finishes in the past seven years. But at the end I told them that they had a project to do for me and that it was their ticket into practice. I wanted to find out a little more about them, so I asked each of them to create a CD for me—not just any CD, but one with their all-time favorite songs. It had to include a minimum of 10 songs, but the important part was that they had to write out why they chose each song. My goal with this assignment was to learn a little more about them as people, and ultimately I got 15 new CDs and a lot of new music! When I explained the project to them, they all looked at me in the way that kids do when they think you're a little weird for saying what you did, but this activity was one of my favorite things I've ever done with any of my teams. Many of their songs gave me insight into some of their values. Many players included songs that reminded them of their parents, their best friends, winning state championships with their high schools, or winning nationals with their summer ball teams. I also learned which songs pumped them up. I created playlists for them to use during our hitting circuits because music has a way of bringing out their emotions. Learning about their music made for great for conversation too. I have to admit that one of my favorites was a song called "Santa Lost a Ho." The explanation was that this kid's father dresses up like Santa every Christmas and makes a playlist of Christmas songs that no one knows and passes them out. Really? It made me laugh when I read this and definitely gave me something to talk about with this student-athlete. The players were open with this project, and I absolutely loved learning more about them.

Everyone knows the saying "Kids don't care how much you know until they know how much you care." I think this was a good step in the direction of my taking the time to start to get to know my new kids and get to know my returning players even better. The CD project was also a way to find a common theme within my team to get them to start coming together. Doing something like this can break the ice in the beginning of the year and help you laugh and connect with your kids off the field.

PRACTICE BEGINS

When we first start practice everyone is enthusiastic! I think it's sometimes how we are programmed. We are excited to start exercising, but a month down the road we lose a bit of that excitement. We are excited when we buy a new car or a new TV, but then we want something else. So how do we keep this enthusiasm with our teams? I hope that the things that we're doing are more motivating than getting a new car or new TV, but we all go through times when the energy doesn't seem to be there because practice has become routine, or everyone is a little more tired, or the practice slot at 5:30 a.m. is not as fun as it was when everything first started.

PRACTICE SLUMPS

We have all played or coached long enough to know the cycles. For those of us who coach college, I can say that the first four weeks are usually good because everyone gets to see each other again after being away for the summer. The weather in Chicago and most parts of the country during fall is amazing, so we get to practice outside. When we hit weeks 4 and 5, we get the first rounds of midterms, so you can start to see the distractions creep in. Because we lift at 6:15 a.m. on Monday and Friday, players are now burning the candle at both ends. I haven't met too many college athletes who go to bed at 10 p.m. get the sleep they need to meet the demands of their schedule. They are staying up late to study, they are still getting up for lifting and practice or classes, and we are playing our fall games, so they get only one day off a week. The excitement may tend to diminish. Here are a few things that I do if I sense that this is happening.

Change It Up

The decisions that you make as a head coach should reflect what you are about. We talk a lot about how important grades are, so I may make practice a little shorter or even give them a day off depending on how many are dealing with a busy week. They always appreciate this! Sometimes I tell them that we have to accomplish certain things at practice that day and when we get through them we are done. This approach offers them the chance to finish early, so they tend to be more focused, which is always a good thing. I'm OK with doing some or all of these things as long as they earn it. Doing some of these things helps build trust between us and lets them know that I want them to succeed both on and off the field. I have also found that the more a student-athlete trusts me, the more she can and will give because she does not hesitate to do what I ask of her.

Money Game

We have put something simple into practice that has worked like a charm during those low-energy times. We call it the money game. Now before anyone turns us in for paying our players, I will tell you that no real money is involved. It is simply like playing 500. Remember? If you caught a ball in the air it was 100 points, one hop was 75, and so on. We said that if they caught the ball in the air it was $1.00, one bounce was .75, and two bounces was .50. An extraordinary play was $2.00! Now if a player missed a fly ball, it was minus $1.00 and so on. We used this in our shagging station for our live hitting station. We have to remember that our athletes are competitive, so any time we can give them a challenge, they are usually excited about it. They were diving for balls, sliding in front of balls to cut them off and get them on the second bounce, and trying to distract each other so that the other would miss. I have to admit that our shorter kids got picked on. They would be set to catch a fly ball and someone taller would simply reach over them and take it right out of their glove! This fun game kept the energy up in a station that usually doesn't elicit much interaction between teammates.

Demonstrate Ideas

Demonstrating something for your players can be really effective. You can incorporate concepts that are important to you into a quick demo that makes the point. One time I brought my dry erase board to practice so that I could draw a concept for them. I talked about a concept called the dip. We all have the outstanding athlete who comes into our program. She goes through her career steadily and does pretty well, but she has trouble ever trusting herself enough to go through the dip, the period when she is learning a new skill or tweaking something she already does, which usually results in her getting worse before getting better. You also have the athlete who is willing to get out of her comfort zone and might even fail for a while. Because she buys into what you're telling her, she ends up going through the dip but eventually becomes a lot better than she was when she started.

The dip encompasses three steps: (1) getting out of your comfort zone, (2) rebuilding, and (3) becoming better than before. Now, most athletes will try something new, but as soon as it doesn't work they come right back to you and say, "See, it doesn't work." They go back to their old ways and never trust enough to find out what they are really capable of doing. Athletes who are willing to get better will understand that they might not succeed right away but that something really good is going to come of this. By going through their struggles, they learn the lesson. They become a little stronger than they were before. When they get the new concept or drill, they have a confidence that will help them succeed again because they learned what they need to do to get better and grow. That process usually starts with their getting out of their comfort zone. This athlete will be able to give you more than the athlete who is not willing to get past the first step.

Open for Change

The other concept and demonstration that is simple but fun is this: Take four glasses of water—three that are almost full and one that is only about a quarter full. Have one of your athletes hold the glass that is almost empty while you take one of the other full cups and start pouring the water into her cup. What happens? Her cup gets fuller. Then take another athlete and have her hold a cup that is almost full. Take another full cup, start pouring your cup into hers, and watch it overflow. Keep pouring so that it spills all over (I made a freshman hold this cup).

I explained that the idea was simple: When the cup is empty, then water can go in, just as an athlete who has an open mind will take in what we tell her. When the cup is full, water spills over, just as the athlete who is not willing to try something cannot take in anything new. No knowledge from us can be absorbed because there is nowhere for it to go. The last thing I tell them is that when they receive more water and their cup starts to get full, get a bigger cup!

These kinds of things are great attention getters and mix things up to help players keep their focus. There is no getting around the fact that you have to put time into developing any skill at which you expect to excel. In a society focused on instant gratification, one thing stays the same. You can't rush mastering a skill! If you want to be the best at something, you are choosing to live a particular lifestyle.

NO GETTING AROUND IT

Laying a solid foundation is the first step in creating good practices, whether you are indoors or outdoors. You might have a brand new group of athletes, or you may be replacing only a few kids, but in looking at laying a solid foundation we can start with expectations.

Here are some questions to ask yourself as a coach that will set the tone for your team. How are they going to look each day when they show up? Are they going to wear the same practice gear with their shirts tucked in, or at the minimum are they are going to have your school or organization represented so that they know who they represent as a team? Understandably, not everyone will have the same budget, but we can make sure that when they show up each day they look like a team. I believe that before you become champions, you have to start acting like champions. How they look is a sign of respect for themselves, the program, your school or organization, and, of course, the game.

What kind of structure or routine can they expect from you? Do you start practice in the same spot each day? Do they know that practice is starting when you say something as simple as, "Here we go." You should do something consistent so that everyone knows that practice is starting. If you like to start practice at a specific spot, do they walk out there, or are they expected to hustle out to you? Do you have the expectation that any time they step foot on the field walking is not permitted? If you were sitting in the stands watching your team practice, what would you want to see from start to finish? Make sure to create that atmosphere.

Again, working backward, we can look at our ideal scenario of where we want our team to be when we start our first game. We know where we need to go, whether we have a three-week preseason or months to prepare.

Each day I start practice by calling my team up and giving them the structure of practice so that they have an idea of what to expect. I then give them a goal to have in mind, usually something more on the mental side. For example, we might talk about focus and refocus and remind them that elite athletes have mastered the process of letting things go and getting back to being in the moment. Because our team has talked a lot about being the best and winning championships, I think it is important to talk to them about the things that successful athletes and people do to get there.

BUILDING A SOLID FOUNDATION

No matter what level you are coaching, you need to work on the fundamentals every day. I believe that coaches need to develop a series of drills that they can have the team go through in a set amount of time. I have created a set of drills called TRs (throwing and receiving progression) and FPs (fundamental progression). Everyone does some drills together, and then I break up the infielders and outfielders so that they get what they specifically need. They do these drills with partners. Depending on your philosophy you can have your middles work together so that they take as many repetitions as possible together, or you can have your partners switch up each day. As they are doing their drills, I am walking around reminding them to do the little things well. I emphasize what they should be doing and reinforce all the good things that they are doing well. They get used to the language that I use, and they are hearing positive reinforcement.

Your philosophy as a coach should be reflected in what you emphasize at practice. For example, if you think it is important to work on good throws, then you should be teaching the proper throwing mechanics and have drills that measure what constitutes a good throw. I believe anything that is measurable can be improved. If the goal of the drill is to have 9 out of 10 good throws to the first, you can have the first baseman simply say, "Yes," when she catches a ball. If you emphasize getting the lead out as part of your defensive philosophy, then you should work on getting the lead out at practice. We use a stopwatch on occasion to make sure that all players have the same internal clock and know whether they have a chance for a play or not. If you have not done this before, I highly suggest using a stopwatch so that your players can understand game speed, especially if you are facing a team that has quick athletes or slappers who will put pressure on your infielders. When working on your slap defense you can say that all plays have to be made in 2.70 seconds or under or whatever time is appropriate for your level of play. When I first started doing this with my team, they thought they had a lot more time than they did. Saying the times aloud started to teach them what 2.70 seconds was in terms of making a play.

LEARNING HOW TO HANDLE PRESSURE

As our team comes together and we start to get to know our kids, we begin to learn who loves to be in pressure situations and who tries to avoid them. We need to know where each kid stands so that we can help the ones who might need a little more confidence to become the person who comes through for the team when needed. We can create these situations in practice to start, so the success rate is fairly high. We create an atmosphere that shows competition as a good thing. As we progress with various drills, we make the challenges more difficult to see how we can get our players to make those plays, to keep their composure, and to be motivated to want to try again at the next opportunity.

For example, I heard about a program that did challenge drills last year, so we tried it. The kids loved it! You can have the challenge be for your defense on

Monday, pitching on Tuesday, offense on Wednesday, baserunning on Thursday, and catching on Friday. One of the aspect that I liked about this is that at the start of the week everyone is eligible to do the challenges, but after a player goes, whether she succeeds or not, she is done until everyone on the team goes. This way, everyone has a chance to do something that she thinks she can be successful at doing, and everyone has to take part throughout the week and knows that she will have an opportunity. When a challenge is presented, the players get together and decide who is going to do the challenge. The only thing you need to do as a coach is tell them what positions will be involved in the challenges that week because if Friday comes and your catchers have already done an offensive challenge earlier in the week, you would have a noncatcher doing a catching challenge. Here are examples of various challenges.

Challenge Drills

Offense

Three players are needed; each player gets to hit five pitches off the machine. The goal is to hit 12 to 15 balls well to the opposite field. (Coaches judge.)

Defense

Two outfielders and one catcher are needed; each player gets two balls hit to her. The outfielder needs to come up clean with the ball and make a good throw to the catcher; the catcher needs to catch the ball and make a tag to end the game. You don't need to have a base runner for this challenge; you simply decide whether the defense would have made the play. The nice thing about this drill is that it puts some pressure on the ones doing the drill because they want to do well for their teammates.

Pitching

You need a pitcher and a catcher, and the catcher can call pitches. For example, the pitcher needs to get a strike on one of the first two pitches. If she does this, then she can continue; if she doesn't, she loses and her challenge is over. If she gets to go on, she needs to hit six out of eight pitches. You can also have a batter stand in to create the same kind of situation. You can have a live situation as well and have the goal be to get the out, however that can happen. If you have a younger pitcher, you can make it less difficult by having her hit three out of six to the right or left side of the plate. You know your kids best, so you can adjust accordingly.

You can put your kids in any game situation and create several challenges to help build their confidence. We usually ended practice with this activity, but we also mixed it in and tried to be unpredictable, just like the game.

THERE'S ALWAYS A NEED FOR FUN

I think some of us who have chosen this profession did not have a coach who really brought fun into practice. We showed up and got the work done, and the reward was getting better, winning! If you ask kids, they inevitably seem to want to have fun. I think a mix of hard work and fun is a great combination! If you think that your team is lacking enthusiasm, then you can start practice by playing a game instead of doing the dynamic warm-up that they usually do. You can play ultimate football or freeze tag. Almost instantly they start to laugh and smile. Let them finish getting loose to make sure that they are ready to go. This kind of activity is especially valuable if you have long periods when you don't have a game or the chance to scrimmage. When we come back in January and start our four weeks of preseason practice inside a gym, the sessions can be monotonous, so we change a part of practice to add a fun element while still getting our work done. You can even modify part of your regular warm-up, such as throwing. After everyone is loose, see how many throws they can do back and forth with a partner in 10 seconds. This condition adds pressure and competition, which are elements of the game.

Another option is to play a Wiffle ball game, especially if you are inside. You can put a ball on a tee or have someone pitch. Play for a couple of innings or 15 to 20 minutes, and require the losing team to do 50 crunches or 20 mountain climbers. Having a winner and a loser will encourage the players to compete.

Let's put some of these suggestions into practice plans and give you some concrete idea of what they look like. The first program, which I call my TRs (throwing and receiving progression), is how we start defense every day.

Throwing and Receiving Progression

Infielders (including pitchers and catchers)

One-knee drills (three positions)

10 open position: Start in an open position with feet shoulder-width apart; step and throw

Long toss: keep backing up to get fully loose and to build arm strength

10 glove to glove

10 underhand flips—hit target, good tag

10 backhand flips—hit target, good tag

10 three-quarter throws—hit target, good tag

10 quick throws

Outfielders

One-knee drills (same as for infielders)

10 open position (same as for infielders)

Long toss (same as for infielders)

1×5 relay throws to cut

10 one-hop drill alternating to target (70 feet, 80 feet [21 m, 24 m])

10 touch throws (throws on the run)

Receiving

Be athletic, in good position for regular catches and tags

Get behind the ball

Transfer from the glove to throwing hand at game speed!

Work both tags: straight down and swipe

You can add whatever you think is important to your throwing and receiving progression. The idea is to incorporate all throws that each infielder and outfielder may possibly make. This activity takes approximately 10 to 15 minutes. I try have both the infielders and the outfielders finish at the same time so that it is easy to manage.

Fundamental Progression

Infielders (Five Reps Each)

On their knees:

Ground balls: middle, forehand, backhand, no glove

Ground balls: middle, forehand, backhand, with glove

Short hops: middle, forehand, backhand, with glove

Standing or ready position:

Short hops: middle, forehand, backhand

Two-step drill: roll to partner and make sure that the ball is fielded at the same time as the glove foot lands

Loopdy: middle, backhand; partner tosses the ball in the air and fielder tries to field it as soon as it hits the ground; same for the backhand

Throws on the run

Groups of three (distance is approximately 20 feet [6 m] from each other):

5-5-5: one person rolls to another, who fields and throws to the third person; five to the middle, forehand (can use flips if close to target), backhand

(continued)

Fundamental Progression *(continued)*

Outfielders

On knee in lunge position:

10 partner rolls, fielding on the outside of the foot

Lunge position (back knee is just off the ground)

Five ground balls: field on outside of glove foot, no glove

Five ground balls: field on inside of glove foot, no glove (stance will be wider)

Five ground balls: field on outside of glove foot, with glove

Five ground balls: field on inside of glove foot, with glove

Five 5-yard (4.5 m) step-throughs, right at, no glove (to throwing shoulder)

Five 10-yard (9 m) step-throughs—three-way, right at, right, left, with glove (to throwing shoulder)

Five 10-yard step-throughs—three-way, right at, right, left, with glove (to throwing position)

Five touch throws (similar to infielders' throws on the run)

Depending on how much time you have you can do your TRs every day and your FPs three times a week, especially if you have only two hours or less of practice. After they do these fundamental drills correctly you can encourage them to do these on their own.

When I say correctly, all coaches have their own philosophy about how they want their team to do their fielding and glove work. Whatever you teach make sure that they do the drills the way you want them done because they will do thousands of these throughout their training.

The reason I gave you a sample of what we do is because when I incorporated this into our team a year ago, we went to the top of our league in defensive stats. Our goal was .975 and we came in at .971, up from the previous two years. When I looked up the best teams in the country, .975 was the fielding percentage for the number one team in the country. The useful thing about this series of drills is that they can be done in a limited space, which most of us have to adapt to at some time during our training. The drills also match up with my philosophy as a head coach that the little things matter. We must be fundamentally sound to have a chance to compete against the top programs in the country.

INDOOR TRAINING

Let's turn to training inside and look at a few examples of what we need to address when structuring our indoor practices. Sometimes things that look like negatives can turn into positives. If we have chosen to coach in a cold climate, then we shouldn't complain about not having the same opportunities as someone who coaches in a warm climate. If we present things to our athletes as negatives or make them feel as if we aren't well prepared, then they will use that as an excuse later. Accountability is one of the things that we try to teach our kids, so we need to be the example of that.

I am going to provide sample practice plans with explanations of what I am trying to accomplish during that practice. We all have different situations, so you can take parts of the various practice plans and merge them into something that works for you.

Modifications for Indoor Training

Many of us use a gym at some point. Even if you coach in a warm climate, you still have to deal with rainy days, so all of us must learn to make the most of our situations. When we are inside, we usually have limited space. I know successful Division I programs that have only a gym to practice in, and they seem to get it done. In this situation you can work on the little things that make a big difference. We do many partner drills and modify the distance. Instead of hitting fungo from a normal distance, we roll balls from 15 to 20 feet (4.5 to 6 m) and still get better each day. We also have our kids take a ball, throw it against a wall, and work on glove work drills. Standing 8 to 10 feet (2.5 to 3 m) from the wall, they can toss it themselves to create short hops, so they don't even need a partner. If they have a partner they can compete against each other by seeing who can go longer without making a mistake.

Communicating Indoors

The acoustics are usually challenging inside gyms, so communication becomes critical. How do you communicate with your outfielders to move them where they need to go? Your athletes need to focus on the voices of their teammates and nothing else going on in that space. This environment is similar to what you will face in the postseason in front of big crowds. We use hand signals, so regardless of the acoustics they know what we are doing with our positioning. For example, in a game-winner situation we have three signals that we use for our outfielders to distinguish nothing over their heads, be able to throw the R2 out, and nothing drops in front. That way they know where to set up, and they can communicate that with one another. Incorporate whatever makes sense for you and your team.

Indoor Practice Surfaces

Another factor is the surface that you are practicing on. If you are on a gym floor you have to decide what ball to use. The surface I have in winter is a gym floor, and we use regular balls. The benefit of that is that the surface plays faster than dirt, so we have to be good at executing our first steps and recognizing the speed and direction of the ball. If you have a turf field to practice on, you can slide and dive and not worry much about the surface. The ball on the turf tends to bounce a little more than it does on dirt, so when you go back outside players need to remember to stay down on the ball.

How can we turn these factors into positives in our training? If your team's opponents play in the same elements, then everyone is in the same situation. If you coach at a university where you travel for the first several weeks of the season, you have to be just as prepared as the team that has been training outside for the entire preseason. How you talk about these factors will be how your team perceives things. You can have a team coming out of a cold climate that had only a gym and batting cages feeling that they are prepared fundamentally with all the glove work they did. You can talk about how well they will hit because the cages made them visualize hitting everything up the middle. Or you can choose to tell them it will take a few games to get used to the field again or that after they've played 10 games outside things will even up. As coaches we always need to keep in mind that we are shaping their perceptions. If we talk about how all the good things we did prepared us, the players will be more confident when they take the field.

Staff Roles for Indoor Practices

When considering how to structure your practices, use your staff and players to make your practices as efficient as possible. When you are in a limited space for practice or have limited time, use your kids during practice so that you can get in the greatest number of repetitions. Players can also learn how to help each other or at least know what to look for, which is an excellent way for them to gain greater understanding of the game. When you can explain something, you have a different level of understanding. I believe that every athlete who comes out of my program should understand the game enough to teach it, whether she does or not.

If you have assistants you can be really efficient because you can split practices and spend more time breaking skills down because you won't have people standing around. For example, if you have a hitting coach and a defensive coach, you can break into two groups. The defensive coach can take the infielders, while the hitting coach takes the outfielders for hitting. A pitching coach, if you are fortunate enough to have one, can pitch to the hitters or be used in whichever way fits your practice plan. After 45 minutes you can switch and give the attention you need to each group. You can bring the groups back together for a short 15- or 20-minute segment so that they get the benefit of working together.

If you are the only coach, I suggest that you take the time to teach a few drills each day in the beginning of your preseason until they understand how you want things done. Then you can let them do some things on their own. To increase the efficiency of your practices, make sure that your drills all have names so that you don't have to describe them each time. You could still split practices. You can have them do tee work and front toss drills for 20 minutes and then switch groups. At the end of that time you can have a longer period with the group working together on defense. When you are finished you can go back to hitting and work more strategy and situational hitting with you there to direct it.

Here are a couple of samples of indoor practices incorporating the ideas we have discussed.

Sample Indoor Practice 1

3:00–3:05 p.m.	Talk to the team about structure and the goal for the day
3:05–3:15 p.m.	Dynamic warm-up
3:15–3:25 p.m.	TRs (throwing and receiving progression)
	Glove work off the wall for IF and OF, 3×10
3:25–3:30 p.m.	Quarterback drill—works on first step, breaking down, and getting to a throwing position
3:30–3:45 p.m.	FPs (infield and outfield split to do their own)
3:45–4:05 p.m.	Infield and outfield split

Infield

Corners: 10 partner bunting, 10 bad throws, 5 pickoff tags

Middles: 2×5 transfer drill working double-play footwork

Reps: no throws

Outfield

2×5 relay drill to cut (about 60 feet [18 m])

Fence drill

3-3-3 with throws—directions are overhead, angled back right, angled back left

Reps: middle, right, left; grounders and fly balls

4:05–4:10 p.m.	Water break
4:10–4:30 p.m.	Infield and outfield together
	Reps with throws—throws to bases

Infield

Throws to 1B, 2B, home

Outfield

Left: 2B, 3B, Home

Center: 3B, Home, 2B

Right: Home or 1B, 2B, 3B

Challenge: Defense

4:30–4:45 p.m.	Baserunning circuit (2)
	Base leads: short game
	R1: run and hit
	R2: beat the ball (any ball hit up the middle get across to 3B)
	R3: sac fly to LF (tag and score)

(continued)

Sample Indoor Practice 1 *(continued)*

4:45–4:50 p.m.	Explanation of hitting circuit
4:50–5:50 p.m.	Hitting circuit
5:50–6:00 p.m.	Clean up, stretch, messages

Sample Indoor Practice 2

3:00–3:05 p.m.	Talk to the team about the structure and goal for the day
3:05–3:15 p.m.	Freeze tag, finish stretching
3:15–3:40 p.m.	TRs and FPs
3:40–4:00 p.m.	Infield and outfield split

Infield

Reps (no throws; change your own footwork)

Reps with throws: first, second, home (R3, bases loaded)

Short game defense with stopwatch

Slapper defense with stopwatch

Split the infield (alternate situations): (1) left side, R12 (get the lead out if you can); (2) right side (no one on, slapper, communication between 1B and 2B)

Outfield

Relay drill off wall (five angle right; five angle left)

Reps (no throws; all directions—middle, right, left; grounders and fly balls)

4:00–4:05 p.m.	Explanation of hitting circuit

Challenge: Offense

4:10–4:55 p.m.	Hitting circuit
4:55–5:00 p.m.	Clean up, stretch, messages

OUTDOOR TRAINING

Let's turn our attention to outdoor practices. Some of the elements we might have outside are variable temperatures, a wet field, sun, and wind, to name a few. Any time we're outside and it happens to be windy, I automatically modify practice so that the outfielders can learn how to stay with a fly ball in the wind. If we have the sun in a bad spot, we intentionally use it to teach kids how to be successful at catching a ball in the sun. We have practice in the mornings a couple of times a week so that we have to deal with the dew from the morning. These conditions are perfect for teaching the outfielders how to adjust when throwing a wet ball. The temperature is another major factor that we deal with where I coach, so we may have to modify the game plan if it is really cold. We have played games in the low to mid 20s Fahrenheit (–5 degrees Celsius), and it is a different game. You have to teach your kids that although the extreme cold can modify a game plan, they can't use it as an excuse because the other team has to deal with the same elements. Have your kids take on the idea that they are always better than the other team at handling any conditions that occur.

Sample Outdoor Practice 1

3:00–3:10 p.m.	Offer motivational quotation or article, explain structure, and give the focus for the day
3:10–3:25 p.m.	TRs
3:25–4:05 p.m.	Split: infielders on defense, outfielders hitting
	FPs
	Slapper defense
	Reps
	Situations: R1, R2, R12, R13
4:05–4:50 p.m.	Switch: infielders hitting, outfielders on defense
	FPs
	Quarterbacks with throws
	Fence drill
	Balls in front
	Reps, no throws
	Reps with throws to bases (five OFs, everyone needs to throw one good one in a row until everyone gets it)
4:50–5:05 p.m.	Together segment
	Situations
5:05–5:10 p.m.	Defensive challenge
5:10–5:50 p.m.	Pitchers' and catchers' workouts
	Baserunning circuit, extra work, stand in for pitchers when they are ready
5:50–6:00 p.m.	Stretch, clean up, messages

Sample Outdoor Practice 2

3:00–3:05 p.m.	Explain structure and focus for the day
3:05–3:20 p.m.	Warm up by playing ultimate football
3:20–3:35 p.m.	Baserunning circuit

(continued)

Sample Indoor Practice 2   *(continued)*

3:35–4:10 p.m.	Pitchers' and catchers' workout with pitching coach
	Everyone else on defense
4:10–4:40 p.m.	Short game live off pitchers
	Incorporate signals for base runners and hitters
	Chart pitcher's first two pitches; one needs to be a strike
4:40–5:30 p.m.	Hitting circuit
5:30 p.m.	Stretch, clean up, messages

FINAL THOUGHTS

I hope you can see that indoor and outdoor practices, when structured well, incorporate not only the physical aspects but also the mental and emotional aspects of the game. The atmosphere that you create for your athletes is just as important as the drills that you are teaching them. The teams that have good chemistry have the edge over teams that don't, so if we can create a fun, challenging, and fundamentally sound practice every day, then I believe we have a good chance of being successful each year. Remember, you know your kids the best, when to push them and when they need a break, so create what they need without compromising your values and philosophy as a coach. Be organized with the structure of your practice, considering the number of coaches you have, your facility, and whether you are inside or outside. Remember that the language you use with your players will shape their perception. Something that can be initially viewed as a disadvantage can become an advantage to your training. Keep the interest of the kids by changing things up occasionally. Varying your practices will be good for you as a coach as well.

Minimizing Monotony

Beth Torina

Although I believe that it is not our job as coaches to entertain our players, I do believe that we should try get the most from them anyway we can. That being said, I think that by planning interesting and innovative practices and engaging them in fun and challenging activities we will get more from our athletes. Although softball is a job for most us, we fell in love with it because we enjoyed the game. As we work with our teams we cannot forget that we need to allow them to enjoy it in the same way that we did. Many will argue that winning is what makes it fun, and, yes, winning is fun. But in my opinion, the process of playing the game is what we all really enjoy.

I use several strategies with my players to keep them focused and interested during practice. The key to all of this is good organization. Each day I have a thorough practice plan set up by practice time and usually balanced between offense and defense. On days when we do not perform a skill well, I may get caught up on one part of the plan, but for the most part I stay with the plan. By moving from one skill and one task to another quickly, I believe that we can hold their attention better and get more out of them. Along with my daily practice plan, I have a weekly and monthly plan. Before the season starts I try to designate how many days we will scrimmage, how many days we will face live pitching, how many days we will need to work on our defense together as a team, and how many days we will need to work on fundamental, position-specific skills. We also focus our offense by knowing how many days we need to spend on outside contact points, lower-half fundamentals, and so on. By setting this calendar ahead of time, I fight off the urge to repeat the same thing over, and I also know that I have covered all the skills necessary to prepare them for the game. This process is how I start to formulate my plan. Of course, you can adjust your plan as your week or month goes on if they need more work in one area or another that you were not expecting.

Before I even start marking up the calendar and organizing our practice weeks, I develop a list of every skill or situation that we need to cover. I make a list for each position, team defense, offense, and baserunning. As we start preparing I check off skills and situations as we cover them. This way I make sure that we do not skip anything. I choose skills off the list for us to cover each day in practice, and these skills form the basis of my practice plan. After I decide what we will cover each day, I choose drills that we can use to practice those skills. I always choose drills that are productive and help us accomplish what we are trying to get done. I love drills as much as any coach out there. I am the first to check out new gadgets and things that are fun for our players to try. I never do a drill just for the sake of doing a drill. We have a purpose and focus for everything we do. First, we put together the task, and then we decide how we will teach it and reteach it each day.

Now that we are sure our practice is organized and productive, we can use several ideas to make practice interesting and fun. Competition, drills, and measurable goals will challenge your team, create some intensity, and increase the focus of your athletes.

SCRIMMAGES

For many of our players, what they love about the sport is the competition. They love to win, and they love to compete. There are many ways to make your practices competitive and challenging while still being productive and accomplishing the task at hand. Scrimmages are the obvious ways to have our players compete. Scrimmages can be presented in many ways. Of course, you have your standard two-team scrimmage, during which we attempt to simulate a live game scenario. These days are important in preparing your team for competition because some situations that occur in games are difficult to re-create in practice. Scrimmages also get your team mentally prepared to compete against another team. Full scrimmages, however, can be lengthy, and many teams do not have the personnel to make up two full teams. For those teams and for coaches not wanting to spend their entire practice on a two-team scrimmage, here are some ideas to get a similar result.

Hustle Scrimmage

This variation is a good way to speed up a scrimmage if you are short on time. All the hitters start with a 1-1 count, and the defensive team stays on the field for six outs. When the teams switch, they have 30 seconds to be at their positions. If they fail to be ready on time, a penalty is awarded (i.e., a ball or a strike on the batter).

One-Pitch Scrimmage

This scrimmage is beneficial for your defense because they will get numerous chances, and it encourages aggressiveness in your offense. We often do this with a coach pitching from behind a screen, but you can do it with a pitcher. Each batter only gets one pitch, which is either a strike for a strike out, a ball for a walk, or a ball put in play. All other rules can be played normally.

Three-Pitch Scrimmage

This variation is similar to the one-pitch scrimmage, but each hitter gets three pitches. The difference in this version is that if the hitter does not swing at the first two pitches, the third pitch becomes a hit-and-run. This drill keeps your hitters in an aggressive, attacking mind-set.

Situational Scrimmage

In this scrimmage you create a specific focus for the offense and the defense. Start with a different situation each inning. For example, if you start with a runner on second, the offense focuses on doing their job of hitting behind the runner, the pitching staff figures out what to throw in this situation, and the defense decides how best to defend it.

Three- or Four-Team Scrimmage

This scrimmage is useful if you do not have 18 players to participate. Divide your team into three or four equal teams. I often divide the team into as many teams as I have pitchers. If I have three pitchers, each one gets a team. This way you know that all your pitchers throw the same number of innings. If you only have 15 players, then you might make three teams of 5. Two of the teams play defense, and one of the teams is at bat. Teams rotate after three outs, so each inning is nine outs instead of the typical six. You get to see different combinations of people working together on defense, and if you have utility players who need to work in multiple positions, you can accomplish that as well.

Short-Bat Scrimmage

This variation is another way to speed up a scrimmage. The offense is given a short wood bat. The hitter still swings with two hands, but the bat is about half the length of a full-size bat. In this scrimmage we usually have a coach pitch. The short bat allows the defense to play shallower because the ball doesn't travel as far. The game moves along faster, and it helps with communication and short-game defense because the fielders have to come get the ball. Some of your stronger kids will still be able to hit the ball well with the short bat, so the defense has to stay honest.

Tee Scrimmage

If you really want to challenge your defense and have a lot of balls put in play, simply let the offense hit off a tee. They can then hit the ball to any part of the field they choose.

Half-Field Scrimmage

In this scrimmage you set your defense on half the field. If you set up on the right side then you play only a first baseman, second baseman, center fielder, and right fielder. If the hitter pulls the ball to the left side, she is automatically out. The hitter must hit the ball to the right side or the area that you are working on. By using this restriction you force your offense to focus on their job and you get some defensive work done as well. The fun part comes when running bases, because hitters are allowed to use only the bases on the right side of the field. They must run from home to first, first to second, and then second to home. The field can also be set up on the left side. This hitter runs the bases as described earlier, and the defense just plays the other half of the field.

Around the Horn

This fun scrimmage focuses on catch and throw with your athletes. It is a great back-up drill for your team to make sure that everyone is in position. The hitter puts the ball in play. The defense must throw the ball around the horn to get the hitter out. The hitter continues running until the ball has gone from first to second to third and then to the catcher. If the hitter hits the ball to the outfield, the outfielder throws to the correct base (the base ahead of the runner). The infielders then throw it around the horn from that point on. For example, it might go from second to third to home and end at first. The offensive team gets a point for each base the hitter touches before the ball goes all the way around the horn.

Backward Softball

This game is entertaining for a day when your team needs to lighten up or take a break. The hitter hits the ball off the tee, off front toss, or however you choose. The key is that after hitting the ball she runs to third. The defense must try to get the force-out at third instead of first. The rules seem simple, but the tricky part is that if the hitter takes one step to first base after she hits, she is automatically out. In addition, as soon as the defensive team gets three outs and gets their entire team off the field (outside the foul lines), they can start hitting. If your team ever needs a good laugh, this one will give it to you!

These scrimmages are just a starting point for creating a great practice. First, think about what your team needs to work on. Is it situations? Communication? Being aggressive? Then use this information to create what you need. All the scrimmages here can be modified in many ways. Be creative and get the most out of your group!

COMPETITIVE DRILLS

Through drills we help break down fundamental skills for our athletes. We try to give them a better understanding of all the parts that make up a skill, and we explain the reason why we want things done a certain way. By learning all angles of the task our athletes understand why they are doing something and will buy in to the current task. We have all had the athlete who understands exactly what we ask her to do on our first instruction. We tell her once to do something, and she instantly gets it. Some players are just extremely gifted and athletic. But this is not the norm. For all the others we are trying to teach their bodies to make a specific movement or trying to teach the timing of an action. By using a drill we often get them to understand the motion more easily. Of course, we always want to spend some time in our practices just taking reps and doing the skill at full speed. Still, we want to spend some time in detailed drill work. This is also a good way to stop your team from going through the motions. By giving them a drill with a specific focus, you can get them to zone in on a particular skill. Also, by switching quickly from one drill to another you can keep their focus for longer periods.

OFFENSIVE DRILLS

When we set up our offensive practice we always include some drill or station work and some live hitting on the field off pitches from either a coach or one of our pitchers. Typically, we have one group in the cage doing drill work, one group shagging (always playing their true positions and working on live reads off the bat), and one group at a live station. While they are at the live station, they are also running bases. They split up at each base and read each ball. They do not run the ball all the way out, but they take their leads and then react to the ball with a few steps. This way they make 10 to 15 decisions at each base. During the drills or cage group, the players split up into stations. We typically have enough stations for each girl, so there is no standing around in the cage. They are swinging constantly throughout this time. Each day the offense has a specific goal and focus. We do hundreds of drills to work on all aspects of the swing. I am going to focus on fun ways that we create competition during our hitting time while still accomplishing our daily hitting goals.

Situational and Partner Hitting

Objective
We do this drill many different ways, and no matter how we do it, the players love it. Modify it to work for your team.

Setup
I usually assign partners for the drill and often try to match a power hitter with a contact hitter or slapper. I then tell them that they must divide up the four situations: no one on, runner at first, runner at second, runner at third.

Execution
Partners must each hit in two of these situations. At the end of the four situations, both players hit in the bases-loaded situation. In each situation they must do their job. For example, with no one on they must get a base hit, with a runner on first they must move her to second, and so on. They hit their situations and continue to get pitches as long as they continue to get their job done.

(continued)

Situational and Partner Hitting *(continued)*

Coaching Points

When they fail at their job they are out. You may want to cap off each situation at a maximum number of points if you are short on time. If anyone hits a home run she gets as many points as the round she is on (runner at second is two points, bases loaded is four, and so on). The winner is the team that scores the most points. Often I make them choose which rounds they hit, and then the next day I keep the same partners and make them switch with their partners and hit the other two rounds. This can also be done as an individual game, and each player can hit all situations. Modify it however you like!

Cones Around the Field

Objective

This drill helps your hitter understand contact points and learn to have good bat control.

Setup

Place six to eight cones around the outfield evenly spaced apart.

Execution

The hitter must hit the ball between all the cones in order. She must even hit to the foul areas. You can start it off a tee and then progress to toss and live.

Coaching Points

Keep score of how many they hit in the correct spot. This drill can also be done in the cage by placing the cones around the base of the net.

Horse

Objective

The cones on the field are the lead-in to this game. After they have mastered putting the ball between the cones, then you can play Horse in the same manner.

Setup

This drill has the same setup as Cones Around the Field.

Execution

This game is played just like horse in basketball. The first hitter calls her shot, such as a line drive in the right-center gap or a ground ball through the 5-6 hole. If she hits the spot, the next player has to hit the same spot. If she doesn't hit the spot, she gets a letter—H. The first one to spell the word *horse* loses the game.

Ground Ball, Line Drive, Home Run

Objective

This drill is similar to Cones Around the Field in that it teaches bat control, contact points, and especially correct extension.

Setup

Set up a tee at home plate on the field or in the cage. You can also do this drill off front toss or live pitching.

Execution

The player must hit a ground ball, a line drive, and then a home run (or deep fly ball) in order.

Coaching Points

You can start off the tee and progress to live. Players can go in rounds of hitting a ground ball, a line drive, and a home run until they do not accomplish the task. They receive points for how many correct rounds they hit.

Long Tee Contest

Objective

This drill works best in the cage and can be done several ways.

Setup

You can hang hula hoops or tape circles on to the back of your cage. Hang one in center, one in left, and one in right.

Execution

The players try to hit off the tee into the hula hoop. The ball must stay on a line and hit the hula hoop without hitting the ground.

Coaching Points

You can devise a point system for this game any way you like and challenge your players to a long tee duel.

Offensive Olympics

Objective

One season our offense really lacked confidence. Instead of doing one of our typical practice routines, I told them to bring only their bats to practice because we were having the Offensive Olympics. On this day all the events involved were aggressive, requiring them to swing hard to produce the result.

(continued)

Offensive Olympics *(continued)*

Setup

You can create any event you like. If your team needs work on the short game or hit-and-run, work those into your event.

Execution

We included events such as self-toss from home plate and hit the ball out of the park, long tee, home run derby, and others.

Coaching Points

After each event we crowned a champion, and at the end of the day we had a gold medalist. This activity was an excellent way to help our players enjoy hitting again and remember that hitting was fun. Also, the change of pace lightened the mood and helped us win the next five straight!

DEFENSIVE DRILLS

The defensive portion of our practices always starts with a short fundamental skill time. This time is position specific, so the outfield has a drill different from the infield. The catchers even have specific fundamental skills that they work on during this time. After this short warm-up we begin our team defensive practice. If we want to break things down more and work fundamental skills with the infield and outfield, we might keep the infield on the field and send the outfield to hit in the cage. Then after 45 minutes or so, we would switch the groups. This approach prevents us from standing around. If we keep them all on the field at the same time, we are typically working on things that we need to do together such as relays, communication, or situations. I always have a specific time frame in which to cover a variety of areas. I try to switch quickly from one to the next to help the players keep their focus. Again, as with the offense, you can use many drills to work on the various aspects of defense, but I am going to focus on just a few that will keep your players on their toes.

Runner at Second Challenge

Objective

This drill pits the outfield against the infield.

Setup

You will need balls, a coach to hit fungo, and helmets for the base runners.

Execution

At first you have one group on the field (either the infield or the outfield) and one group running the bases. The baserunning group starts with a runner on second and a runner at home. Every time the runner at second scores, the baserunning team gets a point. When the infield is on the field, the coach hits hard ground balls between the fielders. The infield has to keep the ball on the dirt to keep the runner from scoring. They try to field the ball and get an out somewhere, either the force at first or the runner going home. When the outfield is on the field, the coach hits ground balls anywhere in the outfield. The outfielders attempt to throw out the runner at the plate or get the runner out at second starting from home, whatever the ball dictates. The outfield needs a couple of infielders to stay on the field to cover bases and act as the cut to home. Each team needs a catcher to cover the plate.

Coaching Points

Each team stays on the field for a designated number of outs, such as 6 or 12. The team that scores the most runs before the other team gets their outs wins.

21 Outs

Objective

This drill gives your team reps, creates communication among them, and forces them to perform under pressure.

Setup

Your team takes their positions on the field, and a coach hits fungo.

Execution

The defense must field 21 balls cleanly and get 21 outs in a row. If they bobble a ball or do not get the out, they must start over at the beginning. The drill ends when they get 21 outs in a row.

Coaching Points

The closer they get to 21 outs, the more the pressure builds!

Hit the Grass or Tweeners

Objective

This challenge creates communication between your infield and outfield and involves not letting the ball hit the grass.

Setup

Your team takes their positions on the field, and a coach hits fungo.

Execution

The coach hits fly balls all over the field or tries to hit ground balls through the infield. Every time the ball hits the grass, the team loses a point or the team owes something (five push-ups, a sprint to the fence, or other task). When the team

(continued)

Hit the Grass or Tweeners   *(continued)*

keeps the ball from hitting the grass, they get a point. The drill ends when the team reaches a designated number of points.

Coaching Points

Remember to set your team in all of their different defenses to do this drill. The space between the players will be different when the infield is in for bases loaded, when you are covering a slapper, and so on.

Throws to Bases

Objective

A simple way to get a lot of reps and work on throws to bases is by having one coach hit to the outfield and one hit to the infield.

Setup

Your team takes their positions, and two coaches hit fungo.

Execution

The outfield always throws a base behind where the infield is throwing. For example, the infield throws to first and the outfield throws to second. Put buckets at each base so that you can collect the balls when they are thrown in and keep them out of the way.

Coaching Points

This alone is a great drill, but then we add a challenge. We have the infield compete against the outfield. Every time a group makes a good throw, they get a point. When they reach a designated number, they win the round. Then the next round begins; the infield throws to second, and the outfield throws to third. This sequence continues until the fielders have thrown to all the bases.

Defend the Island

Objective

This drill works on change of direction, dives, and especially taking the first step in the correct direction and reacting correctly to the ball.

Setup

Place four cones or markers in a square. One player is needed to stand in the square and the coach hits fungo.

Execution

Some people call this drill popcorn because the coach feeds 10 balls up in the air quickly all over the square. Every time the player catches the ball, she gets a point. The player with the most points wins.

Caterpillar

Objective

This game is fun because all the players must react to the sound of the ball hit in case it is their number.

Setup

In this drill the players line up in single-file line. Each player is given a number.

Execution

As the coach hits the ball, she or he says a number aloud at the instant of contact. The player whose number is called must step out of the line and field the ball correctly. If she does not field the ball or misses her turn, she is out. The last player remaining wins the game.

Coaching Points

Players must think about their first reaction step every time the ball is hit whether the ball is for them or not, so they get something out of each rep.

Backward Ground Balls and Fly Balls

Objective

This drill helps your players react correctly to the ball and take the correct first step. It really helps them keep their feet moving on defense and learn to use clues, such as the sound of the bat, to know how hard the ball is hit at them.

Setup

Put your players at their positions and have a coach hit fungo.

Execution

This drill has many variations. One is to have the players start at their positions with their backs to the plate. As soon as they hear the contact of the ball, they turn around and field the ball. If they do not field it correctly, they are out of the game.

Coaching Points

This drill can also be done with the players lying on the ground, facing sideways, or in any other position you can think of.

Infield on Timer

Objective

This was always one of my infield's favorite drills. We often worked on this during the week before we faced a team with a lot of short gamers.

Setup

Before you start, designate the time by which they must get the ball to first base, such as 2.7 or 2.8. Then tell them that they have to get a certain number of outs in less than that time.

Execution

Have a coach hit fungo or have one of your slappers hit off a toss. Every time the fielders get the ball to first in less than the allotted time they get a point.

Coaching Points

I find it hard to create pressure in practice without base runners running to first, but by having the players race the clock you can cause them to rush in the same way they would if a runner were present.

BASERUNNING

Baserunning is a skill that we as coaches often schedule last, and we often seem to run out of time to cover it. But we should never neglect baserunning because it can often change the outcome of games. Each day in my practice I always run bases first. If I schedule it last, I will never get to it, so I always put it first. Each day we work on our paths to the base and making turns at all bases. Then we have a specific skill focus. The skill focus might be fly ball reads or bunt leads, but we cover something each day. Here are a few ways to work on this skill and make baserunning more enjoyable.

Hit and Fetch (or Cat and Mouse)

Objective

This drill works on proper rounds at bases. It also helps your team develop leadership because they must use a strategy that they come up with on their own.

Setup

Split the players into two teams. The team at the plate hits the ball and runs bases. The other team splits into two groups—half at first and half at third.

Execution

As soon the hitter contacts the ball, one player from first and one from third run to where the ball is hit. They cannot pick up the ball, move it, or throw it to their partner. The player who hits the ball runs until both players from the other team have touched the ball. She gets a point for every base she touches.

Coaching Points

By rounding bases correctly and taking proper turns, players can run more effectively and score more points. This drill is helpful for conditioning as well.

Whistle Blower

Objective

This drill helps your players understand the correct timing of their leads and getting off the base.

Setup

In this drill a coach or a pitcher is pitching from the mound and another coach is coaching first base. Both coaches have a whistle. The players are all at first base and are working on taking their leads off the pitcher.

Execution

When the pitcher lets go of the ball, she blows a whistle exactly at release. The coach at first blows her or his whistle right when the player at first base leaves the base.

Coaching Points

If the lead is correct both whistles should sound at the same time.

Base Race

Objective

This drill works on rounding the bases correctly and improves your players' conditioning. Eight players at a time run in this drill.

Setup

One player is on each base, and one player is between each pair of bases.

Execution

When the coach says, "Go," the players start running the bases. When a player catches another player and tags her, the tagged player is out. The winner is the last player left running.

Coaching Points

To make this drill more competitive, you may want divide up your team by similar speeds.

GOAL SETTING OR REWARD SYSTEM

One final idea for motivating your team in practice is through goal setting or a reward system. Both will help keep your players on task and focused on achieving something throughout the day. Of course, the ultimate goal is to win ball games, but to win games we must have many smaller victories.

Goal setting can be done in several ways. One idea is to have a prepractice meeting each day when the team will set goals for that day in practice. The players will decide what they want to do well and what their focus will be. Make sure that the goals are measurable so that you can evaluate the team's performance at the end of each practice day and decide whether they were successful in accomplishing their goals. Another way is to write the purpose of each drill on the practice plan or go over the purpose with them before the activity. Again, we are not just doing a drill. We always have a goal in mind. If your team knows why you are asking them to do something, they will buy into it more. Another way to do this is through a captain's meeting. Pull your captains aside and tell them that you need to do a particular drill that day and explain why. Then, if they hear complaining or if teammates are tentative, they can reassure them by explaining why they need to do the drill. You give your captains power and credibility, and your team may work harder for their teammates.

You might also create a reward system for your players to help motivate them throughout practice and skill work. You can do this in many ways. Create an award for practice player of the day or week. You could excuse this person from field chores that day or allow her to choose uniforms for the weekend. You could hang her photo on a board in the dugout or locker room to recognize her hard work and focus. This award does go to the player who played best; it goes to the one who exemplified the hard work and focus that you were looking for during the week. You can also reward players for outstanding acts, perhaps with stickers for their helmets or by posting their names on the board. These awards can be given whenever someone goes beyond what is required. Maybe they make a great diving catch or help a teammate with a skill that she is struggling to master.

Whatever the task, they receive some type of recognition for their performance. Teammates can also give these awards. I've heard of some teams that place paper bags or banks in their lockers. Teammates can write notes and place them in their bags when they see good work. Peers are the best motivators for some athletes. The players can nominate or vote on who the practice player of the day or week is. This system gives them even more ownership into that week's practice.

FINAL THOUGHTS

Softball is a game of repetition. The more we repeat an action, the better we get at it. Even if we do not have perfect mechanics, the more ground balls we attempt to field, the better we will become at reacting and catching the ball. The more pitches we throw, the better we will become at hitting a location. We can easily recognize that giving our athletes repetitions and having them take swing after swing and ground ball after ground ball is sure to make them better players. By being creative with our practices, however, we make things much more enjoyable. We teach them how to tackle a challenge and how to compete. We keep them engaged and focused. We help them enjoy the sport and maintain their drive to excel.

PLAYER SKILLS AND TEAM STRATEGIES

13

Batting Practice for Power and Consistency

Jenny Allard

Batting is a dynamic and complex skill, one of the most difficult skills in sport because both objects (the ball and the bat) are in motion at the same time. Hitting the ball at the correct time with the correct technique to register a hit does not happen often, which is why a success rate for a hitter of 3 hits in 10 chances is considered a success. Over the last 20 years, run production has increased. We are witnessing record-breaking offensive performances by individuals as well as teams. We have observed improvements in the technology of bats and advancement in batting techniques that have produced more powerful hitters. We are seeing great hitters become increasingly more consistent and teams shattering home run records by developing more power. The three keys to achieving power and consistency in the swing are for the hitter to be balanced, to arrive on time, and to stay on the plane through the ball. Batting practice should stress fundamentals through consistent drill work. Practice should also include execution opportunities that resemble game situations. Creating pressure situations in practice is necessary to prepare hitters to execute in games. By stressing fundamentals in the swing and putting together a quality offensive practice with drills and situations, you can improve consistency and increase power in your hitters.

FUNDAMENTALS FOR POWER AND CONSISTENCY

The following list outlines points of emphasis for coaches as they train their players to achieve both power and consistency. The list is laid out in an order that builds the development of the swing. Individual players may vary in their hitting style, but accomplished hitters consistently execute these key principles.

- **Stance**—The hitter should be balanced with weight distributed on the balls of the feet, knees flexed, body stacked, and elbows loose.
- **Negative move, also known as a load**—The hitter starts with weight at 50-50 and takes weight from the front foot into the back leg, thus loading the back leg. The front shoulder rolls in, and the bottom hand is cocked.

- **Weight transfer**—Being on time is important. The front foot is down and the weight is back at 50-50 before the ball enters the hitting zone.
- **Back elbow and hip connection**—The hands stay inside the ball by keeping the back elbow and back hip connected in a linear movement to contact.
- **Point of contact**—The hands are in correct position (top hand is palm up and bottom hand is palm down) as the ball arrives in the hitting zone; the hitter has good barrel control.
- **Big zone and extension**—The hitter finishes forward and stays through the ball as long as possible.
- **Follow-through**—The hitter releases the top hand off the bat, finishes the swing, and takes the bat off the line of the ball.

Key principles that hitters need to produce a consistent and powerful swing include timing, back elbow and hip connection, and the path of the barrel. Coaches should focus on training hitters to be on time, meaning that the front foot is down, the weight is at 50-50, and the hands are in the proper position at contact. Hitters need to have a good back elbow and hip connection into contact to get to and through the ball. To be as consistent as possible, hitters must direct their energy through the ball up the middle, keeping the barrel in the hitting zone as long as possible. This is also known as staying on plane.

CURRICULUM FOR BATTING PRACTICE

Establishing consistent routines and exercises that athletes perform every day is critical to their success. Each player should establish routines that will translate to success in game situations. The following categories should be included in practices on a consistent basis:

- Warm-up
- Tee drills
- Center toss
- Visualization drills
- Explosive exercises
- Live situations and situational hitting
- Mental game

The following matrix (table 13.1) can help coaches select certain exercises to use in their practice plan. Having consistency is important, but it is also necessary to mix up the drills to keep hitters challenged.

TABLE 13.1 Drill Matrix: Batting Practice for Power and Consistency

Warm-up	Bat stretches
	Dry swings
	One-arm ball tosses into net
Tee drills	Four-corner point of contact
	One-arm
	Bat stop
	Point of contact
	Tee distance (tee to tee)
	Load or dance
	Weight transfer
	Stride, hold, and swing
	Deflated soccer ball or basketball
	Extension
	Double tee (two tee)
Center toss drills	Point of contact
	One-arm
	Upper-body
	Three-plate
	Weight transfer
	Balance step
	Tennis ball bounce
Visualization drills	Stand-in
	Numbered tennis ball toss
Explosive exercises for power	Bridges or planks
	Bat raises
	Medicine ball twists and tosses
	Forearm exercises
Live situations	Situational hitting
	Challenge competition
Mental game	Being patient at the plate
	Hitting your best pitch
	Working counts
	Zone hitting
	Two-strike battle

Warm-Up

A good warm-up is necessary to be both physically and mentally ready to hit. As the athlete grabs the bat, she should begin focusing on the hitting process by stretching out the body, executing the swing, and seeing the ball.

Bat Stretches

Objective

Warm up and mentally prepare to hit.

Setup

Athlete with a bat and an open area to stretch.

Execution

The athlete places one hand at each end of the bat and holds the bat at shoulder height in front of her. She twists left and right, warming up the core through rotation. With the bat overhead, she pulls the right arm down with the left arm overhead and vice-versa. Warming up the body and having a prestretch is important. With one hand she can then hold the bat out in front and draw a small number eight in front of herself to engage the shoulder, forearm, and wrist.

Dry Swings

Objective

Warm up and isolate technique.

Setup

Athlete with a bat and an open area to swing.

Execution

The athlete can start getting loose by swinging the bat back and forth before settling into her formal stance and practicing good technique through her dry swing. Watching hitters take their dry swings offers the coach an opportunity to watch them at various parts of the swing—stance, load, point of contact, and follow-through. A coach can also add resistance at the load phase, point of contact, and follow-through to help them develop core strength.

One-Arm Ball Tosses Into Net

Objective

Learn proper path of the arms.

Setup

Athlete with a ball and catch net.

Execution

The athlete places a ball in each hand to learn the proper path of the arms. Using the front arm the hitter's first move is forward, pulling with the front elbow and moving the hand forward while tossing the ball into a net in front of her in the direction of the pitcher. Similarly, with the ball in the hand of the back arm, the elbow moves into position inside the back hip and the hand tosses the ball forward in the direction of the pitcher.

Tee Drills

The tee is a valuable warm-up, practice, and teaching tool. Working on a tee provides an opportunity to isolate and focus on the dynamic movement of the body while the ball is still.

One of the most important aspects to stress on the tee is point of contact. Often, hitters do not know where to stand in relation to the tee. They are often too far away from the tee (off the plate) and too far behind the ball on contact. The tee should be placed so that the point of contact is slightly in front of the hitter's stride foot before she takes her stride. For younger hitters I like to have them hold the bat in one hand with the end of the barrel touching the ground. While extending the hand forward and up in line with the belly button, the tip of the bat should touch the outside corner of the plate. This action helps position the hitter properly on the tee. After the hitter is properly set up, she should take 10 or 12 warm-up cuts off the tee while working on keeping her hands inside the ball and finishing with the barrel forward.

Here are several tee drills that you can use in developing your offensive practice plan.

Tee Drills for Greater Consistency

Working on a tee provides a valuable opportunity to develop consistency in swing mechanics, which is a crucial element in achieving exceptional results. These drills help athletes develop that consistency.

Four-Corner Point of Contact

Objective

Learn point of contact for different pitch locations.

Setup

Athlete with a bat, ball, tee, and catch net.

Execution

A ball is placed on the tee in the following four positions, and the hitter takes four cuts at each: low inside, high inside, low outside, and high outside. This drill should follow some basic warm-up swings off the tee.

One-Arm

Objective

Reinforce the proper path of the arms to the ball.

Setup

Athlete with a bat, ball, tee, and catch net.

Execution

A ball is placed in a good mid-center position on the tee. The hitter takes her top hand off the bat and, if using a regular-size bat, chokes up to the top of the grip with the front hand. Small or short bats are excellent in this drill, and the hitter using a small bat does not need to choke up. With the focus on the front arm, the hitter emphasizes pulling with the front elbow without opening the front shoulder. This action will help the hitter keep her hands inside the ball. The hitter should uncoil the front arm with the elbow moving forward first. Then the forearm extends forward toward the pitcher, not away from the body, and finally the wrist finishes through the ball.

The hitter should visualize drawing a line with her hands across the letters of her uniform. Be sure to emphasize the forward finish through the ball, having the hitter stay on the plane of the ball as long as possible before opening the front side. Keep the hitter focused on hitting the ball up the middle. A coach can find breakdowns in the hitter's technique if she is not consistently hitting the ball up the middle. Consistent hitters have the ability to let their hands work freely and independent of their hips and shoulders. After several reps (10 to 15) with the front arm, the hitter should switch to the top hand. Have the hitter take her front arm and place it across her waist, which will help keep her front side closed during the drill. As the hitter engages the top hand, she should emphasize a strong wrist and start the elbow below the wrist. The movement starts with the elbow moving forward and into the body close to the back hip. We want the hitter to establish a good elbow and hip connection to maximize power while going down through the ball, not up and under. Again, we want to emphasize the wrist position coming into contact; the wrist should be cocked behind the ball and extend through the ball on contact. Remind the hitter to stay on plane through the ball, extending forward before coming off the line of the ball.

Bat Stop

Objective
Barrel control.

Setup
Athlete with a bat, ball, and tee.

Execution
After the hitter begins her swing ask her to stop at contact. Check where her hands are in relation to the barrel. For inside pitches the point of contact is out in front with the barrel slightly in front of the hands. For middle pitches the hands are slightly in front of the barrel, and for outside pitches the barrel is farther behind the hands on contact. Also at contact, check to see whether the hips are still behind the ball or whether the hitter has cleared her hips too early. The shoelaces of the back foot and the knees should be pointing at contact.

Point of Contact

Objective
Reinforce proper point of contact.

Setup
Athlete with a bat, ball, tee, and catch net.

Execution
The tee is placed in the proper position relative to the plate. For single-location tees that place the ball in the middle of the base, place a home plate under the base to show hitters the point of contact for inside versus outside pitches. Emphasize hitting the ball in the correct location relative to the body. A hitter should focus on hitting an outside pitch farther back in the hitting zone relative to middle or inside pitches. Also, teach hitters to make adjustments on high and low pitches. Low pitches are contacted deeper in the zone, whereas higher pitches should be hit farther in front.

Tee Drills for Developing Power

After an athlete has used the tee for warm-up and point of contact drills, a good next step is to push her to increase the power she generates through tee drills. With the ball stationary on the tee the athlete will have the freedom to use her body more efficiently through the path of the ball.

Tee Distance (Tee to Tee)

Objective

Emphasize proper contact position and power through the ball by moving the tee farther from the catch net.

Setup

Athlete with a bat, balls, tee, and catch net or batting cage tunnel.

Execution

The best place for this drill is in a batting cage. The hitter stands at one edge of the cage and works on driving the ball on a linear path to the other end of the cage. We want to see the ball hit the back of the net rather than the side of the net to emphasize hitting the ball up the middle. The Tee Distance Drill requires the hitter to stay inside the ball and extend forward to hit the back end of the net. If the hitter pulls off the ball or slices inside the ball too much, the ball will hit the side nets and not make it to the back net. This is a good individual and partner drill.

Load or Dance

Objective

Learn proper technique for negative move, or load.

Setup

Athlete with a bat, ball, tee, and catch net.

Execution

Standing at the tee, the hitter steps forward with the stride foot, steps back with the pivot foot, and steps forward again so that the stride foot lands in the same place as the first step. The hitter swings as the front foot lands. This step sequence allows hitters to feel the load, or negative move, back into the pivot leg and the subsequent weight transfer forward.

Weight Transfer

Objective

Emphasize proper weight transfer.

Setup

Athlete with a bat, ball, tee, and catch net.

Execution

The hitter begins with the stride foot touching the inside of the back foot without any weight on the stride foot. The hitter strides forward and falls into the ball (using an extended stride to overemphasize the weight transfer), getting the front foot down before contact. This drill will help with proper weight transfer because by starting with both feet in the load position, the hitter has to come forward more aggressively as she falls forward on the front foot.

Stride, Hold, and Swing

Objective

Emphasize timing in the swing.

Setup

Athlete with a bat, ball, tee, and catch net.

Execution

The hitter takes a normal stride and, with her hands back, pauses for a moment before continuing with the swing. This drill removes the timing element and allows the hitter to focus on getting her hands through the ball. This drill helps the hitter work on getting her hands in the proper position while also transferring weight through the swing.

Deflated Soccer Ball or Basketball

Objective

Emphasize driving through the ball.

Setup

Athlete with a bat, a deflated soccer ball or basketball, tee, and catch net.

Execution

Place a slightly deflated soccer ball or basketball on the tee for the hitter. If the ball does not balance, use a funnel. The point of emphasis is having the hitter drive the barrel through the ball while staying on plane as long as possible. The hitter will feel resistance from the weight of the larger ball that will help produce more power in the swing.

Extension

Objective

Emphasize follow-through in the swing.

Setup

Athlete with a bat, ball, and tee.

Execution

The hitter takes a swing and then focuses on finishing the swing with the end of the barrel pointed at the pitcher. The hitter is forced to direct the barrel through the ball and finish forward on plane, rather than opening the front shoulder too early.

Double Tee (Two Tee)

Objective

Emphasize staying through the ball after contact.

Setup

Athlete with a bat, ball, two tees, and catch net.

Execution

Place a ball on each of two tees, one directly behind the other about 12 inches (30 cm) apart. Have the hitter focus on driving the barrel through the first ball while staying on plane through the second ball. Both balls will be sent forward to the net.

Center Toss Drills

Center toss (also known as front toss) is used extensively by coaches as both a warm-up to games or in practices as a teaching tool. The coach is centered behind a screen about 10 to 12 feet (3 to 3.5 m) from the batter, who is standing at the plate. The coach can then throw pitches to various locations—inside, outside, high, and low—and speeds to prepare and train hitters. For coaches who do not have access to screens or cages, center toss can be performed with small Wiffle balls. The following center toss drills will help hitters achieve consistency and power in their swings.

Point of Contact

Objective

Work on point of contact with a moving ball.

Setup

Athlete with a bat standing at a plate and a coach behind a toss net approximately 10 to 15 feet (3 to 5 m) away with a bucket of balls.

Execution

The coach mixes locations and the speed of the toss to hitters, who have to adjust their timing and point of contact to hit the ball consistently well. This is a great first drill after a brief round of 10 to 15 cuts to get the hitter loose. For center toss to be effective, the coach must vary locations and speed.

One-Arm

Objective

Train proper arm path to the ball.

Setup

Athlete with bat standing at a plate and a coach behind a toss net approximately 10 to 15 feet (3 to 5 m) away with a bucket of balls.

Execution

As with the One-Arm Tee, have the hitter isolate each arm to emphasize the different core fundamentals (refer to One-Arm Tee for technique emphasis on each arm).

Upper-Body

Objective

Emphasize staying through the ball as long as possible.

Setup

Athlete with a bat standing at a plate and a coach behind a toss net approximately 10 to 15 feet (3 to 5 m) away with a bucket of balls.

Execution

Have the hitter start her swing with her balance at 50-50 (she has loaded and is stacked). Now that the lower half is engaged, toss the ball and have her work on bringing her hands inside the ball to and through contact. The emphasis is on contact and getting through the ball while staying on plane as long as possible. Make sure that the hitter has effective back elbow and hip connection before contact.

Three-Plate

Objective

Work on timing and point of contact with balls thrown at various distances.

Setup

Athlete with a bat standing at a plate, a coach behind a toss net approximately 10 to 15 feet (3 to 5 m) away with a bucket of balls, and three home plates set up in front of the center toss net at various locations (close, middle, far).

Execution

Have the hitter take five swings at each plate, moving between the plates in a random fashion. This drill keeps the hitters honest by not allowing them to become too patterned with the speed at one location.

Weight Transfer

Objective

Emphasize proper weight transfer.

Setup

Athlete with a bat standing at a plate and a coach behind a toss net approximately 10 to 15 feet (3 to 5 m) away with a bucket of balls.

Execution

The hitter begins with the stride foot touching the inside of the back foot without any weight on the stride foot. The hitter strides forward and falls into the ball (using an extended stride to overemphasize the weight transfer), getting the front foot down before contact. This drill will help with proper weight transfer because by starting with both feet in the load position, the hitter is forced to come forward more aggressively as she falls forward on the front foot.

Balance Step

Objective

Emphasize weight coming through the swing.

Setup

A coach is located behind a toss net approximately 10 to 15 feet (3 to 5 m) away with a bucket of balls. The athlete stands with a bat at the plate and places a small 6-inch (15 cm) round inflatable balance step under her back pivot foot. She places it toward the inside of the ball of the foot so that as she swings she must pivot on the inside of the back knee to allow proper knee, hip, and elbow connection for power. A decline board or doorstop can also be used.

Execution

The coach tosses the ball toward the athlete, and the athlete swings normally with the balance step under her pivot foot. She resets on the balance step before every pitch if her foot slips off.

Tennis Ball Toss

Objective

Emphasize letting the ball get into the hitting zone.

Setup

An athlete with a bat standing at a plate, a coach behind a toss net approximately 10 to 15 feet (3 to 5 m) away with a bucket of tennis balls, and a flat surface between tosser and hitter.

Execution

Standing behind a net, the coach bounces a tennis ball into the hitter's zone. The hitter works on being on time by getting her front foot down and her hands in the proper position. This drill allows the hitter to work on different points of contact with inside, outside, high, and low pitches. Make sure that the hitter has proper placement of the barrel.

Visualization Drills

Drills that allow hitters to focus on seeing the ball and recognizing the release point, spin, and location are important in developing greater consistency.

Stand-In

Objective

Allow hitters to see pitches and work on timing.

Setup

During the second half of a pitcher's bullpen workout, allow a hitter to stand in at the plate with a bat and helmet.

Execution

Challenge hitters to recognize balls and strikes as they track the ball into the hitting zone. Hitters can also be challenged to recognize in and out pitches and fast or off-speed pitches. They can say yes or no to indicate whether they would swing or not.

Numbered Tennis Ball Toss

Objective

Work on visual acuity.

Setup

Athlete with a bat standing at the plate. A coach serves as side tosser and has a bag of tennis balls with number one or two written on the balls.

Execution

The coach tosses up two balls—one with the number 1 on it and the other with the number 2. The coach calls out which ball the hitter must hit.

Explosive Exercises for Power

One of the best ways to increase power in the swing is to develop your athletes' core strength. Generating an explosive back hip through contact will produce a more powerful swing. The core, defined as the area from the upper thighs to the armpits, is the power base for the swing. Having a strong core allows athletes to stabilize their extremities for greater bat control, extension, and follow-through. Structuring stations during batting practice to improve your athletes' cores will translate directly to better hitting. Listed here are a few core exercises that are simple to integrate as a station in practice.

Bridges or Planks

Objective

Strengthen the athlete's core.

Setup

The athlete lies on her belly with her feet together. She makes a fist with her hand, bends at the elbows, and places her forearms underneath her body.

Execution

The athlete raises up so that all her weight is on her forearms and toes. She holds the position for 30 seconds, rests for 30 seconds, and holds again for 30 seconds. Side planks, a more difficult exercise, would be the next progression. The athlete is on her side (right or left) and raises up on one elbow. Make sure that the elbow is directly below the shoulder. You can adjust the length of time that your athletes hold the position according to their fitness level. This exercise improves inner stability and is one of the best core exercises.

Bat Raises

Objective

Strengthen core.

Setup

The athlete lies on her back with her knees bent. She holds a bat horizontally across her lap with her arms extended.

Execution

Have the athlete lift her torso up and bring the bat over her knees, keeping her arms straight out in front of her. Difficulty can be increased by starting with the bat in both hands overhead. The athlete can bring the bat forward to her waist and then lift her torso up and stretch her arms up over her knees. This exercise focuses on flexion and strengthens the abdominal muscles.

Medicine Ball Twists and Tosses

Objective

Strengthen core.

Setup

The athlete holds a weighted medicine ball in both hands and stands facing a wall or partner about 6 feet (1.8 m) away. If facing a wall, she can move closer to be just a few feet (a meter) away. She holds the medicine ball in front of her body with both hands.

Execution

The athlete moves the medicine ball to the right side of her body by pivoting on her left foot and bending that knee toward the right. She turns her shoulders and twists, passing the right hip, and then, as explosively as she can, throws the medicine ball straight forward to the wall or partner. The side coil to the right (negative move) should be slow and loaded but, as she brings the medicine ball forward, the movement should be fast and explosive. For medicine ball tosses, begin by having the athlete lie on her back with her knees bent and feet on the ground. The medicine ball should be placed at her belly with her hands on the side of the ball. A partner should be standing 2 feet (60 cm) in front of her feet. She generates the toss by raising her torso and extending her arms out as she tosses the ball to her partner. A more difficult toss would have her start with the medicine ball over her head. She generates the toss from the torso and extends the arms forward to toss the ball to her partner. Have the athlete focus on tightening her core as opposed to bending or arching her back. A lighter medicine ball should be used for overhead tosses. This exercise emphasizes rotation and flexion, using both abdominal muscles and obliques.

Forearm Exercises

Objective

Build forearm and finger strength.

Setup

A bucket full of rice.

Execution

The athlete should dig to the bottom of the bucket and then open her fingers continually as she brings her hands out of the bucket.

LIVE SITUATIONS AND SITUATIONAL HITTING

The mark of a consistent hitter is the ability to execute in critical, pressure situations. Center toss is useful for stressing core mechanics, but live hitting is a key element to developing confident hitters. Having a coach or batting practice pitcher pitch live will keep your hitters fresh with their timing. As a coach I enjoy throwing live, even from a shorter distance, so that I can see how my athletes are tracking the ball, when they trigger their load, and whether they are on time with the pitch.

When you have your hitters take live cuts, have them do so in small sets. Their first round might be 12 to 15 swings, but from then on have them rotate through with 5 to 8 swings. When you give them only a small number of swings, they focus better and you will see swings that are more productive because they know that they are taking only 5 swings each round. Some at bats can last 15 or 20 swings, but most are fewer than 5 swings. Train them the way the game is structured. If you have a coach who can pitch to your players, you are able to target areas to work on with each player. If one athlete is struggling with the low and in pitch, target that area and instruct her to hit only those pitches while taking any other pitch, even a strike. You can also target certain situations that you want your entire team to execute regularly. For instance, for a runner on third with less than two outs, have each player in the group work on executing that scenario. Teach them to recognize and execute on a pitch that they can drive to the outfield until they have two strikes. Recognizing the situation and executing is the mark of a consistent hitter.

STRESSING THE MENTAL GAME

The book *Moneyball* told the story of a system put in place by Oakland A's general manager Billy Beane, which stressed the importance of on-base percentage. The author of the book asked an innocent question: "How did one of the poorest teams in baseball, the Oakland A's, win so many games?" The management's system of player analysis was complex, but they focused on something simple. The organization drafted players who excelled at getting on base. Players who consistently got on base produced more runs, which produced more wins. Hitters who get on base consistently incorporate three things in their mental approach: They are patient at the plate, they know their best pitch (specific location), and they work the count (by knowing the counts on which they have the advantage and the counts on which they need to battle).

Being Patient at the Plate

Being aggressive and patient are not mutually exclusive. The key is to be aggressive with the right pitches. Teaching hitters to be selective early in the count will allow them the opportunity to hit better pitches. Oftentimes coaches say, "Hit the first good pitch you see." Encouraging hitters to be aggressive is never a bad idea, but on the first pitch of the at bat we want hitters to see a pitch they can drive rather than react to a pitch that is simply in the strike zone. Hitting a change-up on the first pitch of the at bat is great if the hitter sees it early, makes an adjustment, and is on time. If the hitter is fooled, encourage her to take that pitch and battle until she sees a better pitch to drive. If we want hitters to hit with both power and consistency, we need to develop sophisticated hitters who understand their tendencies, the pitcher's tendencies, and the game situation at the time of their at bat.

Hitting Your Best Pitch

Teaching athletes the location of the pitches that they hit best is simple. A basic round of center toss can give a coach specific feedback that can be passed on to the athletes. I have often found that hitters have little knowledge of which pitches they hit with the greatest consistency and power. Challenging hitters with location drills to hit balls that are not in their strength zones is key to developing more consistent and powerful hitters. An athlete is usually not consistently hitting pitches at certain locations because of a breakdown in technique. The hitter could be opening her front side early, casting her hands away from her body, or pulling off the hitting zone too early.

Working Counts

One aspect to incorporate in practices is hitting with various counts. Take the time to explain to hitters the importance of knowing on which counts they can be selective (when they are ahead of the pitcher, known as power counts) and when they need to expand their hitting zone (when behind in the count, known as consistency counts). Naturally, we do not want our hitters thinking too much in the box or trying to guess what the pitcher will throw, but they must know the situation and the count to execute consistently. You will see results that are more consistent when you regularly work with your hitters on counts, especially counts with two strikes. In two-strike counts, stress to your athletes the need to expand their strike zone and make the necessary physical adjustments to defend against both the pitcher and the umpire. We do not want athletes to leave the last strike up to the umpire.

Zone Hitting

One of the techniques used to help hitters focus on locations within the at bat is called zone hitting. For example, we can train hitters to look to hit the inside pitch and adjust if the pitch is outside. Hitters are at an advantage when they have a game plan for their at bat. If a hitter's strength is on the outside, then we want her looking to hit the outside pitch and adjust to the inside pitch when she has two strikes. Zone hitting can also be used with off-speed pitches. You can instruct the hitter to look to hit the fast pitch and adjust to the off-speed pitch with two strikes. When a team faces a pitcher with a particular strength, the offense should follow a game plan to challenge the pitcher's strengths and take her out of her comfort zone. A hitter who can take away the pitcher's game plan will have both a physical and a psychological advantage.

Two-Strike Battle

Objective

Teaching athletes to widen their zone with two strikes.

Setup

This can be done with tees, center toss, or live pitching drills.

Execution

Have your athletes practice hitting balls slightly outside the strike zone. They can first do this on a tee placed in the proper position with the ball outside the strike zone. Then, using the center toss drill, a coach can train the hitter to be aggressive when managing pitches farther inside, outside, higher, or lower than her typical strike zone. Encourage hitters to waste or get rid of pitches that are close but outside the zone (by fouling them off) and to battle during the at bat. They should focus on staying in the at bat until they draw a walk or get a pitch that they can drive fair.

CHALLENGE COMPETITION

At the college level our pitchers usually do not throw a simple batting practice by just pitching the ball over the plate so that hitters can work on their mechanics. Pitchers should always be placed in opportunities where they can succeed, so we place them in competitive challenge situations with hitters. Having your pitchers and hitters practice certain pitch counts is a great way to practice what they will face on game day. Starting the at bat with the hitter ahead in the count (2-0, for example) will force the pitcher to work hard to get back even with the hitter. Likewise, starting the count with the batter behind in the count (1-2, for example) will force the hitter to expand her zone and battle to look for a pitch that she can drive. Working specific counts with pitchers and hitters in a challenge situation is one of the best preparations for a game. You can also expand the drill to include working situations with runners on base. We always want our hitters to drive the ball hard, but being up to bat with a runner on third and no one out is different from being up to bat with a runner on second and two outs. With the former, the hitter needs to drive the ball to the outfield with a base hit or hit a long fly ball to produce a run. With the latter, the hitter has to be more focused on driving the ball hard through the infield.

FINAL THOUGHTS

To hit consistently with power is a focus of all hitters. Coaches want every hitter in the lineup to be a tough out. Having a team that has a powerful lineup one through nine is the goal of every coach. Stressing good basic mechanics in the swing through consistent drill work, increasing the core strength of your athletes, and improving their focus and mental game are steps toward achieving that goal. Hitters need quality teaching and structured practices that develop their skills and build the confidence necessary to hit with power and consistency.

14

Firming Up Offensive Fundamentals

Ehren Earleywine

I dedicate my section of this book to my favorite ballplayers of all time: Connor, Duran, and Larry Earleywine.

Make no mistake, hitting is personal, and it's a war. And we need to make sure that our hitter knows that the war is not between her team and the pitcher. The war is between the hitter and the pitcher. Neither the coach nor her teammates can do anything to help after the hitter steps into the batter's box. And it's war because if truth were told, the pitcher not only wants to get the hitter out but also wants to dominate her to the point of embarrassment if possible.

The hitter's talent and preparation will be on stage in that moment, and she needs to be fully equipped to deal with that truth. Her talent is what it is, and she can't do anything to change that. But she can control her preparation. So, how does the hitter prepare and respond to a personal challenge?

The best way for a hitter to enter this battle or any competition is to learn everything she can about the opponent (the pitcher). In a time of war, a great general looks at all aspects of the enemy. How many troops do they have? What kind of weaponry will they attack with? When will they strike? What location will they attack from? Hitting is no different. The time that the player spends preparing for her next at bat should be a process of collecting data about the pitcher she is facing and learning her tendencies.

What does the pitcher like to throw when she is behind in the count? What is the pitcher's strikeout pitch? How does the pitcher attack batters like herself? By having that information, the hitter is increasing her odds of getting the pitch that she is looking for and giving herself a better chance for success. Sure, pitchers fool us at times, and we anticipate incorrectly. But the benefits of knowing the enemy will far outweigh the costs over the course of a season.

Many hitters become so caught up in cheering in the dugout or talking to friends that they are unprepared when it's their turn to hit. Can you imagine a military general taking that approach and going into battle knowing nothing about the enemy? The hitter wants to know everything she can about the enemy (the pitcher) before declaring war, so that when she is in the batter's box she is ready for battle.

BAT SELECTION

Finding a good bat takes time. After a hitter finds one, she should treat it with care and hide it from her teammates! She may not find another one like it for a long time. Here are a few things to consider when looking for the right bat.

Bat Weight

First, the hitter needs to find a bat that she can control. When deciding between two different weights of the same bat, she should choose the lighter of the two. Bat control is more important than bat weight, and here's why: A heavy bat must be started early in the swing, so the hitter loses the luxury of waiting on the pitch. The longer the batter can wait, the better off she will be. Bats that are too heavy force hitters to commit to their swing too early, thus making it difficult to hit off-speed pitches and pitches on the outer half of the plate. In addition, bats that are too heavy can alter swing mechanics and create a variety of bad habits that have long-term effects.

Another variable that is important in determining the proper weight is the end-loaded versus balanced bat. Younger, smaller, and weaker hitters should not swing end-loaded bats because the added weight at the end of the bat prevents them from effectively controlling their swings. Obviously, end-loaded bats add power, but what hitters lose in consistency and mechanics isn't worth the tradeoff.

Bat Length

If possible, hitters with short arms should try to swing a longer bat, whereas hitters with longer arms can get away with a shorter bat. The length of a hitter's arms plus the length of her bat equals the overall length of the levers. Longer levers aid in plate coverage and increase power. Keep in mind that we're talking about only 1 to 2 inches (2.5 to 5 cm) of difference. The handle of the bat should be thin for hitters with small hands, but it can be thicker for hitters with large hands. Certainly, there are exceptions to the rule, mostly in the form of hitters with large hands who prefer a thin handle, but more times than not, hand size relates to handle thickness.

Hitters should be willing to consider the idea of having a lighter bat (1 ounce, or 30 g) with them during the course of the season. On days when hitters feel tired or weak and don't have any bat speed, they can drop down in weight to help them through. This concept is more relevant near the end of a season when hitters feel the most fatigue.

POSITIONING IN THE BATTER'S BOX

Opinions vary on this topic, and there are many ways that can work. The two decisions that hitters have to consider when positioning themselves in the batter's box are width and length. Width is how close or far from the plate they stand. Length is how far up or back in the box they get. Here are the most commonly used philosophies of professional hitters that will give hitters the best chance of success.

Distance From the Plate

In determining the first criteria (width), hitters must decide what they are trying to do. In other words, if a hitter likes to hit the ball to the opposite field, she should move farther off the plate. In doing so, most strikes that are thrown will be pitches away from the hitter that she can hit the other way. Any pitch that seems inside to this hitter should be a ball inside.

Likewise, if a hitter likes to pull the ball, she needs to move closer to the plate so that every strike is a pitch that she can pull. A pitch that appears to be a pitch that needs to be hit to the opposite field should be a ball outside. The hitter who stays in the middle of the field (gap to gap) will find herself somewhere in between. The primary factor for that type of hitter is to make sure that she can cover the outside corner of the plate.

Distance Within the Batter's Box

The second criterion (length) is fairly straightforward. Batters want to give themselves the maximum amount of time to see the ball because the longer they can wait, the better off they will be. Therefore, getting to the back of the batter's box (on the chalk) is ideal. Most outstanding fastpitch softball hitters do their work from the back of the box, as do Major League Baseball hitters.

The only negative from hitting in the back of the box is the chance that a pitch will catch a corner of the plate when it crosses the strike zone and then move off the plate for a ball after it gets deep enough to hit. In that scenario, the hitter can scoot toward the pitcher to be able to hit that pitch.

In addition, many players prefer hitting from the front of the batter's box. The argument to move to the front of the box rests on the idea that the ball can be hit before it moves or breaks. This theory is based on assumptions but has never been proved physically. Nevertheless, good pitchers will simply throw a 40-foot (12.2 m) drop instead of a 43-foot drop (13.1) as the catcher moves up to the hitter. Now, the batter not only cannot see the movement but also has her reaction time decreased even further.

An added bonus of hitting from the back of the batter's box is that the catcher must scoot back several feet (up to a meter), requiring her to make a longer throw to second base on a steal attempt. That distance makes a big difference for teams who like to run a lot.

SOFTBALL VERSUS BASEBALL

One of the most common downfalls and destructive beliefs in the softball world is that the baseball and softball swing are significantly different. They're not. Because of increased video technology in recent years, softball people have started to figure out that the two swings are nearly identical. As a result, power numbers and batting averages have never been better than they are today. And the higher the level (MLB and professional softball) is, the more similar the swings are.

So whether a player is hitting a softball or a baseball, the mechanics of the swing are 99.9 percent the same. Certainly, timing can vary, but that shouldn't change the mechanics of the swing, just when to start the swing.

The only major difference between hitting a baseball and a softball is that softball has a rise ball. Rise balls don't exist in baseball because of the trajectory of the pitch. Baseball pitchers throw over the top of their heads, and the mound is 10.5 inches (27 cm) high. Therefore, all pitches in baseball must come down to the hitter. For hitters to get a bat on the plane of the pitch, they must have a slight uppercut.

In softball the mound is not elevated, and the pitcher releases the pitch below the hip. Consequently, a ball can start thigh high and end up at the sternum (technically the top of the strike zone in softball) because of the backspin put on the ball. And because the ball is now going up, the hitter must have a slight downward swing to match the plane of the rise ball. Even so, all other hitting mechanics should stay the same.

ABSOLUTES VERSUS STYLE

We can categorize all hitting mechanics into two groups: absolutes and styles. Absolutes are things that all great hitters have in common, whether in softball or baseball. Styles are various components of the swing that can or will differ from hitter to hitter depending on the hitter's anatomy and physiology. The absolutes are the category of mechanics that cannot be compromised. The greatest hitters in the world all have these elements in common, and all amateur hitters should strive to obtain them.

On the other hand, style components can be changed and experimented with until a hitter finds what works for her. Although these items aren't absolutes, they are arguably as important as the absolutes because they help hitters feel and move in ways that work for their minds and bodies. For example, Albert Pujols has a wide stance, but Ichiro has a very narrow one.

Matt Holliday uses a high knee kick to create his negative move, whereas Jim Edmonds didn't lift his knee at all. Chase Utley has a shorter positive move than Babe Ruth did. At the point of contact, Wade Boggs typically kept his hands in front of his barrel (inside out), but Josh Hamilton has his hands even or behind his barrel most of the time (regular to hook), Mark McGwire had a one-handed finish, whereas Ted Williams finished his swing with two hands most of the time.

These are just a few of many style-related aspects of the swing that differ from hitter to hitter.

Keep in mind that the best hitters in the world experimented with hundreds of different styles in their careers to create the final product that you see on TV. They didn't look like that when they were 12 years old. Developing a style is a process that takes a lot of experimentation. And it requires taking some risks. But don't kid yourself: One change in style can positively or negatively affect the absolutes in a number of ways. Hitters need to put in their time, keep track of the results, and create a swing that works for them.

In regard to absolutes, the good news is that hitters don't have to do all of them right or be perfect to be successful. Although some hitters lack absolutes, they still get hits and experience varying degrees of success. But if absolutes are missing from the swing, the hitter is simply not maximizing her potential. Although many style-related items are relevant to a discussion of the swing, I will address only the absolutes in this chapter.

In addition, I will not be able to cover every hitting phase or topic in just one chapter. Nevertheless, the concepts provided cover a wide variety of information that should prove to be helpful to coaches and players at any level of softball.

THE SWING

We will discuss nine phases of the swing, starting with batting stance and ending with finish. Each of these nine positions is an absolute and has other absolutes within it. The terminology for each of these points differs, but the positions are all the same.

- ◆ Batting stance
- ◆ Negative move (or loading)
- ◆ Positive move (or linear movement)
- ◆ Toe touch (or launch position)
- ◆ Rotation
- ◆ Bat path (or swing plane)
- ◆ Contact
- ◆ Extension
- ◆ Finish

Batting Stance

Batting stances differ from hitter to hitter in many ways. Style is king in this part of the swing, but absolutes are also present in the batting stance of every great hitter. First, all accomplished hitters have their heads turned straight toward the pitcher and have both eyes in position to see the entire pitcher. Have all your hitters get in their stances and close their front eyes. You want to see whether they can see the pitcher with their back eyes. If the head is not turned enough or not straight up and down, the hitter will not be able to see the pitcher clearly with the back eye alone.

Head Position

An astounding number of amateur hitters stand in the box with their heads leaning over the plate. Can you imagine trying to work on a computer or drive a car with your head sideways? Hitting a softball is difficult, but when the head is sideways it becomes even harder. In addition, having the head tilted over the plate puts the batter's balance and posture in immediate trouble.

Back Foot Position

The next absolute of batting stance is related to the back foot. All great hitters have their back feet pointing straight or slightly tilting in towards the plate (pigeon toed). When the back foot is tilting back toward the catcher, getting the hips turned to hit the ball takes longer. This fault is common among female hitters and can be fixed simply by turning the back foot straight or slightly inward in the batting stance.

Elbow Alignment

The third thing that we see in the batting stance of all great hitters is elbow alignment. The front elbow will always be lower than or even with the back elbow. We will never see an exceptional hitter who has the front elbow higher than the back elbow. This position puts the hitter in a tilted-back posture that causes problems as the swing progresses.

Prepitch Movement

Finally, professional-grade hitters all have what we refer to as prepitch movement, which can be with the hands, arms, legs, body, hips, or any combination of those body parts. In making this movement, hitters create rhythm and timing and, more important, stay loose. Loose muscles are fast muscles, and tight muscles are slow muscles.

When amateur hitters try to incorporate prepitch movement after having none, they generally look uncomfortable and "coached." The goal is for the movement to look uncoached and natural. Achieving that end takes time and experimentation with various styles of prepitch movement, but it will ultimately make a difference in the hitter's development.

Negative Move or Loading

The first thing that hitters should do after getting into their batting stance is to move back or away from the pitcher. This action is called negative move, or load. The movement allows the hitter to gather energy, power, and timing before going into the next phase of the swing.

The time when the hitter starts this negative movement will determine the timing of the swing. The start of this load, or negative move, should be based on timing the pitcher's motion and the particular pitch that the hitter is looking for. After the hitter has made her negative move, a few absolutes can be applied to this position.

First, the hitter should have shifted all of the weight to the back leg. Second, the hitter should have proper posture. The upper body should be either level or tilted downward, and the front shoulder should be lower than the back shoulder. Finally, the hitter's head should be in front of the core of the body to allow a good attacking posture before going into the next phase of the swing.

FIGURE 14.1 Negative-move position.

How a hitter gets into this position is style-related (high leg kick, low leg kick, long kick, short kick, and so on). All hitters differ slightly on how they generate the negative move position, but the absolutes remain the same. See figure 14.1 for the absolutes of negative movement.

Positive Move or Linear Movement

If a negative movement occurs, a positive movement must occur as well. Positive movement happens immediately after a negative move. This move toward the pitcher should be a controlled glide. The positive move allows the forward momentum of body energy to send the hitter into a more explosive rotation after the stride foot lands. Technically, rotation doesn't happen until the heel of the stride foot hits the ground, but to avoid getting too detailed, hitters should think about creating a violent rotation at the end of their positive move when the stride foot hits the ground.

From a physics standpoint, objects in motion tend to stay in motion. This basic concept fuels the need for positive movement. Simply stated, positive movement creates power. Some hitters don't move back (negative move) or forward (positive move). Instead, they simply rotate or spin from a stopped dead position. These hitters struggle to hit the ball with any authority because this basic rule of physics works against them.

The distance of the positive move will differ, but all great hitters have positive movement. Most smaller and weaker hitters incorporate a bigger positive movement in an attempt to squeeze every bit of energy they have into the point of contact. Bigger and stronger hitters can get away with a smaller positive move because their size and strength can make up for the difference. See figure 14.2 for the absolutes of positive movement.

Toe Touch or Launch Position

Most hitting coaches argue that toe touch is the most important position of the swing. A good toe touch position can make up for many flaws and shortcomings that a hitter might have in other areas. Toe touch is

FIGURE 14.2 Positive-move position.

defined as the moment when the ball of the stride foot hits the ground. At this point, there are many things to look at, but the big-picture view is that hitters should be athletic and strong at this position. More specifically, weight distribution should be 50-50; the upper body should be directly centered over the lower body in a side or chest view. This guidance is contrary to the teachings of old, when keeping the weight back at 80-20 or 70-30 was the norm. As technology has caught up with the science of hitting, we now see that superior hitters land at a 50-50 weight distribution as the result of a good positive move and the need to be strong and athletic when delivering the blow.

In conjunction with weight distribution is the direction of the stride. Hitters who stride "in the bucket" (away from the plate) will be good at pulling the ball but won't hit it the other way well. Hitters who dive in toward the plate will hit the ball to the opposite field well but will be jammed a lot and have trouble pulling the ball. In either scenario, if the opposition sees the flaw, it could be a long day, season, or career for the hitter.

A stride that goes directly back at the pitcher gives the hitter the best chance of being successful on either half of the plate. Other absolutes of toe touch are keeping the front hip closed, having the front knee inside the front foot, and having the front shoulder turned slightly inward. All these absolutes are connected and allow the hitter to hit to all fields to maximize power. When any one of the hip, knee, or shoulder opens too soon, the hitter loses the ability to adjust to different speeds of pitches and to drive the ball to the opposite field. In conjunction with this, don't assume that the front foot also stays closed at toe touch. The stride foot usually lands at a 45-degree angle (slightly open) to allow later rotation without injuring or tearing the ankle or knee in the process.

When thinking about keeping the knee, hip, and shoulder closed, the hitter should imagine someone pulling a rubber band back to shoot it and then slowly releasing some of the tension before letting go. The result would be a rubber band that is shot with less than maximum velocity. The concept of staying closed with front shoulder, hip, and knee is no different. As soon as the hitter leaks open, power drains.

The positioning of the hands is another critical aspect of toe touch. Some variation will occur, but for the most part, great hitters have their hands back at approximately shoulder height and have a slight bend in the front elbow. Many hitters are overcautious about being short and keep their hands too close to the head and ear. Good contact can be achieved this way, but hitting the ball with any authority is difficult.

Another checkpoint or absolute of toe touch relates to back elbow separation. Some separation should be present between the back elbow and the ribs at toe touch. Back elbow height can vary (style), and power hitters usually have a higher back elbow than nonpower hitters do at toe touch. Regardless, back elbow separation at toe touch is imperative. Next, in looking at bat angle, be mindful of how differing angles create certain strengths and weaknesses. Hitters who have straight bats (vertical) at toe touch are generally good low-ball hitters but poor high-ball hitters. Hitters who have flat bats (horizontal) at toe touch will be just the opposite. Somewhere in between is the ideal positioning to cover both high and low strikes.

As we have seen, the hitter has many checkpoints to think about at toe touch. The overall goal is for the hitter to be in an athletic position that allows her to be strong before the swinging of the bat occurs.

Rotation

The quicker that hitters can rotate, the more bat speed they will generate. All hitters rotate, but what happens before rotation is the key to maximizing rotational speed and explosiveness. We talked about the positive move earlier. The purpose of that positive movement is to create momentum before the rotation, which in turn makes the rotation quicker. When rotation is quicker, hitters can hit the ball harder. It's a simple law of physics. If hitters rotate without any prior positive movement, their rotation will be slower and less powerful.

The rotation of two cars under different conditions can illustrate this point. Car number 1 is at a standstill. Then, with the accelerator to the floor and the steering wheel turned all the way to one side, the car slowly begins to rotate, or to do a doughnut. Eventually the rotation speeds up, but it takes time. Car number 1 represents the hitter who has no positive movement. Compare that to car number 2, which is traveling at 30 miles (50 km) per hour before the driver cranks the steering wheel all the way to one side. Because car number 2 is traveling at 30 miles per hour before the wheel is turned, the rotation will be much faster. Car number 2 is the car with positive movement. The degree or amount of rotation that a hitter will have depends on which field she hits the ball to. When she hits a ball up the middle or pulls it, the rotation usually ends with her back facing home plate.

When the hitter hits the ball to the opposite field, she usually keeps her chest or belly button facing that direction (see figure 14.3). By doing so, she avoids pulling off and cutting across the ball. People have always debated what starts the rotation or swing. Is it the hips? Is it the hands? Now with technology we have found that in great hitters, the hips and hands start at the same time. Actually, the back elbow and the hips begin to move at the same time. Because the back elbow starts the hands, it's safe to say that the hips and hands go at the same time.

A common flaw during rotation occurs when the upper body and lower body aren't connected or aren't working as one. Some hitters rotate the hips ahead of the hands. Others have good upper-body action, but the lower half never rotates. Either way, this disconnection or inability to engage those two gears can cause a number of problems in the swing.

FIGURE 14.3 Avoiding pulling off the ball by keeping the chest pointed to the opposite field is a major component of successfully hitting the other way.

Bat Path or Swing Plane

The goal with the path of the bat is to be on the same plane or path of the ball for as long as possible. Hitters who are on plane for a longer time have a better chance of making contact. Generally, hitters should not have big uppercuts or steep downward chopping angles in their swings. In either approach the bat crosses the path of the ball for only a short time. If the timing is even slightly off, the hitter will miss the ball. That being said, a slight uppercut can be effective when hitting drop balls because the line or plane of that pitch descends. Likewise, a slight downward bat path can be effective in hitting a rise ball because it is going up.

Despite the different swing planes that might be used, most pitches have only minimal up or down movement and require only a slight shift in approach. Most outstanding hitters use fairly level swings. As you can see in figure 14.4, the hitter who is on a level plane with the ball has many more chances for success. From a coaching perspective, when the team is facing a drop ball pitcher, we encourage hitters to try to lift the ball. In doing so, they will probably end up with more line drives and fewer ground balls. Drop ball pitchers are trying to induce weakly hit ground balls. To counter that, hitters must try to lift the drop. When coaching against a rise ball pitcher, we do just the opposite.

By telling your hitters to stay on top of the rise ball and hit hard ground balls, you give them the right ammo. Rise ball pitchers induce pop-ups and strikeouts because hitters continually swing underneath the ball. To counter that, hitters must do the opposite and try to hit ground balls. If the team buys in, we see positive results. Nothing is more frustrating to a rise ball pitcher than to know that hitters are hitting on top of the rise. Likewise, a drop ball pitcher who knows that hitters are getting underneath will have a long day.

FIGURE 14.4 A level swing path creates more opportunity for success.

Contact

Everything discussed previously will add up to a powerful contact position if hitters have good timing. Hitters must be aware of several absolutes at contact, and at the top of that list is keeping the head down. Batters can have great mechanics leading up to contact, but if they don't see the ball, they won't hit it. This concept is a common fault among high school players who later play college softball. They are so used to hitting off pitchers who have little or no movement that the need to keep the head down isn't as important. When they see better pitching in college, the movement happens late and quick. As a result, the high school hitter who hasn't been tracking the ball all the way through the hitting zone has trouble making the physical adjustment.

Next, the front leg needs to be firm, or locked out, to allow the hips to speed up. Despite old teachings that the back foot must stay down ("squash the bug"), we now know through technology that at contact the back foot does not stay down. The forces caused by a good positive move and the back hip and knee driving into the ball at contact cause the back foot to move forward into contact as well. The hands will be in a palm up, palm down position. The top hand will be facing up, and the front hand will be facing down. The arms will have some bend in them and will not yet be fully extended (figure 14.5).

For the inside pitch, hitters should make contact with the ball out in front of the front knee approximately 6 to 12 inches (15 to 30 cm). For the pitch down the middle, the ball should be deeper in the strike zone, about even with the front knee of the hitter. The outside pitch should be hit deeper in the zone but approximately in the middle of the hitter's body. Surprisingly, many hitters at all levels are not aware of the concept of depth and width. Therefore, coaches should revisit this fundamental concept at least once per year.

No matter where they are hitting the ball, hitters should aim for the inside of the baseball. If hitters are early, they will hit the middle of the ball. If they are on time, they will hit the inside of the ball. Both will result in hard-hit balls. Conversely, if batters aim for the middle of the ball and are early, they will hit the outside of the ball, causing them to roll over and hit weak ground balls to the pull side. This common flaw is probably the biggest fault found in young hitters.

Extension

Extension happens after contact, not at contact. Good extension includes both arms being fully extended and pointed back in the general direction of the pitcher. Staying palm up, palm down all the way to extension is crucial because doing so keeps the wrists from rolling

FIGURE 14.5 Proper hand position at contact with the top hand facing up and the bottom hand down; the arms should be bent slightly.

over the ball and hitting weak ground balls to the pull side. In addition, the arms need to be approximately chest high. Some hitters extend their arms down toward the ground, which leads to many well-hit balls being forced into the ground. Likewise, a hitter who extends her arms above the head can produce too many pop-ups.

Another common flaw in extension is extending the arms down either baseline. Hitters who do this hit a lot of hard foul balls because they are cutting across the ball and extending somewhere other than back toward the middle of the field. More common, though, are hitters who never extend their arms at all. Generally, this issue relates to strength, and as hitters get bigger and stronger extending the arms becomes easier. But many strong hitters don't extend either, only because they don't know any better. Through drill work and video, they can overcome the mechanical flaw and see big improvements.

Finish

As discussed earlier, on any ball hit up the middle or pulled, the entire back of the hitter should be facing home plate. On balls hit to the opposite field, the hitter won't always fully rotate because she wants to stay on the ball longer and drive it the other way. In that case, the chest or back shoulder will be facing home plate. Concerning one-handed versus two-handed finishes, it just depends on the hitter. Often, you will find that stocky hitters who have a lot of physical restriction in their finish will release with one hand to allow a bigger degree of finish. They may be unable to do this with both hands on the bat. Leaner, lankier hitters have fewer physical restrictions in their finish and are generally more comfortable finishing with both hands on the bat with full rotation.

A scientific mystery exists about why more left handed-hitters finish with one hand than with two. No one knows why, but it certainly has to do with the wiring of the brain. The concept may be related to the tendency of lefties to wear their hats off center while righties rarely do, or to the fact that left-handers can't throw a straight fastball. Regardless, coaches should note this difference when coaching the finish in left-handed versus right-handed hitters.

We need to be aware of hitters who take too many swings and become tired and lazy in the process. They are prime candidates for releasing with one hand and not fully rotating their core because it's easy. The cure is to have hitters finish with two hands and fully rotate in practice to ensure that they are finishing properly. When it's game time, whatever happens, happens.

TOP FIVE HITTING ABSOLUTES

The abundance of information about hitting mechanics can be overwhelming when a coach attempts to troubleshoot live hitters. To eliminate some of that pressure, here are the five points that top the list in importance. Hitters at every level battle with these critical items on a regular basis. If you and your hitters have mastered these checkpoints, you're way ahead of the game.

1. Positive movement
2. Athletic landing at toe touch
3. Explosive rotation
4. Hitting the inside of the ball
5. Extension

J CURVE

After we begin to coach these new techniques to hitters, they often get worse before they get better. Timing, feel, confidence, and overthinking will all have adverse effects on the hitters' output. These problems exist in high doses for those trying to incorporate new concepts that are contrary to a lifetime of bad habits. If hitters are willing to go through a period of failure in hopes of eventually being better, the results will be worth the wait. The J curve of performance represents the hitter's starting point and the decline that occurs when she begins to work with the new technique. The hitter who is willing to take a risk and work hard will see the numbers start to go back up and eventually surpass the old ones. This period can range anywhere from three months to an eternity. The hitter needs to make a choice. If she works hard and buys into the concepts, the turnaround time can be fairly short. If she straddles the fence between old mechanics and new and doesn't put in the time, it could take years. The time when most hitters give up is at the bottom of the J curve. They can't deal with momentary failure and go right back to their old habits. The downside of not taking the risk and trying the new concepts is that the hitter will always have to ask the question, "What if I would have bought into this?" Anyone who has experienced it knows that what-if is not a good place to be. The better route is to take the risk and go for it. After all, the greatest hitters in the world do it, so the new approach just might work.

NATURAL PROGRESSION

The hitter must follow a step-by-step process if she expects to be a great in-game hitter. Part of that process is what we refer to as the natural progression. Here is what it looks like:

1. Visualization
2. Dry swings
3. Tee work
4. Front toss
5. Pitching machine
6. Batting practice (off live arm at batting-practice speed)
7. Live pitching

If a hitter gets through steps 1, 2, and 3 with mastery but fails at step 4, she can't expect to be able to jump to step 7 and be successful. The natural progression must be followed until conclusion if a hitter wants to see game-time results.

This concept mostly applies to hitters who are working on a particular mechanical adjustment, but it also applies to hitters who just don't have the kind of in-game results they're looking for. As coaches, we often submit advice to hitters and then expect them to implement it immediately off live pitching. That approach can work, but more times than not, hitters need to go through all seven steps to see where they fall short. When they get to that problematic step, they should stay there until they get it right. After that happens, they should move to the next step of the natural progression and continue to the end.

COACHING DIFFERENT TYPES OF HITTERS

All hitters are not the same, nor should they be coached the same. All accomplished hitters have some truths and absolutes in common, but they fall into different categories that require different coaching approaches. By tailoring our coaching to the hitter, we can maximize strengths and minimize weaknesses, depending on the particular skill sets that she brings to the table. Hitters can fall into one or more categories. Regardless, knowing the type of hitter we are coaching is a key aspect in getting the most out of the talent we've been given. Let's look at those categories

Singles and Doubles Hitter

Besides hitting primarily singles and doubles, this type of hitter generally hits for a high average and usually strikes out less than the doubles and home run hitters. We won't get much power from hitters of this type, but their contribution is vital in getting on base and creating RBI opportunities for the power hitters in the lineup.

When coaching this type of player, emphasizing line drives and ground balls is the key. Because these hitters lack power, the last thing we want them doing is popping up or missing underneath pitches on a regular basis.

In addition, shortening up with two strikes is important to these hitters because doing so allows them to put more balls in play, which results in more base hits. Batting practice for hitters of this type should be focused on eliminating fly balls and pop-ups.

Doubles and Home Run Hitter

These are your power hitters. Although they hit singles on occasion, these hitters have power and should be looking for pitches that they can drive in the air. When coaching power hitters, encourage them to hit line drives and fly balls rather than balls on the ground. Ground balls will happen, but if power hitters are going to miss, they should miss underneath the ball to maximize their role in your lineup.

Also, the doubles and home run hitters in most cases should not shorten up with two strikes to put the ball in play. Over the course of a season, taking their regular swings in two-strike counts will add many home runs and doubles that otherwise would not happen. Certainly, by taking this approach the power hitter will strike out more often, but that goes with the territory. In the end, the power hitter has a vital role in a thriving offense, and we have to take the good with the bad.

The ideal candidate for making the change from singles and doubles hitter to doubles and home run hitter would be the bigger and slower hitter who hits the ball hard but mostly on a line or on the ground. Making the change will allow them not only to hit more home runs but also to hit into fewer double plays. After all, if we are looking for a singles and doubles hitter, we are better off getting someone who has good speed who will offer better baserunning and more range on defense. Therefore, the bigger and slower batters in the lineup should be thinking about hitting for more power.

Encouraging this type of hitter to hit the ball in the air can often dramatically increase the number of home runs that she can hit. I've seen players go from 1 or 2 home runs a year to 20 or more in a season by simply taking on the basic approach of hitting more balls in the air.

Pull Hitter

First, the word *pull* must be defined. The pull side of the field for a right-handed hitter is from center field to the left-field foul line. For left-handed batters, pulling the ball means anything hit from center field to the right-field foul line. Pull hitters should make sure to set their feet in the batter's box close to the plate. By doing so, any pitch that is thrown over the plate will be close and inside enough for the batter to pull. Pitches that appear to be outside and would need to be hit to the opposite field are likely balls off the plate that don't need to be swung at.

In breaking this down further, the right-handed pull hitter should think about hitting the pitch on the outside corner up the middle, the pitch down the middle to left center, and the pitch on the inner half to left field. Just the opposite is true for a left-handed hitter. As discussed later in the section "Having a Plan," it is difficult for any hitter at any level to hit the entire plate, but this is the general idea that a pull hitter can apply.

Because of physics, pulling the ball for power is much easier than hitting for power to the opposite field. As a result, this approach is worth considering for the player whom we think could hit for more power. Keep in mind that pull hitters have to hit the ball farther out front, so they need to make their decision to swing earlier. The earlier they have to decide, the more mistakes they will make. Batting average can and will be lower, but power numbers usually become significantly better. The coach has to decide what is in the best interest of the player and the team.

Opposite-Field Hitter

Historically, these hitters hit for the highest batting average. By letting the ball get deep in the zone and seeing it longer, the opposite-field hitter can make better decisions. In addition, the opposite-field hitter usually hits the inside or middle of the ball. Both approaches contribute to producing firmly hit balls.

Hitters who try to pull the ball often hit the middle or outside of the ball. When they are a little early, they hit the outside of the ball, resulting in weakly hit ground balls to their pull side. The opposite-field hitter eliminates that variable by hitting the inside or middle of the ball, which results in a higher batting average.

To maximize their ability, opposite-field hitters should get off the plate far enough to allow every pitch that is a strike to be away or outside to them. Now, all pitches that can be hit hard to the opposite field are strikes. Anything that feels inside or needs to be pulled should be a ball, so the batter can take the pitch.

In breaking down plate coverage for the opposite-field hitter, a right-handed hitter should hit the ball on the inside corner up the middle, the ball down the middle to right-center field, and the ball on the outside corner to right field. Just the opposite applies to the left-handed hitter. Again, few hitters at any level can hit the entire plate, but this is the general thought process of the opposite-field hitter.

The down side to being an opposite-field hitter is that hitting for power is harder than it is for the pull hitter. In short, the coach has to decide whether a hitter is best suited for batting average or power numbers. Opinions vary on this topic, but going with the hitter's strengths and natural tendencies is preferable to creating something that is unnatural for the hitter.

Gap-to-Gap Hitter

Ideally, hitters would strive to be in this category. Gap-to-gap hitters keep the ball in the middle of the field, from the left-field gap to the right-field gap. Most coaches will tell you that the best hitters are the ones who often hit the ball right back at them when they are throwing batting practice. This category of hitter can be a singles and doubles hitter or a doubles and home run hitter.

Inside-Out Hitter

Whether the ball is outside, down the middle, or inside, these hitters try to keep the barrel way behind the hands at contact and hit the ball to the opposite field. Inside-out hitters are singles and doubles hitters because hitting for power with this approach is physically impossible. With the barrel dragging behind and the top hand never releasing fully, power is sacrificed for the ability to hit the inside of the ball. This hitter will generally stand at normal width to the plate or on the plate to ensure coverage of the outer half of the strike zone and to hit the ball the other way.

GENERAL CONCEPTS ON THE MENTAL SIDE OF HITTING

Players lift weights for hours each week. They condition religiously, and they hit until their hands bleed. They are building muscles in preparation to be the best players they can be. But the most important muscle that they should be trying to strengthen is the brain. "Hitting is 90 percent mental," they say. Then why do we only practice and teach it 5 percent of the time? Here are some simple but effective mental concepts that will help develop the hitters' brains.

Having a Plan

Hitters should have a plan about what pitches they want to hit. When hitters don't have a plan, they generally take the approach of swinging at every strike they see regardless of the count. That type of thinking usually results in a whole lot of contact and few well-hit balls. This approach is otherwise known as hitting the entire plate.

Hitters can apply two basic principles in formulating a plan. First is pitch type (rise, drop, and so on). Second is location (in, out, up, down). Hitters can choose either or both of those criteria to develop their plans. For example, if the hitter prefers pulling the ball, she can choose only the location criteria and look for an inside pitch that she can pull. Nothing more, nothing less. If the pitch is a strike on the outer half of the plate, it's OK to let it go. Yes, the hitter can put it in play but probably without much authority.

A more in-depth plan for the same hitter would be to look not only for a ball to pull but also for a rise ball up in the strike zone that she can pull and hit in the air. Now the hitter is combining both pitch type (rise) and location (up and in) to formulate her plan. She should take any pitch that doesn't match those criteria.

Obviously, many combinations of those factors can determine a hitter's plan for that particular pitch or at bat. Much of that plan is a result of knowing what types of pitches the batter hits well and what type of pitcher she is facing. Each hitter has tendencies that will influence those decisions. A critical aspect of having a plan is understanding the count. The fewer strikes a batter has, the smaller the hitting zone should be. With each strike, that zone should expand. After the batter gets two strikes, she obviously has to swing at every strike thrown.

Another criterion that will influence the hitter's approach is the caliber of pitcher she is facing. Generally, the less accomplished the pitcher is, the pickier the hitter can be. After all, bad pitchers shouldn't be able to strike out the hitter, so getting into a two-strike count isn't much of a worry.

At times a hitter needs to do away with a detailed plan and be aggressive on every strike thrown, such as when she is facing a high-caliber strikeout pitcher. If the odds say that the hitter will strike out, then she needs to defy those odds by getting in three good hacks in every at bat. If every hitter in the lineup takes that approach, they may put a few balls in play and scratch out a run or two. That result is the best to be hoped for against exceptional pitchers and is far better than striking out.

The hitters who are most susceptible to not sticking with a plan are those who have great eye–hand coordination and an unhealthy fear of striking out. That combination generally results in far too many poorly hit balls that are easy to defend. Don't be confused; being a good contact hitter has its benefits, but over the course of a season trying to hit every strike thrown will hurt the numbers across the board.

In addition, a plan can change from game to game, from at bat to at bat, or from pitch to pitch. The hitter and pitcher are involved in a constant game of cat and mouse. The hitter just needs to make sure that she is the smarter of the two!

Visualization

Most great hitters practice visualization, although many of them don't do it purposefully. Instead, they engage in visualization because of their love for the game. They dream of big hits, of great at bats, and whether they know it or not, the process helps their game immensely. Multiple studies have shown that visualization is almost as good as the physical act itself.

It has been said that what the mind can perceive, the body can achieve. Therefore, hitters who use visualization can be more prepared than those who don't use the skill. A couple of important aspects of visualization are always to visualize good swings and hard contact and to include as many details as possible (colors, sounds, smells, feelings, and so on).

Believing

As coaches, we need to convey the message that nothing will produce more hits than belief in oneself. Coaches, parents, and friends will all let the player down at some point relative to their belief in her as a hitter. But the hitter must always remain confident in herself no matter how bad it gets. Doing this is far from easy. All hitters have experienced the slumps and struggles associated with hitting, and it's a lonely place to be. Those who can stay confident regardless of the situation will have better success than those who can't. Some call it being cocky, and others call it confidence. Either way, feeling that way is OK. Players don't have to tell others how they feel because most people are turned off by that type of attitude. But make no mistake; hitters need it to be successful at any level.

In-Game Mental Hitting Progression

Coaches: Give this handout to your hitters for an in-game mental approach to hitting.

In the dugout

- What does the pitcher have (up, down, change, and so on)?
- What does she like to throw when she is ahead? What does she throw when she is behind?
- How does she pitch hitters similar to you (right-handed or left-handed, power hitter, slapper, and so on)?
- Formulate your plan from those criteria.

In the hole

- Put your helmet and batting gloves on and get your bat out.
- Stretch.

On deck

- Time and swing with each pitch.
- Anticipate situations and signs that you may be given.

In the batter's box

- Get comfortable.
- Think positive thoughts.
- Use a "Yes, yes, no" approach.
- Between pitches, adjust your plan as needed.

(continued)

In-Game Mental Hitting Progression *(continued)*

After a good at bat

- Leave it alone.

What is a good at bat?

- Hit the ball hard.
- Saw the ball well.
- Swung at good pitches.
- Took bad pitches.
- Had good timing.
- Had good mechanics.
- Saw a lot of pitches.
- Felt good.

After a bad at bat, remove emotion from the experience and ask yourself three questions:

- What was I trying to do?
- What went wrong?
- What do I want to do next time?

Remind yourself of some simple truths if you fail:

- My emotions aren't telling me the truth.
- I am a great hitter.
- I wouldn't be here if I weren't capable.
- I have done this hundreds of times before.
- The best hitters in the world fail 7 times out of 10.
- The best hitters in the world have all struck out and had major slumps.
- I'm one hit away from being happy again.
- Seasons are long; grind it out.
- My hitting doesn't define me or my worth as a person.

PRACTICE COACHING VERSUS GAME COACHING

Practice is for the coach, and the game is for the players. In other words, we teach, coach, and critique as often as we want to during practice, but when game time rolls around, we have to let go. We can suggest adjustments at times during a game, but generally we want our players to react instinctively as often as possible. When in doubt, get out of their way.

FINAL THOUGHTS

As much as has been covered on the topic of hitting, much remains to be discussed. Anyone who has played this game much at all knows that there is no such thing as the perfect swing. No magic pill can transform an average hitter into a great one. Talent, preparation, persistence, determination, attention to detail, and the ability to stay loose and relaxed when it's all on the line are what win in the end.

Players should commit themselves to mastering the absolutes even when it doesn't feel right, even when it's not working at the moment. The best hitters in the world look identical at those key positions. Hitters need to keep grinding those absolutes until they own them. Technology has given us the gift of seeing these truths with our own eyes, and players need to take advantage of that new knowledge. Second, hitters should experiment with styles every time they practice. They can imitate great hitters and let themselves dream, just as little kids have done for decades playing Wiffle ball in the backyard. Players can stand like their idols and emulate the best. A brief experiment or small adjustment may make all the difference. And above all, nothing will produce more hits than believing in oneself. To have a fighting chance, players need to believe in themselves when no one else does.

15

Developing Your Pitching Staff

Erica Beach

Pitching is something that I have been passionate about all my life. I have gone through many phases in my pitching and coaching career, but spreading the love and knowledge of pitching is what I enjoy the most. The bottom line is that I am constantly working to improve myself so that I can give back to pitchers and coaches what I was given throughout my life.

Not every pitching coach was a pitcher in his or her career, but I highly recommend that all coaches try the skills they teach. When I work coaching clinics I ask coaches to stand up and physically attempt to snap or do body-positioning drills. Coaches respond positively to this because they have never tried to do their own drills. You don't have to be a skilled pitcher to get the feeling that each drill involves, but you do need to understand how to communicate with your pitchers.

I have learned throughout my coaching career that every pitcher learns and interprets what you say differently. I have come up with dozens of terms and sayings for various solutions to mechanical errors that occur in the pitching motion. All you need is for one of those terms to click for the pitcher, and suddenly she can make the change.

Developing a pitching staff takes time, patience, and a plan. I work primarily in phases with the pitching staff. These phases are breaking down mechanics, learning the art of deception, building consistency, preparing for game situations, and using dynamic workouts. These phases are further broken down using drills and lessons. When you finish this chapter, I hope that you will feel prepared and confident to take your pitchers to the next level.

PROGRESSION

The first thing I want to discuss is the progression I use to train pitchers. The progression is used to help transfer everything from drills to full motion. If you have ever had a pitcher do something perfectly from half distance and then lose the skill when she gets to full motion from full distance, this approach will help you. Most coaches and pitchers move too quickly to full motion without preparing properly. Most pitchers are effective at making changes from close distance and using only part of the motion, but when they move to full distance and full motion, they are unable to transfer the skill. The progression helps a pitcher relate each mechanic to her full-motion movement by moving back at a slower pace. The following are the steps in the progression:

1. **Wrist snap**: 5 to 8 feet (1.5 to 2.5 m) from the catcher using very little arm swing while standing sideways, or "open."

2. **Curtsey position**: 10 to 14 feet (3 to 4 m) from the catcher with both arms swinging to four o'clock and eight o'clock while in the open position (figure 15.1).

3. **T-position**: 14 to 20 feet (4 to 6 m) from the catcher with both arms in the T-position while in the open position (figure 15.2).

FIGURE 15.1 Curtsey position.

4. **Power position:** 20 to 35 feet (6 to 10.5 m) from the catcher with the pitching arm slightly curved over the head and the glove arm pointing toward the target or slightly higher while in the open position (figure 15.3).

FIGURE 15.2 T-position.

FIGURE 15.3 Power position.

5. **Power position with legs**: 30 to 35 feet (6 to 10.5 m) from the catcher still in the open position but now adding a step and drag while working from the power position.

6. **Superman position**: 30 to 35 (6 to 10.5 m) feet from the catcher having both arms pointing toward the catcher while the feet are still in the open position (figure 15.4).

7. **Superman position with legs**: 30 to 35 (6 to 10.5 m) feet from the catcher still in the open position but now adding a bigger stride and quicker drag into the superman position (figure 15.5).

8. **Superman with swing position**: 30 to 35 feet (6 to 10.5 m) from the catcher with both arms swinging down from the superman position and feet still in the open position (figure 15.6).

FIGURE 15.4 Superman position.

9. **Superman with swing position using legs**: 30 to 35 feet (6 to 10.5 m) from the catcher still in the open position but adding legs to the superman with swing position.

FIGURE 15.5 Superman position with legs.

FIGURE 15.6 Superman with swing position.

The most important aspect of the progression is having the pitcher step back gradually so that she can feel how each spot in the progression is linked together. Using the full progression, you are working from the bottom up, or backward. If your pitcher moves to the next position and loses it, then move her back to the previous position and let her get the feel back before moving on to the next step. You have to be patient while using this progression and not rush your pitcher through each step. If she does not grasp the concept of the skill that you are working on at one position, do not let her move on until she is able to perform at that spot. The most crucial position is the power position. If a pitcher can grasp a mechanic at the power position, then she will usually feel the power position during the positions that follow. When you move from the power position to superman, the verbiage I would use is "Get to power, and then finish the drill." This is the key to a pitcher's ability to relate mechanics to her full motion. If you can make your pitcher feel her power position during her full motion, she should be able to do any mechanic or drill that you are working on.

BREAKING DOWN MECHANICS

Pitchers join your team in many different conditions. Some will have only minor flaws, whereas others may need a complete renovation. No matter what type of pitcher you have, the first step is to identify her key mechanical errors. Some of the common flaws that pitchers develop are the following:

1. **Power line problems:** One or multiple parts of her body are moving in a direction away from the intended target.
2. **Lack of leg drive:** The pitcher may only step out from the mound or is lazy when pushing off the rubber.
3. **Snap issues:** The pitcher snaps with her arm and not with her wrist and fingers.
4. **Body positioning issues:** Her body is at an awkward angle at release or at some point of her motion.

Let's address ways to correct these common pitching problems.

Power Line Problems

The first step is to make sure that a pitcher understands what the power line is and why it's important. The power line is the invisible line between the middle of the pitcher's body and the intended target. On vertical pitches, fastballs, and change-ups, you need to help the pitcher locate her pitches on the inside and outside corners. The three most important things that must remain on the power line during the motion are the stride, arm circle, and glove.

The next thing that you need to do is have your pitcher throw fastballs down the middle to determine whether she is staying on her power line. You can draw a power line in many ways. There are countless pitching mats with power lines painted on them, you can use a string or chalk, and the easiest method is just to draw a line in the dirt. Make sure that her stride, arm circle, and glove are staying as close to the power line as possible.

Lack of Leg Drive

Leg drive is an important part of the pitching process, mostly because it builds energy that should transfer into the snap. The following drills can help improve leg drive. If your pitcher is not using her legs, meaning that she is just stepping off the mound and not creating much momentum, you can do a few drills to help her begin to incorporate her bottom half into her motion.

Walk, Jog, Run-Through

Objective

To help develop an understanding of momentum and train the legs to be explosive.

Setup

The pitcher starts a few feet (a meter) behind the rubber and walks forward into her motion.

Execution

When her drive foot hits the rubber, the pitcher should go quickly into her motion. She will feel the momentum going into her motion. Have her gradually speed up every five pitches until she is running into her pitch. This will help quicken her tempo and get her to push explosively off the mound. After a few of the run-through pitches, have her get back on the mound like normal to see whether she can re-create the momentum that she felt during the drills.

Load and Explode

Objective

To isolate the drive leg and work on explosion off the mound while taking away all momentum from the motion.

Setup

The pitcher starts on the mound and bends forward so that all her weight is on her front foot. Both arms should hang down by her ankles so that all her weight is forward.

(continued)

Load and Explode *(continued)*

Execution

After your pitcher is in position, say, "Go." She has to start her motion with no negative movement. This means that no weight can go backward, and she can use no back arm swing. This movement will isolate her drive leg and work on her explosion off the mound. If she is having trouble getting out quickly and explosively, then stand on her glove side and actually push her when you say, "Go." She will be off balance at first, but challenge her to explode out before you begin pushing, to beat your hand.

One-Legged Pitching

Objective

To focus on the drive leg explosion while slowly adding momentum back into the motion.

Setup

The pitcher stands on the mound on her drive foot with her glove leg off the ground. This drill allows some negative movement and momentum.

Execution

Have your pitcher swing her glove leg back and then swing it forward to begin her motion. The movement still emphasizes her drive leg, but it also allows her to build some momentum and therefore lets her drive out even farther. Draw a line where her foot is landing and challenge her to reach farther on each pitch.

Snap Issues

If you notice that your pitcher is long at her release point or is bending only at her elbow, then she needs to work on snap. This is a common problem, and for some pitchers creating great snap is one of the hardest problems to overcome. The biggest thing that inhibits snap is tension, so always make sure that your pitcher's arm is not locked or straight. Here are some drills to help improve your pitcher's snap.

Towel Drill

Objective

To help your pitcher get the feel of a snapping or whipping movement toward the end of her motion.

Setup

Have your pitcher grip the end of a hand towel.

Execution

Have your pitcher go through her motion from the power position and full motion, focusing on whipping the towel down toward the ground. This action will help her grasp the idea of being loose on the bottom half of her motion, which will help her snap quicker.

Weighted Ball

Objective

To strengthen the fingers, wrist, and forearms using the resistance of the weighted ball.

Setup

The pitcher starts about 4 or 5 feet (1.2 to 1.5 m) from the catcher and stands in an open, or sideways, position.

Execution

Allow your pitcher to use only her wrist and fingers to snap the weighted ball. This action will isolate the snap and make her grip and forearm stronger. Although pitchers should never use a weighted ball overhead or full speed, it's a great tool to work on quickening the snap. After she uses the weighted ball, have your pitcher switch back to the regular ball and go through the same progression. Challenge her to be even quicker with her snap.

Stop Drill

Objective

To help a pitcher feel the difference between the snap and the follow-through.

Setup

The drill can be done from any point in the progression, but the power position and full distance with full motion is typical.

Execution

During this drill have your pitcher stop at her release point. I tell my pitchers to pretend that a wall is in front of them and that the hand can't go past it. Because of the momentum of your pitcher's arm, she will not be able to stop exactly at release point, but she will definitely be able to feel her snap point. Challenge her to make her snap as violent as possible.

Body-Positioning Issues

Body-positioning issues can lead to many other problems and should be one of the first mechanical issues to be fixed. The most common body-positioning issue is leaning forward during the motion. This issue will affect release point, leg drive, and many other parts of the motion.

Drag and Push Back

Objective

To use resistance with the legs to enforce proper posture.

Setup

The pitcher starts in the open position and begins at the T-position.

Execution

Her upper body throws from the T-position, and her bottom half does the following:

1. Her plant foot lands.
2. Her plant leg stays strong and does not collapse.
3. Her drag foot drags hard into the figure four.
4. She resists on her front leg and pushes back.
5. Her drag foot falls back and lands back at its original position.

As your pitcher gets the hang of this, move her through the rest of the progression using the same lower-body mechanics.

ART OF DECEPTION

After your pitcher's basic mechanics have been addressed, you can begin to teach the moving pitches. I recommend teaching one pitch at a time and making sure that your pitcher masters that pitch before moving on to a new one. Too many pitchers out there have six or seven average pitches but have mastered none. I prefer a pitcher to have three or four outstanding pitches that she can throw with command and confidence.

Every pitcher should have the goal of being deceptive. She can achieve this by doing several things—locating her pitches, changing speeds, and moving the ball. A pitcher who uses a combination of these three tools can be extremely effective.

Locating Pitches

To hit locations with fastballs, change-ups, and vertical pitches, your pitcher must make sure to move her stride, arm circle, and glove to each side of the power line.

One way to help your pitcher understand the idea of moving everything side to side is to move a throw-down plate to the corner she is throwing to. After you move the plate, tell your pitcher to throw at the plate as if it's down the middle. This visual helps to simplify the process of using the power line to hit locations.

Changing Speeds

Changing speeds is one of the most important aspects of pitching. Using either a change-up or an off-speed pitch to break up the timing of the hitter not only keeps the batter off balance but also makes the other pitches more effective. There are countless ways to throw a change-up, but they all have one goal—to make the hitter think that a faster pitch is coming by changing the speed without changing the motion.

Most change-ups have a few commonalities, which include limiting snap, keeping the fingers from pushing the ball at release, and using tension in the arm to help slow the ball. Using a stiff wrist is a good way to take speed of the ball. If the wrist is too loose, it will snap the ball, which will give it too much speed. In combination with a stiff wrist, the fingers should not be behind the ball at the release point. One of my favorite change-ups to start with is the horseshoe change-up. It gets its name because the hand is in the shape of a horseshoe while gripping it.

A few key factors in making this pitch successful are locking the elbow, having a stiff wrist, and making sure that the horseshoe is facing the catcher at release. Locking the elbow is one way to eliminate speed. Having a stiff arm means that the pitcher can keep her arm circle speed the same while eliminating the whipping movement in her motion. The whipping movement adds speed, and with a change-up we are trying to eliminate speed. Having a stiff wrist limits the snap that gives the ball velocity. Finally, the horseshoe should face the catcher when the pitcher releases the ball because it keeps the fingers from being behind the ball. When the fingers are behind the ball at release, they push the ball faster, which is the opposite of what we want. By having the horseshoe facing the catcher the fingers are on the side of the ball, which makes it easier to release with minimal snap and speed.

Another valuable tip for the change-up is to release the pitch a little farther forward than the typical release point, which is usually at the hip. The pitcher should feel her arm pull forward slightly and let the ball slide out of her hand at that point. After the ball is released the arm should bend at the elbow. Make sure that your pitcher has a straight stiff arm at release and doesn't bend her arm too soon. The bend should happen after the release, not during. Make sure that the pitcher's wrist never bends during the release, which should make the release feel smooth.

If your pitcher is able to do all these things, the change-up should be about 10 to 20 mph (16 to 32 km per hour) below the speed of her fastball. The faster a pitcher is, the bigger the difference in speed is needed.

Moving the Ball

The ability to move the ball is one of the pitcher's most important tools. Every college pitcher needs to throw moving pitches effectively; therefore, younger pitchers spend their careers developing these pitches. The fastball gradually decreases in importance as a pitcher ages and the hitters improve. Eventually, it is phased out completely and a pitcher is left with her moving pitches and change-up. The main moving pitches are the curveball, screwball, riseball, and dropball.

Curveball

The curveball is a pitch that moves laterally through the zone. For a right-handed pitcher it breaks away from a right-handed hitter, and for a lefty it breaks away from a left-handed hitter. The spin should look like helicopter blades spinning counter clockwise for a righty and clockwise for a lefty. The ultimate goal is to have the pitch start on one side of the plate, break across the plate, and finish on the opposite side. This is a common pitch to throw for a strike and is usually one of the first pitches learned. One of the biggest problems with this pitch is that a pitcher may not be able to make it break enough. Because the ball moves on the same plane as the bat, it has to move really well to make it a pitch that doesn't get hit hard.

A common error with this pitch is the hand position at release. When letting go of this pitch, the hand should be under the ball and the pointer finger should be pushing on the outside of the ball to create that helicopter spin. If the hand is not positioned under the ball, the spin can vary and therefore create odd movement on the ball. Tell your pitcher to keep her palm to the sky and to make sure that her follow-through stays at waist level. This action will help keep the hand at the proper place at her release point so that the ball moves in the proper direction.

Screwball

The screwball moves in the opposite direction of the curveball. It breaks inside to a right-handed batter from a righty pitcher and vice versa for a lefty pitcher. The screwball is another great pitch to throw to establish the corner and throw for a strike. The movement is not quite as sharp as a curveball, but the screwball is still an effective moving pitch. The spin should be as close to a helicopter spin as possible, although the spin will move in the opposite direction of the curveball. The basic release of the screwball has the pitcher's hand moving as if it is twisting a door-knob, but the knob is actually on the ground at release point. The pitcher's thumb would "hitchhike out" below the waist. The palm should be facing the ground as the pitcher's thumb moves from the front of the ball into the hitchhiker position. Here is a drill to help a pitcher understand the release better.

Football Drill

Objective

To help a pitcher understand the mechanics of screwball snap.

Setup

The pitcher kneels down with her pitching-hand-side knee on the ground and a football with the point on the ground.

Execution

The pitcher grips the top point of the football and tries to spin it as quickly as she can so that it spins on its end. Have your pitcher focus on moving the thumb outward as quickly and violently as possible. The football should spin like a top on its point. The drill will help your pitcher keep her hand in the proper position.

Another big thing with the screwball is body positioning. Make sure that your pitcher is completely sideways when she is releasing this ball. If her hip moves forward at all during release, the hand will be forced off the power line and the pitch will break into the batter's box. I tell my pitchers that to be in the correct position, they should release the ball by the front of their quadriceps instead of their hip.

Riseball

The riseball is one of the most deceptive pitches in fastpitch softball. This pitch makes fastpitch stand apart from baseball because the pitcher can make the ball fight gravity and rise. This pitch takes a lot of time to develop, and the pitch must have a certain amount of speed to make it possible for the ball to move upward. If a pitcher's ball still drops because of gravity, it will not be possible to make the ball rise. But it is never too early to perfect the snap and spin, so when a pitcher develops her speed, the riseball will be a natural pitch to throw. The riseball is a fantastic pitch to throw to aggressive hitters and can be thrown in many counts. Great pitchers are able to manipulate this pitch at different heights, which makes it a difficult pitch to hit. If your pitcher can throw a rise lower in the zone, then this pitch can be thrown in just about any count. If she is only able to throw it higher in the zone, she may want to use it as a pitch to throw when ahead in the count.

An effective riseball looks like a strike halfway to the plate before the spin causes the ball to move upward over the hitter's bat. The spin needed to create this movement is backward spin. The ball should spin as close as possible to six o' clock to twelve o'clock. To achieve this spin, the pitcher's fingers must move underneath the ball at the release point. Another key to the riseball is resistance. Your pitcher must resist with her legs by landing on a firm front leg and pushing back. She must also resist with her pitching shoulder by keeping it back and not pulling forward at release. The final point of resistance is with the chest. Make sure that the pitcher's chest does not move forward at the end of her motion. These three points of resistance will help ensure that your pitcher is in the proper position during the release. If she pairs this with the proper finger position, she will be well on her way to throwing a great riseball.

One problem that most pitchers face while learning the rise is body position. Most pitchers have a hard time keeping their weight back and resisting. Here is a simple drill that I like to do to help with this problem.

Knee Drill

Objective

To help a pitcher get the feeling of the resistance during the bottom half of her motion.

Setup

The pitcher kneels down on her pitching-arm-side knee. Her body should be sideways, and her glove leg should be straight and extended toward the plate.

Execution

The pitcher throws riseballs first from the power position, using the straightened front leg to feel the resistance. Throwing from this position will make it difficult for the pitcher to lean forward or have poor body position during release. After she masters the riseball from the power position, have her stay on her knee and do the same drill using the full arm circle.

The closer the spin can get to straight backward revolutions and the tighter your pitcher can make it, the sharper and better the break will be. A good riseball is a devastatingly hard pitch to hit.

Dropball

The dropball is another bread-and-butter pitch that all pitchers should develop. This pitch is usually one of the first pitches learned because pitchers of any velocity can master it. The more your pitcher can make the ball break on the vertical plane, the better the pitch will be. Hitting pitches with vertical movement is much more difficult than hitting pitches with horizontal movement. The purpose of a dropball is to look like a strike halfway to the plate and then drop below the hitter's bat as it approaches the hitting zone. The dropball can be used in almost any count, and if your pitcher can adjust the starting height of the dropball and still spin it enough to drop, it can be extremely difficult to hit. The dropball achieves its movement by having straight up and down spin, rotating from twelve o'clock to six o'clock. The spin should rotate over the top, in contrast to the backward spin of the riseball.

A dropball can be thrown in a couple ways. Some prefer to throw a rollover drop, whereas others prefer to throw the peel drop. The snaps for these two versions are different, although the fingers will be moving up the backside of the ball and finishing over the top of the ball on both. The hand positioning is slightly different on the release, but the result should be the same—straight up and down spin. Another thing they have in common is body posture at the release point. During the release, the pitcher should have her hips over her front foot, her chest over her hips, and her head over her chest. Your pitcher should not bend at the waist while releasing the ball. Naturally, some bend may occur following the release of the ball, but make sure that she is standing tall during the snap. Here is a great drill to work the movement of both versions of the dropball.

String Drill

Objective

To allow the pitcher to see where her ball is breaking and to help her work on adjustments of height on the drop.

Setup

Run a string across the front of the plate. If your pitcher is in a cage, just tie the string on both sides of the cage just below knee height and a few feet (a meter) in front of the plate. I have also used tees as anchors to tie the string. Use your imagination.

Execution

Have the pitcher throw the ball over the string and make the ball drop after it passes the string. Adjust the height of the string to help the pitcher develop command of the height of her dropball.

If a pitcher can throw a good dropball while hitting the corners and adjusting the height of the pitch, then she will be a tough pitcher to face.

BUILDING CONSISTENCY

After you have identified and corrected any mechanical issues that your pitcher has, you can begin to work her consistency. Consistency is the ability to throw pitches effectively and under control to the location that the pitcher chooses on command. Here are some drills to develop consistency in your pitchers.

Repetition Drills

Repetition is the first step in building consistency. By working pitches repeatedly, a pitcher can begin to feel the difference between quality pitches and average ones. She can then begin to learn to make adjustments from pitch to pitch.

In a Row

Objective

This drill challenges your pitcher's consistency and mental toughness.

Setup

The pitcher throws from full distance to a catcher.

Execution

Have your pitcher throw to each of the four corners five times in a row using pitches of her choice. The only rule I place on this drill is that no fastballs are allowed. This requirement will make your pitcher focus on locating her moving pitches and change-up. Most pitchers will struggle with this drill at first. If your pitcher is just starting out, lower the number of times she must hit the spot. After she becomes proficient at this drill, make her work on her weaker pitches or require one of the pitches to be a change-up. You can change this drill in countless ways to challenge your pitcher as she grows and improves.

Out of Ten

Objective

This drill emphasizes quality of pitches and holds your pitcher accountable for each pitch she throws.

Setup

The pitcher throws from full distance to a catcher.

Execution

I challenge my pitchers to throw 10 of each pitch, and we keep track of how many she hits out of 10. Sometimes I ask her to use a mix for 10 pitches, such as curve, screw, rise, drop, and change twice through. Challenge your pitcher to reach 8 out of 10 pitches to attain an adequate level of consistency.

Countdown Pitching

Objective

To add pressure and emphasize executing each pitch.

Setup

The pitcher throws from full distance to a catcher.

Execution

In this drill your pitcher starts by throwing 10 of a certain pitch. You can choose what you would like her to throw. After she throws 10 good ones, she moves to 9 of another pitch. I like to mix the choices by being more specific. Instead of having her throw 10 curveballs, I'll have her throw 10 curveballs on an 0-2 count. Instead of 9 riseballs, I'll have her throw 9 low riseballs inside. Get creative with the choices to keep your pitcher focused and engaged. For her last pitch, I usually let her do pitcher's choice. Here is what my countdown pitching might look like:

10 inside dropballs

9 screwballs for a strike

8 curveballs on an 0-2 count

7 low riseballs outside

6 alternate backdoor curves and curves for strikes

5 outside change-ups

4 outside dropballs

3 catcher's choices on a 3-2 count

2 pitchouts to each side

1 pitcher's choice

Adjustment Drills

Making adjustments from pitch to pitch is a challenging part of pitching. Being able to execute pitches with all sorts of releases is something that pitchers need to master. The following drills work on mixing pitches and making physical adjustments for each pitch.

Opposites

Objective

To work on your pitcher's ability to make adjustments from pitch to pitch.

Setup

The pitcher throws from full distance to a catcher.

Execution

Your pitcher alternates throwing pitches that move in opposite directions. I have my pitcher do 5 or 6 of each pitch for a total of 10 to 12 for each set. Examples of opposites are as follows:

- ◆ Curveball mixed with screwball
- ◆ Riseball mixed with dropball
- ◆ Fastball mixed with change-up

Sets

Objective

To work on throwing all the pitches and keeping track of the quality of pitches that your pitcher is throwing.

Setup

The pitcher throws from full distance to a catcher.

Execution

Sets are five rounds of five pitches each during which the catcher keeps track of how many quality pitches your pitcher throws. An example of the five-pitch sequence I use is curve, screw, rise, drop, and change-up. You can cater it to your pitcher's repertoire however you like. The goal should start at 15 quality pitches out of 25, but eventually your pitcher should be hitting 20 or more to be considered strongly consistent. I also have pitchers sprint between the sets of 25. Have her do four to six long sprints and jog back so that she is out of breath as the workout goes on. This drill is good for pitchers who hit and have to pitch while out of breath from running the bases.

Paint the Corners

Objective

To work on the accuracy of each pitch and make adjustments to hit specific locations.

Setup

For this drill we use a large rectangular colored plate. It has red in the middle, yellow on the middle corners, green on the corners, black outside the corners, and brown on the edges. The pitcher throws from full distance to a catcher.

Execution

I have our pitchers throw each of their pitches to the green, black, and brown colors. They must hit one location to graduate to the next one. The target narrows your pitcher's focus to a smaller area and helps her visualize where the pitches must end up.

Every Other Pitch

Objective

The pitcher makes adjustments from pitch to pitch while still throwing a large number of repetitions of a pitch that we are focusing on.

Setup

The pitcher throws from full distance to a catcher.

Execution

I often have my pitchers throw a change-up or another pitch that they are working on only on every other pitch. Sometimes when a pitcher works many repetitions, especially on the change-up, her motion begins to change, which can throw her off. Mixing every other pitch keeps my pitchers honest with their motions.

Endurance and Conditioning Drills

Endurance and conditioning are a huge component of pitching. Both cardiovascular conditioning and arm endurance are important for the longevity of your pitcher. The better conditioned your pitcher is, the longer she will last in games and the more effective she will be deeper into the season. Here are some drills to train both.

Cycle Pitching

Objective

To work on executing pitches while fatigued. Will boost cardiovascular health and mental focus.

Setup

The pitcher throws from full distance to a catcher. You can use a jump rope, cones, a medicine ball, or a balance ball as equipment for the agilities.

Execution

Your pitcher throws five pitches of your choice; after she finishes her pitches, she does a round of agilities of your choosing. Each round of pitching and agilities is a cycle. You can have her do as many or as few cycles as you want. An example of a Cycle Pitching workout is as follows:

1. Five pitches and then 30 body-weight squat jumps
2. Five pitches and then 50 mountain climbers
3. Five pitches and then a one-minute plank
4. Five pitches and then 25 up-downs
5. Five pitches and then 15 push-ups
6. Five pitches and then 100 jumping jacks
7. Five pitches and then 100 jump ropes
8. Five pitches and then 30 medicine ball slams

The pitcher should begin to get fatigued. After this happens, put more emphasis on the quality of her pitches. This drill will challenge her mentally as well as physically.

One-Minute Drill

Objective

This drill is a great way to boost pitch count, improve mental toughness, and develop arm endurance.

Setup

The pitcher stands about 30 to 35 feet (9 to 10.5 m) from the catcher in the open, or sideways, position. The catcher stands up for this drill.

Execution

For this drill your pitcher throws as many pitches as she can in one minute. This is a good drill to use either at the beginning of practice or after a long workout. Here are a few variations of the drill.

Two-Ball

For this variation the pitcher and catcher each have a ball. The pitcher and catcher pitch and throw the ball at the same time. The goal is to have the ball pop each glove at the same time. When the pitcher catches the ball, she should transfer the ball to her pitching hand as fast as possible and then go quickly into the upswing of her motion. Any negative arm swing takes too long, so push your pitcher to be as quick as possible. In Two-Ball the goal is more than 45 pitches.

Three-Ball

This version starts with the pitcher having one ball in her glove and another in her hand. The catcher starts with a ball in her throwing hand. The pitcher begins by throwing a pitch. After the catcher receives the ball, she snap throws the ball in her throwing hand back to the pitcher, who has transferred the ball from her glove to her pitching hand. After the pitcher receives the ball from the catcher, she moves directly into the upswing of her motion. The goal for Three-Ball is more than 35 pitches.

Run-Through

This variation has the pitcher starting from a few steps behind the pitching rubber with one ball. The pitcher runs into her pitch and goes full motion. The catcher snap throws the ball back to her. The pitcher catches it, runs back to her starting spot, and repeats. The goal for this version is 15 pitches.

Circuit Training

Objective

To increase the pace in pitching practice and have your pitcher throw while fatigued.

Setup

This drill is useful if you have more pitchers than catchers on staff. Have each mound in your bullpen represent a different drill if possible and have one or two agility stations as well. The pitchers throw at each mound for four to five minutes. After the time is up, everyone rotates and begins the next round at the next station.

Execution

An example of the stations is as follows:

Mound 1—Speed work; the pitcher throws fastballs as hard as she can the entire time, working on quicker tempo, leg drive, and snap.

Mound 2—Every other pitch is a change-up; the pitcher focuses on selling her motion by making sure that it looks the same as the motion for her other pitches.

Mound 3—Opposites.

Agility 1—Body-weight squats.

Agility 2—Rotator cuff band work.

Sprint to the Catcher

Objective

To work your pitcher's cardiovascular health.

Setup

The pitcher throws from full distance to a catcher.

Execution

Have your pitcher throw any pitch she'd like from the mound. When the catcher receives the ball, she drops to her knees and holds the ball out in front of her. The pitcher sprints to the catcher, takes the ball from her, and sprints back to the mound to throw again. I usually have players do sets of five to seven of these in a row. After a break, have her do another round.

PREPARING FOR GAME SITUATIONS

After you have worked on a pitcher's consistency and endurance, you can begin to put extra pressure on her and prepare her to face the challenges that she may face in games. There are many ways to train for game situations and game mentality. Some of the things that I focus on are mental toughness, pressure pitching, situational drills, and challenge-based drills. These aspects are all key parts of preparing a pitcher to be her best during games.

Building Mental Toughness

Mental toughness is the key ingredient to an outstanding pitcher. Among a group of pitchers who have the same physical attributes, styles, pitches, and mechanics, the one who has the best mental approach will usually end up being a better performer in games. Pitching is one of the most mentally demanding positions in fastpitch softball. A pitcher needs to perform her best around 100 times per game, which means that she has 100 chances to fail. The position is not for the weak minded because the pressure can be overwhelming at times. Here are some ways that I teach mental toughness to my pitchers.

Mullet Theory

The mullet theory is something I came up with during my playing days in college as a way for me to show my personality on the mound yet maintain focus. For those of you who have seen a mullet, you know the saying, "Business in front, party in the back." Whenever a pitcher's back is facing the plate, which represents "party in the back," she has a chance to collect herself, talk to her teammates, and prepare herself to attack the next pitch. When the pitcher turns toward the plate, everything should be business. Her only focus should be the mound or the catcher. Anything else is a distraction. The party in the back allows a pitcher to have her personality on the mound, whether it is intense, relaxed, or whatever. After a pitcher turns around though, she has to clear her mind completely and think only about making the next pitch her best.

Confidence and Trust

A pitcher needs to feel confidence in her pitches and trust in her pitching coach. She builds her confidence in her preseason workouts when she learns to command her pitches. If you help prepare her, she will trust what you say in games and trust your pitch calling as well. Being a part of her preseason pitching workouts and getting a feel for which pitches she most trusts is helpful. Have an open line of communication with your pitcher about what is feeling good each day and how to correct problems when they occur. I have always given my pitchers the right to shake off any pitch I call, and we always talk after every inning about the pitch calling, how her various pitches are feeling and moving, and how we can continue to get better.

Pressure Pitching

I like to make workouts as hard and as mentally draining as possible some days so that when the pitcher gets to game day, it's easier and she can look forward to it. Pressure pitching is a way to incorporate mental toughness into workouts and prepare pitchers for the pressures of the game.

Pressure Pitching

Objective

To add pressure to workouts and to make sure that your pitcher is focusing on every pitch she throws.

Setup

The pitcher throws from full distance to a catcher.

Execution

In this drill your pitcher throws a six-pitch sequence. If she throws fewer than five excellent pitches during the sequence, she has to do sprints or agility exercises. I put my pitchers through about 10 rounds of this drill to make them mentally and physically tired.

Situational Drills

I use the following drills to help prepare pitchers for situations that they may face in a game. We work on making adjustments in practice so that if the need arises in a game, the pitchers feel prepared. If they face a tough situation in the game, they will feel as if they have been there before. Therefore, they will be more confident that they will succeed in game situations.

Umpire Drill

Objective

To make sure that the pitcher is able to adjust when an umpire's zone may be different from what the pitcher is used to.

Setup

The pitcher throws from full distance to a catcher.

Execution

During this drill we simulate an umpire who takes away a certain side of the plate or tightens the zone overall. We have our pitcher simulate live batters with a zone missing, and we see how she adjusts her pitches. The drill also helps the staff learn when to throw to that zone and when to stay away from it.

Batter Movement

Objective

To prepare pitchers for the instance when batters move around the box. If a batter moves from the very front to the very back of the batter's box, pitches must begin to break at a different point.

Setup

The pitcher throws from full distance to a catcher. The catcher moves from the back of the catcher's box (about 3 feet [1 m] behind the plate) to as close to the plate as possible to replicate a batter's move from the back to the front of the batter's box.

Execution

Have your pitcher practice throwing her moving pitches when a batter is both in the front and in the back of the box. This adjustment happens many times in a game, and most pitchers never train this skill. Your pitcher will need a few rounds to learn how to make the adjustment. The main adjustment when doing this drill is the release point. Have your pitcher vary her release point to see how it affects the pitch.

Challenge-Based Drills

To keep workouts interesting and competitive, I like to incorporate challenge-based drills into some of our workouts. These drills are a fun way to add intensity and toughness to your pitching staff's workouts.

Horse

Objective

To create an atmosphere of competition in the bullpen between pitchers while keeping it fun.

Setup

The pitchers throw from full distance to a catcher. You must have more than one pitcher for this drill.

Execution

Have one pitcher start the rotation and call a pitch and location that she plans on hitting. If she hits that pitch and location, the other pitchers on the staff must do the same. If she hits the spot, she is clear, but if she misses, she adds a letter. The first person to spell *horse* or whatever word you choose loses.

How Many Pitches?

For this drill have your pitcher state how many pitches out of 10 she can hit. Each pitcher wagers who can hit the most. If another pitcher accepts the challenge, then that pitcher must hit the stated number of pitches. If she succeeds, she gets to pick a punishment for the rest of the staff. (We usually make this a fun punishment for laughs rather than a real punishment.) If she fails at the task, then the rest of the staff comes up with a fun punishment for her.

BUILDING DYNAMIC WORKOUTS

Building dynamic workouts is a matter of organizing the drills I have explained in different ways. You can use countless combinations of drills and exercises to keep your pitcher engaged. During the off-season I like to do a few medium-level workouts each week with one easy workout and at least one medium-hard workout mixed in. During preseason I turn up the pitch count to build arm endurance. At this point in the year, I do more medium-hard workouts with medium workouts mixed in and one hard workout. During these weeks we throw five days of the week and mix in two off days. During the season we no longer use the hard workouts and stick to medium and easy workouts. The following are examples of workouts of different difficulty:

Intensity—Easy

Warm up all pitches with regular ball

Long toss

5 of each pitch

Two sets of 25 (50 jumping jacks in between)

3 × One-Minute Drill, all Three-Ball

Running: 10 short sprints (60 feet [18 m])

Intensity—Medium

Warm up

Umpire Drill—the pitcher throws 10 pitches with the "umpire" taking away a location

Opposites—4 × each pitch

6 of each pitch—every other pitch, the batter goes from the front of the box to the back, so the pitch should be a drop with the batter in the front and the next should be another drop with the batter in the back, and vice versa

5 × Sprint to the Catcher drill

Intensity—Medium-Hard

Warm up

Countdown Pitching—the pitcher must hit all 10 before she can go to the 9 pitches. She throws the number of pitches listed. For example, she throws 10 of her best control pitches. Ideally, she needs only 10 to 12 pitches to move on to 9. She then throws 9 up and ins and so on.

10 best control pitches

9 up and ins

8 low and outs

7 change-ups

6 up and outs

5 backdoors

4 black zone curveballs

3 weakest pitches

2 low riseballs for strikes

1 pitcher's choice

5 pitches focusing on leg drive

5 pitches focusing on arm whip on the back and bottom of the motion

5 pitches focusing on wrist snap and finishing

Call the Pitch Drill (pitchers take turns calling the pitch that everyone will throw) × 50 pitches

Running: Indian run × 5 laps, 300 abs any way

Intensity—Hard

Warm up

5 × each spot in row. If she misses, she starts over. She can use any pitch she wants.

Cycle Pitching—five pitches and then each agility for one minute

Jumping or exercise stations:

　　Mountain climbers

　　High knees in place

　　Low squat held in place for one minute

　　Side lunges, stay down for 5 seconds then switch

　　Squat jumps (if a player has knee issues, just body weight squats)

　　Jumping jacks

　　Horse

2 × One-Minute Drill, Two-Ball

2 × One-Minute Drill, Walk-Through

Running: 50 yards (45 m) of each

1. High knee skipping
2. Butt kicks
3. High knees
4. Standing long jumps
5. Walking lunges
6. Side shuffles (switch directions halfway)
7. 80 percent run
8. 100 percent sprint × 10

Allow only a 15- to 20-second break between agilities.

FINAL THOUGHTS

If you incorporate the drills from this chapter into your workouts, your pitchers will be challenged in different ways and will be more likely to stay engaged. They will be challenged mentally and physically in different ways during every workout. They will gain the strength, consistency, and confidence they need to become more effective as pitchers.

Developing a pitching staff is no small feat, but if you take the time to get to know the strengths and weaknesses of your staff, set goals, and put together a plan to reach those goals, you and your pitchers will be successful.

16

Developing Your Receiver

Stacey Nuveman Deniz

Any fastpitch softball coach will tell you that the catcher is one of the most critical players on the softball field. Having a top-tier pitcher is a coach's first order of business, but having a solid receiver behind the plate is a close second. A capable catcher gives confidence to the pitcher and the rest of the players on the field and is an integral part of a team's defense.

Most often, a catcher's physical skills are the primary measurement for how effective she is behind the plate. Beyond the physical aspects, some other more subjective abilities separate the good catchers from the great ones. Mastery of the intellectual, mental, and emotional pieces of the catching puzzle makes for a superb all-around catcher.

Notice that the title of this chapter is "Developing Your Receiver." You might think that the title of a chapter about catching should be "Developing Your Catcher." The reality is that a great catcher does much more than simply catch the ball; great catchers are great leaders, great communicators, and great teammates. Not coincidently, some of the best coaches and managers in NCAA softball and Major League Baseball are former catchers. No other position on the field requires the diverse skill set that is required of a catcher. The physical side of the position will beat up a player—hence the term *the tools of ignorance*—but the intellectual, mental, and emotional aspects are what make the catching position a unique challenge.

This chapter does not focus on the typical how-tos of catching; many fine resources explain how to teach your catchers to block, field bunts, or throw down to second base. This chapter focuses on the more abstract and less obvious components to the catching position and implores you to analyze and possibly reconsider how you train and develop your catchers.

PHYSICAL SKILLS

The foundation for a great catcher is her ability to handle the physical responsibilities of the position. If a catcher cannot block pitches in the dirt, throw out base runners, or frame pitches effectively, the potential for greatness is limited. The physical skills must be mastered first. After the foundation is set, the remaining skills can be taught and refined.

Like any other skill in softball, catching skills need to be practiced on a regular or daily basis to take form. Ironically, however, most coaches admit that they do not allot the same amount of practice time to their catcher's workouts as they do to any of the other defensive positions on the field. The irony in this is that the catcher handles the ball second most on the field, only slightly less often than the pitcher. For this reason alone coaches need to train their catchers daily to hone their skills as well as build their confidence.

Framing

In terms of priority, many coaches spend significant time training their catchers on their throwing and blocking. These two skills are critical aspects of the catching position, but an important overlooked and undertrained skill is framing. Framing pitches is a subtle art and is often considered the next level of training your receiver. Framing is not taking a pitch that is way out of the zone and jerking the glove back into the strike zone; that action will not fool anyone. Framing is the skill of making a ball look like a strike. Framing is not easy to do, and it may be the most important skill that a catcher can possess.

Consider this: A catcher may be asked to throw out a potential base runner somewhere between 25 and 50 times a season, but she will handle between 90 and 125 pitches in a game, and perhaps a quarter of those pitches will be borderline in terms of being a strike or a ball. So roughly 25 times a game a catcher's framing skills can either positively or negatively affect the game. This simple math indicates that spending time on the art of framing would benefit a team much more than working on nearly any other catching skill. Being able to throw out base runners is certainly critical to a team's success, but framing pitches is something that most coaches should work on more with their catchers.

Tennis Ball Framing

Objective

Begin the process of learning how to use body, as well as the hands, to frame pitches.

Equipment

Catcher's gear, tennis balls

Setup

The catcher begins in her receiving position with full gear on except no glove. The throwing hand should be placed behind the back or next to throwing foot so that it does not interfere.

Execution

The catcher begins to shift her weight slowly from side to side, emphasizing a smooth transfer of weight. A coach or another player stands approximately 10 feet (3 m) in front of the catcher and tosses a tennis ball on either side of the catcher in the strike zone. The objective is for the catcher to catch the tossed ball with her bare glove hand and frame the pitch using both her hand and her body.

Coaching Points

The ball should always finish facing home plate to help the catcher understand the concept of getting around the ball when framing. The goal is for the catcher to understand how to use her hand and body to frame borderline pitches subtly, to limit jerky motions of the glove, and to use soft hands when receiving pitches. This drill can progress from tennis balls and bare glove hands to gloves and real softballs.

Throwing

As with most athletic skills, there rarely is a singular way to teach a particular catching skill. Dozens of methods can work for a particular player or within a particular system, but these may not work for others. One skill method in catching that has recently begun to change is that more catchers are throwing to second from their knees rather than popping up out of the catching squat and throwing from their feet. Catchers as young as 12 years old are now trying to throw from their knees.

Throwing from the knees can be done effectively and efficiently, particularly when the pitch is low or in the dirt. But some catchers who are throwing from their knees do not have the necessary strength and are risking future arm injury and generating insufficient velocity by performing the skill in this way. Coaches need to be aware of the physical limitations of their players and not just follow a trend.

To inform the debate about the best way for a particular catcher to throw, the indisputable method is to use a clock. Use a stopwatch and time your catcher from both her knees and her feet. The clock will not lie, and any debate can be settled quickly and fairly. Finally, remember that the best throw to second base is not only quick but also, and more important, accurate! If a catcher cannot be accurate from her knees, then it does not matter how fast she can throw it down. The throw must be on target every time for the defense to have any opportunity to make the out.

The transition of the ball from glove to hand is generally where time can either be lost or gained on the throw to second base. Many catchers think that throwing hard is the answer, but the best way to improve on a glove-to-glove pop time is to increase the speed of the transfer from glove to hand. Arm strength is one factor, but a catcher with average arm strength can make up for lack of power with an efficient transfer.

Glove Transfer for Speed

Objective

To increase the speed and efficiency of ball transfer from glove to hand.

Equipment

Catcher's gear, softballs

Setup

The catcher starts in a receiving position with full gear and glove. A coach or another player stands about 10 feet (3 m) from the catcher and has approximately five softballs at hand.

Execution

One ball at a time but in quick succession, the coach tosses a pitch to the catcher until all five balls have been used. The goal is for the catcher to receive the pitch, quickly transfer the ball from glove to hand, get into throwing position, and then drop the ball and return to the receiving position. One repetition of the drill includes five transfers and should happen in approximately 15 seconds.

Coaching Points

We are training the speed and accuracy of the transfer, but we do not want the catcher to rush! This is a fine line, and as Coach John Wooden would say, "Be quick but do not hurry." The transition should be rapid but under control so that the catcher can ultimately focus on accuracy.

MENTAL SKILLS

As discussed earlier, the development of the complete catcher must be focused on developing the physical game as well as the mental and emotional aspects of the position. Coaches can prescreen the mental capacity of a catcher; the position requires a significant amount of mental processing and cognitive skill, as well as leadership capability. The best catchers in the game understand and recognize the details within the game and have the confidence to communicate openly and honestly with their teammates. All these qualities are not often found within the same catcher, but the goal should be to develop the most well-rounded catcher possible. Many of these skills are innate, but some can be taught or at least improved on.

Leadership

Every team craves leadership, and championships are often won or lost based on the quality of the team's leadership. A team's field general does not have to be the catcher, but a vocal catcher is a bonus for any team. The catcher is the only player on the field who has a complete view of everyone else on defense, and she is close to the dugout so she can communicate the direction being passed on by the coaches.

The best catchers are consistently giving reminders to the defense and providing constructive communication. Examples of constructive communication would be the number of outs, confirming who is covering the bases on a steal, knowing and communicating whether a particular defensive set is in place (e.g., whether the first baseman is staying back on a bunt), which player has the cutoff on a ball to the outfield, and so on. An endless number of possible scenarios may occur, and the more your catcher is communicating, the better off the defense will be.

The other benefit of having a vocal catcher with good leadership skills is that the catcher can become the team's voice so that the players can keep their focus on the field, where it belongs, rather than focusing on the dugout. As coaches our ultimate goal ought to be to prepare our athletes to compete and then set them loose. Players will never reach that goal if they play with one eye constantly on the dugout, always looking for direction and instruction. Ideally, we are teaching our athletes how to think the game as well as play the game. We want them to have a sense of ownership over their play and their team. Great leaders on the field mean that the players rely less on the dugout for direction.

Some catchers confuse leadership with being bossy; these traits are not the same. Great leadership means having good timing and tact, and understanding the skill of being a people person. Yelling at, berating, or embarrassing teammates, opponents, or officials is not good leadership. These points apply to both players and coaches. Good leaders are firm and hold strong convictions, but they understand that everyone does not and will not see things the way they see them, and they are willing and able to adjust accordingly.

Leadership is a skill like any other. Some possess leadership innately, whereas others need a lot of work to develop strong and positive leadership. Being positive is key. No team needs a negative Captain Obvious pointing out all the ways that a team is performing below standards; everyone on the team is keenly aware of the ways that they are falling short. On the flip side, every team needs a positive motivator, someone who keeps morale high, reminds everyone how great they are, and pushes them never to be satisfied with being mediocre. The leader plays a critical role on the team, and whoever fills that role should be a genuine and positive influence.

On-Field Communication

Catchers are often given the responsibility of being the on-field communicator, or on-field coach, who must be willing and able to direct the defense. A catcher's top priority is her communication with the pitcher, but the best catchers also understand the importance of communicating with the rest of the infield and the defense as a whole to create a defense that functions as one unit. Doubt and uncertainty on the part of any defensive player can lead to missed plays, people being out of position, and ultimately to defensive breakdowns.

There is no such thing as overcommunicating, as long as the communication is informational in nature and not chatter. Communication is the responsibility of every player on the field, but the catcher is often the player who ensures that everyone in the infield is on the same page. A definitive voice from behind the plate sets everyone else at ease and likely will minimize costly defensive mistakes.

A specific area in which many catchers could improve is helping make calls after a ball has been hit to the outfield. Catchers often become spectators to the play rather than active participants. The catcher needs to be aware of how hard the ball has been hit, whether there are any lead base runners and how fast they are, which outfielder has made the play, how strong the outfielder's arm is, and whether any cutoff is involved in the play. Having this awareness and being able to manage all this information will help the catcher make quick and accurate calls about where the ball should be thrown. Nothing is worse than throwing behind a runner; heads-up base runners will advance almost every time. The catcher who can communicate the proper calls can help a team avoid making the costly mistake of throwing to the wrong base and giving an extra base to the runner or even surrendering a run.

One way to practice on-field communication is to set up situations by having a coach hitting fungo and using live base runners. Work the drills in rounds. During round 1, only the middle infielders are allowed to make the call. Everyone else is silent. During round 2, only the corner players are allowed to make the calls and everyone else is silent. During round 3, the catchers make the calls while everyone else is silent. Finally, during round 4, everyone is silent and no one is making the calls. In this situation everyone has to use her softball sense to determine where the play should be made, and no one becomes reliant on listening to someone else for direction. This type of drill will help every player immensely in developing the often-elusive softball sense.

Another specific communication portal on the field is between the catcher and the umpire. The first rule for all catchers to remember is that most umpires want to do a good job of calling balls and strikes. It is hard to imagine an umpire walking out on to the field with the goal of blowing calls and having a bad day. Umpires are human and make mistakes, and experience tells us that umpires often make up for a poor call sometime later in the game. They might miss a pitch, but more often than not they will swing the pendulum in your favor at some point.

Some catchers demonstrate the tactless habit of showing up an umpire after a bad call, or a call that catcher or her coach perceives as bad. The catcher might hold her glove for an extended time in an effort to let everyone in the stadium know that the umpire missed the call. This strategy often backfires and ultimately goes back to the point about giving the umpire the benefit of the doubt. Catchers should show umpires respect; they are bound to return the favor. The advisable strategy is to gain and keep a positive rapport with umpires.

One subtle but powerful way that a catcher can display respect for the home plate umpire is never turning to talk to the umpire face to face during the course of play. Chatting between innings or during casual discussion is acceptable, but turning around to face the umpire and dispute a call is a bad idea. Lots of communication can occur between the catcher and the umpire without the other participants even knowing. A catcher can ask about where a pitch missed while facing the field to help the umpire save face. Respectful and subtle communication will benefit the catcher far more than rude and disrespectful behavior will.

Calling Pitches

One of the most critical aspects of a softball game is the way in which the defensive team, whether the pitching and catching battery or the coach, strategize their pitch calling. Having a good game plan and doing proper scouting is critical, but the true measure of greatness for pitch calling is being willing and able to make adjustments as necessary.

First, the pitcher in the circle must have command of a variety of pitches and be willing to use any pitch at any time without fear. Obviously, a pitcher rarely has absolute confidence in her entire arsenal; typically, a pitcher will have superior confidence in a couple pitches, occasional confidence in a couple pitches, and little or no confidence in another pitch or two. The more viable options there are to work with, the more dynamic the pitch calling strategy or game plan can be.

Along with having confidence in her pitches, the pitcher needs to have confidence in her catcher. The pitcher and catcher don't have to be close friends off the field, but the pitcher has to trust the catcher's physical abilities as well as her strategic game plan. The pitcher should be given the option of shaking off a pitch that she does not want to throw; after all, she is ultimately responsible for the pitch. But the goal for the catcher should be to gain the confidence and trust of the pitcher so that the pitcher should never feel it necessary to shake off the call. Ultimately, the battery should work in concert to produce the game plan as well as to adjust it as necessary. It is not the catcher calling the pitches or the pitcher calling the pitches—it is a shared responsibility.

The reality, however, is that most competitive softball programs these days have a coach perform the pitch calling. The pressure to win seems to have increased, so the tendency is for coaches to take control of pitch calling. This trend is a debated topic throughout coaching circles, but in the end most coaches believe that they are better equipped than their catchers or pitchers to make critical pitch-calling decisions.

That may well be true. The coach has in front of her or him the entire scouting book, which contains detailed information about each hitter, results of previous at bats, and tendencies. The coach has likely been around the game of fastpitch softball for much longer than players have and possesses a better base of knowledge of the game. Coaches are faced with tremendous pressure to be successful, so many of them have begun to tighten their grip on the details in an effort to control more of the game from the dugout.

As a challenge to the coaches who do the pitch calling for their teams, this question bears asking: As a teacher, can you not find ways to educate your players and give them the strategic and mental skills to be able to implement the game plan? Why can't we educate our catchers and pitchers on pitch-calling strategy and then empower them to go out and do it?

Calling a great game, whether from the dugout or from behind the plate, undoubtedly requires skills in reading the situation, knowing the pitcher and her strengths and weaknesses, having a feel for the strike zone and umpire, the ability to analyze the hitter, and being able to be one step ahead. These skills take time to develop for anyone put in the position of calling pitches. Logically, as educators, we as coaches should at least attempt to instill these skills into our catcher's arsenal.

During the off-season or even during intrasquad scrimmages you have many opportunities to challenge your catchers and pitchers to take the responsibility of calling pitches in a safe environment. Wins and losses are not on the line, so you can use trial and error during the educational process. Create a game plan before the scrimmage and take a few moments between innings to debrief your players on what happened the previous half inning and what adjustments they need to make moving forward. Then let 'em loose! Let your catcher and pitcher make mistakes and let them be successful. Ask them what their thought process was. Talk about how they might do it differently next time. After all, we are teachers of the game of softball, and making mistakes is part of the learning process.

We have created a worksheet to help pitchers and catchers learn each other's tendencies and preferences in various situations. This worksheet contains a list of questions such as "What pitch do you like to throw when down in the count 3-0?" and "What type of communication do you prefer from your catcher—tough love, encouragement, or specific mechanical tips?" These questions cover both physical and emotional topics and should give an overview of the types of things that a pitcher hopes to get from her catcher. Both the pitcher and each potential catcher should complete the sheet on their own.

This exercise is a vehicle to open lines of communication, help each player understand her battery mates, and create an opportunity for the pitcher to evaluate whether she is perceived by her catchers in the way that she perceives herself. This last point is usually telling because the answers that the pitcher gives are often different from those given by the players who catch her. The pitcher thinks that her best pitch is a curve, but everyone else thinks it is her drop ball. This simple exercise is a powerful way to kick-start the communication process, and it can be repeated to evaluate progress and development in this area.

After this process is complete and the communication and educational process has been put into motion, you may still decide that you are best equipped to handle the job of calling pitches. But through this process, you have fulfilled your responsibility as a teacher and have expanded the skill set of both the pitcher and catcher by helping them see and feel the game on a different level. Even if you are still calling in the pitches from the dugout, the athletes on the field have grown as thinkers of the game, which is powerful and invaluable as you continually develop your program and players.

EMOTIONAL SKILLS

A player's ability to manage her emotions is part of her mental game. Fastpitch softball is a constant battle of managing failure and being able to flush away negative thoughts and move forward in the next moment. The catcher's ability to manage the emotional components of the game is especially critical considering that she is involved in every pitch.

Most coaches or teams do not have the luxury or resources to hire professional sport psychologists or consultants to work with their teams on emotional or mental skills. These coaches must be creative in how they implement mental training into their programs. Even the most basic and simple exercises can have a significant effect on a player's performance and quality of experience.

One exercise that we use in our program is what we call at-bat debriefing. After each at bat, our players fill out a quick survey, or debriefing instrument, that relates to their most recent at bat. This debriefing includes approximately eight statements that players answer on a rating scale from 1 to 5. We ask the player to evaluate herself and her performance in that at bat in terms unrelated to the outcome. Examples of statements are "I was aggressive early in the count," "I maintained positive body language," and "I swung at quality pitches" (i.e., strikes rather than balls). If she gives herself a 1 for a particular statement, she did poorly; a 5 means that she was successful. A player could hit a double to right center and still get a 1 in certain categories, just as a player could strike out and score a 5 in other areas.

This activity, while not specifically an emotional-training drill, is useful in helping players create a game within the game and view their performance as more than hit or no hit. We want them to broaden their perspective on how they approach the at bat as a whole. This process improves their overall success rate and helps them stay positive in spite of a failed attempt to get a hit.

Another exercise that can be a powerful tool is to ask your players to fill out an emotional scorecard. This can also be done as a self-scouting report that focuses more on physical strengths and weaknesses. For the emotional scorecard, a player is asked to describe in detail her emotional strengths and weaknesses. What areas of her mental and emotional game does the player believe are well developed, and what areas need improvement? This exercise will help the player identify her personal strengths, which can be an empowering experience. Further, coaches can gain better understanding of the emotional needs of their players and thus more effectively manage their team's needs.

Separation of the Offensive and Defensive Game

The ability of a catcher to separate her offensive and defensive game from an emotional standpoint is critical to both her personal success and the success of the team. Every player on the field needs to be able to leave her at bat in the dugout and emotionally move on to the defensive side of the game, but that ability is particularly important for the catcher. As a leader and communicator on the field, the catcher needs to play the game outside herself rather than in her head.

For example, if the right fielder has a poor at bat and strikes out with the bases loaded, she may be able to take some time during the defensive half inning to beat herself up mentally, gather herself, and refocus. Of course, this type of emotional pouting should be strongly discouraged. But the right fielder is not likely to see any immediate action during the first pitch or two of the half inning.

The catcher, on the other hand, must be able to manage her emotional response to her previous offensive outing, whether positive or negative, and move immediately into a defensive mind-set. Otherwise, she will be distracted and unfocused as she transitions to defense, and she is likely to be much less effective in her leadership and communication duties.

Keeping a Game Face

One of the best quotations regarding the maintenance of a game face is "Sometimes you've got to fake it 'till you make it!" The ability to maintain composure in the most pressure-packed situations is often the difference between winning and losing. When authentic confidence is waning, sometimes the only weapon left is to fake it.

Obviously, true and authentic confidence is ideal in any pressure situation, but the reality is that confidence and composure are fragile and can come or go at the drop of a hat. This emotional roller coaster is dangerous for any competitor, particularly for a catcher, who is a highly visible player on the field. Consistent emotional output from the catcher is important because it helps the pitcher maintain her composure and engenders a sense of calm in the rest of the defense.

The challenge is for a catcher to be able to fake it when she is feeling less than confident and her composure is shaky. The catcher needs to maintain her outward composure even if she is nervous or lacking confidence on the inside. Her emotions might be raging inside, she might be nervous or excited or amped up, but to anyone looking at her from the outside she looks calm, cool, and collected. She is like the proverbial duck—calm on the surface but paddling like mad under the surface of the water!

A specific area where keeping a game face is critical is in dealing with umpires. Regardless of whether the catcher agrees or disagrees with the call, she has to move forward to the next pitch or play and not display obvious displeasure with the call. Everyone in the stadium knows the umpire blew the call, but the catcher does not benefit herself or her team by making a scene about how bad the call was. This type of emotional outburst often does more harm than good by emboldening the pitcher to lose her composure as well. A much more powerful approach is for the catcher and pitcher to move on as if nothing adverse had happened and proceed to the next pitch with determination and an air of confidence.

Humans are emotional beings, and the pressure of performance during athletic competition can often bring out the worst in people's emotional state. Using a college softball player as the example, her performance can carry a multitude of financial, social, and psychological consequences. She may be fighting to earn or keep an athletic scholarship. She may be striving to earn accolades or a position of status on her team. Her confidence and self-esteem may be strongly connected to her role as a collegiate student-athlete, and this self-esteem may be strongly affected by her performance on the field. As coaches our job is to get the best out of our players on a physical level, but for that to happen, we likely have a lot of work to do in keeping our players in a positive and healthy emotional state.

FINAL THOUGHTS

The separation between good and great catchers is often difficult to measure. Attention to detail and a focus on the mental and emotional aspects of the position are critical to developing a well-rounded and competent receiver. The physical components are the foundation, but the ability for a catcher to integrate the mental and emotional skill sets within her arsenal will take her catching game to another level.

17

Fielding Practice for Errorless Play

John Tschida

Let's begin this journey of developing an errorless defense!

In this chapter, when we talk about errors, we mean anything that takes us away from being the best defensive team we can be. We are talking not just about errors that are recorded in the scorebook but also about unrecorded errors such as throwing to the wrong base.

WHERE DO ERRORS COME FROM?

To discuss fielding practice for errorless play, we must ask ourselves, "Where do errors come from and, in particular, where do our errors come from?" Errors can come in a variety of forms, but when it comes down to it, most errors occur because of poor fundamental physical skills. Players need to master many skills in the game of softball. Later, I will list some of them.

Speed of the Game

Good fundamentals allow us to be efficient and make more plays, but we need to be efficient and fast. We want to be as fast as we're capable of being, so we don't try to go faster just because we are playing against someone like Olympian Natasha Watley. Watching Watley slap and run through first base demonstrates how important both fundamentals and quickness are, but we don't ever want to "step up" to play her—we want to play at the highest level we can all the time.

Inaccuracy

Inaccurate throws are another common form of error. We can be fundamentally sound and quick to get rid of the ball, but it doesn't do any good if we throw the ball away. Being quick without panicking is a good coaching cue. Players need to keep attempting to go faster, but the body needs time to become accustomed to the added quickness. At first, the player is going to be out of control, but later she will be able to coordinate the movements and thought processes to become a finely tuned, highly efficient, powerful player who can play at a speed that is uncomfortable for the opponent. Being specific with the intended target is what pitchers do, and position players should do the same. The throw needs to go at the first-base player's forehead, not to the general area of first base. Few balls thrown at a player's forehead will be missed, but many missed catches will occur when the ball is thrown below the waist!

Lack of Good Working Knowledge of the Rules

Not knowing the rules of the game can create mistakes that may or may not go in the scorebook as errors, but in any case these lapses prevent the defensive team from being as good as possible. For instance, when playing on a field with a collapsible fence, players should know that they are allowed to knock it over and stand on it to make a catch. Knowing this rule and all other rules of softball allows us to know the best way to play a ball.

Poor Knowledge of Game Situations

Softball is a game based on outs, not a time clock. For a defense, a typical seven-inning game means getting the opponent out 21 times. Those 21 outs are accomplished with the intent of not giving up more runs than our team scores. If a defense wants to get the game over quickly because it has a big lead, it needs to eat up the "clock," or in our case, get outs as quickly as we can. We would want the defense to get outs any way they can and take the highest percentage out. Given the option of getting outs at two different bases, we throw to the base that offers the highest percentage of getting the out, even when that means giving up a run, because we are trading a run to the offense for one of the precious few outs left in the game. The score, number of outs, inning, runners on base, pitcher, hitter, and other variables tell us where to go with the ball and which runner to play on.

Poor Prepitch Preparation

Not being prepared on each pitch is one of the more frustrating forms of errors that coaches and teams have to deal with. This area is in our control, but it is often taken for granted and has been the cause of many nonplays or misguided plays. Knowing the game, its plays, and its formations is one thing, but it is quite another to anticipate the plays that are more likely to occur based on the variables of the game. This awareness allows us to react properly and quickly!

VARIOUS WAYS TO WATCH A GAME

Coaches, players, and fans can watch softball games in a variety of ways. How we watch a game will ultimately determine what information we gather and can use. Focusing on one aspect, such as hitting, distracts from the time and energy we would have for another aspect, such as defensive positioning.

Watching for Skill

We can watch a game from the standpoint of a recruiter or coach evaluating talent for picking our future team. We would want to focus on the skills and speed of the skills being displayed. We often look for how sharp a player's tools are. A five-tool player is a player who can hit, hit for power, field, run, and throw. We want to evaluate many other skills, but those are the basics.

Watching for Weaknesses

We can watch a game from the standpoint of scouting an opponent and looking for any weaknesses that our opponent may have. Those weaknesses become opportunities when we have a particular strength that is capable of attacking that weakness. An example of a weakness may be their lack of communication, a weak arm, or a fundamental flaw.

Watching for Fun

The third way that we can watch a game is through the eyes of a fan, looking to be entertained by the talents of the players and the great plays. We may also be there just to support and watch a favorite player or relative. Many coaches focus so intently on making a player better by analyzing what she does wrong that they miss out on how entertaining or athletic she is. Switching off the analytical way that we watch a game can be difficult because we watch most practices and games this way.

PYRAMID OF DEFENSE: A SYSTEM FOR TEACHING DEFENSE

The pyramid of defense is my attempt to list and prioritize in a systematic order what should be covered and when it should be covered to play errorless defensive softball. At the bottom of the pyramid are the fundamental skills that we need to work on the most. By starting with the basics, we will find ourselves staying out of many situations. If we start with situations and bypass, or shortchange, the fundamentals, we will more than likely be in an extraordinary number of situations in which we lack the necessary tools to execute the defensive plays, although our team may know how to run them. The lowest level of the pyramid is for skills that are used most often and are needed to execute at the next level.

The whole idea behind a teaching progression is to keep players constantly growing from a strong base. Difficulty is added progressively and systematically to create failure and thus the need to grow and adapt. This process leads to a building of confidence, self-discovery, and mastery.

When organizing practices, a coach should consider all the skills needed. As noted in the pyramid, the lack of development of any of these skills leads to an incomplete defensive player, opening the door for a variety of errors. Each of us has lost games in part because of fundamental breakdowns, tactical ineptitude, and poor psychological skills.

Simplified Pyramid of Defense

Looking at all the details of the defensive pyramid can be overwhelming. When we cover anything in detail, the learner can easily get lost in the small things and lose sight of what we really want to get out of the lesson. For this reason I first provide a basic defensive pyramid. A simplified pyramid of defense (see figure 17.1) has three main levels:

Level 1: fundamental skills

Level 2: defensive formations (where players should start and then go on each play)

Level 3: situations of the game and the way in which they affect which skills and formations we use

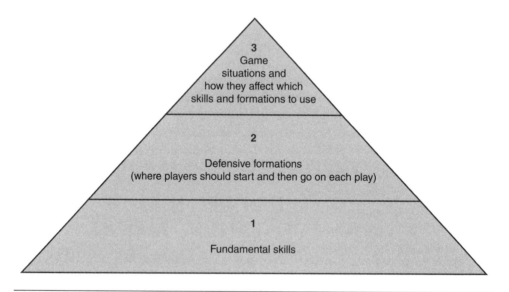

FIGURE 17.1   Simplified pyramid of defense.

Advanced Pyramid of Defense

To play softball at a high level, a defensive player or team needs to learn the basics, but then the player or team needs to learn how those basics can be adjusted to various skills and situations. For example, knowing how to throw comes before knowing where to throw. Understanding where to throw may change according to the number of outs, score, inning, and so on, which is yet another advancement from the basic pyramid. For this reason we provide both a basic and an advanced defensive pyramid. The advanced pyramid contains six levels and categories within each level.

Level 1: Fundamentals

This level is simply the basics of every game. Level 1 represents fielding, catching, throwing, running, and advanced variations. Let's go through the six levels of the pyramid of defense.

Level 2: Combined Group Skills With Individual Skills

This level includes skills such as covering bases on force-outs and tag plays and fundamentals for fielding various bunts, slaps, passed balls, wild pitches, dropped third strikes, and so on.

Level 3: Predetermined Defensive Formations

This level represents formations that are predetermined in every game. Where to go with and without the ball on fly balls, line drives, ground balls, and hits are the basics of level 3. Start with singles and extra-base hits. Then move on to where to go on short-game plays, steals, and more advanced first-and-third steals. This level also includes communication systems and priorities.

Level 4: Reads and Reactions

Players constantly have to read and react to instances when predetermined defensive formations and skills are adjusted in game situations. Players adjust to the speed and direction of the ball, fielders, and runners. The techniques and abilities of the offense and defense also are factors that affect the play.

Level 5: Game Situation Adjustments

Game situations always affect predetermined formations. These types of situations include number of outs, inning, runners, elements, field, hitters, count, pitch, pitcher, bench, coaches, philosophies, umpires, and alignments.

Level 6: Trick Plays

Most teams don't use and rarely need trick plays. An example of a trick play would be throwing the ball straight in the air to the pitcher when a base runner gets a great jump or when the catcher drops a pitched ball. Another example would be middle infielders who fake fielding a ground ball and turning a double play when the batter pops up with a runner stealing. Some teams take advantage of a first-base coach who yells, "Back," when she sees a second-base player leaving early to get in position at first for a pickoff. With a runner on first and an offensive team who likes to bunt runners over, a defensive team could send the second-base person early, giving the impression that a pickoff is on. Instead of throwing a pitchout pickoff, the defensive team throws a pitch that is easy to bunt, hoping that the first base coach's yelling to go back causes the base runner to dive back to first. The defensive team then fields the bunt and easily throws out the lead runner, who dove back into first.

1. FUNDAMENTAL SKILLS: THE BASE OF THE DEFENSIVE PYRAMID

When teaching, I like to build systematically on the technique being taught. We build on the details of the skills and begin with those most commonly used. We then add speed to the skill and the ball and learn how to use these skills in a game setting where the environment is no longer controlled and static, but very dynamic.

Teaching Progressions Based on Fielding Techniques

The teaching progression I use for fielding techniques begins with routine plays and progresses to the forehand and backhand plays. The basic areas of skills covered for errorless defense include the following:

- Approach to various balls hit
- Sprinting and movement skills with and without a glove
- Various force-out footwork
- Picking a good hop
- Fielding various ground balls and fly balls
- Making throws of various types and distances
- Applying various tags at bases and many other skills

Teaching Progressions Based on the Ball

Techniques are taught first without a ball, then with a nonmoving ball, then with a controlled slowly rolled ball, then with a controlled bouncing ball, and finally with random types of contacted balls. Starting without a ball allows players to focus solely on the fundamental physical skill. Adding a ball that is not moving adds the need to time the setting up of those same fundamental physical skills and to do so in a way that aligns with where the ball is. After the ball starts moving, the timing becomes more difficult because the physical skill must be executed based on the speed of the ball being hit. Going through the actions of fielding a ground ball too early or too late can cause either missed balls or much slower release times. Therefore, more runners will be safe. Going from controlled rolls and bounces to randomly thrown balls with various speeds and bounces requires the player to have not only the physical fundamentals but also a higher level of timing and judgment about where the ball will be at any given time. Great fielders have the ability to pick good hops by adjusting their own speed and direction.

Teaching Progressions Based on Speed

The following is the progression used when dealing with speed. Techniques are first taught by defining and learning a perfect, static fielding position. The ultimate goal of the fielder is to be in this position when fielding the ball. After learning what the destination or perfect fielding position is, we cover how to get there. We do this first in slow motion and then progressively get faster until the fielder is a bit out of control. The fielder is then taught to slow down slightly to become comfortable. Then we again slowly increase the speed and build the comfort level. Getting quicker while staying smooth and in rhythm is a constant challenge.

Teaching Progressions Based on Pressure

Staying with the philosophy of building a defense one step at a time, we now include pressure. We begin in a controlled setting where there are no consequences for errors. As technique and speed improve, we begin to add consequences. These could be as simple as winning or losing or more substantial such as sitting out, running, or doing push-ups. Defensive players thus experience pressure and the need to control arousal level, much as they would in a game.

Fundamental Skills Applied to Situations

Here fundamentals meet up with the needs of the situation. With a runner at second and a ball hit to the right fielder, the right fielder would need to know the speed and direction of the ball, fielders, and runners to know what to do with the ball. Having a rhythm of the game refers to knowing when to use each of the fundamentals based on the speed and direction of the ball, fielder, and runner.

Speed of the Ball

The speed of the ball may be fast, slow, or anywhere in between. The ball may take the fielder toward the direction she wants to throw or away from her intended target.

Speed of the Fielder

The speed of the fielder may be a full-speed sprint, half-speed sprint, controlled jog, fast walk, slow walk, or standing still. The direction of the fielder may be toward the play or away from the play.

Speed of the Runner

The runner's speed may be fast, slow, or anywhere in between. The direction of a runner may be toward a base or away from a base, or she may be standing still.

2. COMBINED GROUP SKILLS WITH INDIVIDUAL SKILLS: ONE STEP UP

After players master the fundamentals, we combine those individual skills with a small team unit and finally with the larger team unit. For example, pitchers, catchers, infielders, and outfielders all do individual drills to develop their own skill sets separately and at the same time in practice. In separate spaces on the field, the pitcher works on spinning a rise ball correctly, the catcher works on blocking balls in the dirt, the infielders perform a quick-hands drill, and the outfielders work on over-the-head catches.

The next step brings the pitchers and catchers, middle infielders, corners, and outfielders together in small groups. Going further, the whole infield works together, and then the infielders work with the pitchers and catchers.

Finally, the entire team works together using drills such as playing intrasquad scrimmages, running through cutoff and backup responsibilities, and engaging in various competitions in which one team of hitters is matched against the defense. Some of the skill areas may be worked on in small defensive groups, and I would work on them in the order of the frequency with which they occur.

Playing high-level catch

Ground balls with throws to bases

Fly balls and pop-ups

Communication and priority systems for fly balls and ground balls

Backup responsibilities, covering open bases, and communicating

Slappers, bunters, short-game formations, and priorities

Relays and cutoff responsibilities for singles and then extra-base hits

Steal coverage

Passed balls and wild pitches

Rundowns

Signs and communication systems: alignments, plays, and pitches

Defensive positioning: count, outs, up by a lot, down by a lot, catching fouls, and so on

First and thirds (traditional and nontraditional)

Pickoffs and pitchouts

Double plays—feeds and turns

Intentional walks

Small groups that commonly work together:
Pitcher and catcher

Middle infielders

Shortstop and third-base player

Second-base player and first-base player

Pitcher, catcher, first-base player, and third-base player (corners)

First-base player, third-base player, shortstop, and second-base player (whole infield)

Pitcher, catcher, first-base player, third-base player, shortstop, and second-base player (whole infield, pitchers, and catchers)

Pitcher, catcher, and third-base player

Pitcher, catcher, and second-base player

Left fielder, third-base player, and shortstop

Right fielder, first-base player, and second-base player

Center fielder, shortstop, and second-base player

Right fielder and center fielder

Left fielder and center fielder

Here is an example of how to organize a system for teaching individual fundamentals in a small group. The example prepares your team to defend a first-and-third situation.

1. Basic throwing and catching: Start with the technique done in slow motion without a ball. Then add a ball and later add speed.

2. Throwing and catching from various distances and angles: flips, dart throws, short and long throws using the upper body, and then throws using as much of the lower body as needed for more power.

3. Rundown skills, rundown execution rules, and communication systems.

4. Basic formations for first-and-third defenses (where to go with and without the ball). Dry runs are done with no runners. Later runners who have predetermined routes are added.

5. Adjustments to basic formations for first-and-third defenses based on reads of the speed and directions of the ball, fielders, and runners (where to go with and without the ball).

    a. Live run-through with the defense knowing what the runners are going to do

    b. Live run-through with the defense not knowing what the runners are going to do

    c. Live run-through with the defense knowing what the runners or hitters or bunters are going to do

    d. Live run-through with the defense not knowing what the runners or hitters or bunters are going to do

3. DEFENSIVE FORMATIONS: TWO STEPS UP

At the start of each pitch, the defense can choose to position the fielders in any position on the field as long as they are in fair territory and not in a position to purposely distract the hitter or obstruct the runner. A player at any position may move, or a defensive team may choose to move small groups or even the entire team to encourage or discourage the offensive team from executing a particular play. The defense may be positioned in close or back, on the lines or off the lines. Good team defense requires players to know what their teammates are doing and who has backup responsibilities for each play.

Some of the better-known formations for defenses include the following:

1. Standard—The pitcher, catcher, first-base player, and third-base player play in tight to the hitter to field bunts.
2. 1-back defense—The first-base player plays deep.
3. 3-back defense—The third-base player plays deep.
4. All-back defense.
5. Sidekick defense—An infielder positions in the first base and pitcher alley, up close, side by side with the pitcher. Typically, the first- or second-base player is the sidekick.
6. Fifth infielder—An outfielder plays in the infield to close the gaps and keep the ball in the infield.

Each of these defenses has strengths and weakness. These defenses require players to know their responsibilities. Other more specific formations come out of the first-and-third and bunt defense situations.

4. READS, REACTIONS, AND ADJUSTMENTS TO PREDETERMINED DEFENSIVE FORMATIONS AND SKILLS: THREE STEPS UP

After learning what to do and where to go in a structured, predetermined practice, players must learn to do it when we do not predetermine the actions of our opponent. Fielders need to read and react to endless possibilities. They have to read the position, body language, skill, ability level, and movement of the runners to determine where to go. For example, when a bunt is laid down to sacrifice a runner, the defense may choose to get the lead runner because of her lack of speed or inability to slide properly. Another example is throwing home on a base hit with a runner starting on second. The throw starts home, but when the runner stops, the relay turns into a cutoff and relay to third base instead of home. Each player must be ready to call these "defensive audibles," much as a quarterback does in football. The defense would have to read and adjust to the offensive weapons that our opponents use to score runs. These weapons include the following:

Bunts: sacrifice, suicide, drag bunt, push bunt, and fake bunt

Slaps: hard slap, soft slap, chop slap, fake slap

Hits: hit away, step or shuffle step and hit, fake hit

Baserunning: steal, delay steal, slides, rundowns, and lead and trail runners providing confusion

Taking a pitch

Any of the preceding can be combined.

The defense may defend itself with weapons such as pitch selection, pitch location, and various defensive alignments to encourage or discourage the offense from doing what it wants to do. In a bunt situation, the defense may move the corners in to discourage the offense from bunting or move them way back to encourage or entice a power hitter to bunt.

5. GAME SITUATION ADJUSTMENTS AND PREDETERMINED FORMATIONS: FOUR STEPS UP

First, we covered fielding fundamentals. We proceeded to apply those fundamentals to small and large groups. Our next step was to use both of them while reading and reacting to the offense. We now climb to the top of the defensive pyramid by learning how these ideas change based on the situation of the game. Here the defensive player makes use of her ability to stack all the pertinent information. I will explain stacking in a few paragraphs.

How Can I Use the Defensive Pyramid?

How much time do you have to master playing errorless defense? Some of us have one day, whereas others have nine months. With more time, we can master one skill before moving on to the next. Many of us do not have the luxury of developing in phases and must settle on being adequate in certain areas. The less time you have, the more you need to combine individual skill development with team defense. You will be doing two things at once and making sure that both get sufficient time.

W-I-N

The question "What's Important Now (W-I-N)?" is significant. It implies that we are, to some degree, limited in time, so we have to choose which skills and formations we need to practice now and which we can save for later. Great coaches excel at controlling the controllables. An uncontrollable is time, but how we spend that time is something we can control. Because of time constraints, we may not be able to master a particular skill or play, but we need to evaluate what is more likely to affect our ability to play errorless softball. The defensive pyramid was created to help us decide "W-I-N." We consider where we are now, where we would like to be, what it takes to get where we want to be, and how much time and how many resources we need to get to the level required or desired. Sometimes we must consider what skill development will produce the best return on investment. With all these things in mind, we are able to make better decisions on what to focus on and when.

READY POSITION AND STACKING

To be ready to make a play, a defensive player goes through two steps before the pitch. Both are seen as forms of stacking. The first step is preparing mentally, and the second step is getting ready physically.

Mental Stacking

Mental stacking precedes physical stacking. Mental stacking is what separates high-level players from lower-level players, and many of the errors that are not recorded in the scorebook occur because of poor mental stacking.

Mental stacking involves getting the mental state of the athlete into not only moving quickly to the ball but also knowing what to do with it after she gets it. Mental stacking can be explained by thinking about a stack of playing cards or music CDs. Imagine that you love music and have 500 CDs. You have them in a large box but in no particular order. If I were to ask you if you have a particular song by Pearl Jam or Elvis Presley, you may know the answer off the top of your head. But if I wanted to play that CD right now, you may have to rummage through the box for 10 minutes before you come up with the proper CD. Now imagine that you have those same CDs in alphabetical order by artist and then by album. Finding a particular CD take a lot less time when the information is organized in a way that you understand.

Having knowledge and organization of knowledge is relevant to the defensive player or any athlete who needs to have knowledge and the ability to process it quickly. Players may have a lot of knowledge about the game but have a tough time deciding what to do in a timely manner. They have all the CDs, but they just can't find the right one! When questioned about making or not making a play, these players respond with, "I know. I know. I know!" They know, but they just couldn't apply what they know within the appropriate time, which is just slightly better than not knowing at all. What we need to do is teach them how to put their CDs, or knowledge of the game, in an order that will allow them to pick the right one, quickly. Mental stacking improves when we have developed a stack of knowledge and put it in an organized form.

Do Great Players Have Instincts, or Have They Learned the Behaviors or Reactions?

Mental stacking involves knowing all the many variables that may potentially affect the game. Just knowing the variables is not enough; we must also know how those variables affect each other. Mental stacking involves sorting through the game variables to determine which are more relevant and which are less relevant based on the score, inning, number of outs, the hitter, the hitter who is potentially coming up later, and so on. A defensive player then takes that information and decides what possible actions she could take if this or that happens and what the best, worst, and most likely result of her actions would be. This mental process happens before each pitch. Finally, after all that, she gets physically stacked to react to the batted ball and the developing play.

Knowing and sorting through these thoughts and considerations allows the player to make not only good decisions but also quick decisions. Knowledge combined with the ability to think quickly is what many call instincts. I don't like the term because it insinuates that one is born with this knowledge and the ability to sort through it quickly. I think that the trait is learned and processed through playing and watching games in a specific way. Watching and playing with the intent of winning or finding the best way is different from watching to be entertained or to admire athleticism. When something doesn't work for high-level athletes, they evaluate and think about ways that may have worked better and why they might work better. I believe that people who "know" the game have watched it with the intent of figuring out how to win. They process games in a way that makes sense, and this allows them to make quick decisions and take quick action. On a side note, I worry about the generation of players who are growing up playing in friendly games or showcases that are not about finding a way to win, but about showcasing talent. They are losing many opportunities to develop this mental stacking. My guess is that their knowledge of how to win will not be as strong as it was in players in the past.

Using Mental Stacking in a Game

The score is tied at 1-1 in the seventh inning. There is no one out, and no one is on base. The opponent's leadoff hitter hits a double to lead off the inning. She has good but not great speed. The next hitter, the number two hitter, is a good bunter with good speed but no power. What will your opponent do, and what should you do? Should you take a proactive stance, or should you just counter what they do?

Offensive Stacking—What Will the Offense Do?

1. Bunt the runner from second to third and let the number three and four hitters hit the runner in.
2. Bunt the runner over and suicide squeeze the runner in.
3. Let the number two, three, and four hitters swing away and attempt to knock in the run.
4. Attempt to steal third base and let the number two hitter suicide squeeze the runner in.
5. Attempt to steal third base and let the number two hitter safety squeeze the runner in. If the defense fakes a throw, keep the batter–base runner going to second base to create a first-and-third situation.
6. Attempt to steal third base and let the number two hitter safety squeeze the runner in. If the defense fakes a throw, keep the batter on first base and the runner at third base so that we can hit away with the number three hitter.

7. Attempt to steal third base and let the number two hitter safety squeeze the runner in. If the defense fakes a throw, keep the batter on first base and the runner at third base so that we can hit away with our number three hitter. If the number three hitter fails to get the runner in, let the number four hitter hit the runner in. If she gets a strike or two and is looking bad, we can run a first-and-third play to attempt to get the run in.

Table 17.1 provides a brief example of what goes through the defensive player's mind and how she might use stacking to help predict how to perform during the game.

TABLE 17.1 Mental Stacking Used for Playing Defense

Score	What is the score of the game, and what do I think the score will be at the end of the game based on both teams and the elements of the day?
	Are we ahead or behind by a lot, tied, or ahead or behind by a little? Is it a low-scoring or high-scoring game?
Outs and inning	How many outs are there in the inning?
	How many outs are left in the game?
Runners	What bases are occupied?
	Which runners are important based on the score and inning?
	What is the speed and baserunning experience of each runner?
Elements	Is the playing surface wet, dry, fast, or slow?
	Is the weather rainy or dry? Is the wind blowing in, out, or whirling? Is it cold or warm? Extreme or mild?
Field	Is the field is hard or soft, fast or slow, wet or dry, familiar or unfamiliar?
	Are the fences and backstop close or far? Do they have a trampoline or deadening effect? Are they high or low? Permanent or collapsible?
Hitters and the count	What type of hitter is up and what types of hitters, potentially, will be coming up? Is the hitter in a positive hit count, neutral hit count, or negative hit count? Where will we be in our order? What types of hitters are on deck and in the hole, and whom do they have as pinch hitters? What skill sets do the hitters possess?
Pitch and pitcher	What location, spin, and speed are being called, and what do I think the hitter will do? How does our pitcher match up with their hitters?
	Does she have control or strikeout ability?
Bench	What does the offensive team have on the bench?
	Do they have quality or depth in the following areas: hitters, slappers, bunters, runners?
Coach's and team's philosophy	Is the offensive coach's philosophy an aggressive one or a conservative one?
	How often do they hit, bunt, slap, steal, take pitches, make no call, or execute a combination of these strategies?

Umpires	Are the umpires consistent or inconsistent, aware or unaware, generous or stingy, poised or rattled?
	Do they have favorite rules to call?
Defensive alignments and responsibilities	What defensive alignment are we in? What are the base coverage responsibilities? Do we have any defensive players who are going to be in a position that they cannot handle physically or mentally, and what can we do to prevent this?
	What will I do with or without the ball based on the speed and direction of the ball, fielder, and runner?
Ball	What is the speed and direction of the ball hit? What will I do if the ball is hit to my left, my right, ahead of me, or behind me? If the ball is hit in the air, on the ground, or not hit, what will I do? If the ball is hit extremely hard, extremely soft, or somewhere in between, what will I do with it?
Fielder	What will I do if I am going full speed, half speed, or somewhere in between when I field it? What will I do if I am going to my left, right, forward, or backward? Do I have momentum going to a base? How much momentum do I have, and with how much control? What is the speed and direction of the defensive player going to the ball when fielding the ball, and what was the speed and direction of the players not fielding the ball? How far did the defensive player run to field the ball, and how much time elapsed? Was the ball fielded cleanly, or was it booted? Does the defensive player who fielded the ball have good arm strength and accuracy, and is she aware of where to go?
Runner	What is the speed of the runners at the time of the play, and in what direction are they going? What is the overall speed of the runners before the play develops? What is the intelligence of the runners? Which runners are of primary importance and to what extent, and which runners are of secondary importance?
	Were the base runners moving on the pitch? In what direction and how fast were they moving?

Defensive Stacking—What Should the Defense Do?

1. React to what the offense does and get outs where we can while preventing the run from scoring.

2. Call a pitchout pickoff. If it doesn't work, intentionally walk the number three hitter to increase our chances of turning double plays, getting easy force-outs, and eliminating the need to face the dangerous number three hitter.

3. Let the number two hitter bunt the leadoff hitter over and then intentionally walk the number three and four hitters. This strategy will eliminate their two most dangerous bats and go after the less dangerous number five and six hitters. If we get out of the inning, we will face their number seven through nine hitters the next inning, tipping the scales in our favor.

4. Execute any combination of the preceding strategies.

5. Move an outfielder into the infield to prevent the bunt or steal. Pitch according to the defense; in other words, throw outside if we bring in the pull-side outfielder.

6. Play a 3-back defense to better defend the steal of third base and have a better chance of picking the runner off if she strays too far.

7. We should consider a seemingly endless variety of options that could happen.

Physical Stacking

Physical stacking involves getting the body in an athletic position to be quick to the ball. The fielder bends her knees, gets her glove and throwing hand out in front, and has both elbows bent approximately 90 degrees. How low she goes depends on how close she is to the hitter. Whether the fielder is up close and low or farther back and higher, when she bends to get into an athletic position, both her shoulders and hips should rise and lower at the same rate. If she lowers or raises one faster than the other, she loses the athletic position of being physically stacked with a slight lean forward to the point where her toes grab the ground. As the pitcher rocks back in preparation to drive forward, the infielder takes small jab steps forward and then makes a small hop when the ball is approximately halfway to the plate. She thus lands in a good athletic position just as the ball is entering the hitting zone. This hop is very small, typically only a couple of inches (5 cm), and is not a jump. In doing this hop, the hands are separated and the feet land almost parallel so that the glove-side leg is slightly forward just a couple of inches (5 cm) to allow for a staggered stance that will maximize range in every direction.

Having covered stacking, we can move forward and stack it into our "book." What exactly is meant by saying, "playing by the book," and where can I pick up a copy?

MENTAL ERRORS

Mental errors can occur when players or coaches don't know what their strengths and weaknesses are, how they match up versus an opponent's strengths and weaknesses, and how that fits into game situations. The percentages that apply to the best thing that could happen, the worst thing that could happen, all the other things that could happen, and the most likely thing that could happen are important to weigh in making good decisions. This concept is what they call playing by the book or playing against the book. The problem is that everyone has a different book because each player or team not only has a different amount of information but also has a different capability for processing that information during the game. The more information that the player and coach can process effectively, the more unpredictable they become. Therefore, they are using a bigger book to play or think the game.

The average fan uses CliffsNotes to make decisions, whereas the advanced player and coach use a thick manual that they have acquired over a long time. Not everyone will acquire a book like this. Knowledge of one's own team, the opponent's team, the game itself, and the elements that relate to today, right now, is what makes a good strategist, both offensively and defensively. Making good decisions is about more than just making the right decision; it is about making the right decision based on all the variables available, not just a couple of the variables. So a poor decision is not necessarily a wrong decision; it is one that was incomplete because of the variables that were not considered. Players and coaches can make better decisions if they are able to know and process all the important information in a timely manner.

SWOT ANALYSIS

The SWOT analysis is a tool that can be used to evaluate your progress in developing an errorless defense. A SWOT analysis will help you identify what areas of your defense might be attacked. Knowing your opponent and your team will help you make better game decisions. SWOT stands for strengths, weaknesses, opportunities, and threats. A SWOT analysis starts with getting to know your team's strengths and weaknesses and then comparing them to your opponent's strengths and weaknesses. Strengths that may be used to expose your opponent's weaknesses are called opportunities. Opponent's strengths that may be used to expose your weaknesses are considered threats.

To begin the SWOT analysis, we need to evaluate and ask some questions.

What kind of player or team are we? (The more specific we can be, the better our analysis will be, but here is a basic model.)

Are we a team deep in talent, with just enough talent, with limited talent, or with no talent? Are we talented or deep enough in talent at all positions? Are we a team with great, good, average, or poor defensive fundamentals? Is our knowledge of defensive formations or play sets great, good, average, or poor? Does our team have great, good, average, or poor knowledge of how to play the game based on its situations and variables? What are the defensive skills or plays needed to be successful when playing fastpitch softball? Where are we presently with regard to our sport psychology skills, team chemistry, strength of schedule, and game experience? We covered the preceding topics throughout the first three-quarters of this chapter.

Will we need to be masters of all the defensive skills to compete against our best opponent?

What do we need to cover before we start our practices, games, or playoffs? Will we ever be capable of mastering these defensive plays or skills? Will we ever master these plays, or should we just worry about becoming adequate so that our opponents don't notice the lack of mastery as an opportunity that they can exploit? Will simplifying what we work on make us a better team? Are we trying to be masters of everything while being good at nothing? Would it be better to be great at a few things and just adequate in others? Ironically, when we get good at answering the question "What's Important Now (W-I-N)?" we begin to put ourselves in a position to win more consistently based on the quality of our practices and what we cover in those practices.

For the level we are playing, what is considered average, what is the best, where are we now, and where could we potentially be with proper training?

Some areas to evaluate are bat speed, arm speed, and running speed. This list can go on to cover many aspects of the game, but they should be relevant.

How much time is available and what resources are available to master the skills and plays?

What is the likelihood that we will get to a particular level given the time and resources available?

What is the best way to acquire the skills necessary with the resources available?

Prepare short-term and long-term solutions. A long-term solution to having no pitching is to recruit more quality pitchers or develop the pitchers we already have. A short-term solution is to practice less on our short game and more on our power game and big-inning offense. We could also practice our pickoffs more so that we can get our pitchers out of jams.

FINAL THOUGHTS

Developing a flawless defense requires more than having a working knowledge of what makes an outstanding individual defensive player. It requires knowing how to develop individuals, small teams, and the larger nine-player defensive team, both individually and as a unit. It requires knowing the best way to progress in both the physical and mental aspects of defensive play, taking into consideration all resources, including time. Ignoring the way that players think about the game and the way in which the score, number of outs, and inning affects their decision-making process is a sure recipe for frustration for the coach, players, and fans. Coaches will use different systems for teaching defense, but I hope that after reading this chapter, you will reevaluate the order in which you teach defensive skills, the amount of time you spend in each area, and the extent to which you have prepared your team in both the physical and mental side of playing flawless defense. After all, we all enjoy a well-played game!

18

Strength Training, Conditioning, and Agility

Teena Murray

When it seems nothing is happening I go and look at a stonecutter hammering away at his rock—perhaps a hundred times without as much as a crack showing in it. Yet at the hundred and first blow it splits in two, and I know it was not that blow that did it—but all that had gone before.

Anonymous

I often use that quotation, one of my favorites, to explain the importance of commitment to training. Everyone wants immediate results—a more explosive first step, stronger legs, less body fat. What is often lacking is appreciation for the process involved in making those things happen. Training always stimulates change—whether neural adaptations, positive changes in energy production and utilization, or processes that remold and rebuild tissue—and it is the combination of those subtle incremental changes beneath the surface that over time leads to outward progress. Just as with breaking the rock, the key is consistent dedicated effort!

Training is a process, a process that relies on the interaction of many complex factors. The process should unfold to prepare each athlete technically, tactically, psychologically, and physically for the highest level of performance at the most important times of the year. The process relies on focused planning, individualization, and the management of a wide variety of factors that extend well beyond the weight room and the softball field. Rate of development or progress is influenced by many factors: (1) training frequency, volume, and intensity; (2) exercise selection; (3) rate of progression of these training variables; (4) quality, quantity, and timing of nutrition; and (5) sleep, stress, and the influence of other lifestyle factors. Optimizing athlete development and maximizing sport performance depends on the structure surrounding and commitment to all of it!

This chapter discusses the training process as it relates to developing the softball athlete. This information will be organized in seven innings (sections). The goal is to present an overview of an organized system for developing the bulletproof softball athlete.

INNING 1: PHILOSOPHY

Just as there are many philosophies on hitting and baserunning, there are many approaches to athlete development. For me, the number one goal of the training process is to produce bulletproof softball players, to build physically tough, mentally tough, and above all injury-resistant (or durable) athletes.

The second goal of the training process is transfer to sport, in this case, to softball. Does it really matter that Maggie's squat has increased by 20 pounds (9 kg) if she's slower on the base path? Or that our pitchers have higher vertical jumps but lack the stamina to throw a complete game? Of course not! Designing training programs that prepare athletes for the specific needs of their sport and position (while reducing injury risk) is all that matters.

This I know for sure: Talent alone does not win championships. Likewise, being bigger, faster, and stronger alone does not make a great athlete. Rather, the athletes most likely to succeed are those who have prepared meticulously, know and play to their strengths, have the skills to manage adversity and their weaknesses, and are trained to perform under pressure. Therefore, creating opportunities during training to develop those qualities, in addition to the physical components, is a priority for us. Showing up and doing the sets and reps is never enough!

At the University of Louisville we are committed to creating a culture and a training system that develop the entire anatomy of a champion—body, mind, and spirit. This process has been, and will continue to be, a work in progress. But we are invested in an approach that educates, motivates, inspires, and empowers every athlete to achieve her full potential. To this end, our methods are athlete centered, evidence and assessment based, coach driven, and performance focused. We base our training model on the latest research and employ cutting-edge strategies and technologies in the areas of medicine, athlete development, nutrition, and mental conditioning. We use a variety of traditional and nontraditional methods (as we see fit) to have the greatest possible effect on our three performance outcomes: (1) reduce noncontact injury risk, (2) optimize athlete development, and (3) maximize team success.

Of course, implementation of this holistic approach to performance requires a team effort. At Louisville our performance team includes a variety of professionals, from athletic trainers and performance specialists to physical therapists, chiropractors, massage and other soft-tissue experts, nutritionists, team physicians, and mental conditioning specialists. It takes a village, and we are committed to using every resource to accomplish our goals!

Building Bulletproof Athletes

Let me begin by saying that there is no perfect or magic training plan for developing (great) athletes. I do believe, however, that the best programs have a few things in common. First, training begins with a comprehensive evaluation or assessment of every athlete. This information is then used to drive appropriate program design. Second, the program uses a systematic progression of training that is individualized. This progression is designed to peak athletes (physically) for the most important time of the year, the competitive season, but it recognizes that every athlete responds differently and that rates of progress vary. Finally, philosophy, athlete assessment protocols, and training methods are strongly connected. Too often, a disconnect is present between what is stated and what is done. If injury prevention is the primary training goal, then the evaluation and methodologies should reflect that. Throwing in a few prehab exercises along the way is not what I'm talking about.

As performance specialists we often make the mistake of treating every athlete the same way, regardless of training age, strengths and weaknesses, position, injury history, or even deficiencies identified by screening and testing. We often use the same starting point for training all athletes and progress everyone at the same rate regardless of adaptation or readiness. We are, at times, married to certain exercises (e.g., squatting and Olympic lifts), believing that they are appropriate for all. And I say "we" because I am guilty of all of this. Fortunately, experience has taught me a few things. Namely, lack of individualization may increase injury risk by exposing athletes to mechanical or metabolic stresses that their bodies aren't prepared for.

So, here is my action plan for building bulletproof athletes:

1. Physical development plans are based on the specific needs of the sport and position being played, the training age of the athlete, and results from a comprehensive assessment.

2. Mental conditioning, leadership development, and team-unifying tactics are emphasized throughout the design and implementation of training—from accountability measures woven through workouts to competitive finishers at the end of workouts and entire workouts dedicated to strategy, competition, and toughness training.

3. Injury resistance (or durability) is the top priority, and it is a by-product of assessment-based and systematically progressed training methods that emphasize the individual athlete's movement quality and readiness for training.

Performance and Prevention

Performance and prevention are not mutually exclusive training goals involving or requiring separate methods. Rather, they can be seamlessly integrated, because they have a common denominator—movement. Therefore, improving movement (quality and control) should not only reduce injury risk but also provide a foundation for increased performance capacity. For this reason, assessing and correcting movement (patterns) is central to everything we do. After we establish clean patterns, sustaining them throughout training and competition, while enhancing strength and power, becomes the priority.

The performance pyramid, shown in figure 18.1, demonstrates the importance of athletes' having a broad base of functional movement skills. This foundation of functional movement acts as a buffer zone essential for protecting the body during high-impact and high-stress activities. Without it, no level of strength or speed training matters because those qualities will never be developed safely and optimally. Think about a center fielder who has a rocket of an arm but throws with poor mechanics. She may be effective for a portion of the season but will likely break down or develop an injury related to the unhealthy motion. Poor movement patterns can never be sustained without consequence. Where performance and prevention are concerned, a bottom-up approach is required.

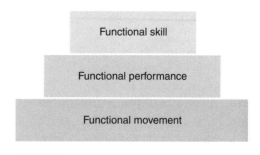

FIGURE 18.1   The performance pyramid.

Source: Gray Cook, 2010, *Movement: Functional movement systems* (Aptos, CA: On Target Publications).

INNING 2:
HIGH-PERFORMANCE ATHLETE ASSESSMENT

Driving blind is unsafe. So is training blind! For this reason, our goal is always to accrue as much information as possible on every athlete before training begins. At Louisville we have implemented a high-performance athlete assessment plan that includes three components.

Our three-pronged approach begins with screening, which is qualitative in nature and is used to identify injury (or health) risk. This area involves significant collaboration with our sports medicine staff. The second component is performance testing, which is used to quantify performance capacities in a variety of relevant areas (i.e., strength, power, speed, conditioning). The third component is tracking, which involves monitoring key performance variables throughout the competition season (because we do not do any testing during this time).

Screening

Because minimizing injury risk is a top priority, screening any items that are known to increase risk is essential. Research indicates that the top four predictors of noncontact injury are (1) previous injury, (2) asymmetry (in movement), (3) lack of neuromuscular control (balance), and (4) body composition (Plisky, Kiesel, and Voight 2007). In accordance, we focus our screening on those four items. We also look at specific health parameters that have potential to influence performance—vision, gait, iron status and nutrition, and lifestyle habits.

Previous Injury

Although previous injury is the single best predictor of future injury, we can do little preventatively on that front. Just the same, we do analyze injury history and verify that movement patterns and strength levels have either been restored or achieved according to specific return-to-play guidelines.

Movement and Balance Screening

Our softball movement screening protocol includes three components. First, and most important, is the Functional Movement Screen (FMS), which has quickly become the gold standard in our industry for assessing movement. The screen includes a battery of seven tests that are qualitatively ranked. These tests take athletes through fundamental movement patterns (e.g., squat, lunge, push-up) to identify either mobility or stability deficiencies or asymmetries that may exist. Each test is scored on a 0 to 3 scale to produce a total score out of 21. We use 16 out of 21 (with no significant asymmetries) as a passing score. Scores below 16 result in mandating individualized corrective work.

The second movement screening tool is a vertical hop and stop test performed on a Just Jump mat. This test looks at single-leg landing mechanics after a maximum-effort vertical hop. Success clearly relies on balance (or neuromuscular control). In addition to scoring the quality of landing on each leg, we look at the height of the hop on each leg and the difference between right and left legs. A difference of less than 2 inches (5 cm) is the goal. When landing-quality issues or a significant asymmetry exists, supplemental work on landing mechanics and balance is incorporated into training.

A third screening tool that we have recently begun using with our softball team is shoulder and hip range-of-motion measurements. Using a goniometer, our athletic trainer measures internal and external range of motion on both shoulders and both hips. Because these areas are among the most injured in the game, we want to identify mobility limitations that may exist. When internal and external range of motion is added together and compared right with left, the goal is less than a 10 percent difference. Asymmetries greater than 10 percent are addressed and corrected on an individual basis with soft-tissue (self-massage, stretching) and targeted corrective exercises.

Body Composition

Though larger athletes can be successful softball players, we know that being overweight can increase injury risk and impact performance. Monitoring body composition, not just body weight, is a consistent priority for our softball program. It allows us to track progress with training and tailor effective nutrition education according to specific athlete needs.

Performance Testing

When it comes to performance testing, the key is creating a meaningful battery of tests that will predict success on the field and implementing it at the right times during the year. Baseline data is gathered at the beginning of each new training year. In the college season this can be challenging because typically after we play our last game our players leave town for the summer. The first opportunity we have to test everyone is in August, when we are three months into our off-season training. In an ideal situation we would test within one to two weeks of the end of the season.

You cannot improve what you cannot measure.

We know that softball is a game of speed and power, so these tests ultimately mean the most to us. But strength is a precursor of power, so our strength data are also important, especially gains made between August and November (our max strength phase). An overview of our performance-testing menu is shown in table 18.1.

After collecting testing data, we analyze it a variety of ways. We look at short- and long-term comparisons (within and between years), player rankings by test, positional rankings by test, and performance scores derived from our softball performance index (see table 18.2). The index attaches a point value (0–10) to scores on each test. A total score for all 10 tests is then calculated (out of 100). This score is a reflection of overall softball athleticism and is the best way to assess and rank players.

TABLE 18.1 Louisville Softball Testing Battery by Category

Power	Strength	Speed	Conditioning
Vertical jump	Power clean (1RM)	10/20 yards (turf)	1/2 mile repeats (2)*
Long jump	Back squat (1RM)	Home-1st (field)	
4-jump elasticity	Close-grip bench (1RM)	Home- 2nd (field)	
	Pull-ups (max reps)	Home-home (field)	
August/November/ February			

*August only

TABLE 18.2 Louisville Softball Performance Index

Points awarded	Long jump (in.)	Vertical jump (in.)	4 jump (% VJ)	Power clean (% BW)	Back squat (% BW)	Bench press (% BW)	Pull-ups (reps)	10-yd sprint (sec.)	20-yd sprint (sec.)	1/2 miles (2) average time	Points awarded
10.0	97	26.0	94	125	200	100	10	1.70	2.90	2:45	10.0
9.5	96	25.5	92	122	190	98		1.73	2.94	2:50	9.5
9.0	95	25.0	90	119	180	95	9	1.75	2.98	2:55	9.0
8.5	94	24.5	88	116	170	93		1.78	3.02	3:00	8.5
8.0	93	24.0	86	113	160	90	8	1.80	3.06	3:05	8.0
7.5	92	23.5	84	110	150	88		1.83	3.10	3:10	7.5
7.0	91	23.0	82	107	140	85	7	1.85	3.14	3:15	7.0
6.5	90	22.5	80	104	130	83		1.88	3.18	3:20	6.5
6.0	89	22.0	78	101	120	80	6	1.90	3.22	3:25	6.0
5.5	88	21.5	76	98	110	78		1.93	3.26	3:30	5.5
5.0	87	21.0	74	95	100	75	5	1.95	3.30	3:35	5.0
4.5	86	20.5	72	92	95	73		1.98	3.34	3:40	4.5
4.0	85	20.0	70	89	90	70	4	2.00	3.38	3:45	4.0
3.5	84	19.5	68	86	85	68		2.03	3.42	3:50	3.5
3.0	83	19.0	66	83	80	65	3	2.05	3.46	3:55	3.0
2.5	82	18.5	64	80	75	63		2.08	3.50	4:00	2.5
2.0	81	18.0	62	77	70	60	2	2.10	3.54	4:05	2.0
1.5	80	17.5	60	74	65	58		2.13	3.58	4:10	1.5
1.0	79	17.0	58	71	60	55	1	2.15	3.60	4:15	1.0

Performance Tracking

After the competitive season begins, we track key performance variables to ensure that athletes are maintaining essential performance qualities and are recovering appropriately. To this end, tracking becomes a weekly or biweekly event.

In any power athlete, the most important qualities to maintain during the season are lower-body power and lean mass. Both of these can decline over time unless adequate loading is taking place (in the weight room) and solid nutrition is implemented. The result of declines in these two areas is compromised speed and power on the field.

Losses in strength will eventually manifest as reduced power output, but a decline in power is not always caused by a loss of strength. For that reason, body mass and lean mass are also tracked in season. A decline in power output with no change in body mass may be a sign of (nervous system) fatigue, because the body will struggle to produce peak power levels in a fatigued state. This data should be used in conjunction with qualitative information derived from conversations with athletes—about sleep, soreness, appetite, desire to train, and commitment to regeneration methods—to differentiate cause.

Power Tracking

There are multiple ways to track power during the season. Our preference is to use a Tendo Weightlifting Analyzer for a loaded countermovement squat jump on the day after the team's day off (when their bodies should be the freshest). The analyzer measures and reports power output (in watts) immediately postjump. Each athlete is given three jumps, and the best attempt is compared to a baseline value from preseason. A team of 20 athletes can roll through this protocol in 10 minutes using one Tendo or 5 minutes using two.

A second option for power tracking is a countermovement vertical jump test on a Just Jump mat (much faster than using a Vertec). Likewise, three jumps are given to each athlete, and the best jump is compared with a baseline value. The key on either test is ensuring that a max effort or best effort is given (after a solid warm-up, of course).

Another option for tracking (nervous system) fatigue that we have started to play around with is a reaction time test, such as a five-second react drill on a *Quickboard*, because reaction time is one of the qualities most sensitive to (nervous system) fatigue. For this test the player stands in the center of a *Quickboard*, a large board with five yellow dots placed in a grid on a black background, and reacts to lights on the display by moving her closer foot to the appropriate yellow dot. In the course of five seconds, she aims to get as many foot touches as possible. Performance is scored against a baseline performance from preseason.

Lean Mass Tracking

We weigh our athletes weekly, on the same day that we do our power tracking, which is typically the day after our NCAA day off. In addition, we do body composition assessments every three or four weeks during the in-season phase. We look at this information in conjunction with our power data. When losses equal to or greater than 1 to 2 percent of baseline body weight are seen over two consecutive weeks, we intervene to determine cause. We might talk with the athlete about how she is feeling, sleeping, and eating, and we may adjust workouts, typically by reducing volume and increasing recovery work.

Our tracking data are critically important for in-season success. They not only guide decisions about nutrition, supplementation, and recovery but also allow appropriate individual training adjustments to be made.

We know that the following qualities cannot be improved in a state of fatigue: (1) absolute speed, (2) refinement of new skills, (3) speed–strength, and (4) max strength. Without tracking data, we are left to guess about readiness to train these items. Our tracking data allow us to adjust not only the types of exercises and activities but also total training volume (to allow fatigue to subside and fitness to rebound).

The consequences of continuing to push athletes who are fatigued include injury, suppressed immune function, reduced desire to train, weight loss, and reduced performance potential. At Louisville we use the following guidelines and pay particular attention when jump performance and body mass are depressed for consecutive weeks.

Training Guidelines Based on Tracking Data

Greater than 90 percent of baseline (low fatigue)—train strength and power

80 to 90 percent of baseline (moderate fatigue)—train strength

Less than 80 percent of baseline (high fatigue)—prehab work and light aerobic conditioning (regeneration emphasis)

INNING 3: SOFTBALL NEEDS ANALYSIS

Before designing and implementing a training program, we analyze the game, from biomechanics to psychology, to gain full understanding of how to build the bulletproof player.

Elite Player Profile

For me, it always starts with trying to create a physical profile of the elite player. What do the best of the best look like? What should they look like? Players of all shapes and sizes can play the game, but what does a great slapper–outfielder look like? How strong is strong enough for a great catcher? How fit is fit enough for a power pitcher? This information can sometimes be hard to find in the literature (and that is definitely the case for softball), but we work hard to build the most accurate profile possible and use it to create training standards and set training goals.

Needs Analysis

Next, we study the physical demands of the game, offensively and defensively, and by position when necessary. We analyze the types of movements performed, planes of movement, speed of movement, and mechanical stresses created by those movements. I often use the force-velocity curve (shown in figure 18.2) to discover exactly where various movements and skills fall and then make training decisions accordingly. This curve helps answer the questions posed earlier: How strong is strong enough? How fit is fit enough?

If we look at specific movements in the game—throwing speed (arm internal rotation velocities over 4,000 feet [1,200 m] per second) and bat speed (80–90 miles [130–145 km] per hour), in particular—we find that most fall on the lower right quadrant of the graph. They are under speed and under speed–strength. As a result, these areas are performance priorities, especially as we get closer to the start of the season. But when injury prevention or durability is concerned, strength is essential to decelerate the arm and the body from those incredibly high-velocity movements. Strength also plays a key role as a foundational component of power (power equals strength times speed) and must be prioritized, especially during the off-season.

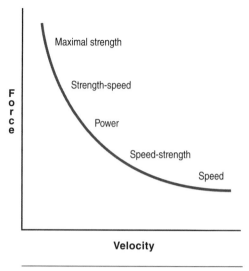

FIGURE 18.2 Force-velocity curve.

Offensively, we know that the top performance priorities (see table 18.3) include bat speed (rotary power) and starting speed. Defensively, multidirectional speed and quickness (which includes reaction time), throwing velocity, and stamina prevail. On the mound, pitchers need exceptional lower-body power and power–endurance. Creating training plans to develop and peak these qualities is our goal.

TABLE 18.3 Performance Priorities

Offensive priorities	Defensive priorities	Pitcher priorities
Rotary power (bat velocity)	Multidirectional speed	Lower-body power
Starting speed	Throwing velocity	Throwing velocity
		Power endurance

Conditioning Needs

What about conditioning needs for a softball player? How fit is fit enough? This topic has been controversial for years. If you look at figure 18.3, you can see that the predominant energy system for baseball (the closest option available) is ATP–PC (or anaerobic–alactic), which predominates during high-intensity activities of less than six seconds. This makes sense because most actions in softball are explosive and last less than three seconds. But if we base our conditioning programming on this information alone, we will miss the boat!

Sport/Activity	ATP-PC	Glycolysis	Aerobic	
Baseball	80	15	5	
Basketball	80	10	10	
Field hockey	60	20	20	
Football	90	10	0	
Golf	100	0	0	
Gymnastics	90	10	0	
Ice hockey	80	20	0	
Rowing	20	30	50	
Soccer	60	20	20	
Diving	98	2	0	
Swim (50 m)	95	5	0	
Swim (100 m)	80	20	0	
Swim (200 m)	30	65	5	
Swim (400 m)	20	40	40	
Swim (1.5 km)	10	20	70	
Tennis	70	20	10	
Field events	90	10	0	
Run (400 m)	40	55	5	
Run (800 m)	10	60	30	
Run (1.5 km)	5	35	60	
Run (5 km)	2	28	70	
Marathon	0	2	98	
Volleyball	90	10	0	
Wrestling	45	55	0	

FIGURE 18.3 Percent ATP contribution by energy systems.

Reprinted, by permission, from N.A. Ratamess, 2008, Adaptations to anaerobic training programs. In *Essentials of strength training and conditioning,* 3rd ed., by National Strength and Conditioning Association, edited by T.R. Baechle and R.W. Earle (Champaign, IL: Human Kinetics), 95.

In addition to the intensity and duration of actions on the field, an equally important aspect to look at (where conditioning status and standards are concerned) is the duration of games, volume of actions during those games, frequency of games, and conditions under which games are played. For example, how many pitches will be thrown in a game? In a weekend series? What is the temperature? Humidity? How many hours will be spent at the field, including warming up and waiting around between games? All these factors affect mental and physical fatigue and are influenced by aerobic fitness. Likewise, executing highly technical movements over time and under stress relies heavily on an athletes' aerobic conditioning status. To this end, we overemphasize aerobic conditioning, especially for our pitchers and catchers. For them, we use a $\dot{V}O_2$max of 48 to 50 milliliters per kilogram per minute as a general standard for aerobic capacity. And the rest of the team shouldn't be far behind.

At Louisville we use a simple aerobic field test to determine conditioning status. The pass–fail test involves running two half miles (805 m) with three minutes of rest after the first one. The goal time is less than 3:30 on both. We also do a 5-mile (8 km) bike test consistently throughout the year to monitor changes in fitness with training. Our pitchers always do two or three extra conditioning workouts per week, emphasizing aerobic capacity and power–endurance. These workouts include high-resistance bike rides, resisted incline (hill) strides, and lots of sled work (pushing, pulling, and dragging).

Softball Injuries

An understanding of injury trends, sites, and mechanisms in the sport (by position if possible) is the next step in a comprehensive needs analysis. Fortunately, recent research contains significant softball injury data.

First, we now know that softball injury rates are higher than those in baseball (Powell and Barber-Foss 2000). We know that more injuries occur during games than in practices; the game injury rate is 4.3 per 1,000 athlete exposures. And we know that half of those injuries occur from noncontact mechanisms, primarily overuse. The shoulder, ankle, and hip are the most common sites of injury.

A 16-year study of college softball injuries conducted by the NCAA between 1988 and 2004 provides the clearest representation of injury trends across all divisions (Marshall, Hamstra-Wright, Dick, Grove, and Agel 2007). Their data suggest the following:

1. Preseason practice injury rates are double regular-season injury rates.

2. In-season practice and game injury rates are higher than postseason rates.

3. Practice injuries were more associated with noncontact mechanisms (55 percent), whereas game injuries were more associated with contact mechanisms (51 percent).

4. Severe injuries, which accounted for 10 or more days missed, accounted for 22 percent of the total. Knee and ankle injuries represented the greatest percentage (30 percent).

Pitching Injuries

On the pitching front, we now know for sure that the softball pitching motion is not more natural than the baseball pitching motion and is not less stressful to the arm. In fact, research has shown that forces on the shoulder joint are equal to or greater than the forces related to the overhead pitch. Specifically, shoulder distraction stress near ball release was calculated at 94 percent of body weight in a study of 53 youth softball pitchers (Werner, Jones, Guido, and Brunet 2006), increasing risk for posterior cuff injury. This stress, combined with high magnitudes of elbow extension torque at ball release, also increases risk to the biceps labrum complex. Where the lower body is concerned, significant ground reaction and braking forces are experienced by the stride leg, peaking quickly after contact in the range of 115 percent of body weight. When we combine these mechanical stresses with higher throwing volumes and less recovery time between appearances (compared with baseball), the exceptionally high injury rates (72 percent) and rates of overuse injury (53 percent) are no surprise (Hill et al. 2004).

Developing a structured action plan to prepare pitchers for the physical stresses of the position is essential for durability. This plan includes assessing and correcting range-of-motion differences between the throwing arm and the nonthrowing arm (see the section on screening). Likewise, working with sport coaches to monitor weekly pitch count and implementing a consistent recovery plan is paramount for limiting unnecessary overuse injuries.

To summarize, based on our softball needs analysis, our training goals are the following:

◆ Increase total body strength
◆ Increase lean mass
◆ Increase power output
◆ Increase starting speed (multidirectional)
◆ Develop a moderate level of aerobic capacity

INNING 4: ATHLETE DEVELOPMENT

The obvious goal of all training is to maximize performance potential, which is a combination of physical preparation, technical (or skill) preparation, and tactical preparation. Where physical preparation is concerned, we are focused on building the best athlete for the game.

I think we can all agree that a better athlete makes a better softball player. We can also agree that a better athlete is typically a more durable softball player. So, what makes a great athlete? What are the qualities that separate good from great? And how should they be developed to maximize performance success?

At its core, athleticism is movement. Specifically, it's the ability to coordinate movement with

1. high levels of force,
2. high levels of speed,
3. high levels of accuracy, and
4. combinations of all the preceding.

Building bulletproof athletes, therefore, requires focused training on various aspects of movement following a systematic progression toward the qualities most important for sport success. At Louisville our progression begins with mastering fundamental movements with body weight and light loads and progresses toward developing explosive sport-specific movements (our athlete development model is shown in figure 18.4). Note that even as we move forward from one block of training to the next, we never leave behind the cornerstones of our foundation. Rather, we continue to reinforce those elements as we build on them.

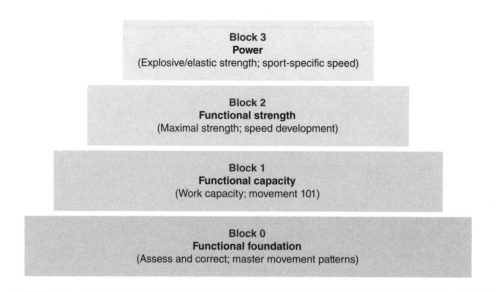

FIGURE 18.4 Athlete development model.

Block 0

Our training system begins with block 0, when we assess, correct, and then build the movement foundation for everything else we do. We know that movement (quality) is limited by two things—lack of mobility (or range of motion) at segments of the body where it is needed and lack of stability (or motor control) at segments where it is needed. If an athlete lacks the mobility or stability to do the things that she needs to do (like throw or run), her body will compensate for that deficiency by finding what it needs elsewhere (usually at a joint above or below), often causing a problem at that site. For that reason, the site of pain is almost never the site of the problem. A great example is knee pain, which is typically the result of a lack of ankle mobility or hip mobility. Likewise, shoulder pain is often the result of limited thoracic spine mobility. This is the main reason that we do the Functional Movement Screen (discussed in "Inning 2: High-Performance Athlete Assessment") with every athlete and prescribe individualized corrective work as needed based on results. It's also the reason that we spend a lot of time on joint-by-joint prehab work (shown in table 18.4) to develop and maintain mobility and stability where it's needed. Developing appropriate mobility and stability is our primary focus during block 0 and becomes the basis of our daily preworkout and prepractice warm-ups thereafter.

The fundamental movement patterns we strive to perfect in block 0 include (1) squat, (2) lunge, (3) step-up, (4) hip hinge (Romanian deadlift), and (5) push-up, as well as multiplane variations of them. We teach and reinforce those movements with an isometric and slow eccentric emphasis during this phase. We want our athletes to be able to get into these positions, stabilize (and hold) them, and get out of them safely and effectively with body weight and light external loads (vest, medicine balls, and light kettlebells and dumbbells).

TABLE 18.4 Joint Needs

Joint	Needs
Ankle	Mobility
Knee	Stability
Hip	Mobility
Lumbar spine	Stability
Thoracic spine	Mobility
Scapula	Stability
Gleno-humeral	Mobility

Movement, Gray Cook, On Target Publications, 2010, pg. 319

Block 1

After solid movement patterns have been established and any deficiencies or asymmetries have been corrected, the next step is building work capacity. The role of a sport performance program is not just to improve strength or conditioning but also to increase an athlete's potential to produce energy. This increased capacity to produce energy provides the foundation for athletes to perform skills with greater force and velocity over time.

Capacity is developed simply by gradually increasing volume. We are still building our workouts around multijoint and multiplane movements with body weight and light loads, but we are increasing the density of training by doing more work per unit of time. We accomplish this by using complexes and circuits during which athletes perform exercises continuously with limited rest. Manipulating time under tension is another tactic used to increase work. For example, a repetition of a body weight squat might involve a 5-second eccentric hold and a 10-second isometric hold (at the bottom) before an explosive concentric action, making this a 15-second repetition for one squat! We might follow 5 of these with 10 squat jumps and a 30-second bike sprint for 2 minutes of continuous work.

In block 1 we also introduce the first phase of our speed development system, Movement 101, which focuses on teaching basic linear and lateral movement mechanics (see table 18.5). I'm always amazed at how many incoming freshmen

TABLE 18.5 Sample Block 1 Week of Training

Monday	Tuesday	Wednesday	Thursday	Friday	Saturday	Sunday
Prehab	Prehab	REGEN	Prehab	Prehab	Extra needs	REGEN
Linear speed			Lateral speed			
Work capacity	Work capacity		Work capacity	Competition		
ESD	ESD		ESD			

do not know how to run! Literally. They just run however their bodies felt best as they were growing up. During this phase we teach basic body positioning, leg action, and arm action. We also spend considerable time teaching stopping and landing mechanics, because most injuries occur at that time. We always focus on stopping and landing before we worry about starting and jumping.

Finally, we also do nonspecific conditioning (energy systems development) during this phase to develop each athlete's aerobic capacity. Softball may be an anaerobic power game, but the ability to sustain high power output for extended periods relies on energy being regenerated through aerobic processes. We believe in building a solid foundation of aerobic fitness before shifting toward more anaerobic, softball-specific conditioning.

Block 2

By the time we get to block 2, when our emphasis shifts to maximum strength and speed development, our athletes have already gotten stronger. They've typically been working hard for a minimum of 6 to 12 weeks. During this time they've established a solid foundation of movement quality and work capacity, and they've typically added a few pounds of lean mass. They are ready to start pushing heavier loads!

Block 2 is characterized by two or three days per week of heavier loading with a maximum strength emphasis. Within these workouts we place a secondary emphasis on speed–strength (or power). Because our training is based on a conjugated method of periodization, we always are attempting to develop two main qualities. In block 2 those qualities are maximum strength and speed–strength. A fourth day of lifting (typically the last day of the week) has a work capacity and competition emphasis.

Our speed training during this time focuses on starting speed (0 to 10 yards). We dedicate 30 minutes one day per week to linear speed and a second day to lateral speed. Within these workouts we increase plyometric volume and shift toward an emphasis on power output with our plyometric exercises.

Finally, our conditioning (ESD) during this time also shifts toward an anaerobic capacity emphasis, which is limited to two days per week at the end of our workouts. We keep our conditioning volume relatively low during this time (except for our pitchers and any players who need to improve body composition) because our priorities are strength and speed. A sample overview of a block 2 week of training is shown in table 18.6.

TABLE 18.6 Sample Block 2 Week of Training

Monday	Tuesday	Wednesday	Thursday	Friday	Saturday	Sunday
CNS activation	Mobility	REGEN	CNS activation	Mobility	Extra needs	REGEN
Linear speed/plyos	Max strength		Lateral speed/plyos	Work capacity		
Max strength	ESD		Max strength	ESD		

Block 3

In block 3 we shift toward more softball-specific work in all areas—lifting, movement training, and conditioning. Most notably, we change our training schedule to include five consecutive days. Two days are dedicated movement and conditioning days, and only three days are spent in the weight room.

Goals during this phase are speed and power, which means that explosive and elastic exercises predominate—plyometrics, medicine ball throws, and dynamic strength movements. Speed and quickness training is mostly game and position specific with a reactive emphasis, and our conditioning (ESD) priority is anaerobic power. An overview of a block 3 week of training is shown in table 18.7, and more detail on this phase is provided in "Inning 5: Softball Specific."

TABLE 18.7 Sample Block 3 Week of Training

Monday	Tuesday	Wednesday	Thursday	Friday	Saturday	Sunday
Prehab	Activation	Prehab	Activation	Prehab	Extra needs	REGEN
Speed-strength	Linear speed/plyos	Speed-strength	Lateral speed/plyos	Max strength		
	ESD		ESD			

This is probably the most appropriate place for a quick comment on specificity. Coaches often think that simulating sport-specific movements in training is essential for improving performance on the field. Not true. Although specificity has a place in training, increasing overall athletic capacity, with an emphasis on the biomotor qualities that relate to the game, must come first. This point is especially relevant to high school and college females, who may have played the game for years but have a low training age and limited physical development. Here again individualization is essential. Our older players, juniors and seniors, and those who have achieved higher levels of relative strength progress to more advanced and specific training (characteristic of block 3) sooner. Younger players continue to focus on increasing relative strength and improving movement skills.

INNING 5: SOFTBALL SPECIFIC

All softball programming begins with a heavy emphasis on the areas most prone to injury in the game—the shoulder and the hip and low-back area. Our top program design considerations or strategies for developing the bulletproof player are listed next.

Shoulder

Where the shoulder is concerned, we correct asymmetries or imbalances identified during screening first. These issues are often easy to identify in the throwing athlete (even without screening) because they present as poor posture, specifically rounded shoulders or excessive internal rotation. This poor posture affects the position of the scapulae and ultimately the stresses that are placed on the shoulder during the throwing motion. In training, excessive pressing (bench press, incline press) reinforces this poor posture and further increases injury risk.

We know that overhead or throwing athletes have a tendency toward tightness and dominance in the anterior muscles (pectorals, anterior deltoids) and a tendency toward overstretching and weakness in the posterior muscles of the shoulders and upper back. Moreover, many of the muscles important for decelerating the arm and stabilizing the shoulder joint are neglected by the traditional pushing and pulling movements commonly done in training. To address this issue and create stability in a joint that is designed for incredible mobility, we focus on activating the underactive stabilizers (rotator cuff); strengthening the long, weak upper-back musculature; and lengthening the overactive and tight prime movers (pectorals) in the front of the body.

We do this simply through exercise selection. The goal is to choose exercises that minimize risk while maximizing reward. First, let's talk about exercises that we avoid. The list includes shrugs, upright rows, flies, front and lateral raises, and, during the season, bench presses. Bench pressing is done only after our fall season ends and before our spring practices begin, so it never coincides with periods of heavy throwing. In addition, our athletes rarely do it with a traditional grip (close-grip emphasis), and they do it a maximum of once per week, ever. Our favorite pressing exercise is push-ups, and we love push-up variations. The push-up is valuable because it is a closed-chain exercise that recruits and strengthens the stabilizers in the shoulder. We often start athletes on an incline until they develop perfect technique (no scapula winging or shoulder abduction). Overall, pressing always takes a backseat to pulling in our upper-body training. We typically do twice as much pulling (vertical and horizontal variations) as pushing in our programs, and we have found this approach to work well, especially with our female athletes. In our chin-up variations, we have the athletes emphasize scapula depression (pulling the scapulae down) at the top of each rep. Inverted row variations and single-arm dumbbell row variations are big exercises for us. Finally, we spend time daily on thoracic spine mobility (extension and rotation) and stretching the pectorals and anterior deltoids.

Hips, Low Back, and Core

The second area prone to injury and critical for performance is the hips and low back. What we often see in this region is a lack of hip mobility (internal rotation deficit) and a lack of core stability and pelvic control. These issues lead to compensation patterns that affect every joint above and below the hip. Remember that the site of pain is rarely the site of the problem!

We know that most athletes need a stronger posterior chain—erector spinae (low back), gluteal muscles, and hamstrings—and better core stability. Most rotary athletes (like softball players) also lack hip mobility (internal rotation in particular). This is where we begin. After athletes establish mobility, we reinforce this new motion with stability and control exercises. Athletes do these mobility and stability exercises at the beginning of every workout and practice. Examples of stability or gluteal activation exercises include resisted miniband walks, band-resisted abduction and external rotation exercises, and hip extension exercises in a variety of starting positions.

Within our lifts we put a premium on lower-body pulling movements, on two legs and one. We emphasize deadlift variations, using the trap bar deadlift as a measuring stick. Our goal is to get all players to the point where they can pull 150 to 200 percent of their body weight. We do most pulling exercises with shoes off to train the stabilizers in the feet and promote greater muscle recruitment.

Where core stability is concerned, it is all about progressing toward functional (dynamic) stability. We begin with isometric or static stabilization exercises, like bridging, and progress toward more functional (standing) variations of dynamic stabilization. Most people fail to realize that the core is designed to stabilize the pelvis and spine. That's it! Sit-ups, crunches, and many of the traditional floor-based exercises that just keep hanging around do nothing to improve core stability and actually reinforce poor posture and tight hip flexors.

Our core training programs focus on antirotation, antiextension, and anti-lateral-flexion, We want the spine and pelvis to stay in a neutral position while the arms and legs perform a variety of pushing, pulling, chopping and lifting, and carrying movements.

Rotational (Hip) Power

Rotational movements are a huge part of softball, so preparing the body to generate rotational power is a programming priority for our softball athletes. Because rotation is a chain reaction in which energy is transferred sequentially from the feet to the head, incredible core stabilization is a prerequisite. Lack of core stabilization strength results in energy leaks and compromised power output.

Teaching rotation begins by emphasizing core stability, gluteal strength, and the use of the hips (not the lumbar spine) during rotation. We accomplish this by having our athletes use bands, medicine balls, and cables, progressing from slower and more controlled hip rotation exercises to more explosive and elastic (high-speed) variations.

Grip Strength

Research does not show a connection between grip strength and bat velocity, but that does not mean that grip strength is irrelevant or unimportant! We are currently training grip strength more than ever because it is often the weakest link in the kinetic chain of our female athletes. And what good comes from a strong body that can't express that strength through the hands? We also know that the hands are loaded with nerve endings. Stimulating those nerve endings leads to greater recruitment of muscle fibers and stronger muscle contractions. So, a stronger grip means a stronger woman!

From an injury prevention standpoint, we also know that when we challenge the hands and the grip, we get greater recruitment of stabilizers in the shoulder joint. Talk about great bang for your buck!

To develop grip strength, we do things like towel hangs and towel chin-ups. We put Fat Gripz (www.fatgripz.com) on dumbbells and bars to force a wider grip and greater activation of hand and forearm musculature.

Olympic Lifts

When training power athletes like softball players, the Olympic lifts seem like a no-brainer. After all, they are among the most athletic and most explosive exercises we know, and when they are performed properly they are one of the best ways to improve rate of force production (power). For this reason, the three Olympic lifts—clean, snatch, and jerk—have long been cornerstones of most collegiate strength and conditioning programs. But they aren't for everyone, and they aren't always the best choice for softball athletes, especially softball pitchers.

Olympic lifts are highly technical exercises that place significant stress on the shoulders, elbows, and wrists. We have already discussed the excessive stress placed on pitchers' shoulders and elbows during the windmill motion. Adding to this stress is probably not a low-risk, high-reward strategy. As a result, our pitchers do not do Olympic lifts. They do rack pulls in the off-season to develop lower-body power, but that's as close as they get. Instead, we do more plyometrics, medicine ball throws, kettlebell swings, and sled push, pull, and drag variations.

Field players do one-arm dumbbell snatches—a great exercise for developing unilateral shoulder stability and trunk stability—and most players progress to doing power cleans (from a hang position) during the off-season (depending on movement quality assessed by the FMS). We use them during our maximum strength development phase from mid-September through January but take them completely out of our program during preseason, when throwing volume increases.

Pitcher Considerations

As previously mentioned, exercise selection is critical for performance and prevention, especially with pitchers and especially as we get closer to the start of the season. We want our pitchers strong, so we push strength development with them just as we do the rest of our team. But we limit excess stress to the shoulder, elbow, and wrist, and they do not do Olympic lifts. Likewise, we take bench pressing and pull-ups out of their program during preseason. Instead, we spend more time on mobility (thoracic spine and hips), horizontal pulling, core stability, and lower-body strength work. In addition, we spend more time on conditioning.

INNING 6: IN-SEASON TRAINING

In-season training (in the weight room) is all about complementing what's happening on the field. The force-velocity curve discussed earlier tells us that players spend most of their time on the field at the absolute speed end (or far right end) of the continuum. Hitting, sprinting, fielding, and throwing are all high-velocity movements. So, during the season more high-velocity movements are not needed in the weight room. Rather, the weight room emphasis should shift back toward more of a maximum strength and strength–speed emphasis.

Because on-field activities are repetitive and are all done with light loads, typically body weight only, we do the opposite. We keep training volume low and use higher loads to stimulate higher threshold motor unit activation to maintain strength levels.

In season, less is more, and quality definitely takes precedence over quantity. At Louisville we reduce our workouts to two or three lifts per week, and rarely do they last longer than 40 minutes (after warm-up). Extra time in the weight room beyond that is for soft-tissue work and extra mobility only. With regard to exercise selection, we eliminate Olympic lifts and bench pressing at the beginning of the in-season phase. Likewise, we back off on exercises (prehab and strength) that stress the shoulder joint. Players are typically getting their fair share of work, and more volume only increases the risk of overuse injury.

Finally, the bottom line with in-season training is consistency. We make every effort not to skip workouts (even during periods of significant travel and weeks with midweek games) to minimize detraining and associated muscle soreness that occurs when training resumes. In addition, we make sure that we are tracking lean mass and power weekly to stay on top of any changes with our athletes. Ultimately, we want to prepare for a physical peak at the end of the season when the most important games are being played.

INNING 7: THE 24-HOUR ATHLETE

In the world of sport performance the crucial question is this: What's the fastest possible way to gain muscle mass, strength, stamina, and power? Well, making rapid progress is a function of two interrelated variables: (1) training stress and (2) rate of adaptation and regeneration. You can typically accelerate progress either by improving training or by improving the body's capacity to recover from training.

In North America we often make the mistake of focusing our attention on training and the methods for manipulating volume, intensity, and load. We devote limited time and attention to recovery. In other parts of the world athletes and coaches prioritize regular regeneration sessions in their planning. Russian coaches take three semesters on massage and regeneration in their physical education coursework! Guess how much we take here? Right, zero!

I tell my athletes all the time that to maximize the benefits of training, they must be 24-hour athletes! What I mean is that they must commit to doing the right things away from the weight room and the softball field during the other 20 to 22 hours of the day, everything from soft-tissue restoration to nutrient timing, sleep, and mental and emotional recovery. Creating structure around those items and designating appropriate times to do them can be the difference between being good and being great. I tell our players that we create a performance edge by taking better care of our bodies, day after day.

Regeneration

Training and competition both place significant physical stress on the body. The product of this stress is muscle shortening and stiffening, accumulation of waste products (in muscle tissue), and localized inflammation. All of these promote muscle soreness, challenge the immune system, and delay recovery. Regeneration is the timely application of specific techniques to minimize or counteract these processes, on both a local (muscle) and systemic level. These techniques are most commonly applied within the first 30 to 60 minutes postexercise, but they can also be used as part of an active recovery session between workouts or games. (Research has shown that active recovery is much more effective than passive recovery.)

Soft Tissue

At Louisville our regeneration protocol begins with addressing soft tissue (muscle and connective tissue) by self-massage with foam rollers (one of our most valuable pieces of equipment). We roll from head to toe, hitting every major muscle group, but spend particular time on the areas hit hardest during training. Self-massage lengthens muscles by releasing tension accumulated in the fascia (layer of connective tissue surrounding muscle). Self-massage also increases blood flow, helping with the removal of waste products from muscle.

Step 2 in our recovery protocol is stretching, but not static stretching. We go through either a dynamic stretching series (just as in preworkout) or a series of active isolated stretches. (We know that static stretching does little to assist with recovery.) Our goal is to move the body through large ranges of motion to reestablish mobility and movement patterns after continuous repetitive muscle actions and significant mechanical loading. Active isolated stretching involves activating the antagonist (opposing muscle) before stretching a particular muscle and then holding the stretch for a series of 5 to 10 reps of only two seconds. An example would be turning on the gluteal muscles in a half-kneeling or lunge stance before stretching the hip flexors.

After rolling and stretching we hit the cold tub. Cold-water immersion has long been known as a great way to reduce inflammation, thereby reducing soreness and accelerating recovery. Even though it's not always popular and definitely takes time to get used to, this is one of the most valuable regeneration tools. The water should be 50 to 55 degree Fahrenheit (10 to 13 degrees Celsius), and athletes should submerge their bodies as deeply as possible (ideally chest deep) for 8 to 12 minutes for best results.

Yoga is another tool that we use for recovery. It serves as both a physical and mental recovery tool and has become a favorite of our players. During the off-season we do a private team yoga session on Wednesday mornings for midweek active recovery.

Nutrition

Eating to optimize health and performance is always a top priority, but where recovery is concerned nutrient timing and density is critical. We educate our athletes and provide supplementation based on the R4 system outlined here:

- ◆ Rehydrate
- ◆ Replenish
- ◆ Repair
- ◆ Reduce

Rehydrate   To monitor fluid losses during exercise, we weigh in before and weigh out after practices. For each pound lost, 24 ounces of fluid (water or sports drink) is consumed as soon as possible (for each kilogram lost, 1.5 liters of fluid is consumed). We also encourage our athletes to monitor hydration status by monitoring urine color and output. We post urine charts on the back of bathroom stall doors in locker rooms to make sure that they know what to look for.

Replenish   We know that the first 30 minutes after exercise is a critical time for muscle recovery. During this window of opportunity the body is efficient at replenishing muscle glycogen, the body's preferred source of energy during exercise. Consuming fast-absorbing sugars (with a small amount of protein) during this window accelerates glycogen repletion and ultimately recovery. At Louisville we provide a recovery shake that has a 3:1 carbohydrate to protein ratio and fresh fruit and bagels for our athletes immediately after their workout.

Repair   Besides replenishing the body's fuel supply, postexercise carbohydrate and protein consumption changes the hormonal environment in the body from catabolic (muscle breakdown) back to anabolic (muscle building). The rapid consumption of carbohydrate and protein (not fat) postworkout allows the body to begin repairing and rebuilding immediately. In addition, we know that protein enhances carbohydrate uptake, assists with glycogen repletion, and plays a role in keeping the immune system strong in the face of exercise stress.

Reduce   Finally, reducing the effects of oxidative damage (inflammation) is essential for recovery. Unstable molecules (free radicals) produced during the metabolism of oxygen promote cell damage and inflammation within the body, leading to muscle soreness and delayed recovery. Because exercise greatly increases oxygen consumption, it also increases the production of these unstable molecules. Antioxidants are known quenchers of free radicals, so ingesting antioxidants postexercise is a valuable strategy. The most effective antioxidants are vitamins C and E and a variety of other phytonutrients found in fruits, vegetables, nuts, and seeds. Omega-3s found in fish oil are also effective antioxidants known to have anti-inflammatory properties. We provide fresh fruit postworkout and encourage our athletes to eat lots of fresh fruits and vegetables in addition to supplementing with fish oil.

Sleep

On the topic of regeneration, I'm convinced that the most underrated factor in promoting recovery is sleep! Physically, not getting enough sleep affects reaction time, absolute speed, fine motor skills and coordination, and stamina. More important, it affects mood, attitude, and desire to train. We know that most high school and collegiate athletes do not get enough sleep.

Where sleep is concerned, the first priority is getting enough, ideally a minimum of seven to eight hours per night. Next, developing a sleeping plan (just like an eating plan) is key. To set the circadian rhythm around the sun, going to sleep and waking up at approximately the same time each day based on when the sun rises and sets should be the goal. Most athletes go to bed far too late, wreaking havoc on many key hormones. It's been said a thousand times that every hour before midnight is like two hours afterward, so all attempts to front-load sleep are encouraged.

And what about napping? Power naps are great, but they should never extend beyond an hour. Longer naps shift the body into REM sleep and may affect sleep at night. We tell our athletes that if they feel groggy after midday or pregame naps, they should soak their feet in cold water right away. The feet are loaded with nerve endings, so the cold water perks people up in no time.

FINAL THOUGHTS

Every day we gain new insight into the complexities of the human body. As performance specialists we work endlessly to evaluate, adjust, and implement new techniques, tools, and strategies to help our athletes gain a competitive edge. Yet, at the end of the day, the effectiveness of any program rests with the athletes' motivation and willingness to do the things they need to do consistently. Although committing to a process can be challenging for young athletes who want immediate results, there are no shortcuts to becoming bulletproof. A well-organized program, well executed, is often the difference between being good and being great, between being healthy and being injured. Athletes need to stay the course, to appreciate the process, and to trust the wisdom of the body. Then, as with the stonecutter, momentous events will be sure to happen!

PART FIVE

PLAYER MOTIVATION AND LEADERSHIP

19

Establishing a Positive Player–Coach Relationship

Donna Papa

People don't care how much you know, until they know how much you care.

John Maxwell

Coaching is about building relationships. Genuinely caring about your players as people first will go a long way in building those relationships. At the end of your players' careers, the interest that you took in their day-to-day lives off the field will mean more to them than the great play they may have made on the field. During their collegiate years, they are growing and changing as people. They will have obstacles to overcome on a daily basis while they are away from home for the first time. They may receive their first poor grade or feel like a little fish in a big pond. One way to build positive relationships is to do something as simple as sending a handwritten note or a text to acknowledge something that a player has done well. I make it a point to congratulate my players with notes regarding their academic achievements or their progress in a skill that they have been working on. Recognizing birthdays, doing community service together, going to lunch with them, or even dressing up for Halloween shows your players that you care about them and their lives while having some fun along the way.

For their book *The Seven Secrets of Successful Coaches*, Jeff Janssen and Greg Dale (2002) interviewed a number of successful coaches. Many of the coaches interviewed for chapter 1, titled "What It Takes to Be a Successful Coach," recognized that the Xs and Os of coaching are important, but they insisted that their success depended more on their ability to relate to and motivate their athletes. The authors also talk about the definition of success as a coach. They believe that you will not be judged solely on the number of wins you have but on the quality of relationships that you develop with your athletes.

In the same chapter, the authors discuss interviews they had with athletes about successful coaches. In these interviews, the athletes confirm that successful coaches do more than win games; they also win their athletes' respect. Many athletes were eager to share the profound effect their coaches had had in their lives as athletes and people. Here are a couple of their statements:

"Coach brought out the best in me."

"I have the utmost respect for Coach."

Still talking about success, Janssen and Dale indicate that the primary reason successful coaches win is that they have earned their athletes' trust.

Another chapter in the book is titled "Credible Coaches Are Caring." In this chapter the authors talk about people who make the biggest difference in our lives. They are not necessarily the ones with the best credibility, the most money, or the greatest success. The people who have the biggest influence are the ones who truly care about their players.

In the introduction to the book *The Carolina Way* (Smith and Bell 2004), University of North Carolina basketball coach Roy Williams talks about former Carolina coach Dean Smith, referring to him as a servant to his players. Williams states that Smith cares deeply for his players and that his devotion to them continues to this day. Phil Ford, a former great player and assistant at North Carolina, was quoted in the book, stating, "I knew when I signed with North Carolina that I was getting a great coach for four years, but in addition, I got a friend for a lifetime." According to Coach Williams, that pretty much sums up the relationship Coach Smith had with his players.

THE SEVEN Cs OF CREDIBLE COACHES

Janssen and Dale's list of the seven Cs of credible coaches includes the following: character, competence, commitment, caring, confidence, communication, and consistency. I believe that these characteristics, besides describing a credible coach, are important in building relationships with players. I think that each of these characteristics can be expanded on to give better insight into what it means to be a credible coach.

Character

According to Janssen and Dale, character-based coaches look to do the right thing. They are guided by integrity and ethics. They conduct themselves in a professional manner and take pride in representing their teams and themselves with class. They value having people with solid character in and around their program and consider character as important as talent.

Competence

Competent coaches have a strong understanding of the fundamentals and strategies of the game. Although they are students of the game, they remain humble and are able to keep their success in perspective.

Commitment

Committed coaches have a true passion for sport and coaching, which fuels their intense drive and enthusiasm. They are usually highly competitive and enjoy winning at the highest levels.

Caring

Caring coaches care about their athletes as people. They want the best for them and look to help them in any way possible. They invest the time to get to know athletes on a personal basis, showing interest beyond the field or court.

Confidence

Confidence builders continue to help build the confidence of their athletes. They work with them on being successful in challenging situations and try to build them up as much as possible. Although they may be demanding and set high standards for their athletes, they also know how to guide them with patience as they are trying to achieve their goals.

Communication

Communicators have open, honest communication with their athletes. They look to be good listeners by trying to understand where their athletes are coming from. They need to be in tune with their athletes so that they can understand any conflicts or concerns that might be present.

Consistency

Consistent coaches develop and have a sound philosophy of coaching that stays fairly consistent over the years, although they are able to adapt and be flexible over time. They are consistent with their attitude and the mood that they bring to practice and games.

All of the preceding characteristics are discussed in detail in *The Seven Secrets of Successful Coaches*. I paraphrased some of them to give you an idea of what the authors meant by their description of various qualities of coaches. As a coach, I strive to weave all these characteristics into my coaching style as well as into my interactions with my athletes.

BONDING WITH YOUR TEAM

Getting to know your players at different levels will take some work, but the investment in time will be worthwhile. Bimonthly academic meetings are a way that I have built relationships with my players. My philosophy since I started coaching has placed academics first. I am most proud of a player when she completes her degree. We have outstanding academic resources for student-athletes at our university, including an academic center as well as academic counselors and tutors. I like to have a check and balance in our program as well. We divide our team into small groups of four to six players who are assigned to one coach. At the beginning of the semester, I give the players a blank calendar on which they can fill in all their upcoming tests, quizzes, and papers. My staff and our athletes meet every two weeks to discuss how things are going with tutoring, test taking, and so on. In the spring semester we change coaches and groups so that we get to know other players better. Many times, these meetings lead into our having an opportunity to ask them questions or find out more about them as people. The players also know that we are committed to one of the goals of our program, which is graduation with a degree.

On a recent team-bonding trip, Jeff Janssen provided a worksheet that our players used to get to know one another better. The coach also can use the worksheet to get to know the athlete better. Our coaching staff has used many of these questions with our players in fall meetings to help us get to know them better.

Involve the Families

Allowing the student-athlete's family to be part of your program is important. I am not talking about having helicopter parents. We allow our players to spend time with their families while on the road, although at times we require our players to be at team-only dinners. We have players from all over the country on our roster, and parents may have only one opportunity in a season to watch their daughter play. I believe that allowing them that time together is helpful in building relationships with both the player and the family. As long as you set your parameters in terms of curfews and other responsibilities, allowing family time will go a long way in solidifying a positive relationship with your team.

Our senior weekend is an important season-culminating family event for our program. This special recognition weekend begins with acknowledging our seniors on senior game day. We introduce parents and family members over the PA system and lead them out on to the field. Our juniors honor their teammates by presenting flowers to a specific senior. A prerecorded audio clip giving some insight into their special relationship with that senior and what they have meant to the program is played over the PA for all the fans. Seniors are presented with a framed jersey, and, of course, they receive a hug from me. Later that evening we host our senior banquet, which includes individual senior videos prepared by the families of the seniors. We started this tradition early in my career. Videos are made chronicling the life of the player through her time in our program. Seeing players as infants, toddlers, and in their first uniform is entertaining. We have many laughs and, of course, some tears. The next day we have our family picnic, at which our dads cook and our moms prepare all the side dishes and desserts. Typically, we have a group of at least 200 family members and friends. This wonderful tradition of our program has been built over time.

Show Your Human Side

In developing my relationship with our players and the team in general, I have found that I need to let my guard down. They need to see that I am human and can have fun. I have been known to dress up on Halloween or play board games with the girls when we are on team-bonding trips. I have done Zumba or other workouts with them as well. As coaches, however, we need to remember to keep that line drawn between coach and friend. We can do this if we have done the things needed to earn the players' respect.

Another way that we build relationships is investing time every week in what we call Fun Fridays. We pick a 10- to 15-minute activity that typically is not related to softball. It might be a problem-solving event or just some type of crazy relay, such as having players lie on their backs in a line and pass a banana using only their feet. Starting practice with this type of activity is just plain fun, and it draws everyone in.

USING TOOLS FOR TEAM BUILDING

As part of our team development, both coaches and players complete a DISC (dominance, influence, steadiness, conscientiousness) assessment. The DISC assessment provides an appraisal of behavioral profiles and helps us build stronger relationships with our players by giving us better understanding of their personality styles. It also gives us information that helps us communicate effectively with each person. From a coaching perspective, we use it to gain a better understanding of each player and to help players gain more respect and understanding for one another. The DISC assessment can help you become more familiar with your personal style, strengths, and limitations, and it gives you tools and strategies that you can use right away. By understanding the behavioral characteristics of each their teammates, players learn to treat others how they want to be treated. This is a valuable tool for our coaching staff because it helps us relate better to our athletes and helps our athletes better understand the coaches.

Choosing a Team Theme

Every year, we choose a book to represent a theme for our team. The premise behind this activity is that these books will help guide us through the season with messages about leadership and the importance of developing core values. Reading a particular book allows us to have a common language or theme and will help coaches and players have a good dialogue. Books we have used include *Energy Bus* by Jon Gordon (2007), which highlights accountability and having a positive outlook in all situations—an important in being a good teammate; and *Pulling Together* (2010) by John J. Murphy, which emphasizes putting team first.

Leadership Tools

We have an outstanding leadership program at our institution called the Baddour Carolina Leadership Academy, which been used by many institutions around the country. One of the by-products of this program is that it has given us a common language to communicate with our athletes about where each one is in terms of commitment. The program encourages us to converse at a deeper level that goes beyond just asking how someone is doing. We have created a Carolina Softball Leadership Council on our team. This council includes representation from each class—freshmen, sophomores, juniors, and seniors. One of the council's missions is to facilitate communication among the classes and the team with the coaching staff. This initiative allows us to address any issues and facilitates the growth of our program and the culture of our team. Allowing your players to have ownership in the program with activities such as these is another way to help build a positive player–coach relationship. When athletes know that you are invested in them and that their investment in the program is important, you tend to get more buy-in to your program.

Involve the Players

Providing players the opportunity to be a part of setting the team's foundation lets them know that you care about what they think. To continue to build player–coach relationships, I allow our seniors to help develop and revise our team rules and expectations. The whole team participates in developing our core values and team goals. The coaching staff reserves the right to have the final say in the content of the rules and expectations. I am more focused on core values and standards than on rules.

Throughout the year, we assign each coach and team of players, called TPS teams (Tar Heel Performance Series), a quotation of the week. The TPS teams are teams within our team. They are composed of freshmen, sophomores, juniors, and seniors and are identified by specific names—Bats, Heels, Rams, and Swoosh. We try to make them even in terms of having hitters, slappers, a pitcher, and so on so that they can compete for points in practice, in scrimmages, and in other activities. We also use them in hosting recruits or community service. The coach or TPS teams are responsible for finding a quotation, reading it to the group, and telling why the quotation is significant or how it applies to our team. This activity is another opportunity for players to participate in setting the team's foundation. Letting players know that you care about what they think leads to a sense of ownership in the program.

BUILDING TRUST

Building trust is important. Again, it is not about how much you know; it is more about how much you care and whether they can count on you throughout their careers. They may not always agree with your decisions about playing time and other issues, but if they can count on you to listen to them, that goes a long way. Sometimes the effect that you have on a player is not apparent to her until she graduates and has time to reflect on her experience. Seeing things is sometimes difficult when you are living it. When players have time to reflect, they appreciate what you did for them and what type of effect you had on their lives. An example of this follows. I received a card from a former player that illustrates how influential a coach can be and how important it is to have a good player–coach relationship.

> Coach, I want to thank you for all you've done and for the role you played in my life. You were not only a coach but a mother away from home. I knew you were always there for me if I ever needed anything. As a coach, you taught me valuable lessons that have shaped the person that I am today as well as helped me be effective at my job in the hospital. You taught me about teamwork, determination, trust, dedication, inspiration, and most importantly that hard work will get me anywhere and anything I want in life. I can't do my job at a high level without my team, and I know that a positive outlook attracts positive energy and opportunities. Thank you for everything and the impact you had on my life.

I saved that card and pull it out occasionally to remind me why I do what I do. It really doesn't get any better than that.

Mike Candrea, head softball coach at the University of Arizona, offers another example that highlights the importance of trust between a player and coach: "Rings don't mean that you are a champion. It's that kid 10 years from now who calls you up and says, 'You know what? You were special in my life.' That is what it is all about."

My mom passed away a few years ago from cancer. She was not a coach; she was a teacher's aide in a K–5 elementary school. One of the things that impressed me most about my mom was how much she loved her job and looked forward to being at work every day. She gave her best effort every day because that's how she lived her life. Students never got cheated with my mom. She believed that the teachers and children at her school were part of her family, and she treated them that way. They reciprocated that feeling by making her feel as if she was a part of their family. Whenever people found out who my mom was or that I was her daughter, they would say, "She's the best," "We love her," or "She makes us smile." She had the uncanny ability of making all the people she met, young and old, feel as if they were on top of the world. She was definitely a confidence builder. Some things that happened during the time when she was sick have stayed with me and were meaningful to her, my family, and me. On Shirley Papa Day at school, students in each class made a video that contained heartwarming messages for my mom. Each child in every class made cards and wrote loving messages to my mom for that day. My mom and I read every one of those together. She was amazing in that she could tell you something about each child in every class. In my mom's eulogy, which I wrote, I closed with two quotations that summed up her life and the influence that she had on me as a coach. I realized how successful she was by understanding the effect she had on so many lives, because she touched so many. I share this story because it is an example of someone who left an imprint on my life about how to treat everyone with respect and kindness while not expecting anything in return.

The first quotation was written by Maya Angelou:

> **I've learned** that people will forget what you said. People will forget what you did. But people will never forget how you made them feel.

The second one is by Ralph Waldo Emerson:

> **To laugh** often and much, to win the respect of intelligent people and the affection of children, to earn the appreciation of honest critics and endure the betrayal of false friends. To appreciate beauty, to find the best in others, to leave the world a bit better whether by a healthy child, a garden patch, or a redeemed social condition. To know even one life has breathed easier because you lived, this is to have succeeded.

Work With Individuals

As a head coach, you may work only with a certain group on a daily basis, such as the outfield. To connect with the rest of the team, you may need to meet individually with each player or have your players fill out questionnaires that give you insight into what is important for them in building positive relationships. Periodically, I go into the infield a couple of times a week to interact with that group on the field. I have taken time to go to our pitchers' workouts before a team practice to watch a workout or interact with them, even though I don't specifically coach that position. Then I may follow up that observation with a text or e-mail that acknowledges something they may have done well in the bullpen that day.

Going to lunch with a player or having small groups over for dinner, all within NCAA rules, is another effective way to build and form relationships. When one of our best hitters was experiencing a slump last year (her first ever), I invited her to meet for lunch away from the field just to talk and see what was going on other than the hitting slump to help build her confidence. Taking the time to do something like that is invaluable in continuing to develop a relationship.

Ask for Player Involvement

I thought that it would be insightful and interesting to ask my current players a few questions regarding positive player–coach relationships. The first of three questions I posed was, "What do you think is the single most important area for a coach to focus on in building a positive player–coach relationship?" My players' responses were consistent with what I have read in the literature. Among the responses that my players shared were the following:

"Being understanding."

"Believing in them."

"Respect—there is a level of respect that must be maintained throughout the entire relationship."

"Trusting that the coach sincerely believes in their ability."

"Trust—it is the backbone to positive communication and stabilizes the relationship."

"Treating players fairly."

"Open communication."

Relationships in sport can often make the difference between success and failure. A recent and compelling study on the topic was conducted and written by Penny Wurthner (Hanson n.d.). The study was funded by the Own the Podium initiative of the Canadian Olympic Committee. The research was undertaken after the 2008 Summer Olympic Games in Beijing, China. The purpose was to identify the factors contributing to successful and, in some cases, unsuccessful performance from the perspectives of both the coaches and the athletes. The study consisted of interviewing 27 Olympic and Paralympic athletes and 30 coaches. Five key themes emerged from an analysis of the interviews.

1. Athlete self-awareness
2. Strong coach–athlete relationship
3. Optimal training environment
4. Strong financial and human resources support system
5. Excellent management of the Olympic environment

Of the five critical themes, a strong coach–athlete relationship was viewed as the most crucial factor in winning an Olympic medal or producing a personal best performance.

The second question I posed to my players was, "What was something that one of your former or current coaches could have done better to help build a relationship with you?" Their responses seemed to center on having trust and open communication.

"Trust me and believe in my ability."

"More respect shown, verbally and nonverbally—then will be more receptive to change and criticism."

"Open communication with everyone on team, not focusing on just a few players."

"Communication is key and helps form a bond between the coach and player."

"How you talk to or approach a person is key. Get to know how to get the best out of them."

"Learn how each person responds to criticism and encouragement."

To be successful in any walk of life, you have to know how to build and maintain relationships, and this guidance applies to the player–coach relationship. Respect is an important ingredient of building and maintaining the relationship.

BUILDING STRONG RELATIONSHIPS

The Canadian study referenced earlier supports the responses that my players had to the previous question I posed, "What was something that one of your former or current coaches could have done better to help build a relationship with you?" The coaches in this study were already proven in the sporting arena and had exceptional technical skills. Additionally, they had strong knowledge of their sport. The determining factor in creating strong coach–athlete relationships was the importance placed on trust and communication. A number of the athletes surveyed spoke of the open-mindedness of their coaches and their willingness to listen to what each player needed and thought. The other thing that was determined was that their coaches cared for them not just as athletes but also as people. The information that my players shared with me corresponds to some of the information found in the study.

The third and last question that I posed to my team was, "What are some examples of things that coaches past or present have done that helped you build a relationship with them?" Here are some of their responses:

"I really like when we split up into small groups and go to dinner with Coach— it's more personal."

"Understanding me and how I work."

"Being friendly and approachable, but also direct and assertive."

"Showing interest in the individual."

"Telling the truth and not sugar-coating information."

"Being supportive and encouraging to help build self-confidence."

"Coach always said the right things and really built up my confidence. This helped me play my best and I saw great results."

In *The Carolina Way*, Coach Smith states that the most important thing in good leadership is truly caring. He goes on to say that the best leaders in any profession care about the people they lead and that the people being led know when the caring is genuine and when it's faked.

One of the quotations in *The Seven Secrets of Successful Coaches* comes from one of my colleagues at North Carolina, head soccer coach Anson Dorrance. He sums up relationships between players and coaches and the importance of caring about players.

> As long as you give praise and support to the athletes who are making a difference, and you are genuine about it, I think the people who follow you will always die for you. . . . Treating your people with this kind of respect and letting people know why your teams are successful is important. . . . I think that ends up winning the respect of everyone.

I have not coached men, but I would think that building a positive relationship between the player and coach may be different for males compared with females. It is said that women have to feel good to play good, whereas men have to play good to feel good. I have also heard it said that women bond to battle whereas men battle to bond.

FINAL THOUGHTS

As a coach, you play a big part in your athletes' lives both on and off the field. The relationships that you develop with your athletes are probably the best investment you can make in your coaching career. This aspect of coaching will have the most long-lasting effect on you, your athletes, and your program. I have gained a great deal of knowledge over time about the importance of positive coach–athlete relationships. As a young coach, I wish that I had known more about the seven Cs that I referred to earlier in the chapter. All of them have an effect on how successful you are as a coach in delivering your messages. Certainly, success has many definitions, but having a solid relationship with your players will allow you to have more success overall. To know that you had a positive effect on your players' lives is the part of coaching that will give you the greatest satisfaction and worth. The values that you instill can shape a person in many facets of her life. I value having that opportunity as a coach.

Understanding Today's Athlete

Carol Bruggeman

As a coach, especially an experienced coach, at some point you've heard yourself mumble, "I just don't understand players today!" Whether the comment originated from a communication issue, a perceived work ethic issue, or a leadership issue, the feeling is the same. As the bestseller *Who Moved My Cheese* reminds us, one constant you can count on is change! Players evolve and change over time, as does everything else in the world. Change is part of life and part of athletics. Therefore, coaches need to continue to find ways to understand, motivate, and teach current players. At its core, coaching is a profession of servanthood. Coaching is not about you; it's about someone else. To reach ultimate goals, coaches must be able to understand and relate to current players. If coaches and players can get on the same page, everyone involved can have a positive experience and earn success together.

The overall goal in understanding today's players is to evaluate, educate, and embrace in many areas. Evaluate the situation, educate yourself on current trends and ideas, and embrace new challenges. In an ever-changing world, coaches must keep standards of excellence high and continue to challenge players to raise expectations. Today's players are smart, driven, and motivated, and they will jump on board if they feel understood. Most important, if you can build trust with today's player, you will have a high probability for success.

HERE COME THE MILLENNIALS

Before we can truly understand and therefore coach our current players, we need to interpret the demographics and details surrounding this particular generation. Although the exact dates may vary slightly, Generation Y, also known as the Millennial Generation, refers to anyone born between 1984 and 2002. The following statements will help you gain an initial understanding of this generation.

- They cannot imagine a time without personal computers, digital cameras, e-mail, cell phones, ATMs, and video games.

- They have always had access to cable.
- Google is where they have always found information. Roller skating has always meant in-line skating.
- Popcorn has always been prepared in the microwave.
- They never owned a record player.
- They have only known a world with AIDS.
- They think that the Vietnam War is as ancient as World Wars I and II.
- They can understand "c u b4 2nite"
- Their biggest health issue is obesity.

Generation Yers' overall attitude is "Let's make the world a better place." They are tolerant and caring, and they accept family structures that are both traditional and nontraditional. Fewer than half of their meals are consumed at home, and smartphones constantly interrupt those meals. They spend a great deal of leisure time on computer games and surfing the Internet. They want to know what you think right now because Generation Y has had instant feedback from birth.

They aspire for new experiences and challenges, yet they are anxious and not trusting. They are eager to stand out but still want to fit in. They want more freedom and fewer restrictions, yet they value discipline. They are heavy consumers of media and embrace technology and music. They think more globally than any other generation.

Tim Elmore, a leading expert on the topic, refers to Generation Yers born after 1990 as Generation iY because of their constant exposure to technology. Because of technology, members of Generation iY do not think that they need adults for information. The result, Elmore believes, is a generation who knows too much, too soon, but has no context to process the information. They aren't bad kids; they simply know too much. They have content without context.

Generation Yers crave independence. Why is independence so important to Generation Y? To answer that question, we have to understand that Generation Y could really be called Generation Why.

Why are my parents not together?

Why are there metal detectors at my friend's school?

Why am I not allowed to stay with Pastor Dave?

Why am I not safe on an airplane in America?

Why are polar bears going to be extinct?

Why are my grandparents working when I thought they were supposed to retire last year?

Why do shootings occur at colleges and high schools?

Why is my best friend still in Afghanistan?

The world can be an incredibly unsettling, radically changing, unsafe place for Generation Y. Because of this perception, they value independence. Generation

Yers struggle to trust people in their lives or the world in general. Understanding this sociological data is important, because one of the primary traits that coaches want to develop within their teams is trust. Developing trust must be given high priority for today's player. If trust can be developed, the foundation for a successful program will be in place.

TALK TO ME

Because of the ambiguity and uncertainty of the world for Generation Y, they ask lots of questions. They truly do want to know why your bunt defense is set a certain way or why your hitting drills develop power. Coaches can answer these questions by using numerous forms of communication. Communication methods have evolved at a rapid pace over the past decade as the world of technology has exploded. Coaches must embrace these new forms of communication and educate themselves on the benefits of varying methods. Coaches can communicate in more ways than ever with today's players.

When communicating with today's player, we must quickly grab their attention. Within the first four minutes, we must grab their heads or their hearts if we want to sustain interest. Being an effective communicator is nonnegotiable for coaches. To be a successful coach, you must be able to communicate! Excellent communication systems need to be in place with players, parents, support staff, media, boosters, administrators, and others. In the sport of softball, if you cannot catch and throw, you cannot play (and win!) the game. In coaching, if you cannot communicate, you won't be able to develop a successful career and sustain a championship culture.

When talking about the importance of communicating with players, one of my favorite lines is this: "Have you ever heard of one problem because of overcommunication?" In trying to get the point across that it's usually the lack of communication that causes problems, the question makes players realize an important fact. We cannot have too much information or overcommunicate. In today's world, many forms of communication are available to ensure that our messages are sent and received. With all the methods available, coaches need to set guidelines. For example, is it acceptable to text a coach about being absent from practice? Or do you expect a phone call? Be clear about what forms of communication players should use in various situations so that everyone is on the same page.

So How Do I Reach You?

The team meeting before and after practice used to be the only way to reach all players at once. Everyone had to be in the same place, at the same time. Today, we can mass text, mass e-mail, Facebook, Twitter, put information on our websites, or make a phone call. The ease and convenience of these communication methods has certainly helped us keep in touch with players and get information out quickly. One positive for coaches is that we should never hear "I didn't get the message" because most players have smartphones and have access to all the previously mentioned forms of communication on one device.

Today's players want to upload their thoughts. They want to express themselves, learn through dialogue, participate fully in the process, and work toward the achievement of outcomes. They are constantly connected.

Because they are constantly connected and available through technology, face-to-face communication is used less and less. Interpersonal communication can be a challenge for today's players. Simply sending a teacher or professor an e-mail or sending a coach a text may not be appropriate for a serious situation. Body language, eye contact, and engaging in conversation are becoming unused communication skills. If today's player can master face-to-face communication skills, they will separate themselves from the masses when competing for a job and when competing for wins on the softball diamond. After all, technology isn't found on the field! Players must use nontechnological forms of communication to be successful on game day.

One way that we attempt to enhance face-to-face communication with our team is by putting all cell phones in the front of the bus on road trips. If our players want to communicate, they must communicate with team members or coaches without using a cell phone. If we didn't do this, the majority of our team would live on their phones the entire trip and miss an opportunity to converse or share ideas and stories with their teammates.

So how do coaches communicate and relate to today's player in this ever-changing world? Coaches need to teach and mentor constantly (they want immediate feedback) and consistently (we need to build trust). Remember that "telling and yelling are not selling anymore." If you are always a drill sergeant, they will tune you out. For today's player to listen, you must motivate and direct, remembering that how you say something is as important as what you say. Bottom line, you must be a teacher, not a teller.

In terms of communicating with today's player, research shows that leadership models are moving away from an autocratic model and toward a team or whole model. This model represents teamwork and group decision making while still having someone (a coach) in charge.

Because players are excellent collaborators today, effective communication models should include team input while still having a leader take charge. At Louisville, we have found success with a team leadership model called the leadership team. Each year, our team has a few seniors, juniors, and possibly a sophomore who meet once per week for leadership training and provide a leadership avenue for our program.

Hurry Up Already

Generation Y is part of a Google society. Players want information, and they want information now. But they only want it when *they* want it, just as they use Google. They learn on a need to know basis. Because they have this Google mentality, coaches need to give immediate feedback. Players want relevant information, and they want to know what you think right now.

Today's players grew up with YouTube, videos and video games, digital cameras, the Internet, and cell phones with cameras. They think in images and want their communication to be either image based or image enhanced. Generation Yers could be called screen teens because almost everything they use on a daily basis has a screen. In today's world, coaches have many fantastic options readily available to help teach and give feedback in images. Right View Pro software and the Coach's Eye app are terrific image-based teaching tools that have exploded in our sport. The iPad can be used to video a player performing a skill, and an athlete can immediately see what she is doing or not doing and make corrections. The old teaching creed "I hear and I forget, I see and I remember, I do and I understand" is important to implement in coaching and communicating with today's players.

Coaches need to use all methods of communication appropriate for the situation. Send your player a text and tell her that she had a great practice! Meet with players regularly on and off the field and give constant and immediate feedback. In today's workplace, annual reviews and end-of-the-year evaluations are becoming outdated. Today, employees are given quarterly or even monthly quality reviews, and immediate feedback comes on a daily basis. Our softball programs should also reflect our culture's new method of evaluation and communication.

One way that we have embraced the idea of immediate feedback is by adopting the 24-hour rule in our softball program at Louisville. This communication tool demands immediate attention and encourages face-to-face interaction. We use the 24-hour rule for our entire team in terms of winning and losing because we have that amount of time to enjoy a win or feel bad about a loss. After the time is up, we move forward. We use the 24-hour rule as individuals as well. If a player has an issue, she must address it with the appropriate person within 24 hours of the incident and work things out. If she does not address the issue, she has to move on. Holding issues against others is unfair if they are not aware! We use the 24-hour rule for positive feedback as well. If a player has a great practice or did something special, we compliment her within 24 hours. Players will forget what you say, but they will always remember how you made them feel.

WHERE'S MY PHONE?!

Today's players were bathed in technology from the womb and do not understand a world without it. When they text you and you say, "I'm not tech savvy," your inadequacy is as absurd to them as their lack of interpersonal skills is to us. Coaches need to embrace the world of technology and all the wonderful conveniences it can afford. To thrive in today's world, we have to accept and understand any technology that will help us better communicate with our players and perform our jobs at a higher level. As coaches, we want our players to try new ways of doing things, and we will earn their respect if we do the same. Because of technology, today's players can do everything faster, access everything faster, create everything faster, and therefore can outperform all of us in technological areas. Embrace their intelligence and understanding in those areas and get on board!

With unlimited exposure to media and technology, Generation Y has developed an unrealistic picture of adult responsibility. They believe what they see: TV dilemmas can be solved in 30 minutes, you can block a friend you don't like on Facebook, or, if boredom sets in, simply turn it off. Today's players embrace the world of technology, and they expect easy and instant results. They catch on to new ideas and technology quickly yet struggle with long-term commitments. They are good at multitasking yet have difficulty focusing. Today's players are social beings yet can be isolated by technology. They live in an online, artificial world and branch out in every direction, but they find it hard to go far in any one direction.

To combat the unrealistic pictures that the media present, coaches must set daily goals and expectations. Coaches must relate those goals and expectations to a bigger picture of the overall program. Players need to understand that short-term goals lead to long-term results. Not everything happens now, but small changes that do happen now will pay off in the long term.

iPhones, iPods, iPads, blogs, smartphones, Google, Instagram, Snapchat, YouTube, social media—just a few years ago these items didn't exist! Today's player enjoys the freedom of using laptops, mobile phones, and the Internet. Expression and acceptance are highly important. Although new forms of technology can be beneficial, we must educate them on the positives and potential negatives of using worldwide technology.

As stated earlier, today's player has grown up learning in images. As Dan Tudor of Tudor Recruiting Strategies suggests, "We must tell a great story about our program." Make sure that technology used within your program is telling the story that you want told. Being a great storyteller as a coach can also help you teach, because stories allow the players to think and learn in images.

Many programs now incorporate video scoreboards, flashing and revolving TV monitors, and eye-catching websites to tell their stories. Today's players and youth will remember those lasting images much longer than they will remember anything you said to them.

WHAT'S YOUR HASHTAG?

> Cards Win 5-4 & Now in 1st Place in the league! Hit a home run and played the hot corner. Next game 2morrow at 3 pm—C U there! #lovemyteam

Today's players love social media! Whatever event happens, it must be posted immediately on Facebook, Twitter, Instagram, Snapchat, or YouTube for the event to be validated. Educate yourself and your players on the positive and potential negative effects of social media. By the way, the title of this section contains 140 characters, the maximum amount allowed for a Twitter post.

Social media is about storytelling and creating a brand. Ask today's players, "What story do you want told about yourself?" Facebook, Twitter, Instagram accounts, and YouTube videos should accurately reflect that story and protect the image of any program they represent.

Social media have many positive attributes. These sites can increase communication, increase the awareness of your program, and get your message out to the masses quickly and cost efficiently. On the negative side, without proper control, the story told on these social media sites can be damaging to a player, a softball program, and an institution, and it can potentially have a negative effect on future employment.

One of my friends in the business world had an interview set up with a strong candidate for a position within her company. Because of her resume, the candidate was immediately among the top three choices for the position. Two days before the interview, my friend Google searched the candidate's name and checked out her corresponding Facebook page. Because she found far too many inappropriate pictures and inappropriate language in posts, the interview was cancelled. Social media follows wherever you go.

PICK ME . . . PICK ME!

To understand today's player, we need to examine the recruiting process. Pure economics of supply and demand are alive and well in the recruiting world. The demand for scholarships and positions on post high school teams is much higher than the supply. To be seen by recruiters, players are now playing year-round. Ten years ago, a 16-year-old softball player played a fall or spring high school season (depending on her home state) and played travel ball on a select team during the summer months. Each age level had one national tournament, and earning a spot in the national tournament was a big deal.

Nowadays, a 16-year-old player plays high school softball and a travel ball schedule that includes every weekend during the summer and every weekend during the fall until Thanksgiving. There are even travel ball tournaments in January! Various national tournaments run from mid-July through mid-August. Organizations and individuals are hosting showcases, exposure camps and tournaments, and national tournaments at every available opportunity.

On a positive note, because softball is so popular, more opportunities have been created for players to compete. The growth of softball in the past two decades has exploded as both players and parents have discovered numerous benefits from playing the sport.

On the other hand, players who compete in the year-round travel ball circuit miss many of the high school rite-of-passage events. Most players cannot discuss homecoming or tell you about their high school football team because they were playing softball every weekend. I would be hard pressed to find a collegiate coach who believed that this youth playing schedule was favorable. More is not always better. Overuse injury rates and burnout levels are extremely high. The number of games that travel ball players play all year, year after year, is astronomical. They certainly get exposure to recruiters, but it can come at a high price.

Today's player is being recruited in a fast-paced recruiting cycle, especially at the Division I level. Softball players now make early verbal commitments, just as athletes do in basketball, soccer, volleyball, and other sports. Players are committing to play for a college as early as their freshman year in high school. We would all agree it is difficult for a 14-year-old to make a decision about a high school, let alone a college. This process is occurring earlier every year because of the competitive level of our sport. More money is spent on college programs, college softball stadiums, TV and media exposure, and coaches' contracts, so competition for top players has heated up accordingly.

A decade ago, if a coach ran a clean program in which players graduated and stayed out of trouble, and the team finished above .500, administrators were pleased. But today, because of the tremendous amount of money pumped into programs, the extensive media exposure, and the high level of softball played on the field, expectations are higher. "To whom much is given, much is expected" is now a theme surrounding softball at the collegiate level. Another is "What have you done for me lately?" With increased financial support and public interest, pressures have escalated in all facets of softball programs, including the recruiting process.

Today's player has always watched softball on TV, has always known that scholarships are available, and has attended many games in beautiful stadiums. As players and coaches negotiate scholarships during the recruiting process, if everything fits—the school, the scholarship, the location, the academics—then an early commitment brings some real positives to both the prospect and the program. The prospect can prepare academically and athletically for a particular school and stop stressing (*stress* is a word used often with Generation Y) because she has her college decision behind her and can just play and get better.

On the other hand, committing early can be a real risk for both parties. For the college coach, committed young players can lose interest and passion because they have reached their goal of earning a college scholarship. Many travel coaches take only uncommitted players to top tournaments and leave the committed players at home. I don't believe that collegiate programs committed to prospects so that they could stay home for the next few years! Coaches need to have conversations with committed players about what is expected after the commitment. Also, we would hope that committed players would desire to play against a high level of competition because they love to play, compete, and help their teams win. They also should want to prepare for the next level.

Many travel coaches have found early commitments to be problematic as well. Some young players feel pressure to commit early because they think that they may not get a better opportunity later. Collegiate coaches may present a short timeline. Others commit because of peer pressure; all their teammates are committing. Many travel coaches also voice frustration about committed players who stop wanting to play every weekend. Additionally, a college coach can leave a school before a committed player gets to play for him or her, the player may find new academic interests, or the collegiate program may move to a higher or lower level.

In the current recruiting landscape, collegiate coaches must spend a great deal of time keeping committed recruits, not just getting their commitment or signing them. Officially, a verbal commitment means nothing. I have a friend in the football coaching world who says, "All a verbal commitment does is confirm that someone else thinks the player is good, too. Now the real recruiting begins!"

Today's player, even a young, verbally committed player, needs to feel valued and appreciated, so coaches have to continue recruiting the player or she may not be committed for long.

Recruiting today's player at an earlier date is here to stay; therefore, coaches must reinvent ways to recruit. Because of NCAA rules and because of the age of prospects, coaches must develop more relationships with travel ball coaches, high school coaches, and parents. These people influence who is in the recruiting mix and how a collegiate program is received. Coaches must embrace unofficial visits and be creative with technology and social media in the recruiting process.

IF IT DOESN'T MATTER WHO WINS AND LOSES, WHY DO THEY KEEP SCORE?

The youth softball structure, especially at a high level, deemphasizes competitiveness. Today's softball player has only played showcases with time limits and exposure tournaments that have no bracket play or no winners of games. We have to teach today's player how to win and how to compete! Nothing is more frustrating (and unproductive, I might add) for a recruiter than to be watching a youth game in the bottom of the sixth inning, two outs, 2-2 count, tie score, runners on first and third and then hear the umpire call, "Time," ending the game. No one gets to see how the hitter or pitcher or defensive players compete and perform in this pressure situation.

If a game ends because of a time limit, whether a player's team is ahead, behind, or tied, many players begin to subscribe to the "Oh well, what field is our next game on?" mentality. For today's player, whether they win or lose really doesn't matter because the system is set up for apathy toward competitiveness. Because of the current structure and format, the "survive and advance" and "find a way to win" mentalities are gone. If winning and losing didn't matter, we wouldn't have a scoreboard, which, by the way, most youth tournaments do not.

Because incoming players lack competitiveness, our practices have changed dramatically at Louisville. After the players learn the fundamentals, individual drills and especially team drills are set up with pressure and competition. The drills have winners and losers, and consequences. We compete every day against each other, against a clock, against some challenge that matters. Something else has emerged as we've changed our practices to increase competition—the players love it! They embrace the challenges and enjoy the competitions.

As coaches, we need to give today's players real, meaningful tasks that require them to work toward a challenging solution. Our head sports performance coach, Teena Murray, created a team competition at Louisville called the Oklahoma City Challenge. Oklahoma City is the home of the Women's College World Series, and the dream of every Division I program is to win a national championship. Two captains are selected to lead two teams, and a draft is held for the remaining members of the team. The two teams engage in four different competitions over four days. The events require teamwork, strategy, physical fitness, mental toughness, and competitiveness to win. Coach Murray speaks only with the captains of each team and informs them of the tasks required for the day. The captains must inform their respective team members about the challenges for the day. A fierce loyalty develops within each team and the program as a whole. Every year, each player desperately wants to be able to sign her name on the Louisville Slugger bat that will be displayed with a picture of the winning team. To win the OKC Challenge, players must strategize, work together, and believe in one another, thus creating and celebrating healthy competition.

Student-athletes today are high performance and high maintenance. These combined characteristics can be a challenge for coaches to manage. We must walk the delicate line between nurture and challenge, understanding the value in developing both areas. Competitive settings can provide the backdrop for this progression.

I GOT YOUR BACK

Loyalty in athletics is a sacred and revered ideal. If you asked coaches to rank order important attributes in athletics, you would be hard pressed to find a coach who would not rank loyalty in the top two. To be truly loyal, a person must be faithful and devoted. A team can earn much success if a coach has players who have bought in to a program and are loyal.

According to research, loyalty, commitment, and trust are words with different meanings for Generation Y. Because today's players value independence and have minimal trust and therefore minimal respect for authority or hierarchy, they rarely acknowledge a chain of command. For the most part, titles and flow charts are meaningless to them. As an authority figure, a coach must earn a relationship with today's player. Most important, today's players live in a culture that values convenience more than commitment. This culture makes developing loyalty a challenge for coaches.

These apathetic views of loyalty have spilled into softball at all levels of competition. Many youth players switch travel ball teams on an annual (or sometimes semiannual) basis. I remember speaking with a successful Division I softball coach about eight or nine years ago who said, "I will never recruit a player with more than two uniforms in her closet." This coach wanted players who had played for one or at most two travel ball teams because that background showed loyalty. Today, a softball coach would struggle to find youth players who have only played for only one or even two organizations in their careers.

Many youth players switch travel ball teams often, always looking for the perfect playing situation. We are all familiar with the game Where's Waldo?—collegiate softball coaches feel as if they are playing this game when evaluating prospects in fall because numerous players switch teams. Finding who is playing where presents a challenge.

Why is this happening? Where is the loyalty and commitment? Today, many youth players (and parents) are simply looking out for number one. Many times it becomes what's best for me, not what's best for the team. I'm not sure when the transition occurred from the mentality of working hard to earn a position to the idea of just leaving and going where the player has a guaranteed spot. If something isn't perfect or exactly the way the player wants it, the grass must be greener elsewhere. With new people constantly being thrown in the mix, this mentality presents a challenge for coaches at every level to develop team spirit, team chemistry, and loyalty.

This mentality has invaded the collegiate game. Transfer rates from college to college are increasing annually. For today's players, if things aren't perfect, an acceptable solution is to go somewhere else. Parents play a huge role in this mind-set. With prospects making their collegiate decisions earlier, this trend will only continue to grow.

Futurists believe that Generation Yers will make approximately 10 career changes in a lifetime. This generation doesn't believe that career changes are moves up the ladder. They might leave their influential job in one corporation to learn another skill in a different area of another corporation. We are seeing this same trend in softball in multiple transfers at the youth and collegiate levels. Additionally, a youth player may leave an elite travel team to play a different position on a less competitive team.

Recently, a coach at a top 25 program had a verbal commitment from a high-level pitcher dating from her sophomore year in high school. One week before the early national signing date in fall (the player was now a high school senior), the prospect called the coach to inform her that she was going to a different top 25 program and would be signing with them the following week. This example illustrates many ethical issues and is a real-life story of the decline in loyalty.

So what can coaches do to develop loyalty? They must spend time on team building and on communicating with players honestly about their roles on the team. Realistic expectations must be presented. Coaches must help players understand that true success requires time and lots of hard, unglamorous work. Collegiate coaches need to be honest during the recruiting process.

One thing that Carol Hutchins does with her softball program at the University of Michigan is to have the incoming freshmen write a paper on the history of their respective jersey numbers and take a test on the Block M. These small tasks become huge loyalty builders because players have to connect the past with the present. In addition, Michigan players learn that everything is about the program, not about the individual.

When I was coaching at Purdue, we had a senior dinner and team skits night every February right before the first games of the season. Our seniors would make dinner for the whole team (it's amazing how much they learn to cook in college!). Over the years the dinner became a real competition to one-up the seniors from the year before. Usually, the dinner had a theme, and some classes even went so far as to dress the part and send invitations! The videotaped skits were the best part. Every class had to perform a skit of their choice. We would watch the senior class skit from when they were freshmen, the junior class skit from when they were freshmen, the sophomore class, and the grand finale of the evening was the current freshmen class skit. This dinner and skit night connected all the classes and was a tremendous experience for everyone to build loyalty and a sense of belonging to the program.

Today's players want to belong before they believe, they want an experience before they want an explanation, and they want a cause before they want a course. Anything we can create as coaches to facilitate these ideals will go a long way in building loyalty.

BE ALL YOU CAN BE

A current trend in softball is that players are developing a tremendous amount of softball skill but lack overall athleticism. Because of intense pressures to be seen by recruiters, today's softball players play softball at an alarming rate with no time off. They play in tournaments every weekend as well as weekly showcases and camps all year long. Because of these pressures, athletes believe that they need to pick only one sport in high school, so they play softball year round to improve their skills. Certainly, softball is a technical game, and players can improve technical skills through repetition. Softball players who specialize and play only softball throughout their entire high school career can certainly develop a high level of softball skill.

On the down side, specialization in softball can cause overuse injuries. Injuries of high school and college freshman softball players are at all-time high levels. Softball is a one-sided sport for most players (e.g., hit right, throw right), so movement patterns can be lopsided or overdeveloped on one side. By playing multiple sports in high school and by adding quality strength training, many muscle groups can be developed, thus reducing the potential for injuries.

Multisport athletes bring a higher level of overall athleticism. They develop additional teamwork skills, stay at higher fitness levels, and learn to work with different coaches and athletes. Players in their 8th, 9th, and 10th grade years often ask me, "Should I play other sports in high school or specialize in softball?" My response continues to be the same. If they enjoy playing another sport in high school, they should play it, especially if they are a significant contributor in that sport. If the high school team is a winning team with a history of success, they have even more reason to play. The more an athlete can learn how to win and be around a competitive environment at a high level, the better off she'll be.

OLDER VERSIONS OF ME

Views have changed dramatically over the past 40 years with regard to young adults and parents. Research states that 85 percent of Generation Yers claim to be extremely close to their parents, whereas 40 percent of Baby Boomers in 1974 claimed that they'd be better off without their parents. Because of these beliefs, Dan Kiley named Generation Y the Peter Pan Generation because they tend to delay many events into adulthood. They would define the word *adult* based on certain personal abilities and characteristics rather than more traditional rite-of-passage events. Researchers believe that the age at which members of Generation Y reach adulthood is now closer to age 30 than age 20! Based on the economy and other factors, college graduates strongly consider moving back in with their parents as a viable option. This trend does not have the same negative stigma it did a generation ago.

Today's player grew up in a guaranteed world—in a failure-proof, risk-free environment. They live in a structured and adult-planned world. Consequently, recent graduates struggle with making adult decisions. For the first time in their lives they have to make real decisions on their own.

Because of the structure of youth softball, parents are highly involved in the lives of today's softball players. Parents drive players around to various cities to play, eat meals with their children on the road, stay with them in hotels, take them to lessons, spend every minute of every weekend together, and are just around all the time. Because of this intensive time commitment, the prospect wants parental input in the softball playing and recruiting process.

Parents and their offspring are closer than ever, which can be a real positive in terms of involvement in a child's life. Some parents, however, want to handle their daughter's battles and issues. These inclinations are detrimental to a young female's preparation for real life. Additionally, because of the astronomical amount of money that parents spend on youth softball (equipment, lessons, travel team fees, and so on), they tend to believe that their daughters are entitled to full scholarships. High school and travel ball coaches deal with parents on a daily basis. Collegiate coaches may not have the same issue, but they still must set boundaries for parent. At Louisville we send parents a letter that states expectations and guidelines to make sure that everyone is on the same page as we head into the season.

I WANT IT AND I WANT IT NOW!

Generation Y has been described as an entitled group. They expect to have nice things, and they expect to have nice things now! Today's softball player has been raised in an era of prosperity. Parents have been able to afford high-performance equipment throughout their daughters' careers. They have the financial means to provide hitting and pitching lessons, personal trainers, recruiting services, and camp fees. Although many young players appreciate those items, they have little or no meaning for others because they were not earned.

Because parents have handed those items to their daughters on a regular basis, impressing today's player is challenging. New shoes? Check. New bat? Check. Video equipment? Check. Personal trainer? Check. Specialty coaches? Check. The list goes on and on. They have always known a softball world of opportunities and scholarships, and they expect to receive those items.

From time to time, we share a list of everything that a University of Louisville softball student-athlete receives and attach a corresponding dollar amount to each item. When players see what a tutor costs per hour or what a complete uniform costs, let alone what tuition costs for the year, they begin to see the bigger picture. We attempt to eliminate entitlement by constantly discussing the time and effort put into all the benefits our softball players receive and by having our players understand that items are earned, not given. Our players also participate in a Cardinal Athletic Fund Thank-a-Thon when they call our donors and thank them personally for their contributions to Louisville athletics.

Discipline within a program is critical for success. Today's players want structure, although at times they will complain about it. The most effective way to discipline a player in an era of wealth and prosperity is to take away the only things that really matter—time and money.

Because members of Generation Y think globally and truly desire to make a difference, they have volunteered more time to the world than any previous generation. Although they are entitled with things, they are generous with their time. Your program must be dedicated to making a difference or to contributing to society. Find out what community service activities really light a fire under your current players and get involved. It's a win–win situation. Your players will respect your desire to get behind something, and society as a whole will benefit as well.

One year at Purdue, we hosted a softball game for special needs children. Every player on our team was assigned to a special needs child, and we played a softball game. The children involved were on cloud nine because most never imagined that they would play on a Division I softball field. To see wheelchairs on the field alongside our Division I athletes was a sight that everyone in attendance would remember forever. One of our players was so moved by the whole experience that she later chose a profession in social work. She felt a calling to help those in need. Making a difference matters to today's players.

WHO'S THE BOSS?

If you want to develop leadership within today's players, you must invite them, include them, and involve them. Remember that their participation has been adult driven and adult structured their entire lives. They were not given playground opportunities to pick teams, pick sports, make up the rules, and settle conflicts. Today's player has not had opportunities to develop leadership and take on responsibilities. They have minimal skills in leading various personalities. We must teach leadership, and not just from a book. A book can provide a good foundation, but teachable leadership moments come to life on the field and in daily activities.

Bill Edwards, NFCA Hall of Fame coach at Hofstra, rarely coaches in fall practices during game situations so that his players learn to think the game and make decisions on their own. He believes that not enough free play occurs. Many players go to hitting lessons, pitching lessons, and conditioning lessons during which coaches tell them what to do and how long to do it. No decision making occurs. Coaches should put players in leadership and decision-making positions and let them figure it out from time to time.

At Louisville we have a subtle way to flush out leadership. Every time we do a team drill at practice, everyone on the current defensive team always meets at the pitcher's mound. Why, you may ask. Because at some point, while they are all standing there staring at each other in a tight space, somebody is going to say something! The team finds out every day in practice who is willing to be vocal, to step up and say something. They also find out who they are going to listen to. We want to figure out every day the person who the team looks to for positive encouragement and who the team looks to for a strong redirect. We don't want a tight game setting to be the first time the team addresses those situations. We practice it every day.

YA GOTTA LUV EM!

Today's players thrive on a healthy balance of work and play. Balance is critical, because work and play are not viewed as separate entities for Generation Y. They believe that they can have fun while they are working. Because of these beliefs, coaches need to add fun and enjoyment into their programs. Remember that fun does not mean goofing off, although at times it may be appropriate. Fun can also mean healthy competitions and new challenges on the softball field.

Young athletes today are technologically savvy, civic minded, visionary, confident, smart, optimistic, moralistic, and values driven. They are tolerant, caring, honest, open minded, and balanced. They believe that their work will help change the world! As coaches, we know that they will change ours.

Assessing Your Team's Mental Makeup

Kyla Holas

Assessing your team's mental makeup is often easier than changing it. As coaches, we have a solid perspective about how our athletes interact as a team, what situations they will perform well in, and which ones could possibly cause them to crumble.

On a daily basis, we watch our athletes perform, thus being spectators to their failures and successes in a variety of situations. What lends to this is the process of identifying strengths and weaknesses in our athletes, which usually seems easy and natural to most veteran coaches. But if you are newer to the coaching profession, it is the ability to create opportunities for change that can generate difficult situations in terms of identifying strengths, weaknesses, and changes that may need to be made.

During my first few seasons as a head coach, I believed that the team was supposed to emulate my ideas and possess my approach to the sport. As an athlete, I was an intense competitor who hated to lose and loved to work hard. As a head coach new to the profession, I expected my team to have this approach.

Instead of meeting my expectations, the teams of my first years crumbled under pressure and lost games that they should have won. I had players who hated practice and truly believed that they practiced too hard. Therefore, I was lost, frustrated, and disconnected from my players. I thought to myself, this is not what I was taught, nor do I have athletes who are playing or responding as I did when I was an athlete. At this point I began to look at each player more closely, really trying to understand where the breakdown in my approach was happening and how that affected each of my athletes. I wanted to understand where the disconnect was occurring in each of the athletes.

I began to discover that by mentally assessing each athlete, I could enhance my ability to motivate and understand each person on my team, thus having an effect not only on each individual but also on the team as a whole. As I came to understand how essential this piece of the puzzle was to the overall picture, it became important to me, even somewhat of an obsession, to implement my new knowledge.

As part of this, I read motivational book after motivational book. I made it my business to talk with one sport psychologist after another, striving to understand how to motivate my athletes (and, thus, my team). Additionally, I wanted to understand why they were not mentally playing softball in the same way that I approached it, in a way that would offer greater opportunities to win more games. And there it was: the outcome versus the process. I completely overlooked the process, maybe even took it for granted. What I had was a team full of players who were operating in the mind-set of trying not to lose instead of playing the game one pitch at a time and focusing on the process of winning. After I arrived at this realization, I gained an element of opportunity for my athletes and, in turn, my team that I had never possessed before.

After discovering that I had a new tool in my toolbox, I completely changed my approach to coaching. Looking back, this is when the winning started. I began my new approach by evaluating the players on the team in a three-step approach. I made it my business to discover and learn about each athlete. I wanted to know who they were, what made them want to play softball, and how committed they were to reaching their goals. I saw this as the beginning point of understanding who my team was and how I could offer them opportunities to achieve not only their individual goals but also our goals as a team, which in turn would enable us, together, to achieve a winning perspective.

As I have gained additional years of experience as a head coach, the method of evaluation has now become the easy part, but the implementation process is still a work in progress. Armed with this knowledge, my staff and I started to focus on how to tailor practices to produce quality repetitions and reach all our athletes in the most effective way possible. We measured their quality reps to allow them to compete against themselves daily. We transformed ourselves with the mind-set that when game time comes, we never compete against an opponent, just ourselves, and we focus on our best effort on that particular day. As a result, each year, we must adjust our perspective and reevaluate our athletes based on the makeup of our current team. As a staff, we understand the importance of our team's mental mind-set and the way that we go about producing it daily.

EVALUATION PROCESS

The first stage of assessing your team's mental makeup is evaluation. This first stage includes three aspects, and the achievement of each stage propels you into the next. The first aspect that is accomplished during the fall of each year is a personality test. Many personality tests are available, and they vary in content and price. As a coaching staff, we have tried two of these personality tests with much success. The primary test that we use is the Insight model, which assigns colors for each person to identify with. We have found this test the easiest to implement and discuss with our team. The other personality test that we have employed is known as the Myers–Briggs, which assigns four letters that describe each person. Based on these two personality tests, our coaching staff and team are able to learn about and gain a holistic understanding of each person. As a whole, the coaching staff and team have a lot of fun with this. They learn which team members think alike and who shares the same letters or colors. More important, it helps us understand and work with each other, especially when our thoughts and behaviors do not match.

Public Persona Versus Private Personality

In most situations athletes want to impress and please coaches. This sometimes means that athletes change or act differently in the presence of coaches. As an example, I coached an athlete in the past whom I thought I knew well. I also thought I had a good grasp on how to approach and work with her. After she completed the personality testing that we engaged in that year, I was shocked. What I had seen in practice and games was a timid introvert who always took the cautious route. This behavior was completely contradicted by her personality assessment, which labeled her as an enthusiastic extrovert who was getting lost in our daily practice routines, details about the game, and self-evaluation system. I learned from the results that I had been approaching this athlete in the wrong way to meet her where she was a person. From that point on, we tried being more stimulating in our practice drills and more open and flexible in the details that we applied to skill input. This new approach allowed the athlete to grow, open up with the team, and ultimately improve her performance.

We have all had those athletes who were unreachable or athletes who did something that we thought of as way out of character but in all actuality may have been exactly who they were. A particular event may really demonstrate a person's true being, and the difference is that we are seeing it for the first time. Knowing what encourages an athlete to perform her best helps you, as a coach, to have more accurate knowledge about how to reach the athlete and how to handle her in times of stress and pressure, when her personality traits are really tested.

Assess the Team's Motivations

The second stage of assessing your team's mental makeup is motivation. Knowing what motivates each individual and, in turn, your team is of utmost importance. Understanding why each athlete plays the game of softball is a vital tool in understanding her personality. For example, as a coaching staff we have employed the Competitive Pyramid. We ask each athlete to place herself in one of the following three categories that they truly identify with: competitive actions, competitive mind-set, or competitive motives.

Competitive Actions

I received the Competitive Pyramid from the Jeff Janssen Leadership Academy. After I learned of its existence, I used it to help us reach our athletes, learn how to challenge them, and identify what angle to approach them from. A competitive actions person is motivated each day by her work pace and actions. Players in this category will be your pace setters at practice and will base their confidence on the work they did that day. I make sure to keep these players motivated with challenging practices and appeal to their hard-working mentality.

Competitive Mind-Set

A competitive mind-set person tends to be the kind of player who hates to lose and plays softball with the idea that there is something to prove. Players with this mind-set will take full responsibility for a loss. With competitive mind-set players, I try to make daily practice drills become more gamelike by increasing competition during drills. Mind-set players will thrive on game day. If you talk to the team about something that they need to improve and the situation does not pertain to a player with a competitive mind-set perspective, you must be sure to go back and talk one-on-one with that person. Otherwise, a competitive mind-set person will likely take everything addressed to the team as personal. This point could be important because such players are usually not the ones you are talking to.

Competitive Motives

A competitive motives person tends to be more internal, takes things more personally, and ties her self-worth to her performance. Athletes in this competitive mind-set need the most help in maintaining balance during practice and competitions. With too much failure, this type of athlete attaches her self-worth to those outcomes and tends to be emotional. Motive players, however, are the most loyal to their team, and as a coach, you should try to appeal to that quality. Having these types of people in charge of another player or partnering them up on challenge days to keep them focused on someone other than themselves can be beneficial. Because their self-worth tends to be tied to performance, make sure to praise these players because it matters more to them than it does to others.

To put this all together, the Competitive Pyramid has armed our coaching staff with a tool to meet our student-athletes where they are, which in turn empowers them to achieve. After we have gained a good understanding of team personality and recognized the players' motivations, we use another evaluation tool to determine each athlete's level of commitment. We have our team and our staff rate each player on the Jeff Janssen Commitment Continuum Scale. The scale ranges from resistant–reluctant–existent to compliant–committed–compelled.

This process has each player rate where she thinks she is and where the team and coaches think she is. This motivating tool is an eye-opening experience for players, especially those who perceive themselves differently from those around them or the ones who work really hard and think that no one notices their efforts.

As a coach who employs this tool, I have a goal to have everyone on the committed side by the start of the season and have a team that buys in to the philosophy and established goals of the program. In trying to achieve this, I have to keep in mind and understand the starting point. In doing this, I strive for the leaders first and then build to the starting nine. From there, we work one at a time to get any remaining players on the right side of the chart. That single athlete on the right side of the chart can be the jump to success that you have never had or the key to a team's downfall. Those one or two players will be the toughest to work with and often take the most time, but when they make the move toward buying into the mind-set that is being established, they will make the most difference in your team. This important measurement tool can help your team work as one toward a common goal and use a mentally sound approach.

At times during a season, players may need a model to identify with. I usually save this model for a time when these players are struggling with the balance of focusing on the process while still competing. For these situations, I created a questionnaire for our athletes to promote thought about how competitors operate and a spot to rate themselves on three key points. I ask them these questions: What differentiates competitors? What motivates them? What frustrates them? How do they handle adversity? How do they prepare daily?

They then rate themselves on the categories of self-belief, self-discipline, and competitive fire. I have noticed that the questionnaire has helped us open up discussion on competitiveness being a combination of intensity and intelligence and something that is attainable for everyone.

In completing this endeavor, remember that this evaluation stage happens on a daily timeline. Personality tests, commitment scales, and other tools are important elements that enable you, as a coach, to know where your team and players really are versus where you want them to be.

Having a pulse on the mental makeup of your team will be the only way to move through the stages of changing your team's mental makeup. As a reference, keep in mind that on average it takes 21 days to transform a change into a habit. What that means for the team is that we must have consistent days of using who they are together to establish a mentally solid and sound team that works and functions as a unit.

To enable changes to occur and help us advance toward having a well-oiled team that has all the motions working together to function as one unit, we have established a variety of opportunities and situations that help us work toward that goal. These include a multitude of team activities, player routines and releases, the establishment of team leaders, practice challenges, and the institution of game-day processes. All the work that has been previously addressed is a starting point. The knowledge base has been established; now it must now be implemented.

TEAM ACTIVITIES
(TEAM BONDING AND CHALLENGES)

As a coaching staff, we start each year using an established pattern, but one that is flexible and can be adjusted to work with each athlete and, in turn, the team. Every year, we use the fall and recruiting-visit time to bring our team together, spend time with recruits, and observe how those individuals may fit in to our system. We also use this time to begin building the mental makeup of our program. As part of this, we create situations and challenges to bring our athletes together, challenge them, and divide them at times. This process helps us, as coaches, to observe and determine which players demonstrate leadership skills, to understand how our team works as a whole, and to identify the issues that we might need to improve on. This is also the time when we consult the Internet to find anything and everything out there in our surroundings to do. We have tried just about every possible activity; some of them cost money, and some we do ourselves at little to no cost.

We usually plan four team events each year that are staff lead and then pass it on to the team to lead for the remainder of the fall. We therefore have a semester-long process of building the team's mental makeup. A few examples of things that we have done as a team are photo scavenger hunts, a game known as Bigger and Better, the Cougar Cup, Minute to Win It, Fear Factor, Mind Games, the Dating Game, and an outing to Sur La Table, in which we went to our local store and attended a cooking class, where we divided into teams and baked an appetizer, meal, and dessert. After tasting, we voted on the best entry.

Photo Scavenger Hunt

The photo scavenger hunt was done by creating a list of items around town to take pictures of. After teams were established, rules were given (such as observing all traffic laws and wearing seat belts). Time lines were set, and ideas about bonus points were offered. Finally, all team members were off in and about town to take pictures to complete the photo scavenger hunt list.

Bigger and Better

Another game, Bigger and Better, has also been used as a team activity. This game is played by having groups start with a single small item, like a pencil, and then go out to trade the pencil up toward bigger and better items. It is important with this game to establish a set timeline and require that when the groups return, they own the last item outright.

Cougar Cup

The Cougar Cup includes a multitude of physical challenges that cross all sports and have a fun twist to them. Rules are listed, and a point system is established. The team is divided into two groups. Coaches and players have a lot of fun seeing how people work together as a group to achieve these physical challenges. At the end we award a trophy cup that is kept by the winning team for the year.

TV Games

Other favorites, Minute to Win It and Fear Factor, are taken straight from the television shows. In Minute to Win It, favorite challenges are chosen. Then a timer is set for one minute as players try to achieve the challenges. An adaption of Fear Factor is another activity that we have used. For example, after making sure that we know about food allergies beforehand, food items are wrapped in foil. Then challenges are drawn to see who can eat the items the fastest. An additional challenge that we have previously implemented is the Dating Game, in which we adapt the television show for our needs by having two people partner up and learn everything they can about each other. We then separate them and have them answer questions on cards. Finally, the partners are asked the questions that they previously discussed to see whether they have the same answer. If the answers match, they are awarded points for their work

Mind Games

Mind games, in which athletes are asked to compete with a different set of skills, puzzles, riddles, mazes, and so on is one of the toughest ones for athletes because they prefer physical challenges. But this activity can be a good change of pace and bring out some leaders who may not have excelled in the physical challenges. We pull together some of those tough brainteasers and award points for the team that solves them the fastest.

After we finish play in the fall and the players go back to their individual schedules, we keep them focused on staying as a team and working together as a team by creating situations each week in which the athletes are offered opportunities to plan weekly team-bonding events. Two player's names are drawn, and they have to coordinate and organize something for the week that the team can do, based on the available free time left in the week. The activity can be as simple as a pizza and movie night, a birthday celebration, a night of bowling, or an old-fashioned board game challenge. These events create situations in which you can start to learn what interests your athletes possess. The activities not only build team atmosphere but also afford players the opportunity to each be in charge of bringing the team together. In turn, this helps them invest in their team and take ownership of their team's mental makeup.

With these activities, the athletes begin to invest into the team concept because they are helping to create the atmosphere. Sometimes they find that they have a lot more in common with someone whom they might not have known very well before the team activities began. Later in the season, the activities could be an ally in getting a struggling player back on track by taking her for a mental timeout to revisit her success in one of the activities.

PROCESS-BASED PLAYER APPROACH

Player routines are important because to have a sound mental makeup, a player must have an established routine and a release. A routine is something that a player does every pitch, whether on defense or offense, to create consistency in the prepitch moments. The routine enables an athlete to remain in a consistent mind-set and approach before the ball moves.

Routines

Routines should be simple, have a fluid movement to them, and include a deep breath to settle the internal systems. An example of a hitting routine would include taking two warm-up swings outside the box, getting the signal from the coach, facing the batter's box, and finding a focal spot on the bat. The athlete would then take a deep breath, step into the box, be loose and relaxed in the body, and have a focused facial expression to be ready for the pitch. This established routine should be the same for every pitch, keeping in mind that no at bat, ground ball, or pitch is more important than another. The entire process of a routine provides the consistency that is needed to allow a release.

Releases

The release is an action that gets the athlete back into the normal routine when something did not go as planned, such as an error, a bad pitch, or maybe a swing and a miss at a ball. Releases should be physical so that the action can signal that the moment is over. The release promotes the idea that the athlete is moving on from what did not go as planned. The player also demonstrates to coaches and teammates that she is now ready for the next pitch.

Input Versus Output

Another item to note about routines and releases is that you need to know your athletes and your team well. As coaches, we take time to know each player's routines and releases on defense and offense. With this knowledge, we are able to know where each athlete is during a game. We can determine when we might need a time-out to slow the game down for the players and help them refocus on the input, not the output.

Routines and releases usually become inconsistent or nonexistent when players are focused on outcomes. For example, a pitcher's routines can speed up between pitches, and before you know it you have had back-to-back hits. Some players do not release and take their defensive mistake into their offense and vice versa. Another issue that can happen is that the lack or inconsistency of a release can cause a player to forget all the other things that she did right that day. She may begin to engage in the negative self-talk that usually puts a mentally weak player on the bench, pouting about her performance that day.

Quality Counters

One way to stay on the input of the task at hand and the quality of reps is a quality counter. Our coaching staff uses this idea because our coaching model is based on the belief that measurement equals motivation. During practice, reps are important, but quality reps matter much more. For instance, imagine a practice in which reps during a defensive drill, batting practice, or pitching sets were measured for quality. You would go through them differently, correct? That is the objective here. Make everything that you do count, instead of just counting everything that you do. It is not just 10 fastballs, but 10 quality fastballs. The same goes for every other instance.

As a coach, if you remain focused on the process, then the outcomes will take care of themselves. For example, we chart pitchers and hitters during practice to demonstrate clearly where the athlete is in terms of the quality range of reps. This is a simple thing to chart. All the chart must contain is a slot for total reps, a place for quality reps, and the percentage total for that day. Our players know their goal number for the day, and each day their goal is to try to beat their personal best number.

"What Else?" Mentality

This charting system allows us to have a better gauge of lower-quality days, when the athlete may have needed more focus. That focus and the "What else can I do?" mentality is where we, as coaches, want those lower-quality days to be for our players. We want our athletes to think for themselves, "OK. It wasn't a great day. What else can I do today for my team?" This allows us to focus and remain in a working mentality, which is our goal for our athletes and the key to being a mentally sound player every day.

CREATING LEADERSHIP

The area of team leadership has been a primary focus for our team during the past few seasons. We have all had teams that had specifically designated captains, but they were present in name only. In other words, these players had the title of team captain, but they did not consistently demonstrate any real sense of leadership for the team to follow. We had captains who had little or no power to lead, or captains who were disconnected from the team. Those instances created a need for change.

Captain of Peers

Our old process of choosing team captains was to have the team and staff choose two leaders each year. At the beginning of the selection process for captains, we would distribute a copy of the job description for the captain positions, offer applications, and encourage team members to apply. After applications were submitted and players were chosen, the newly appointed team captains attended a 10-week leadership program with me, as their head coach, to learn a variety of techniques and skills about how to become a better and more effective leader. Despite the selection process and the leadership-training program, the problems described earlier kept finding a way into the team during the season.

Four Versus One or Two: Power in Numbers

As a coach I have observed a difference in seasons that had effective leaders. I have come to believe that the team leaders, usually your team captains, are your lifeline to your team. During one challenging season, I altered our team leadership system from a two-person job to a four-person job. My belief in the power of numbers proved successful and is now our current approach to team leadership.

Our team selects four class leaders: one freshman, one sophomore, one junior, and one senior. These four leaders still attend the 10-week leadership program together, but now we demonstrate our leadership based on class rank. A freshman is the liaison for the freshman, a sophomore for the sophomores, and so on. This approach has enabled us to have a better grasp on what is happening for each person and thus the class as a whole. It also offers the opportunity to grasp the possible differences in class issues; the issues that a freshman might be working through will be different from the possible issues for a sophomore, junior, or senior.

This new approach to team leadership has given us, as coaches, a new and more personal perspective into the mental makeup of our team. In addition, four people are now working together for the betterment of the team. This lends itself well to the idea of leaders having more support and additional options of approach to work with during tough times.

Weekly Meetings

We meet each week with all four team captains to discuss where they see themselves as leaders, where the team is, what has gone well, and what has not gone well. We also discuss who may be in need of special attention and what we need to prepare for in the coming week. The meeting usually takes about 30 minutes, but it sets the tone for the rest of the week. It offers us, as a staff, the opportunity to discuss and reflect on any changes that we need to address in regard to team issues, such as the need to push an athlete or ease up on a struggling player. Overall, these meetings offer the chance to talk with team captains in a personal and open atmosphere about the direction of team for the week. All this sets up a scenario in which the team begins practice with four players and three staff members who are buying into your plan for the week. That adds up to seven people at practice all on the same page. Power in numbers!

HABIT OF COMPETING

Having a mentally stable team that can overcome the ups and downs of a season usually requires more work on the part of the leaders, rather than the players. Leaders must know each player as a person. A leader must also know what motivates each player and then must employ that knowledge to encourage commitment to the program plan. This dynamic process is in a constant state of change and can be greatly enhanced during daily dealings with the team. To offer an example, as the head coach I implemented practice challenges a few years ago. At first, practice challenges were an occasional thing in which athletes tried to bargain to reduce the amount of a task, like baserunning, or get out of something altogether, like weight lifting. What really stood out during those practice challenges was how the dynamics of the team would change and how hard and competitive the athletes would become to try to achieve the challenge. But I would not get that kind of energy from the team during the course of the practice. Because of this discovery, I began to search for ways to create practice challenges on a more frequent basis. What has transpired are daily practice challenges. We now use these daily challenges as a way to see how athletes respond to pressure, to determine who thrives in the various competitions, to expose weaknesses, and to challenge the opponent. The challenges started out as something simple, such as the team versus the coaches, but it morphed into infield versus outfield, right side versus left side, or pitchers versus hitters. Eventually, it evolved into a leader board that ranged from simple awards like baserunning leader or offensive leader to web gem player of the day.

Some examples of favorite challenges include situational hitting, in which we create small teams and go through situations while awarding points for runners advanced, and a bat control contest in which we challenge athletes to ground ball, fly ball, and line drive days. Another favorite challenge is known as total bases day, when points are added up for how many bases are touched.

We have also competed in a bunting challenge in which we attempt to advance and score runners with sacrifice bunting, drop bunting, push bunting, and slapping. One Ball is a challenge in which normal batting practice rounds are achieved using only one ball (points are added or subtracted when another ball has to be taken out of the bin). Defensively, 21 Outs is a challenge in which we see how many balls have to be put in play to get 21 outs.

Infield versus outfield is another challenge that the team enjoys. This adaptable challenge can become whatever you want it to be. It is similar to another challenge that we have used, known as right side versus left side. Rather than establishing the teams as infield versus outfield, teams are labeled as right side and left side. The defense versus base runners challenge focuses on baserunning to see how many bases the teams can get. Another challenge that we have had success with is having two pitchers do the workout and compete to see who can get the workout down first. This is great for a perfects day, when pitchers cannot move on to another pitch until they hit the location.

Finally, two other challenges that we have used include Cougars (played like a game of horse, but with throwing pitches) and pitchers versus hitters day, in which we keep track to see who wins the count. Overall, the institution of practice challenges has been a big hit with the players. As coaches, we are able to watch as they work hard to win at their daily activities that they once went through so mindlessly. As previously mentioned, challenges energize athletes. Adding to this is the fact that throughout the season, the staff maintains a running total of the challenges. At the end of the year, points are totaled to determine the first- and second-place winners.

GAME-DAY APPROACHES

All the team bonding and practice work that has been put into routines, releases, and challenges will pay off on game day, but that does not mean that all the work done before game day will guarantee that the team will show up and play a men-tally tough game. As we all know, game days are the toughest days to stay focused throughout. When the going gets tough on game days, athletes may disregard all the mental preparation that has been established.

There Is No Big Game

When an athlete feels pressure, she demonstrates her true character. Given this, as a coaching staff we operate with the thought of making sure that there are no big games. We make a concerted effort not to talk about our opponent. Instead, we focus on the keys to what we need to do this week. Additionally, we give priority to preparing to win and to making the necessary adjustments. To further this, we set goals that need to be accomplished for the game or inning by inning. This plan is determined from the scouting report that we have obtained. All this work increases our chance of success.

Process and Routines

During the game, focus is given to routines. Those individual routines slow the game down for a player. When it seems as if the game is moving too fast, I have my athletes take a deep breath to settle and refocus themselves. During the huddles, we focus on things that can be done to add speed to the game and take every inch that we can. An example of speeding up the game is our display of energy in hustling on and off the field. This also allows us the opportunity to gain an advantage over the opposing pitcher by picking up on timing, knowing the other team's signals or defensive shifts, and observing the tips that a pitcher is giving.

Deal With the What-Ifs

As a coach I believe that a team can be beaten before the first inning is over just by speeding up the other team to an uncomfortable pace that gets them out of their comfort zone. Despite using these techniques, however, we have had games in which we did everything correctly yet still lost. Because those losses are the hardest to forget, we prepare for them and try to attack them head on, beforehand. As part of this process, we have a board that has two sides labeled "What Is the Worst That Could Happen?" and "What Can I Do to Prevent That From Happening?" The goal in having this board is to have each player report what she is most worried about and then what she can do to prevent that from happening. An example of a fear could be "What if I give up a home run?" The corresponding action is "Focus on one pitch at a time."

FINAL THOUGHTS

Overall, the daily implementation of the previously mentioned components can be tedious and time consuming for the coaching staff. They must spend a great deal of time thinking of challenges to bring and ways to calculate results so that things remain within the established perspective. Other things may seem more important, but the commitment shown to the process and the players will be the commitment that you get back from your team. Taking time to step back and listen can develop an entirely new perspective toward creating an effective method of developing a mentally sound team. Keeping in mind that the process is dynamic and evolving is a recipe for success and a way to focus on what we started with—the process, not the outcome. With the process in place, the outcome will take care of itself in creating a mentally sound team.

22

Building Team Chemistry

Kelly Inouye-Perez

Competition thrives in softball. Our sport has grown, and I am the first to admit that the strides made in the last decade are unprecedented. From coast to coast, the sounds and sights of softball are accelerating the development of players striving to gain competitive excellence. All coaches, no matter the level of competition, work tirelessly to make their teams faster, stronger, and mentally tougher so that their players are ready to compete for softball supremacy. They introduce drills on the mechanics of hitting, defense, pitching, and catching. They attend clinics, conduct softball camps, and hire experts to teach the fundamentals and finer points of playing softball.

As coaches, we should never stop learning. We should constantly look for ways to make our teams compete successfully. That is our ethos, and we should never apologize if we burn with that desire. The reality is, however, that even with talented players on the field, winning is not easy. More is needed to get to the highest level of competition and ultimate success. That element is team chemistry. It's the final ingredient needed to get your team to play at a championship level. Barring injuries, incredible bad luck, or overwhelming competition, a team imbued with great team chemistry will win. It's as simple as that.

Why is that? Why is team chemistry, in particular great team chemistry, critical to success? From my vantage point I believe that the reasons become clearer as we view our environment. We are surrounded by efforts that fail. We document our failures just as much as we herald our successes. We archive and compile statistics of every player, every inning, and every ball game throughout the entire season. Errors, strikeouts, losses, and pitching details are tracked just as religiously as we track successes. We work in a field that defines a great hitter as one who fails 60 to 70 percent of the time. To see through all this requires a disciplined mind and the support and focus of the entire team. You need great team chemistry.

Can you imagine what it looks and sounds like to have your players consistently communicating with loud voices on defense? Can you appreciate your player hustling to the dugout after a failed attempt at the plate and being received with true compassion by her teammates? Can you imagine your team fighting back from a losing position and then leaving an opponent on the field in the bottom of the seventh? Can you imagine practices when players work with great energy and enthusiasm? Witness these things, and I will show you a team with great chemistry. At the conclusion of each championship season, no matter the sport, I frequently hear someone say, "This team had great chemistry!" or "We all got along," or words to that effect. And the star of the game is usually the one who says those words. Those watching the proceedings may conclude that winning leads to good team chemistry, but I believe that it is the other way around. A strong team culture leads to great team chemistry and is the key to championship softball.

In this chapter I share three things. First, I describe how we got started in developing our unique team chemistry. I then offer examples of what we used to maintain our team chemistry throughout the season. Finally, I explain how despite the lack of a guarantee of a championship season, a team can use team chemistry to make the season an enjoyable experience.

START WITH THE PHILOSOPHY

Every program starts with a philosophy about the core values that guide and support all efforts to be successful. These core values allows coaches, team members, and all involved to keep their respective priorities straight through all the ups and downs that college softball represents. For example, at UCLA our philosophy is as follows: Family comes first, then school, and then, finally, softball—the fun part. We believe deeply that a healthy family structure enables our athletes to compete at the highest levels. We define family to include the entire softball family: players' families, administrators, coaches, support staff, and our alumni. It's corny, but it works. Every decision we make is based on ensuring that each player receives the best support and guidance to make her career here successful.

Academics at UCLA are not insignificant. It challenges our players, who in turn need our support to ensure their success. We support them in many ways including mentoring, counseling, and, yes, even attending their classes to make sure that they are there learning and paying attention to details. With commitment to their studies, players get to enjoy softball on the field. Lack of commitment in the classroom has consequences for the individual and the team. For example, a player who is faltering in school is not allowed to practice or compete with the team. We do this to emphasize the importance that we place on academics. It hurts if your star players are not allowed to compete, and it should. Avoiding these consequences remains a high priority and a cornerstone of our philosophy. Softball is the fun part, and we try to make the softball experience at UCLA enjoyable and rewarding.

WHERE ARE WE HEADING?

Although our philosophy does not change, our vision can change each year. By vision we mean getting the team to a better place from where we were at the start of the season. For most teams, at any level, it usually starts with a vision to win a conference or national championship. I had the great fortune of knowing Coach

John Wooden. I asked him a question he probably answered many times: "How do you create the championship tradition?" He kept it simple with one of his famous aphorisms, "Yesterday is as old as dirt, and we have no control of tomorrow, so make today your masterpiece." I took his advice and spent a lot of time trying to figure out how to accomplish what he made appear so simple. I realized that his focus was on the process of how to become the best you are capable of being. He knew that he had no control over the outcome. His pyramid of success was how he documented the path to competitive greatness at the top of the triangle. Each word on that triangle stood for the qualities needed to be a champion in life.

Realizing the Vision

Our focus to realize our vision was not as elaborate as Coach Wooden's pyramid of success, but it had meaning to our program. Three concepts became our daily challenges: One, we honored our Bruin culture by inspiring each other with work ethic and enthusiasm both on and off the field. Two, we developed our competitive excellence by working on the skills that would allow us to compete at the highest level. And, three, we realized that we were here to win in life, so we strived to be the best in all that we did both on and off the field each day. Because we could not measure a championship in October, this vision allowed us to focus on how to create a masterpiece each day that would be our backbone in June. This vision gave us direction and purpose to improve ourselves throughout the season. It was not easy. It took the better part of the season to understand what each part of the vision looked like and felt like, and how it made a difference in our drive to the championship in 2010. But I am getting ahead of myself.

Creating Our Own Language

After we defined how to keep our priorities straight and where we were heading as a team, the next step was to learn how to do this on a daily basis. This task was especially daunting because we knew we would not get an outcome until our season was over. Yet we were determined to move forward. I was fortunate to have a leadership coach, Dr. Foster Mobley, to call on to help us define the steps that we needed to take to make our vision a reality. He sat with my coaching staff and made us define what we believed were the most important things to focus on with our daily actions. He asked many questions. What it would look like? What would it sound like? What would it feel like? He made us dig deep into ourselves and write down what we believed were the critical factors that we needed to do as a staff. He grilled us for clarity by asking each of us to explain why we believed our concepts were important. We had pieces of paper taped to the wall and wrote everything that was important to us. On each paper was a list of words or actions that we wanted to see both on and off the field—words and phrases like hustle, compete, take care of each other, focus, concentration, discipline, be a team player, and mental toughness. Our job was to distill these words to their lowest common denominator. From this process emerged our guiding principles. These would be

> ### Our Guiding Principles to Uphold the Tradition of Excellence of UCLA Softball
>
> - We live "team over self."
> - We have each other's backs.
> - We hold ourselves accountable to our commitments and our efforts.
> - We create our masterpiece in every moment.
> - We are each here to be "the one"—to be a difference maker when it counts.
>
> These concepts and words represented our core beliefs of what we expected and wanted our players to represent and believe in. Knowing the process that we underwent with Dr. Mobley, we knew that we needed a way to communicate those concepts to our players and support staff. We started with our seniors. We made time to discuss with each individual, class, and position what those guiding principles represented, what those words looked like and felt like, and how important it was for everyone to understand that the principles were the essence of the program. Team chemistry was born as we explained the principles.

the phrases that we would use to guide our day-to-day journey to accomplish our vision. The five phrases represented what we wanted our team culture to represent and how we would pursue competitive excellence to win. Here is how we stated it:

Practicing the Language

The next phase proved equally challenging—how to maintain team chemistry. We decided to have team meetings in which each player was to give an example of a teammate who lived up to those concepts. For example, a player would state, "I choose Katie for the guiding principle of *creating a masterpiece in every moment* because she comes early and stays late, focusing on her mechanics. Another example: "I pick Drea for preparing to *be the one* because she is always challenging herself by practicing her weakness in drills at practice. Another example: "I pick Monica for *having my back* because she called me for morning weight training to make sure I wasn't late." We were able to create a picture of what it looks like and feels like to be a part of a strong culture. Each meeting every player had to recognize someone who exemplified a guiding principle. The team chemistry became strong because players were recognizing each other for actions that allowed us to accomplish our vision.

This process accomplished two things. First, players were getting credit for their hard work. Nobody talked about outcome; the statements were focused purely on actions. Second, those who were not being recognized were getting feedback that they were not being recognized for their actions, which spoke volumes. Both starters and role players were recognized. For example, "I pick Grace, the bullpen catcher, for having a *team over self* mentality for giving to the pitchers without getting anything in return." Others were recognized for actions off the field. For example, "I pick Sammy for *holding me accountable* in the classroom by studying with me to help me keep up with my readings." We started to see things off the field, which strengthened our culture and team chemistry. Players were now looking for things to notice so that they were prepared to share with the team one of the guiding principles, which is to give credit to a teammate. The meetings were powerful, and I was impressed with how the language of what was important created a clear picture.

Maintaining the Language During the Season

All of this was easy to do in fall ball and into preseason. Would it work during the heat of battle? As a coach I made an important decision on how to maintain our culture when the team was challenged on the field as the season began. I made this statement to the team: "We cannot fail because each challenging opportunity prepares us to be at our best when we need to be our best, at the end of season." Therefore, each practice and game would be a positive learning experience if we could see where we fell short and what we did well to prepare for the next opportunity. Equally important was my desire not to be a Captain Obvious coach. No longer would I tell the team what we did poorly after each game. I simply asked them to be accountable and describe where we fell short and what we would do next time. This approach was powerful for all because it was clear that we could have done things differently to affect the outcome of the game. Even after a win, we identified things that we could have done differently. We created a positive culture with strong team chemistry because players were not afraid or embarrassed to be called out after a game. Instead, players would step up and say, "My bad for not getting the bunt down and moving the runner." Another example: "My bad for not working ahead as a pitcher. I know it made the innings too long." The accountability allowed the team to have each other's backs rather than be frustrated with how the game was affected. But I need to be clear here; this wasn't just a meeting to say, "My bad," and move on. The culture was created that if a player is accountable, then the team has her back because they see her working on her shortcoming every day. And something better be done about it next time. So repetitive accountability for a weakness was not OK!

Focusing on the Little Things

Now that we addressed how to manage the challenges of failure and accountability in front of the team, the next step was to address what we did well. My assistant at the time, Gina Vecchione, came up with a great idea to focus on the little things that made a big difference. For example, moving the runner was more important than the hit that brought the runner home. We created a standard that if a teammate sacrificed herself to give another teammate an opportunity, then credit was given to the player who demonstrated team over self. So a standard was created on how to focus on the little things that allowed us to succeed. Home runs are an exciting part of the game and a gut punch to your opponent. But the leadoff batter who went six pitches into the count allowed the dugout to see the pitcher's weapons, which ultimately led to the success of the hitters who followed. So a little thing like having a quality at bat was given credit. We changed our focus from outcome oriented to process oriented. Our focus and recognition of the little things gave the team the strength to produce the big things that followed. Making this change was not easy because the history of many of our players was just that—doing the big thing when it counted. The team needed time to recognize the importance of doing the little things and have it become part of what was expected each day.

Other examples of little things were energy in the dugout, defensive players backing up bases, and runners taking an extra base to get in scoring position. The focus was on things that were in our control. Our expectations were high in this area. We developed a powerful culture and team chemistry because the focus was not on clutching up; the focus was on controlling what was in our control. The guiding principles were also used for actions that were not always in our control, such as picking up a teammate after a failed opportunity. For example, "Thank you, BB, for *having my back* and coming through after I struck out." Another example: Thank you, offense, for *having my back* after my terrible first inning on defense as a pitcher." The team chemistry was directed toward picking up a teammate because that action was more powerful than just clutching up or trying to be perfect. The individual felt less pressure because she knew that her teammate would have her back.

Many coaches may say, "I already do this, but then the language and meaning loses its novelty. Now what?" I agree that the effectiveness of good ideas can be lost when the outcome just isn't there. The temptation is to be Captain Obvious and say, "We were inconsistent." The statement may be correct in most cases, but it is not a great motivator for better performance.

CREATING MOMENTUM

There are ways to battle the inner demons of inconsistent play and highlight the need to get better. We as coaches have to create momentum from within the team. Coach Sue Enquist was a momentum creator and inspirational leader. She always stated, "Don't try to get everyone to buy in, just the critical mass." That is great advice. We know who our leaders or core players are, and if we get them to buy in to anything, the rest of the team should follow. The problem comes when the leaders don't know how to get off the roller coaster themselves. Then what? The leaders become frustrated, the team is frustrated, and you can bet your last dollar that the coaches are frustrated as well. I would hear people say, "I know something needs to be done, but we don't know what to do." Does that sound familiar? Several concepts are available to get groups refocused. Here is what I did. I read a book titled *The Tipping* Point by Malcolm Gladwell, first published by Little, Brown in 2000. Gladwell shared how small changes can make a big difference. He introduced the 80–20 principle, which is exemplified in the idea that in any group effort roughly 80 percent of the work will be done by 20 percent of the participants. These people are described in the following ways:

- Connectors are people with a special gift for bringing the world together. They are "a handful of people with a truly extraordinary knack [for] making friends and acquaintances. . . . Their ability to span many different worlds is a function of something intrinsic to their personality, some combination of curiosity, self-confidence, sociability, and energy."

- Mavens are "information specialists," or "people we rely upon to connect us with new information." According to Gladwell, mavens start "word-of-mouth epidemics" because of their knowledge, social skills, and ability to communicate. As Gladwell states, "Mavens are really information brokers, sharing and trading what they know."

- Salesmen are "persuaders," charismatic people who have powerful negotiation skills. They tend to have an indefinable trait that goes beyond what they say, which makes others want to agree with them.

I used these concepts by identifying who could serve as these important role players. I needed them to get us focused on moving in the right direction using the same language. For example, I identified the player who had the best interest of the team at heart and was always looking out for her teammates to make sure that everything was OK. This person was my connector. This player had to have the gift of communicating with all groups on the team regardless of age, position, or social standing. Usually this is a player who says what the team wears on game day, when we will meet for an event, and so on.

My maven was the one who was always asking for an explanation in drills and strategy discussions during practice. This player needs to know why we are doing something before she buys into performing the task. As a result players would go to her for information when they were confused. Most times you would like to say to this player, "Do it because I said to," but I realized that answering the question was important.

The last role player I needed to identify was the salesman—the voice of the team or the most influential person. The influential person can be described in many ways. I needed that person who the team really listens to and follows. This person may not be the one you want the team to follow, but be that as it may, they follow her.

GETTING EVERYONE HEADED IN THE SAME DIRECTION

Now the key was to get all those people together with the coaches and explain how this critical mass was going to lead us to success as a team. We defined the ingredients desired and what we needed to work on to improve as a team. For example, we decided as coaches that we needed to work on our mental toughness. We wanted our players to practice hitting using the machine that had the most movement. This was going to be a challenge. We needed buy in and acceptance that this drill would develop our mental toughness. So, I would explain to my maven that hitting off this difficult machine would be a challenge and that the players would have to recognize that continuing to battle the machine would make them better. What we didn't want was for players to give up and say, "It's too hard." We wanted to focus on what we had control of rather than outcomes.

For clarity, mental toughness was defined as the players' ability to battle the machine and not show frustration regardless of outcome. Subsequently I would ask, "Do you understand, Maven?" I had to answer any questions at this time because the players will later ask Maven, "Why are we doing this? This sucks!" Maven has to have the answer: "Because we are working on our mental toughness, and your goal is to battle without showing frustration and it will improve your success rate if you accept the challenge rather than give up." Next, the connector comes in to tell the team that the goal is not to show frustration no matter how hard it is. "We all have your back, so go for it!" she says. Last, the salesperson says, "I'm up first! I will be great at this station! Watch me beat this machine."

Using this approach we were able to focus on the drill, clearly communicate what was expected, and infect the environment with the enthusiasm of the salesman. I knew that we would get mentally tougher after this drill because they proceeded with the proper attitude and team chemistry.

High Ropes Course Challenge

Challenging a team in a different environment from the ball field can be great for team building. We take the team to a challenge course to climb a 40-foot (12 m) pole and jump out into the air to grab a floating bar—harnessed, of course. Teammates below are supporting the climber by holding the ropes that safely secure her. We build trust with a language to "Go for it" because teammates literally have the player's back.

We also present challenges to accomplish a task while certain players are muted. Teammates must find a way to communicate by voicing commands or by finding creative ways to communicate directions. Here is an example of a challenge: We asked all the players to stand on a wooden log approximately 25 feet (8 m) long. Then we gave the instruction for players to arrange themselves on the log by birthdate in ascending order. Nobody could touch the ground in the process. We also muted everyone so that they had to find a way to communicate birthdays and trade places without falling off the log. If anyone touched the ground the players had to start over in their original places. We had a lot of fun watching them communicate, balance, and not fall off the log, laughing the entire time. They also demonstrated adherence to a team standard and accountability by starting over when they touched the ground.

All this takes work, probably much more work than if I just demanded it. Every situation that became confusing or hard to accept required us to meet as a group, get feedback on what we needed to do to change behavior or action, and set up a plan with the coaches. As many would tell you, getting buy in is the hard part. Barking instructions is easy. The team chemistry and culture created powerful momentum because we all knew where we were going, why we were going in that direction, and how we would stay on track, because our leaders were first in line! It takes time as a staff to explain expectations while being open to suggestions from within the team to build momentum for when it really counts. It is a coach's dream to have leaders from within who are working with you to get the team to go in the same direction and speaking the same language.

FINAL THOUGHTS

As I stated earlier, this work does not guarantee a championship, but it sure makes coaching more enjoyable throughout the season when you work together with great team chemistry and a positive culture. You can just play softball, knowing that your team has learned throughout the season how to focus on the little things that brings success at the end. Because you will not be able to measure a national championship until the last week of your season, I believe that you need to find ways to define success daily. As Coach Wooden stated, "Do the ordinary things extraordinarily well." Your culture and team chemistry is where you start. Good luck!

23

Developing Student-Athletes off the Field

Sandy Montgomery

Playing softball for Coach Montgomery at Southern Illinois University Edwardsville was about more than just softball. Through the grind of playing a college sport, I learned valuable life lessons that went way beyond the softball field. Coach instilled in me the importance of accountability, toughness, and commitment on a daily basis. She expected more of me than I ever thought was possible. During my four years as a member of the team, I did not always understand why she was so adamant about the little things. But, looking back, I realize that the dedication to detail is what molded me into the person I am today. Sadly, my years of playing college softball are over, but thanks to Coach, I will always hold onto those values that have become such a big part of my life.

K. Griffith

The Cougars softball program at Southern Illinois University Edwardsville (SIUE) has evolved significantly over the 24 years that I have served as the head coach. As with many young coaches, early in my career I focused on the on-the-field skills and strategies such as hitting technique, pitching improvements, and getting the most out of each player.

Those technical skills are important, some might even say critical, to having a winning season. But as I developed as a coach, I discovered that players can learn many valuable life lessons through the sport of softball. I believe that as a collegiate coach, I play an important role as an educator. It is my responsibility to make sure that my players learn many life lessons. I also believe that a team that truly gets it, that takes those lessons to heart and makes them part of who they are as players, teammates, and young adults, can be a competitive force.

THE TOTAL PLAYER

At SIUE we have built a program that focuses on the total player. The goal is to embed within each young woman the kind of person she should aspire to be in life, using the sport of softball as the tool. When we execute this strategy well, our players are successful off the field and have the opportunity to achieve greatness as a team. Let me share a story with you. In 2007 I took the perfect team to the NCAA Division II World Series and won. They weren't the perfect team because they were the most skilled players whom I had ever coached. They were the perfect team (on that given day) because they knew that although other tournament teams had players with more talent, they understood that if they poured their hearts and souls into achieving greatness they would succeed. They understood that everything they had worked hard to achieve was within their reach. Because they were all on the same page, success was so close they could taste it. Being committed, selfless, and passionate all made sense, and the result was a national championship ring that I still wear on my finger.

BEGIN AT THE BEGINNING

The total player concept begins with the recruiting process at SIUE. As a staff we are clear about program expectations to both potential players and their parents. We deliver this message directly to recruits, and their coaches communicate it to them as well, based on their knowledge of our program. Our current players and alumni also have opportunities to share their understanding of what they consider our tradition of excellence, and they all know it isn't just about winning.

The expectation that each player will demonstrate an understanding of this mind-set comes the day she signs the letter of intent. Even before our future team members graduate from high school, we expect them to start behaving as members of the Cougars softball program. The first lesson we teach is that they are representatives of the program and that how they carry themselves in the community, as well as online through social media, has both direct and indirect implications for the team. They are expected to grasp the fact that their actions affect the program. As freshman, most of them are somewhat immature and do not have the ability to comprehend the bigger picture of this lesson. They cannot see how their actions will affect the perception of others, future employment, and other aspects of their life. In this day and age, this lesson reminds players what one simple mistake can do to someone's future or the reputation of a group.

OPENING DAY

Each year, after the new players (freshmen and transfers) have arrived, we bring them quickly into the fold through a team gathering. During this first encounter our new players begin to feel as though they are members of the Cougars family and start to understand their responsibility to one another and to the program.

Following dinner, our associate head coach shares lesson number two with the players—how to get along with the head coach. Although this lesson seems easy in concept—work hard on the field and in the classroom, represent the team in the best light at all times, be honest, hold yourself to a high standard, be a good teammate, be on time, and so on—execution is sometimes a challenge. The sophomores, juniors, and seniors all know that life's little missteps have consequences, and they are happy to share stories of running the berms in the rain for a week solid, sitting on the bench during an important game, or calling Dad to drive a pair of spikes across two states because that important piece of the gear didn't make it to the bus with the rest of the equipment!

During the first team meeting, players receive a softball survival guide that is full of information designed to give insight, goals, and tangible guidelines to all players, both new and returning. Most of this information remains the same from year to year, but as our program has evolved some of the specific policies have evolved as well. Although all these expectations are specific to our program, our new players soon discover that they also pertain to their daily lives.

We continue educating them on expectations at the first team meeting. We provide information about practice expectations and perceptions of our program both on the field and in the classroom and community. At this time, players are made aware of the perception that the faculty and administration have of our squad. The culture of being a Cougars softball player has become a standard for those who have come to expect excellence from our team, and each player is expected to understand that we do not tamper with this perception. When the 2011 freshmen class was asked to describe the softball program at SIUE, here was their response:

> Coach Montgomery pushes us to recognize ourselves as athletes on daily basis. She shapes us not only as softball players but also as respectable young women. As a freshman class, we've learned that no performance on the field is more important than our performance in the classroom or in the community. She pushes us to be the best that we can be in all aspects of being a student-athlete; this entails being responsible and taking care of the important things in life, no matter how large or small.

Faculty, administrators, students, and members of the community who are exposed to our players have seen (and now expect) a consistency of traits throughout the years: responsible, honest, accountable, conscientious, "good people," and, of course, winners. For better or worse, that is our legacy, and every day we work, both on and off the field, to continue the tradition of excellence of our program.

> The opportunity to play for SIUE has taught me much more than any tangible item could have accomplished. Among other things, three words distinctly stand out when thinking of my time as the center fielder: trust, responsibility, and, most important, accountability. Coach set the bar high on the field but equally stressed the importance of being a good person to your teammates, to your family, and to the community. Without a doubt, Coach Montgomery's coaching philosophy has taught me life lessons far beyond the scope of the game of softball. (C. Mall)

HERE WE GO

For collegiate softball players, the season really has three parts: the fall season, the off-season (individuals), and the regular season. As we prepare for our fall competition, the lessons continue. All involved are reminded of how hard we must work to achieve greatness as a team and how hard each individual must work even to make it to the field of play. The fitness test is administered the first week of practice. All returning players know the difficulty of this test and realize that summer is not a time for rest and relaxation, but a time of preparation for the coming year.

Accountability

Freshmen traditionally have the least amount of trouble with the fitness test because they are coming off an active summer of playing ball and are motivated by the fear of not being prepared for their first collegiate experience. Occasionally, however, we will see a junior or senior who didn't take the responsibilities of the summer seriously and pays for it during the fitness test. The lesson of accountability is typically first demonstrated here. We hold our players accountable for their actions by upholding the no pass, no play rule.

As coaches, we want our players to be successful on and off the field. We will do our part to help them reach their goals. If they aren't prepared for the fitness test, we schedule them extra time with the strength coach, customize their eating plans, and motivate them all we can. If grades are a concern, we schedule extra time in study tables and make tutors available when necessary. But in all circumstances, we never waiver on the no pass, no play rule. This lesson in accountability is important for both the players and the coaches. If, as a coach, you break one of your own rules to win a game, you have lost. Not only have you lost the opportunity to teach your players an important life lesson, but also you have whittled away at your own integrity as well as the respect of the team. You have sent the message to your players that the outcome justifies the means, that living a life without integrity is OK as long as you win. My advice to coaches is not to break your own rules.

Responsibility

Accountability is one of approximately 12 positive character traits that we work to instill in our players; another is responsibility. Playing softball at the collegiate level is a whole different ballgame for freshmen, and the fall season is ripe with opportunities for learning responsibility. We expect our returning players to take responsibility for guiding new players through their first year as Cougars, and we expect our new players to follow those positive examples. Basic responsibilities that must be learned quickly include being on time, working hard, and paying attention to details. These simple skills sometimes take a while for players to grasp and execute to their fullest.

Our returning players are expected to lead by example and remind the rookies that we demand certain behaviors from each team member and that we are consistent with the expectation. Although this is an established practice on our team, we still must go through the learning process each year. Inevitably, someone will forget an appointment with the academic advisor, leave a glove on the field or in the dugout after a practice, or miss a deadline required of all players. These mistakes come with a price.

Failure to care for equipment requires payment of a $5 fine, and other items require physical activity following practice. Being responsible for their own actions as well as the actions of their teammates is an important component of getting a group to achieve as a unit. We expect players to assist each other with the aspects of being a responsible person. They can achieve this by phone call reminders, conversations in which certain behaviors are prompted, or even by a little hand holding. Any method will work as long as the message is delivered and received.

> As sophomores and playing for Coach Montgomery, we are able to reflect back on our freshmen year and see how we have grown and matured not only as players but also as individuals. When we were freshman, Coach was persistent in establishing our sense of responsibility on and off the field. We were held to the same standards as everyone with our schoolwork, workouts, and life outside of softball. This helped us develop a sense of pride not only for our program but also in how we carry ourselves. We now know that to achieve what we want on and off the field, we need to take to heart Coach Montgomery's words because we are not just becoming better players but better people.

Work Ethic

The first few days of practice is a learning experience for all involved. The new players begin to realize just how much they still have to learn, and the returners are grasping the fact that the new players are going to push them for playing time. As each day goes by, every player either learns or is reminded that work ethic is a staple of our program. This lesson is reinforced with every activity in practice, every class attended, and every opportunity they are given to represent our program. Being lazy or uncommitted is not an option, and each player is held accountable for the type of effort she demonstrates in every aspect of her life.

Being a good teammate is an essential step in building good team chemistry. Both the coaching staff at SIUE and team members are expected to facilitate this process. Most collegiate athletes were the elite players of their high school and summer ball teams. At this level of play, however, most discover that they are 1 of 19 talented players, giving the phrase *good teammate* a new meaning. Putting the good of the team before self is a tough lesson to learn, but it is important to success on and off the field.

I believe one of the reasons that the SIUE softball program has been so successful is because of the team chemistry. Since I came here as a freshman, Coach Montgomery has stated time and again, "Great teams have great teammates." I know I can count on any of my teammates to be there for me on and off the field. At the end of the game, when the skill levels are equal, it is the team that believes in each other that will succeed.

S. Stanicek

TEACHING THROUGH SERVICE

Another staple of the Cougars softball program is community service. Many college teams across the country use service projects as team-building exercises, but for our program community service is the opportunity to develop the player into a person who possesses compassion and an appreciation for the opportunities that she has been given.

It is challenging to teach humility and selflessness to young women who get to do something they love everyday while earning a college degree, so community service is a great vehicle for instilling a little humility in our players. Each new member of our team learns quickly that community service is a requirement of the program. They have difficulty wrapping their heads around what it has to do with softball, but we find that community service helps develop them into caring people on and off the field.

Over the years, we have participated in many service projects and events. Some require manual labor, and some require only time, but they all have a purpose. We have participated in Habitat for Humanity, worked in a women's shelter, packaged canned goods in a food pantry, participated in a Pen Pal program for K–2 schoolchildren, and adopted a family for the holidays. All these activities have been beneficial in developing well-rounded players and people.

One particular organization that we work closely with is Special Olympics. Our players work with the Special Olympics athletes through the bowling program, and the entire Southern Illinois University Edwardsville athletics department supports the Special Olympics track and field regional competition. Here again, our players give up personal time with friends and family to influence, in some small but meaningful way, the life of someone else. Although some of the players might rather be doing something else, when the event is over, 99 percent of the time they have had a great day. They talk a lot about the athletes and the strength and courage with which they compete, and that experience stays with them for a long time.

As college athletes, our players want to win all the time, they are extremely competitive, and they put a lot of time and energy into what they do. What our players see through working with the Special Olympics athletes is that they too are dedicated and focused on competing and winning. Seeing those athletes compete puts tears in our eyes, and my players and coaches have those memories for a lifetime. As a coaching staff, we always talk about what inspires them as people, and they know what that means by the end of the day.

DEVELOPING AS PLAYERS AND PEOPLE

Commitment to the program is an integral part of achieving success, allowing the team to move from pretty good to great. Strength of commitment is demonstrated daily not only in performance at practice and in the weight room but also in everyday actions with team members, classmates, friends, and recruits. Commitment means being the best player one can be and helping teammates realize the same potential. Throughout the fall season, we are gratified to see new players make this transition and watch returning players reaffirm their commitment to one another and the program. Our players come to rely on and trust one another and the coaching staff at a deeper level as they experience this commitment to and from the team.

As coaches, we have to understand the emotional development of our student-athletes as much as their physical development. Although we sometimes wish our new players would arrive on campus with the essential character traits fully developed and deeply ingrained, they do not. A process of months and even years is needed before our players fully realize their potential. For example, we expect our players to be loyal to the uniform that they wear and the team for which they play, but we understand that loyalty exists primarily at the surface when they first arrive on campus. As our players make that deeper commitment to one another and to making the program stronger, we see their loyalty to the program strengthen, and we see them become truly invested in the program.

INSTILLING LEADERSHIP

Of all the character traits we try to instill within our players, the one that is the most difficult to achieve is often leadership. We expect that by the senior year, our players will be ready to lead. In fact, this expectation is so strong that our senior players are automatically our team captains. We challenge them to lead by positive example, to work with younger players, to motivate them while making sure that they follow the standard of behavior expected in our program, and to step up and be role models. If our players arrive at their senior year not ready or unwilling to lead, we see it in the performance of the team. In all honesty, it can be ugly. The senior player who forgets appointments, who doesn't do the little things in practice that are expected, and who doesn't place the team first is not getting it. But when the entire senior class embraces its leadership role by demonstrating on a daily basis all the character traits that we have worked to help them develop, they and the entire team experience a great year. Team chemistry, trust in one another, and a high level of commitment contribute to achieving greatness as a team.

To facilitate positive thinking about leadership, each year we draw from the works of experts in the leadership field. In the book *Coaching the Mental Game:*

Leadership Philosophies and Strategies for Peak Performance in Sports and Everyday Life (2003), H.A. Dorfman outlines leadership attributes that we have adapted to fit our leadership development program. We use these leadership statements to help our players grow into their leadership role with the team, in the classroom, and in life:

1. The leader is focused with great intensity on the team's values and objectives. The other is focused on herself.
2. The leader admits her mistakes. The other never makes mistakes and blames those who do.
3. The leader arrives early and stays late. The other comes in late and leaves on time.
4. The leader is consistent and steady under pressure. The other points fingers and places blame on others.
5. The leader often takes the blame. The other looks for a scapegoat.
6. The leader gives credit to others. The other takes it for herself.
7. The leader truly believes the team comes first. The other may say the same message but doesn't act accordingly.
8. The leader is tough and confronts team issues. The other is elusive, avoids as many problems as possible, and says what others want to hear (pp. 351–353).

We strive to instill each of these eight leadership qualities in our players through a series of conversations and activities to facilitate the process of making meaning out of what it is to be a leader. To make the concept of leadership real for them, we put the eight leadership qualities into a more tangible framework through a series of discussions. We find it helpful to talk about former players whom they considered great team leaders and why. Players can readily identify a great team leader; they know it when they see it! But when they are asked to articulate why someone is an effective leader, they often can't put their finger on it; they are making a decision on gut instinct. By taking those real-life examples and assigning them to the various leadership qualities, they begin to understand the leadership qualities on a deeper level and begin to process the role of leadership that they must assume as a senior Cougar. We see our players move through three stages during this process: think it, believe it, and demonstrate it.

Seniors who embrace the leadership role have an easier time demonstrating their responsibilities. They quickly learn that their actions, more than their words, are what inspire the younger players to want to follow. Living as a leader is not easy because it involves considering how every decision made affects the credibility of a leader and how both good and bad decisions of the leader affect the team. Although actions play a significant role in leadership, strong communication skills are a key indicator of leadership success. Communicating the standards of behavior that are expected of all Cougars is a critical role of the senior leader. The most effective communication technique is peer-to-peer mentorship, which can be highly effective in supporting the coaching staff.

PRESSURES OF THE GAME AND LIFE

As the games begin we experience all the ups and downs of competition and the way in which each player responds to these emotions. Life is full of challenges, and the many stresses of softball prepare our players for the trials that they will face in everyday life. The added pressure to win that athletes endure is a constant reminder that they must face adversity with courage and determination. Life is no different from what we experience within our program. We have a staple expectation every season to win the conference championship, and each player handles this in many ways. The ability to handle this kind of pressure is different for every person, and the responses can determine the successes that the person may achieve. We spend a lot of time discussing being self-motivated, determined, mentally tough, and handling all the pressures that the game presents, but the ability of each person to cope with and manage these emotions will be the deciding factor in her success. The game itself doesn't really present the challenges; it's the fear of failure and the ability to handle disappointment through the course of a season that creates success or enables failure.

IT IS WHO YOU ARE

Coaching for me is much more than teaching a set of skills or the end result of winning or losing. It is about being a role model and living the qualities that you try to develop within your players while they are part of your program. Coaching shouldn't just be something that you do; it should be a significant part of who you are and how you live your life. The same qualities that we work hard to instill in our players are the qualities that guide every decision that I make in life on and off the field. Leaving a player home from a road trip when you know that she might be the difference in winning and losing is a sign of integrity and something that your entire team will respect even though they might not like the decision at the time. For young coaches, establishing this mentality early in your coaching career will give you the foundation on which to build a successful program. Showing your players that true character makes a difference will have a lasting effect on their lives for years down the road. They will gain the ability to become people of true integrity.

> Over the past four years that I have played for the SIUE softball program, Coach Montgomery has been more than just a coach to me; she has been a mentor, a motivator, and even a friend. She has provided a guide of strength and motivation throughout the struggles, strife, and tribulations that being a student-athlete brings. Softball at the collegiate level is more than just a sport; it brings about a mentality of winning, in more ways than just on the field.

Throughout my collegiate career, I have made my fair share of mistakes, most of them being outside of the chalk. As I have progressed into the confident senior I am today, the coaching staff at SIUE has been, other than my parents, the main structural support that I have had. The lessons learned have been more than just the sport-specific skills of hitting the ball or fielding a grounder. It has been the growth from an immature, loud, obnoxious freshman into a role model, leader, and positive senior that has been the most important part of this experience that I can take away. When I put my cleats away for the last time and my final season comes to a close, it won't be what my batting average was or how many home runs I hit in my career that mattered; it will be how strong I became as a young woman and how I learned to become a leader to help myself and my team succeed. I've taken away many things from this program, but the one thing that I will never forget and that I will use throughout the remainder of my life is what softball has taught me about strength and perseverance and never giving up. I've realized now that even when everything has fallen to the ground, there will always be someone to pick me up, and for the past four years that has been Coach Montgomery, the coaching staff, and my teammates who are my best friends. (W. Davis)

FINAL THOUGHTS

If there is one thing that I hope to give a young coach who reads this chapter, it's the ability to develop a mind-set to guide her or his program by demonstrating strong character and integrity. I believe that positive character traits can not only guide someone toward becoming an outstanding person but also be the framework to develop a positive team atmosphere that will result in a winning attitude and program. Coaching gives you the platform to touch the lives of young people in many ways. Your influence affects who they become and what decisions they make long after their collegiate careers are over. Becoming a coach is a career choice that should not be taken lightly; it comes with significant responsibility, occasional heartbreak, and many challenges. But if you do it well, you will develop quality people on and off the field.

COACHING CHALLENGES, PRESSURES, AND OPPORTUNITIES

24

Handling Each Season's Highs and Lows

Rachel Lawson

Several years ago, my sister Dr. Lenore Doster, a licensed psychologist, took it upon herself to assess my personality type. She compared my demeanor with that of the tortoise in the fable "The Tortoise and the Hare." At the time, I remember thinking that my sister should have demanded her tuition money back because her psychology training was clearly lacking. How on earth could she compare my temperament to a slow-moving turtle? I had recently earned a Women's College World Series ring, had completed my master's degree, and had already embarked on my career as a Division I softball coach. In my mind I was moving fast; I was the hare!

Now, as I write this chapter examining how to handle each season's highs and lows, I have come to understand that Dr. Doster was correct in her assessment of my character. I am the tortoise. One basic premise from which I coach is that if I want my team to achieve at a consistently high level and avoid long periods of low moments, then as the true leader of the program, I must be systematic and steadfast in my approach. As a head coach I have come to appreciate that no forward movement is too small. It is my responsibility to stand firm on what our team's foundation is built on. No matter how I feel about the outcome of a game, I must ensure that the team keeps moving forward on its intended path with as few detours as possible.

APPROACH

I operate under the belief that involvement in all softball games, practices, and events should be one of the best parts of the day for my team and my staff. Without question, a team needs to win a lot more than it loses to have a good time. One of the greatest feelings in the world is winning a big game. With that said, for a program to sustain great play over a long period, the athletes must feel as if they are a part of something exceptional and they must have balance in all aspects of their lives.

Consistent Play Starts in the Off-Season

If an athlete feels strong, dresses well, and believes that she is intelligent, then she will have more confidence and play with more certainty and aggression. Each fall I remind my team that they can have it all. They can feel great, excel on the ball field, and obtain the education that they need in order to enter their chosen profession.

Confidence Starts in the Weight Room

Most of our athletes become more confident as they tackle small goals while competing in our strength and conditioning program. The program is designed to maximize the potential of each athlete. Without question, if the athlete puts out tremendous effort, she will be successful. As the player increases the amount of weight that she can lift and improves her running times, she feels stronger and more athletic overall. Another great benefit of our strength and conditioning program is that everyone is miserable at some point during the workout, so they bond together as a team. Nothing brings people together more than a common enemy. In our case, the enemy is team running.

Learning to Play with Certainty Starts During Off-Season Practices

The off-season is also a great time to empower an athlete to think for herself. I want my players to grow to become independent and intelligent women who believe that they have options. On the ball field, I ask question after question. An example of such inquiry starts with me stating, "Pretend I am a third grader. Now explain to me how I should take my barrel to the ball to make square contact." I will admit that most of my athletes hate answering questions. The majority of my players simply want to be told what to do so that they don't have to think. Granted, when my athlete feels uncertain and I can tell that they are on the cusp of panic, I will make a quick decision for them to remove their sense of anxiety. But, most of the time, I want them to know that they can come up with the answer themselves. This process takes weeks and possibly months for many athletes, but when that time comes, it has a huge upside. When an athlete is confident in her intelligence, she is more comfortable making decisions. If an athlete makes her own decisions, she learns to play with certainty. Often, when we have a streak of below-average play, the cause is that the athletes are unsure about what they are doing and are worried about the potential outcome.

I have found that these moments of uncertainty manifest themselves both in the batter's box and on defense. Players go in slumps or teams go through long streaks of poor offensive production because they are not certain of their approach at the plate. They are guessing when to swing instead of committing to a plan before going to the box, assuming that they are going to get that good pitch and just trusting that they have made the right decision.

Defensively, teams often make fewer plays when both the pitchers and the defenders are not committed to throwing their pitch or attacking the position on the field where the ball is hit. In these moments, I stress to the team to make a decision, commit to the play, and accept that what happens, happens. I reiterate to them that if they make the wrong decision, we will simply process the information, make a different decision next time, and accept that what happens, happens. I have found that eventually, if we have a well-thought-out plan and consistently put out great effort, things will turn in our favor.

During the off-season, the focus at practice is solely on improving each player's strength and skill. The daily purpose is to make the play, execute the pitch, and put a good swing on a hittable pitch. Our entire squad and coaching staff operate under the assumption that if we are going hard, mistakes will happen. We are also under the impression that if we focus on the little things, we will get smarter and physically better each day. So we quickly process why a mistake occurred or what it was that made it work and then move on to the next pitch. Over time, confidence grows as each athlete begins to realize that she is capable of making elite-level plays. The athletes are constantly reminded that if they want to beat a top 10 team, then they must individually make top 10 plays. We begin the process of making top 10 plays during count drills. For example, if I am working to improve my shortstop's range, I will set up the drill so that she must get five balls between these two cones before moving on. I set the cones so that the player is challenged physically, but the cones are still within her normal range so that she can accomplish the task. This drill will be set up several days in a row. As the athlete gets better at reading angles and more efficient in her motion, her range will improve, and she will see the distance between the cones increase. In seeing the distance increase, she knows that she is making the right reads, and in doing so she naturally becomes more confident.

When creating the practice plan, the objective for each skill is highlighted. The plan emphasizes both the fundamentals of the specific skill and which opponents we will need to stop by using that skill. For example, several times a week our infield works toward mastering a game called 2.6 seconds. The purpose of the game is to field the ball cleanly and throw it to first base within 2.6 seconds or better. We make the team aware that we play this game because the University of Tennessee has at least three athletes in their lineup who can run from home to first in under 2.6 seconds.

By consistently using a practice plan that improves individual skills and discussing the need to stop the other team's best players, our team feels more comfortable when facing that opponent during the regular season. The confidence gained through preparation helps us anticipate the play before it unfolds. As a result we avoid the panic and inevitable lows that come with uncertainty.

Get Good at Something

I often have to remind the players on the team that I am not too concerned about what they cannot do. I can walk across campus and find 20 people who are incapable of playing softball at a high level. What I am particularly interested in is what they can do. After a player figures out what she is good at, this becomes her identity. Softball is one of the few sports that have a place for errors on the scoreboard. One of the unfortunate by-products of this tradition is that players grow up with the mentality that they need to spend most of their practice time focusing on improving their weaknesses. If a team wants to win a championship, then the athletes on that team had better become very good at something and the coach had better be smart enough to put those various assets together. A pitcher needs to develop a good out pitch. A hitter needs to be able to drive her pitch every time it is thrown. In fact, a team needs to be so good at their strengths that few people can stop them.

After mastering a skill, the athlete then has the ability to expand her strengths by adding more skills to the list of what she already does well. If a team spends most of their time minimizing weaknesses instead of maximizing their potential, then they are too easily defeated by an opponent who has a well-executed game plan.

Developing the Team's Identity

During the fall of 2010 I spent weeks trying to pinpoint what my team was missing. I loved my team. We had just come off back-to-back regional appearances, and everyone was doing what I was asking of them, but I just didn't feel as if we were going anywhere. Then suddenly, it hit me—our team identity was simply ordinary.

Like any crafty coach, when I did not know what identity we should create or how we were going to create it, I shifted the responsibility back on the team during a team meeting. I asked the freshmen to sit on one side of the room and the returners to sit on the other. I asked the freshmen to tell the team all the things they had learned from their teammates since coming to Kentucky. As I wrote their list on the whiteboard, it became obvious to everyone that the only thing the eight freshmen thought they had learned was to be on time and not to quit on a team run. At that point, I asked the returners if that was how they wanted people to see them. Of course, the answer was no. Next, I asked the returners to list words that illustrated our identity. We listed the following: punctual, responsible, good students, excellent in community service, and overall nice people. Finally, I stated, "Now that we have an idea of who we are, we need to list everything that we want to be known for." The final list read this way: intimidating, relentless, aware, aggressive, prepared, consistent, committed, flawless in execution, possessing a championship mind-set, and, above all, exuding a strong presence.

After we established the identity that we wanted to create, it was my job to make sure that everything we did on the field reflected one of those qualities. I needed to hold the athletes to a standard consistent with the agreed-upon characteristics. In addition, the language I used when addressing the team either repeated the words or reflected their true meaning.

Interestingly, the identity that we set out to create was not the identity that the 2011 team was known for. We were seen as the ultimate underdog. We worked hard, made plays, and were fun to watch. And then, somewhere in the middle of trying to win softball games, players on the team came up with our unofficial team motto: "Woots and dubs."

To this day, I am not sure where this identity came from. And I am not sure how it relates to the original list that we came up with in the locker room. All I am certain of is that after we established this dynamic identity, we were a much better team. And as I suspected, a team who is confident in who they are might lose a game but it would take a lot more than one loss to keep that team down for long.

Focus Always on the Task at Hand

When we concentrate on the immediate task in front of us, our focus stays in the present. If we allow our minds to get stuck on past performances or wander too far into the future, we run the risk of becoming derailed. Through this consistent approach our team finds their comfort zone.

We need to learn from the past. If we make a mistake, we quickly learn from it and move on to the task at hand. An error, no matter how detrimental, is simply a mistake; it is not personal. No athlete wakes up in the morning with the intention of making an error. I have learned to tread lightly and swiftly when choosing to point out past mistakes. Often, acknowledging an error and examining why it occurred can prove to be a valuable teaching moment. But I am careful about spending too long highlighting the mistake or about using words that are hurtful because I run the risk of damaging the athlete's self-esteem. When an athlete has low self-esteem, she is hesitant to expand her range, to take the extra base, or to go deep in the count. This uncertainty can lead to multiple errors and offensive slumps and ultimately creates long periods of low moments for the athlete. If these emotions rub off on her teammates, the downward spiral gains tremendous momentum.

A great illustration of this steadfast approach can be seen in my coaching career. UK was opening SEC play with our freshman pitcher throwing a no-hitter going into the seventh inning. During the inning, a fly ball was hit to deep center. Our center fielder turned three times and tripped, and the ball landed in the grass for a hit. At first, you feel the devastation of blowing the no-hitter, and then you wanted to rip her head off. But instead, our pitcher brushed it off as if it were her fault for letting the hitter get such a good piece, and the staff later showed the center fielder how to approach the ball better. During that season, our outfielder went on to make several similar bad reads. Each time, we pointed out the flaw and continued to hit those types of fly balls in practice until eventually she became proficient at catching them. A couple of seasons later, this same center fielder had not only improved her range significantly but also had a 1.000 fielding percentage, was recognized by the SEC for several awards, was a team captain, and was one of the best athletes ever to wear a Kentucky uniform. Her tremendous play propelled the University of Kentucky to its first ever appearance in the super regionals.

One of the biggest challenges I have as a coach is helping athletes maintain their emotional stability even when things are not working out as planned. Had the approach of the staff been to yell at the center fielder and remind her how she was continually hurting the team, she never would have become a great player. She was already an A student and at the top in the weight room and at team running. Simply stated, she was a perfectionist. She didn't need to be reminded that she had failed; she already understood that it was her fault. What she needed was for someone to acknowledge why the error occurred and to work tirelessly with her at improving so that she would be better in the future. When the athlete buys into the fact that a mistake is not a measure of self-worth but rather an indicator of a skill that she needs to improve on before the next outing, then she will be more likely to remain focused on the task of defeating the next opponent.

Most of the time, we are trying to create our own highs. We are trying to win a championship, defeat a higher-ranked opponent, win individual awards. We need to realize that because softball teams play many games, any player can make one great play and any team can beat even the toughest of opponents one time. And if a team does something amazing, we want to analyze how that play or win occurred so that we can continually re-create that greatness over the course of a season. If we do something awesome, we learn from it, spend a little time enjoying the moment, and then move on to the next task. A coach can never replicate the feeling of winning a big game or the satisfaction that people feel after finally achieving a goal that they have worked hard to accomplish. In these moments an athlete discovers her self-confidence. For a short time, I find it best for the team if I move to the background and allow them to become lost in the revelry of winning. Soon afterward, it is my responsibility to bring the team back to the present.

Every game is different. Just because we won does not mean that we will win again. And just because we lost does not mean that we will lose again. Each game brings new challenges. To stay consistent, we must take nothing for granted and plan for the next game.

Game Plan

Our game plan is simple. Our goal is to stop the other team's players from accomplishing the skill or skills that make them great. Two days before any game day, the entire practice plan is designed to slow down our upcoming opponent. Offensively, we work toward attacking the opposing pitcher's weakness with one of our strengths. Defensively and in the circle, we methodically prepare to control each hitter in the lineup. No matter who the opponent is, we discuss each of their player's strengths so that we feel prepared the second they step in the box, on the mound, or in the field of play. The last thing we want to happen is to stop the other team's best player but then lose the game because we did not prepare properly for the other athletes in the lineup who were less statistically formidable.

Earlier in my career, I would hear other coaches give game recaps such as this: "We got the cleanup hitter out, but then we lost because our pitcher let the number eight batter crush a home run over deep center field." Or, "We would have finished in the top two, but the worst team in the league beat us the last weekend of the season." The more I heard comments like these, the more I came to realize that these teams lost because they did not place the same value on each opponent or on each hitter in the lineup. A ball ripped in the 5-6 hole is the same hit, whether it was hit by the leadoff batter or the number eight hitter. And a loss is a loss, whether it was at the hands of an out-of-conference opponent or your hated rival.

The great aspect about competitive athletics is that the outcome is often unpredictable. Because of this uncertainty, every athlete and every opponent deserves the same level of concentration; no player or team can be taken for granted. The scouting report and pregame video is always prepared the same way, and we always adhere to the same practice timeline for each opponent.

The scouting report illustrates the relevant statistical data and includes a brief summary of the opponent's tendencies, including who is hot and what we can do to stop them. Like all information, the scouting report and corresponding video is helpful only if we can execute the plan on the field. Two days before the start of the game we always focus heavily on stopping our opponent. The day before a game, we continue to implement our strategy, paying particular attention to making sure that our team feels confident about the game plan. For example, a few years ago a pitcher in our league threw 80 percent curveballs when she needed a strike. Because of this high percentage, we decided that the best strategy for our hitters was to sit on this pitch. We implemented a practice plan in which our hitters worked on putting their toes on the chalk until they could drive the curve. In addition, we worked to foul off the inside pitch from this position in the box so that the hitters would not get jammed on a two-strike count. The next day during the game, we were able to beat the pitcher for the first time in school history. In defeating this pitcher, our team not only enjoyed winning a game but also began to buy into the concept that by having a good game plan and executing it, they could beat anyone in the league. In such ways an underdog can defeat even the highest ranked opponents.

Over the past three seasons, I have come to understand that my team embraces the process of preparing to compete against the next opponent. And because their mind-set is on winning the next game, their emotions stay even. More often than not, a team's emotional stability creates what we perceive as highs and lows. Because our team is fixated on an immediate goal, our players stay on point, work hard, and need little external motivation.

Team Practice Versus Individual Practice

To evolve throughout the course of the regular season, we blend individual practices with team practices. When things are going our way and we are winning a lot more games than we are losing, we tend to work out more often in a team practice setting. During these practices, the players love each other's company, they move fast through the drills, they give each other positive feedback, the music sounds great, the weather isn't that bad, and every silly comment is funny. The overall attitude of the team is positive, and, as a result, practice is productive.

When an athlete or the team is struggling, or we have just lost a big game, I schedule individual practices. Often, when a team is swept in a series or loses three or more games in a row, the immediate response by coaches is to schedule more practice. Many members of the team believe that they need to embark on a team-bonding activity or have a group meeting. But I have found that when we lose, the players and staff are grumpy and in some instances oversensitive. Every song over the radio is overplayed, every play requires great effort, we can't wait until it is warm with a slight breeze, and our teammates and coaches are getting on our nerves. During these times, I try to minimize the amount of time that we spend together, so I set up practices of groups of four or six. In this small-group setting we give each player a lot of individual attention, try to build up their confidence, and make them feel that they have improved.

Individual practice time allows an athlete who is under a lot of pressure to change her focus back to the task at hand. During team practice, the mind can easily wander to places that are not productive. During individual time, the repetitions are specific and continuous, so the athlete must pay attention to the ball that is in front of her. During these practices, the coach can help a struggling athlete rediscover her comfort zone because the focus is placed on the talents that she possesses that allow her to be successful.

An additional benefit to individual practice time is that all people want to feel special. When a coach spends extra time helping an athlete work through a perceived problem, that athlete often feels important. Few people who need attention can find what they are looking for in a group setting. Sometimes, all a player needs to bring her back to a positive mental state is for a coach to show her that she matters and tell her that if she stays the course, things will eventually work out for the best.

MAINTAINING PERSPECTIVE

I often remind my team that anyone can play well when things are going her way. But, I continue, how a player reacts when things are not going as planned reveals the true measure of a person's character.

Play Fearless Softball

Early in my coaching career, I realized that it was a lot easier to lose my temper after a bad play or a bad loss than it was to maintain my composure. As a coach one thing I do not tolerate is lazy play. I would often yell across the field during a game at a player who would forget to run into a backup position or would not run hard after a ball. Consequently, I found that in losing my temper and yelling at them to make the play, I instilled a sense of panic throughout the team. This feeling of panic not only distracted the players from the task at hand but also chipped away at their confidence. I came to find that when I maintained my composure, delivered the message calmly, and then factually pointed out what went wrong and what steps would be required to reverse the outcome, the team was able to stay focused on the upcoming challenge. In extreme cases when the athlete did not adapt to the speed I wanted her to play at, I reduced her playing time instead of yelling. I found that this approach helps the athlete hear my message better.

Fear is a powerful motivator, and the response to fear is often unpredictable. In many instances, fear slows down the athlete. Over time, when an athlete feels afraid, she begins to worry. She worries about past mistakes, she worries about what the team is thinking, she worries about striking out, she worries about the 10 poles she will have to run if she misses this ball, she worries about losing, and through all this worrying she creates self-doubt. It is in this self-doubt that panic sets in. I usually see this panic take root when players are reprimanded for swinging at bad pitches. In time, the hitter becomes so afraid to swing at a bad pitch that her approach in the box becomes defensive and she starts second-guessing her approach to hitting. The result is often a period of weak contact and low offensive production.

For a team to play fearless softball, the anxiety associated with panic and self-doubt must be removed. Even in the rockiest of times, coaches need to have trust in the program and in the athletes in the system and know that in time the team will move forward.

The quickest way to restore an athlete's trust in her play is to have her focus on the defensive side of the ball. Defense is often a product of awareness and hard work. As a result, if athletes are willing to concentrate and put in the effort, they can quickly see positive results in this part of their game. The team will make more plays, which will not only increase their confidence but also keep the score low. I have found that in periods when we sustain a number of loses, if we can work to keep the opposition's scoring down, all we need to do is string together a few hits or get a lucky break and then we can win. That one lucky win can change the course of a team's season.

During defensive practice, the coach controls the setting and ultimately has the ability to push the athlete in an area where she can be successful. The drills can be implemented first off a roll or toss to emphasize the fundamentals of the task. After the athlete has accomplished the skill, the difficulty of the drill can be increased by incorporating a stopwatch or base runners.

When the self-confidence created because of small successes augments the sense of worth that was established in the weight room and the classroom, the athlete often comes to realize that she possesses many strengths. A resilient person rarely gets too high or too low. She instinctively knows that all bad times will soon go away and that all accomplishments will happen again in the near future.

Athletes Need Balance

In athletics we can fall into the trap of simplifying everything that we do into two categories—winning and losing. At times, this oversimplification creates the certainty that is needed to keep moving forward. But to produce more wins than losses over the course of a season, we need our players to maintain a healthy balance as athletes, as students, and as social human beings.

This perspective helps to create an environment that the athlete enjoys coming to day in and day out. An athlete generally produces results much closer to her actual potential in this type of atmosphere because she is free from negative distractions and becomes lost in the sport that she loves. I believe that our 2011 squad was able to change the face of Kentucky softball forever because as a team, win or lose, they brought their A game all but five times. In sustaining such a high level of performance, they were able to defeat many teams that had a higher ranking.

Adjusting Practice Demands to the Athlete's Workload

To get the most out of our student-athletes, we adjust their practice demands to their academic workload. If a player has several tests or projects due during the same week, she will generally be more worried and as a result will sleep and eat poorly. If an athlete has made many mistakes or is just not bringing her A game in the batter's box, the first thing I examine is her academic situation.

Adjusting the nature of the team's practice to be less time consuming and physical in nature during busy academic weeks will help minimize the risk for injury and provide more time to study so that the athletes will feel less overwhelmed. As a result, they will play at a higher level for a longer time. During finals week we do not play a midweek game, and we give the team Monday and Tuesday off. Wednesday will be a lighter hitting day, and Thursday will be a heavier offensive and defensive practice. Regardless of the fact that we often play a big series on the weekend, I have found that spending less time practicing during finals week produces better results on the weekend.

Becoming Lost in Something Greater Than Yourself

The best part of being in a team sport is that the individuals can lose themselves in something bigger. The loyalty developed toward that larger purpose generates tremendous momentum and becomes part of the team's identity. This identity, if dynamic, often nudges the team over the top for a big win and helps the squad bounce back faster after a crushing loss.

When I first came to Kentucky, I immediately noticed that our team did not know the fight song and we did not pay much attention to the other sport teams on our campus. We had not embraced the value of being part of Big Blue Nation. And, above all, we did not appreciate how awesome it was to be afforded the opportunity to compete in the SEC.

In the fall of my first season as the head coach, I required each class to present the fight song to their teammates. I sent constant text and e-mail messages about the other sport teams and athletes who were part of UK. Every poster, media guide, and picture that was created emphasized the color blue. I forced our athletes to take notice of all the great athletes and plays that made the SEC exceptional. And I worked my hardest to get them to understand that they too were members of that elite class.

We didn't need much time to buy into the belief that we are Kentucky and we are the SEC. And if you are wearing Kentucky blue, you are one of us. To continue to facilitate this loyalty, the team must generally enjoy being together and participate in activities that allow them to bond. The feeling of camaraderie is a balancing act that must start the minute the roster is solidified. Like holidays, the functions that bring the team together have greater meaning if they are on a regular schedule so that the players can look forward to them.

Hunger Is a Distraction

In moments when I hope to relay a significant message to the squad, I always wait until they are fed before proceeding with any coaching points. Because hunger can be a huge distraction, food should be an important aspect in both game and practice preparation. From the moment when our athletes wake up in the morning until they go to bed at night, they are on the go. If an athlete doesn't have a break before the start of practice, her warm-up time does not start until she has a chance to grab lunch and change into her practice clothes. If an athlete has a night class, she should be released from practice with enough time to grab dinner before class. To maintain consistency in our play over the course of the season, we stick with all routines before and after games regardless of the outcome.

To maintain healthy team dynamics throughout the school year, we incorporate a good meal on a routine basis and as often as allowed. One tradition that most people take part in is gathering with their friends and family in the kitchen. Although we might not have the ideal kitchen, the right food often helps to bring our team together and make those who feel anxious more comfortable. During the spring season, we often provide a pregame meal in the locker room or at the hotel. This meal is incorporated as the players are putting on their uniforms. The music is blaring and the uniforms are all hanging in their lockers while they are sitting together laughing and snacking on a meal. This ritual has kept families together for centuries, and it has helped get our players minds' right for the upcoming game since 2011.

Everyone Needs a Break

To perform at a consistently high level, we try to maintain a forward-thinking and productive working environment. When the team is winning, softball feels better and both the coaches and the athletes find it easier to stay the course. A team's harmony is often only challenged after a big loss or series of losses.

By nature, when competitive people lose, they believe that the only way they can turn the outcome in their favor is to put in a lot more time on the ball field. Depending on the circumstances that surround the loss and the disposition of the athletes in terms of how they relate to each other, often a better approach is to give the team the day off. No matter how poorly the day went or how poorly someone played, reality always seems a little brighter the next morning. After a day off, a feeling of newness is associated with the team. The hurt of the loss, although still present, doesn't have quite the same sting. As a result, the players can more easily bounce back and focus on the game plan needed to beat the next opponent.

Create Moments Worth Remembering

An athlete has only a small window during her lifetime to compete. Because time is precious, I want to provide an environment where they have the opportunity to win softball games and make the most of their four years. Idealistic as it may sound, competing should be an amazing experience. Athletics is one of the few places where we can help create moments of greatness and excitement for those who have trusted us to lead them.

Every decision I make moves us in one direction or another, and every time we come together as a team a moment is created. So before I choose to react to any situation, I try to ask myself whether the decision I am making is moving the individual and the team closer to our ultimate goal. Are my choices bringing out the best in my players as athletes and as people? Ultimately, if most of the decisions I make are good ones, then in these moments the athletes become engrossed in the present and the team subconsciously learns to bond together.

FINAL THOUGHTS

The bonds of an elite program are not cemented overnight. Tremendous faith and patience are needed to stay the course and stay together. As competitors, we know what we want and we want it now. Often, if we hit a low, it is too easy to get off track and start over. If we witness something exceptional, we believe that the only way to re-create its greatness is to copy it, even if it means that we abandon what we do well. Sometimes we forget that no coach starts as a hall of fame coach and few teams start with the staying power required to win a championship. Day by day and pitch by pitch, most great teams take small steps. The key is that the steps move them forward on a course toward their ultimate goal.

25

Continuing to Learn, Continuing to Develop

Kristi Bredbenner

In business, it is often said that what got you where you are today won't keep you there. As you well know, being an excellent coach requires ongoing learning and development; it doesn't stop with winning a conference championship. Achieving true excellence in your sport demands inspiration, motivation, leadership, education, and the ability to adapt and develop professionally.

How can I get better? How can I improve?

> The best coaches see where there is room for improvement, and their humility and passion drive them to improve. The average coaches, however, don't see it or don't want to see it. They think that after they arrive at the door of greatness, it will stay open forever, not realizing that if they don't improve, the door will shut and in some cases will even fall on them (Gordon, 2009, 45).

> The first thing that you as a coach must understand is that your coaching philosophy can always change. Change is good. It means that you have evaluated experiences, listened to the beliefs of others, and tried new ideas to see what you think is the best way to approach coaching softball. Every coaching philosophy is unique and ever changing. Learning from your experiences, mentors, players, and mistakes molds that philosophy into something that you hold true to your teaching.

> Complacency is a choice—a way of giving up, of stopping, and of not taking the risk of living into greatness. It's not that there's anything wrong with taking a breather. We go through natural rhythms of activity and rest. We need rest periods to function at our best—like taking the time to sharpen a saw. Complacency arises when these rest periods extend beyond what is necessary for replenishment. Complacency becomes a habit—a conditioned pattern of avoiding doing what we can do because it's easier to do nothing (George, 2006).

For coaches, complacency is not an option. Student-athletes are changing, the game is getting faster and more powerful, and administrators are expecting greater success. To keep up with the pace of the game, you have to continue to learn and develop as a coach. You can develop your knowledge of the game in a variety of ways. Some require you to get outside your comfort zone, some require you to pay it forward, and some require you to be a follower instead of a leader. Throughout your career you can continue to learn and grow in your sport in a multitude of ways. Love of the game and willingness to learn from peers, players, and mentors can make a good coach great.

LEARNING FROM EXPERIENCES

An effective leader is forged by event, experience, observation, and education.

John Wooden

On August 18, 2001, I received a phone call that would change my life. As a fifth-year senior at Truman State University, I was looking forward to being a normal student during my last year in college when the athletic director, Jerry Wollmering, called me into his office. Former head coach Kristy Schroeder had taken a job at the University of California, Santa Barbara in June, and her replacement had just called to tell Jerry that she had decided not to take the job. School was starting, and the softball program had no one to manage fall practices. Jerry asked if I could step in as the interim head coach for the semester until they had time to do another coaching search. I accepted his offer, and my life changed as soon as the office door shut behind me.

Talk about a learning experience. After four years of catching at Truman I was now the person developing practice plans, recruiting, running a booster club, and ultimately writing out a lineup card for a group of girls who were depending on me to make the right choices. I had no college coaching experience, yet here I was at the helm of a successful NCAA Division II program. The administration checked in on a regular basis to make sure that I was staying afloat, but ultimately it was up to me to keep the team going in the right direction.

After the season ended I had two options—stay at Truman as the full-time head coach or move my life to Santa Barbara, California, to be an assistant coach under Schroeder at UCSB. After weighing the pros and cons of both offers, I decided that I would benefit more from being an assistant coach at a Division I school on the West Coast than I would as head coach at Truman.

Truman proved to be a great experience for me. I realized that coaching was my passion and that softball would always be part of my life. The challenges that I faced helped me to grow as a person and prepared me for the next phase in my coaching career.

After two months as the assistant coach at UCSB, Kristy informed me that she was pregnant with her first child. Although this was exciting news for the Schroeders, the timing presented a slight problem. She was due in February, sometime between our trip to San Diego State and the Softball by the Beach tournament that we hosted in Santa Barbara. In February, with great mentoring by Kristy and the help of a student assistant, I again stepped into the third-base coaching box. My experiences at Truman and UCSB shaped my coaching philosophy. Throughout those four years I had the opportunity to pick the brains of some of the greatest coaches in the country.

One of the main ways that we learn and develop is through our failures and mistakes. In many instances the first thing you have to do is acknowledge a mistake. The ability to be open-minded and make adjustments is one of the most important attributes a leader should have.

LEARNING FROM YOUR PLAYERS

*An **effective*** leader is good at listening. It's difficult to listen when you are talking.

Coach Wooden did not learn only from great coaches. He learned from his own athletes, from coaches of no particular celebrity, and from people beyond the world of sport. He was open to learning from whoever had valuable information that he could use to elevate his team.

Each day that you get to interact with your players is a new chance to find out who they are and learn from them. Coaches who take the time to listen to their players will get better insight into their personal lives, the team, and any other issues that are affecting them. Opening the lines of communication with your players encourages discussion, feedback, and problem solving for everyone.

To learn and get the best out of your players, you have to understand them and the generation in which they were raised. If you ask coaches who have been in the business for the last 20 years, they will tell you that the athlete of today is significantly different from the athlete of their first couple of years of coaching. Today's athlete grew up with showers of attention and high expectations from parents. They display a great deal of self-confidence to the point of appearing cocky. They started out playing in little leagues that had no winners or losers, or all winners. They've since grown up and put all their emphasis on being recruited by the biggest and best colleges they can. To do that, they have to play every weekend in an exposure tournament, where everyone gets to play and there are no winners. If they aren't getting the playing time that they are looking for, they quit and join a new team, or one of their parents starts up a new program. How are you going to get the best out of this generation and the generations to come?

In October 2012 the administration at Wichita State University brought in Tim Elmore. Tim changed my perspective of the student-athlete. Ironically, in December of that same year the NFCA chose Tim to speak at the coaching convention. Generation iY (so called because of the influence of iTunes, iPhones, iPods, and the Internet) offers insight on what could happen to our society if we don't change the way that we relate to today's teens and young adults. The Habitudes series offers a different approach to teaching leadership, changing culture, and communicating through images. Tim and many others are presenting material that gives us insight into something important in coaching—how to communicate, relate to the current generation, and help them take on leadership roles on teams and in their lives.

COACHING CONNECTIONS

After working at four colleges I've gained some perspective on whether my department is a team or I am an individual. After being at Wichita State for almost two years, I can see the direction that our athletic director Eric Sexton and senior women's administrator Becky Endicott wants our department to go. They want the entire department to be the best, and one way they try to get that point across is through our coaches' round table meetings. Every other week we have a coaches' meeting or a coaches' round table. Although coaches' meetings are somewhat formal, the coaches' round table meetings are used to get the coaches talking and sharing ideas that can improve every program. We cover topics such as marketing our programs, developing booster relations, and defining the mission of the department. The meetings are not mandatory, but they provide a great deal of feedback from coaching peers.

In addition to attending meetings like our coaches' round table, take it upon yourself to get to know the other coaches and the administration in the athletics department. Many of them have been in your shoes and can provide advice on how they handled various situations.

PROFESSIONAL DEVELOPMENT

It's what you learn after you know it all that counts.

John Wooden

We may not have a few hours each day to commit to our professional development, but we all can find at least 10 minutes. One significant way to develop as a leader is by reading. When we seek opportunities to learn and enhance our perspectives, we discover inspiration, enrichment, and even opinions that challenge and expand our own. You may say to yourself, "I don't have time to read." Although you might not have an hour every night to spend with a book, you can reprioritize your life to free up a few minutes.

Here are five quick ways in which you can carve out time to learn:

- Limit your e-mailing to a few select times during the day. Constant e-mail checking is a time-consuming productivity killer.
- Be disciplined at the break room. Cut out a few minutes from each visit, and you have just uncovered time to pick up the paper!
- Search the web with purpose. There's more than 10 minutes of worthy reading material online. Make it a priority to discover it.
- Schedule reading into your daily routine. Keep a book on your iPad by your bedside and promise yourself that you will read 10 pages each night.
- For those who use mass transit, pick up a magazine or swap the music on your iPod for an enriching podcast.

Leaders are on a constant quest to improve. New ideas and concepts can allow you to develop continuously, all the while igniting your imagination (Morgan and Lynch 2011).

In 2002 I attended my first NFCA coaches' convention. As the four-day convention grew closer I remember thinking about how great it would be to get away from the office and enjoy the warm Tampa weather. After attending my first coaches' caucus and listening to two passionate coaches go back and forth about the hot topic of the day, I knew that the convention was more than just a four-day vacation. This meeting was a chance for me to network, learn from some of the best in the sport, and have my voice heard. I have attended all but one convention since, and each year I look forward to seeing old friends, hearing the various perspectives that the speakers bring to the table, and witnessing a raging debate on the NCAA rules or recruiting opportunities.

In 2010 Sue Enquist and Annie Smith introduced an evening mentoring session at the NFCA convention. The inaugural mentoring session included 61 current and former head coaches and NFCA Hall of Fame members. Young head coaches and assistants had an opportunity to learn from the best. Whether it was hitting strategies, practice organization, or dealing with today's player, the topics and conversation were the talk of the convention. All participants, including the mentors, learned from the conversations in the room and were able to network with people they may never have talked to before. In 2011 the number of attendees who signed up for the mentoring session was larger than expected. Eighty-four veteran coaches, Hall of Fame coaches, and Olympians mentored over 400 participants.

In 2000 the movie *Pay It Forward* starring Kevin Spacey, Helen Hunt, and Haley Joel Osment taught moviegoers what it meant to create good will. Spacey, a social studies teacher, challenges his students to change the world for the better through good deeds. Recipients of good deeds, instead of returning the favor, were asked to pass it on to someone else. Many coaches and organizations are paying it forward in the softball world. The late, great Mary Nutter, founder of National Sports Clinics, is an example of someone who paid it forward. Mary provided affordable clinics all over the country for coaches to learn from some of the most passionate and experienced coaches in the game. Although her booming voice made her a recognizable figure at the clinics, Mary was all about teaching the sport and making sure that those attending the camps were getting the best information they could. Mary brought in the best the sport has to offer to speak at each clinic and provided instruction for all levels. National Sports Clinics have provided me with great information, and I look forward to attending them in the future. Take some time each year to pay it forward in the sport. If we want the game to continue to improve, we have to take the time to teach the game. Whether you are speaking with a T-ball coach wanting to learn about the game for the first time or a Division I head coach looking for a new perspective, your willingness to provide insight and knowledge about softball paves the way for the future.

One of the best ways that I have learned throughout my 11 years of coaching is through books. Each year I pick two or three books to read from an assortment of topics including sport skill books, coaching biographies, business strategy, and leadership. Books are inexhaustible sources of knowledge and wisdom about life, the human condition, the world around us, history, philosophy, and more. In books, we find the lives of great leaders, successful entrepreneurs, brilliant thinkers, and people of action and accomplishment. A library of good books is a wise collection of friends, mentors, counselors, advisers, and encouragers.

Ten Tips for More Effective Reading

1. Schedule a daily reading time, preferably an hour a day or more.
2. Be a discriminating reader.
3. Keep books handy wherever you are.
4. Don't just read books; interact with them.
5. Furnish your home with good books.
6. Set aside a portion of your vacation time for a reading sabbatical.
7. Share your reading experiences with other enthusiastic readers.
8. Use what you learn.
9. Widen your reading horizons.
10. Encourage reading in others, especially the young.

(Williams 2011, 105)

THE BEST LEADERS ARE GOOD FOLLOWERS

Before you can be a good leader, you have to be a good follower.

John Wooden

Most full-time, graduate, student, and volunteer assistants are continuously learning through their experiences.

Characteristics of Great Followers

1. They are clear. They understand their role. You can't be a good follower unless you have clearly identified the leader. Although you may be a leader in your own realm, everyone has a boss—including you. Great followers not only accept this fact but embrace it.

2. They are obedient. Although obedience may be a politically incorrect concept, it is essential for the organizational effectiveness. No one who can't obey orders should be allowed to give orders. This is how great leaders model to their followers the standards of acceptance.

3. They are servants. This is crucial. Great followers are observant. They notice what needs to be done to help the leader accomplish his or her goals. Then they do it—joyfully, without grumbling or complaining.

4. They are humble. Great followers don't make it about them. They are humble. They shine the light on the leader. They make their own boss look good—especially in front of his or her boss.

5. They are loyal. Great followers never speak ill of their boss in public. This doesn't mean that they can't disagree or even criticize. It just means that they don't do it in public. Great followers understand that public loyalty leads to private influence.

NFCC TEXAS WOMEN'S UNIVERSITY MASTER'S PROGRAM

In 2002 the National Fastpitch Coaches Association teamed up with Texas Women's University to offer a master of science degree in kinesiology with an emphasis in coaching. TWU and the NFCA developed a curriculum that combined coaching theories with practical experience. The master's program is made up of eight NFCC courses, 24 hours of professional development coursework, and four TWU graduate courses totaling 12 credit hours.

Throughout the year eight NFCC courses are offered in a multitude of cities, including two at the Women's College World Series in Oklahoma City and several at the NFCA convention site. They cover such topics as the art of championship coaching, offensive game strategy, and winning strategies for game-day coaching. The classes focus on the fundamentals and strategies used in today's game. The NFCC registration fee includes the cost of an in-depth course manual, which supplements the material being taught during the class. The manual is considered part of the course and is not written as a stand-alone resource because of the analysis and discussion presented by NFCC instructors.

These classes are not only an excellent way to complete the master's program needed to coach at the collegiate level but also offer coaches a chance to network with other softball coaches across the nation and listen to various perspectives on the sport.

BUYING IN AND LIFE LESSONS

Each member of your team has the potential for personal greatness; a leader's job is to teach them how to do it.

John Wooden

Coach Wooden tells us that his favorite thing about coaching was teaching. He was a teacher of the game and life. Getting your student-athletes to buy into your teaching, whether you are teaching the fundamentals on the field or life lessons, can be a daunting challenge.

In the summer of 2009 the mother of one of my freshmen came up to me at a summer softball tournament. She thanked me for teaching her daughter some manners. Never before had her daughter said please and thank you on a regular basis. At Emporia State one of the first things we talk about when we go over team rules is manners and what a privilege it is to be a student-athlete.

My first year at Emporia taught me the importance of manners. After starting the season 40-1, we ended up at Missouri Western State College for a tournament. Between games I decided to take the team to Chili's for lunch. Any time you take a large group to a restaurant, you are going to have timing issues. Several of the girls were done eating before the coaches had been served their food. Our waitress was running around trying to make everyone happy without any pleases or thank-yous from the girls. Halfway through my meal I looked down the table and could not believe what I was seeing. Three of my players were stacking their leftover food on one plate as high as they could, and my senior captain was talking on her cell phone. After we finished eating I went out to start the bus. As I opened the door I had one player thank me for lunch. I had heard and seen enough. After pulling in to the parking lot I had all the girls sit down in their seats, and I laid into them about their manners or lack thereof.

Unfortunately, the ramifications of that talk resulted in our second loss of the season, but the pleases and thank-yous that I heard from that point forward never got old. Those girls learned the hard way, but every team I have had since knew that we were going to treat everyone with respect and that no one was entitled to anything. When that mom came up to me that summer, I knew that I had had an influence on her daughter even if it had nothing to do with softball.

FINAL THOUGHTS

No matter how much we know, we can never know it all, for one simple reason: Our athletes and situations keep changing. What works in one situation with one group of athletes may or may not work in another. So we have to expand and polish our teaching and leadership skills to equip our athletes to face new situations.

Whatever you do, whatever you hear or don't hear from those around you, you absolutely have to stay committed to one thing. You must never stop learning. It's something you control completely. Do it every single day.

> ***The best*** are always looking for ways to learn, apply, improve, and grow. They are humble and hungry. They are lifelong learners.
>
> John Gordon (2009, 45)

26

Coaching, Family, and Personal Priorities

Deanna Gumpf

I write this chapter as a spouse, a mother of two, and an NCAA Division I head coach. I write this chapter while trying to win a conference championship, a regional championship, and a national championship. I write this chapter trying to make sure that every player in our program graduates in four years and receives the best possible student-athlete experience. I write this chapter as a parent whose ultimate goal is to raise well-behaved, happy, and healthy children who will learn to make good choices for themselves and take responsibility for their actions as they mature. Lastly, I write this chapter as a parent and a coach who has learned, and is still learning, to deal with uncontrollable external forces that make balancing family and career even more difficult.

BALANCING ACT

We all know that balancing a family and a job can be a challenge. When you are the head coach of a softball program, the balancing act becomes more difficult, especially at the higher levels of the sport. I have seen numerous young coaches who chose to start a family get out of coaching because being both a coach and a parent can be just too difficult.

If you were asked why you began your coaching career, your answer would most likely come easily: love of the game, passion, determination, drive, competition, teaching, winning, teamwork, building a team, and so on. Your answer most likely would not include convenience, work hours, stress, pay, or vacation time.

Life is constantly changing. Whether you have a growing family, have pets, or are taking care of other family members, you have to deal with the stresses and priorities of this career. In all cases, a growing family can mean anything from your own children to other people in your life who are important to you.

When you have a growing family, you need to ask yourself why you got into coaching and what is keeping you in coaching. Ideally, your answers are close to being the same. I believe that to be successful as a coach and as a parent, you need to keep these priorities at the forefront. When things seem difficult, appreciate your drive and determination to stay focused on the things that brought you into this profession and motivate you every day.

I have often asked myself how I can be the best coach for my team when I have to go home and be a spouse and parent. How can I balance family and work? How can I possibly give my best to my team, to my partner, to my children, and to everyone else in my life who needs my attention? When I get home, I have to help with homework, make dinner, make sure that the kids are bathed, read a story, talk with my kids about their day, talk with my spouse, watch film, call a recruit, put the kids to bed, work on the scouting report, and so on. The packed schedule leads to exhaustion, pure exhaustion.

You need to find an appropriate balance between career and family. The challenge is to figure out what works best for you, your family, and your team. What is optimal for you as a parent, spouse, and coach? You have to think about this balancing act every day. Your best reward? You can have an amazing personal life and an amazing career. We are the lucky ones. Ours is a life that is rewarding on and off the field, the best of all worlds. How many people do you know who get to have a spouse and family and go to work at the softball field every day? We are blessed, and we can't forget about it when times get tough.

It takes a special person to be married to a coach. Your spouse is the one left at home weekend after weekend. He or she is the sounding board when things are going well and when things are going poorly. Your spouse has to recognize that being a coach isn't the type of career that allows you to leave things at the office. He or she also has to understand that your hours are never going to be nine to five with weekends off. And most important, your spouse goes through the highs of winning and the lows of losing.

Adding children into the equation changes the dimensions of your coaching career. Some people believe that being a father and a coach is much easier than being a mother and a coach. Whether you are male or female, being a parent and a coach brings on challenges that are extremely difficult to negotiate, whether you are prepared or not. If you look around, you can see that it can be done effectively. It's not easy, but it can be done.

> *Balancing the* needs of my players and the program as a whole against my love for my family, my commitment to being fully present in my daughter's life, and my need to find some rejuvenating time for myself, is the most difficult struggle I face as a professional woman, and when I'm able to find that balance, it's also the most rewarding success I enjoy.
>
> Jacquie Joseph, head softball coach, Michigan State University

When you see a successful head coach who is also a full-time parent with small children, you know that an effective and dedicated supporting cast is behind the scenes. Whether it is a spouse or partner, a full-time nanny (day-care provider), or other family member, someone is always there for the children when the coach is out of town or otherwise unavailable to be at home.

Life definitely changes after you have children. Whatever the circumstances, life changes. Finding the balance that works for you as a coach and parent is the key. Whether your children become a major part of your team or you choose to keep team and family separate, only you can decide what is right for you. You need to determine how to bring balance to your life, to let you be the best coach, spouse, and parent you can be.

A major part of coaching is travel—team travel, recruiting, camps, clinics, and so on. This area causes major conflicts for most coach–parents. The best way to deal with travel is to figure out what works best for you as a parent and coach. Some coaches choose to have their children travel with their team. Other coaches keep their private life separate from their work life. And others find a balance whereby their families occasionally travel on road trips.

Coaches usually use one of two thought processes:

1. Keep the kids at home and keep softball and family separate.
2. Bring the kids along and make them become part of the fabric of the program.
3. Either can be a good choice; it just depends on which one works best for the individual and the program.

Leaving the Kids at Home

Leaving your children at home allows you to focus on the task at hand while traveling. The most difficult part of leaving the children at home is just that—you are leaving your children. Coaching requires time, commitment, and focus. Traveling without your children allows you to be available to do all those things without interruption or distractions. Unfortunately, being away from your family also causes an emotional ailment, which we often refer to as guilty parent syndrome. The bottom line is that many times you aren't physically there for your children.

Luckily, with advancements in technology you can stay in contact in many ways, even though you aren't physically with your children. Skype and FaceTime have become popular among parents who are away from their children. They are easy to use and fun. My family designates a specific time for our video calls before I leave town, and we are able to spend a few quality minutes together every day while I'm gone.

Bringing the Kids Along

As a coach and parent you cannot have a better moment than to look up in the stadium seats and see your children waving and cheering on your team. When the game is over, you are able to go back to the hotel and be around your children. Spending this quality time with your family is a definite plus, but this arrangement also has its drawbacks. As a parent you must decide what works for you.

Here are some things to think about:

- How many road trips are you taking throughout the year?
- How long are the road trips that you are taking?
- Is there someone who can come along to help care for your children while you are on the field?
- Do you scout or review video while on the road? If so, how many hours do you spend doing those things?
- How many quality hours will you be able to spend with your children? You have to exclude all game preparation, actual game time, postgame activities, scouting, team meals, and so on.
- Are you comfortable having your children around while you are unable to be actively engaged with them?
- What is truly better for your children? Are you making the choice to bring them for you or for them?

The positive aspect about having your children travel with you is that you don't get guilty parent syndrome. They are with you. When the working day is over, you are able to be with them.

The negative aspect that occurs is the issue of having them around but not being able to spend the time with them that you would like. Although your children are with you, you can't give them your undivided attention. The children become a distraction. You find that you aren't quite the best coach when you're being pulled in another direction by your children, especially when children are young, require more attention, and don't realize why you aren't able to give them the attention they need or want.

Other Factors to Consider

If you choose to bring your children with you on the road, many potential road blocks may get in the way, and you should be prepared to take those challenges head on. Make sure that you know your rights as a coach and parent.

1. What are your institution's policies and procedures on family travel?
2. Is your institution prepared to pay for your children to be on the road with you?
3. Does your institution allow your children to be with you on the road? Are they allowed on the team bus, in vans, in hotels?
4. Find out how to get support from your institution when you choose to bring your family on the road with you.

One of the biggest factors when dealing with this issue is making sure that your student-athletes remain a priority in your decision making. Your players are the ones who play the game, and they are the ones who help build a successful program and a successful coaching situation. Regardless of the decisions you make about bringing your family on the road, you need to keep your players connected to the decision-making process.

Coaching and parenting are strikingly similar. Success in either job isn't a solo mission; it requires the help and support of many people. My support staff includes an athletic director who encourages a family atmosphere at work to grandparents willing to drop everything at a moment's notice to watch my girls. The championships, my daughters' growth and development, and my sanity are all dependent on these factors. My support staff is truly the source of my success.

Laurie Nevarez, head softball coach, University of Redlands

I was eight months pregnant with my son when I accepted my first head coaching position. The best decision for my family and me at the time was to have my son with me as much as possible and travel with my team. With that decision came many challenges and burdens for me, my coaches, my players, and my spouse. But at that time in my life, I thought it was right, and we made it work.

My goal as a parent was never to spend more than three nights away from my son (this lasted about three years). I have vivid memories of him vomiting on my head during a flight home from a tournament. I also remember many sleepless nights and many diaper explosions while my players were holding him. We had some difficult times along with a lot of laughs that accompanied the small disasters. At that time, my son became part of our program.

Four years later, my daughter was born. This time I did things differently. I chose to take my children only when the road trip would be more than four nights. I learned through time that the quick weekend trips were just too brutal for my children, my spouse, and me; too many activities were packed into this short period. Although I didn't want to admit it for a long time, I have realized that I am a better coach when my children are home while I am on the road, and my children are happier staying within their routine. I also believe that I am a better mother for it. I know that during the time that I am with them, I make every effort to give them all my attention. I try to value the quality of time, not the quantity. It doesn't mean it's easy, and I find myself missing them desperately when I am on the road with my team. But I wholeheartedly believe I am doing what is right for my family.

WHEN LIFE THROWS YOU A CURVEBALL

Uncontrollable outside forces thrown into the mix can threaten the balance that you've tried so hard to achieve. Are you prepared for the unexpected? How does your institution deal with family illness or personal illness? You hope that you never need to ask those questions, but I had to face those issues last year when my daughter was diagnosed with leukemia.

You are never prepared to deal with a life-threatening illness. When it happens to your own child, it takes your breath away and makes time stand still. Although the rest of the world was moving forward, I couldn't. The diagnosis took over my world. Life changed in an instant, and so did team dynamics.

When I hired my staff, I had no idea how much I would depend on them and how much trust I needed from them. I spent over a month away from my career. During that time, my two assistants literally took over the program. They did everything—recruiting, administrative duties, meetings, everything. Throughout that time it became clear to me exactly why I hired those two people and how incredibly important it was to have great assistants. My experience supports the notion that as a head coach you need to make sure that you have hired assistants whom you trust and who could step in and take over at a moment's notice.

My team's response to my daughter's illness and the subsequent upheaval in our lives has been phenomenal. Sometimes student-athletes' lives can become extremely narrow. Their focus is on sport and academia. But my daughter's diagnosis not only shook up my world but also greatly affected my team. Their coach's little girl who had cheered them on from the stands and sung the alma mater with them down on the field was now seriously ill. Her illness was a terrible thing, but I think it helped them understand that their coaches are regular people, not just instructors and authority figures. The relationship that I had with my team went to a whole new level. I think that the experience helped us all gain a new, broader perspective and grow as people.

My daughter's diagnosis has also changed me in many ways and has definitely changed my perspective on many areas of my career. Before her diagnosis, winning was everything to me. When my team lost, I would not be able to sleep for days. I would make myself sick over it. I would also lose my temper over little things. I was a much angrier coach.

Now, I still get frustrated when we lose, but I have a much better perspective on the loss. I have replaced anger with disappointment. I enjoy the time I am out on the field, and I appreciate my team more than ever. I try harder to listen to my player's perspective. I believe that my daughter's diagnosis has made me a better coach. I have realized that when I am a better parent, I am a better coach and vice versa. For me, they go hand in hand. My time demands are different. I don't spend as much time in the office and have become more creative with my time. I definitely lean on my coaches and players more than ever.

My philosophy is simple: Family comes first, then school, and softball is last. I believe the key to success is having a philosophy and sticking to it. Being a coach is not a job; it's a lifestyle, and my family allows me to enjoy each day as a working mom.

Kelly Inouye-Perez, head softball coach, UCLA

MAKING IT ALL WORK

Sometimes it feels as though personal challenges and priorities get in the way of being the best possible coach for your players. But only you can determine what makes you the best coach for your players and your university. Every coach has different challenges to deal with. Having challenges and different personal priorities doesn't mean that you can't be the best possible coach for your team. We know that people who spend countless hours at the office and neglect their personal lives are not necessarily the best in their professions. Realistically, the smartest objective is to be the best at your profession during the hours when you are at work. You want to be productive with your time, not just put in hours.

Before having children, I spent at least two to three more hours a day in the office. To make up for the time that I had lost, I had to figure out how to become more efficient and smarter with my time. I had to learn to delegate more responsibilities, trust my assistants, and let go of trying to do so much myself. At times, this didn't come easy. At times, I flat out failed. At times, I still struggle.

A valuable piece of advice that I want to pass on is that you should surround yourself with people who know you and understand and share your values and perspective on coaching and family. It just makes sense. You and your coaches spend entirely too much time together not to enjoy them on and off the field. Coaching is much more fun when you enjoy the people you are with and have similar goals. Conversely, coaching a team is much more difficult if you are part of a staff that is not in sync. The time and energy that you are putting into a staff that does not mesh should be spent on the team. Coaching with people who have unlike goals is aggravating.

Within our coaching family we have four different family dynamics, so our personal priorities are all different. Each of us is in a different phase in our personal lives. Three of us are coaches, mothers, and wives who have children ranging from 15 years old to 3 years old. We also have a coach who is single and in the dating world. We make it a priority to give each other space, but we also try to support each other through various life challenges and changes. The coach who doesn't have children has become part of our extended family. Our staff is fortunate in that we are very close.

I feel so lucky and blessed to be a coach and a mom. I really feel that each one makes me better. I am a better mom because I coach and a better coach because I am a mom. Once I became a mom, coaching wasn't just about the X and Os or even winning, but more importantly about building a team and molding the players to be successful after college. I am a strong believer that what it takes to be a great college student-athlete—the hard work, discipline, dedication, commitment, and drive—are what make you a great person who is ready to tackle the real world. I learn just as much from my team as they do from me. I am so impressed by them each day, and they make me want to work harder for them to see their dreams come true.

Bridget Orchard, head softball coach, Fordham University

BURNOUT

Coaching 18- to 22-year-old women is a challenge, no matter the sport or level. These young women go through many emotions and obstacles during the four years that we have them. As their coaches, we are also mentors, teachers, and sometimes psychologists. We have the opportunity to have a major influence on their lives. Being parents, we also see how important it is to help these women grow as individuals off the field. One of the realizations I have come to is how my student-athletes help me be a better parent to my children and how being a parent helps me be a better coach to my players. These two jobs go hand in hand.

The reality of balancing coaching and family is to be the best you can be without getting to the point of burnout. Sometimes you can just have too much on your plate, so something has to give. Unfortunately, for many women in coaching, it's the coaching that is given up. Through my 16 years in the profession I have seen more mothers leave coaching than stay in coaching. I am biased, but I believe that our young student-athletes can have no better role model than mothers who are coaching at the highest levels. These young women will learn many life lessons without even realizing it. They can see and believe that they can be anyone or do anything. They can be mothers and wives and be able to do something they love. They learn that they don't have to give up one thing for the other, that they can be everything they aspire to be.

Burnout is the harsh reality for many coaching mothers. Women in coaching need to get a handle on where to draw the line and how to avoid spending too many hours at work and trying to do too much. Coaching isn't a nine to five job, and as a coach your work is never really done. You always have something else that needs to be done to make your team and program better. As a coach you always want to improve your game so that you can improve your team's game.

Like everyone else, I struggle at times. Parent–coaches cannot be afraid to get advice. Do research on what other coaches are doing. Reach out to others who are in your shoes or have been successful as a coach–parent. Join coaching groups and alliances. Recognize that you are not alone and that resources are available to you.

RISING TO THE CHALLENGE

Without a doubt, this career presents many challenges. The number of hours we put in to be successful and the time commitment we make throughout the year is the reality of this profession. We miss weekends, we sometimes miss evenings and mornings, we miss Little League games, parent–teacher conferences, birthdays, special events, and so on. Fortunately, we gain huge benefits and advantages that make up for the events we miss. We typically have flexible hours, we get a generous winter holiday break, and we get to play softball every day as a career. Not many people can say that.

Coaching as a career also offers huge benefits for your children. Your children are part of something special. They are surrounded by fantastic, young, goal-oriented student-athletes who are striving for something that takes hard work and dedication. They are great models for our children to learn from! One of my favorite experiences occurs when our alumni return to town and hang out with my family. My children are fortunate to grow up in the college environment, surrounded by amazing young people who have already accomplished a great deal and are striving to accomplish much more personally and through softball.

> **My feeling** is that the more loving people there are in my son's life, the better. Just because I am not home with him does not mean he is not loved. Being around his grandparents and family gives him another outlook on life compared with what solely we can teach him. I am thankful every day for all the people he interacts with and learns from to make him a better human being. I believe that the ultimate goal is to give him all the tools to be independent and successful in life. The EMU family is also my son's extended family. He sometimes goes with me to workouts, fund-raisers, and other events. While some people say it takes a village to raise a child, I like to think of it more as a team!
>
> Karen Baird, head softball coach, Eastern Michigan University

FINAL THOUGHTS

Although it will always be a juggling act, especially when extra challenges are thrown in, I wholeheartedly believe that having a career in coaching and an enriching family life is possible. With a bit of adapting and prioritizing, we can be successful at both.

Perspective is everything in coaching. Finding peace and getting to the point where we can sleep at night knowing that we have done our best each day is vital. Being present in every moment, never taking anything for granted, and enjoying our successes on the field and at home will bring fulfillment and satisfaction.

Works Cited

Chapter 2

Bennett, Bob, ed. 2009. *Practice Perfect Baseball*. Champaign, IL: Human Kinetics.

Cain, Brian. 2011. *Toilets, Bricks, Fish Hooks and Pride*. Peak Performance.

Chapter 3

Carter, Wanda H. *To Achieve Your Dreams, Remember Your ABC's*. http://InspirationMotivation.com.

Kushner, Harold. 1996. *How Good Do We Have to Be?* Boston: Little, Brown and Company.

Chapter 5

Burns, James MacGregor. 1978. *Leadership*. New York: Harper & Row.

Chapter 13

Lewis, Michael. 2003. *Moneyball: The Art of Winning an Unfair Game*. New York: Norton.

Chapter 18

Kiesel, K., P.J. Plisky, and M.L. Voight. 2007. Can serious injury in professional football be predicted by a pre-season functional movement screen?, *North American Journal of Sports Physical Therapy* 2:147–158.

Marshall, S.W., K.L. Hamstra-Wright, R. Dick, K.A. Grove, and J. Agel. 2007. Descriptive epidemiology of collegiate women's softball injuries, *Journal of Athletic Training* 42:286–294.

Powell, J.W., and K.D. Barber-Foss. 2000. Sex-related injury patterns among selected high school sports. *American Journal of Sports Medicine* 28:385–391.

Werner, S., D.G. Jones, J.A. Guido, and M.E. Brunet. 2006. Kinematics and kinetics of elite windmill softball pitching. *American Journal of Sports Medicine* 34:596–602.

Chapter 19

Gordon, J. 2007. *The Energy Bus: 10 Rules to Fuel Your Life, Work, and Team with Positive Energy*. Hoboken, NJ: Wiley.

Hanson, B. n.d. *Success of Coach Athlete Relationships* (Canadian Olympic Study). Athlete Assessments.com.

Janssen, J., and G. Dale. 2002. The Seven Secrets of Successful Coaches: How to Unlock and Unleash Your Team's Potential. Cary, NC: Winning The Mental Game.

Murphy, J. 2010. *Pulling Together*. Naperville, IL: Simple Truths, LLC.

Smith, D., and G.D. Bell with J. Kilgo. 2004. *The Carolina Way, Leadership Lessons From a Life in Coaching*. New York: Penguin.

Stein, A. 2009. *Player/Coach Relationships*. Stronger Team.com.

Chapter 22

Gladwell, M. 2000. *The Tipping Point.* New York: Little, Brown and Company.

Chapter 23

Dorfman, H. 2003. *Coaching the Mental Game: Leadership Philosophies and Strategies for Peak Performance in Sports and Everyday Life* (351–353). Lanham, MD: Taylor Trade.

Chapter 25

George, Kim. 2006. *Coaching Into Greatness: 4 Steps to Success in Business and Life.* Hoboken, NJ: Wiley.

Gordon, John. 2009. *Training Camp.* Hoboken, NJ: Wiley.

Morgan, Angie, and Courtney Lynch. 2011. *Never Stop Learning.* http://coachandrea.com/2011/07/22/never-stop-learning.

The Best Coaches Never Stop Learning. n.d. http://chsolutions.typepad.com/elevatingathletes/2008/08/the-best-coache.html.

Williams, Pat. 2011. *Coach Wooden: The 7 Principles That Shaped His Life and Will Change Yours.* Grand Rapids, MI: Revell.

Wooden, John, and Steve Jamison. 2007. *The Essential Wooden: A lifetime of Lessons on Leaders and Leadership.* New York: McGraw-Hill.

About the NFCA

The **National Fastpitch Coaches Association (NFCA)** is the sport's leading professional growth organization for coaches at all competitive levels of play. The NFCA works to formulate guiding principles, standards, and policies for conducting competitive fastpitch softball programs for girls and women. It encourages players to participate in softball with the highest tradition of competition and to become leaders in their fastpitch programs. The NFCA recognizes outstanding members through its Victory Club and Coach of the Year awards programs, in addition to All-Region, All-American, and Scholar-Athlete awards programs for members' college and high school players. The NFCA also works with *USA Today* to produce polls for NCAA Division I, II, and III and high school softball teams, and it hosts collegiate tournaments and recruiting camps across the nation.

The NFCA headquarters are located in Louisville, Kentucky.

Gayle Blevins served as head coach for Division I collegiate softball programs for 31 years, coaching at Indiana University from 1980 to 1987 and at the University of Iowa from 1988 to 2010. She brought the two teams to the Women's College World Series seven times and never had a losing season at either university. She led her teams to eight Big Ten championships, winning five of them. She amassed 1,245 wins overall. Additionally, she has seen nearly 80 of her former players become coaches of their own teams across the nation.

Blevins was named NCAA Division I Coach of the Year by the National Softball Coaches Association in 1986 when the Hoosiers finished in third place in the Women's College World Series under her tutelage. Blevins was inducted into the National Fastpitch Coaches Association Hall of Fame in 1999. Twice she has been selected as the Division I National Coach of the Year.

Blevins now works as a National Fastpitch Coaches College instructor. She also serves as a public speaker for national conventions, service organizations, educational institutions, and corporations across the United States.

About the Contributors

Jenny Allard is the Ivy League's longest tenured coach. She has spent nearly 20 seasons as the head coach of the Harvard softball program. She is also one of the Ivy League's most successful coaches, boasting a 462-342-2 overall record, including a 213-74 Ivy League mark. All six of Harvard's Ivy League titles, each of its six 30-win seasons, and its five NCAA championship berths have been under the watch of Allard. Her teams have produced 45 first-team, 51 second-team, and 30 honorable mention All-Ivy selections as well as 6 Ivy League Players of the Year, 5 Ivy Pitchers of the Year, and 3 Ivy Rookies of the Year.

A 1990 graduate of the University of Michigan, Allard was named the Wolverines' Most Outstanding Player and Most Outstanding Pitcher. Allard was a four-time All-Big Ten Conference selection and a two-time first-team Mideast Region selection. She was named Big Ten Player of the Year and a Division I All-America selection. Named to the Big Ten all-decade team in 1992, Allard ranked in the top four all time in 15 hitting and pitching categories at the time of her graduation from Michigan.

Erica Beach has been head softball coach at the University of Mexico since 2010. Under her guidance, the Lobos have set Mountain West Conference records for most home runs (95) and best team slugging percentage (.568), and the team has been ranked no. 1 among NCAA Division I softball programs for home runs. Beach worked as an assistant to the Ohio State Buckeyes from 2006 to 2010. With her assistance, the team advanced to the NCAA regional championship game four times, including one super regional appearance.

As a player, Beach pitched for the Arizona State Sun Devils, helping advance them to NCAA tournament all four times, including two Women's College World Series appearances. She was named to the 2002 WCWS all-tournament team and was a three-time All-Pac-10 honoree. Beach played professionally for the Sparks Haarlem in the Netherlands, leading the team to the 2003 European Cup championship, for which she was named the European Cup Most Outstanding Pitcher. In 2004 and 2005, she played for the Arizona Heat in the National Pro Fastpitch League and was an all-star in 2004. From 2006 to 2008, Beach helped lead the New England Riptide to the NPF championship.

Chris Bellotto is the head softball coach at Florida Southern College, where she has led the program for over 30 years. Under her guidance, Florida Southern has won more conference titles than any other Division II program. In 2012 the team made their 20th trip to the NCAA tournament. Overall, Bellotto's teams have won 24 conference titles, 8 regional titles, and 1 national championship. The Moccasins remain the only Sunshine State Conference (SSC) softball program to go undefeated through conference in any season, doing so seven times. Twenty-six All-Americans have played for Bellotto, winning a total of 45 All-American awards, including 24 first-team selections.

Bellotto's 1,110-362 record in fastpitch competition and .754 winning percentage put her among the all-time leaders in every coaching category in the NCAA record book. She has been named the SSC Coach of the Year 15 times, regional Coach of the Year 10 times, and NFCA Division II National Coach of the Year 2 times. She was named the head coach on the SSC silver anniversary team in 2007. Bellotto has been inducted into the National Fastpitch Coaches Association Hall of Fame, the Sunshine State Conference Hall of Fame, the Florida Southern College Athletic Hall of Fame, and the Polk County Sports Hall of Fame.

Kristi Bredbenner is the head softball coach at Wichita State University. Before joining the Shockers in 2012, Bredbenner spent six seasons leading Division II Emporia State University. Under her tutelage, Emporia State had a winning percentage of .763 and appeared in the NCAA postseason seven straight years, including a trip to the NCAA Division II national championship game in 2006. The team went to six straight Mid-America Intercollegiate Athletics Association championships. Bredbenner was named MIAA Coach of the Year twice, and she and her staff were named NCFA/Speedline Regional Coaching Staff of the Year two times.

Bredbenner spent three seasons as the top assistant at the University of California at Santa Barbara, guiding them to their first NCAA tournament and a second-place finish in the Big West Conference. She served as interim head coach at her alma mater, Truman State University, during the 2002 season. That year the team won the MIAA tournament championship. As a player, Bredbenner was a four-time All-MIAA pick and two-time Division II All-American, and she was named MVP of the conference in 2000. She claimed nearly every hitting record at Truman, and her three-home-run game on April 7, 2000, is tied for fourth on the Division II single-game list.

Carol Bruggeman has been the associate head coach at the University of Louisville since 2005. She has helped guide the Cardinals to three Big East Conference championships and seven straight NCAA appearances. She has helped produce 45 All-Big East selections, 13 all-region team members, 6 All-Americans, and 3 conference Players or Pitchers of the Year. In 2012 Bruggeman was part of the Big East and NFCA Great Lakes Regional Coaching Staffs of the Year. That year Louisville captured the Big East regular-season and tournament titles, spent the majority of the season ranked in the top 10 of both national polls, and ended the season with a program-best 55-5 record.

Before joining the Cardinals, Bruggeman spent 12 years as head coach at Purdue University and 5 years as assistant coach at the University of Michigan. As an athlete, she played at the University of Iowa, where she earned All-Big Ten, All-Mideast Region, and Academic All-American honors. She has served as president and Division I representative on the executive board with the NFCA. Additionally, Bruggeman has produced instructional DVDs on softball-specific athlete development.

Ehren Earleywine, head softball coach at the University of Missouri, has taken the Tigers softball program to unprecedented levels of success. Earleywine has led Missouri to three Women's College World Series, making five straight NCAA super regional appearances. Heading into the 2013 season his .750 winning percentage was ranked eighth among active Division I coaches. He was the fifth fastest coach to reach 100 wins in NCAA Division I softball history. Previously the head coach at Georgia Tech (2004–06), Earleywine has led every team he has coached to the NCAA tournament. A three-time conference Coach of the Year, he and his coaching staff have twice been named National Fastpitch Coaches Association Midwest Staff of the Year.

As a player in men's fastpitch softball, Earleywine was a four-time member of the U.S. team and was named captain for his final two seasons with the national team. He collected four medals—one gold, two silver, and one bronze. A six-time American Softball Association All-American, Earleywine was an all-world selection in 1999 by the International Softball Congress. Earleywine won the ASA Softball national championship title with the Decatur Pride in 1999, taking ISC world championship honors in 2001.

NFCA Hall of Fame coach **Patty Gasso** has served as head coach at the University of Oklahoma since 1995. Under her leadership the Sooners have reached the Women's College World Series seven times and in the process advanced to the postseason every season. Gasso has a career collegiate coaching record of 1'032-338-3 (.753) and holds an overall record of 871-279-2 (.757) at the University of Oklahoma. Gasso's Sooners teams have finished second or higher 13 times since the inception of the Big 12 and have claimed five Big 12 regular-season titles and four championship titles.

Of Gasso's players, 41 have been named All-Americans, 87 have earned all-region honors, and 118 have been all-conference selections. Seven Sooners have been named Big 12 Player of the Year. Gasso has received three Speedline/NFCA Midwest Region Coaching Staff of the Year awards—the national honor in 2000 and the Midwest honor six times. In addition, Gasso has been named the Big 12 Coach of the Year five times. Before coming to OU, Gasso spent five years at Long Beach City College. Her accomplishments there led to her induction into the LBCC Hall of Champions and the inaugural class of the Long Beach City Baseball and Softball Hall of Fame.

Stetson University's **Frank Griffin** has been head coach of the Hatters since 1996. Griffin has led the Hatters to 543 wins, 14 appearances in the Atlantic Sun softball tournament, two regular-season championships, one conference tournament title, and an appearance in the NCAA tournament. Five times the Hatters have eclipsed the 40-win mark. Griffin has coached 29 A-Sun Pitchers of the Week, 19 A-Sun Players of the Week, 19 first-team all-conference players, 22 second-team all-conference players, 4 third-team all-conference players, 4 all-freshman team players, 1 A-Sun Player of the Year, 2 first-team all-region performers, and 5 second-team all-region players. He also earned 2001 A-Sun Coach of the Year honors.

Before arriving at Stetson, Griffin spent seven years as head softball coach at Winthrop University in Rock Hill, South Carolina. With the Lady Eagles, Griffin compiled a record of 225-87, won six conference titles in seven seasons, and led Winthrop to three NAIA national tournaments. Griffin also played fastpitch softball for the Rock Hill Merchants for five seasons, pitching his team to the South Carolina state championship in 1988, for which he was named team MVP. The Merchants went on to win the Southeast Regional championship in 1988 and again in 1989.

Deanna Gumpf is the head softball coach at Notre Dame University. Under her tutelage, the Fighting Irish have made 11 trips to the NCAA championship while claiming four Big East Conference tournament titles and six Big East regular-season championships, the most recent occurring in 2010 and 2011. As of 2013 Gumpf had a record of 465-192-1 (.707) for the highest victory average of any Big East skipper. She became the program's all-time winningest coach with her 378th victory at Notre Dame in the 2010 NCAA tournament.

Under Gumpf's guidance, the Notre Dame coaching staff was named the NFCA Mideast Region Coaching Staff of the Year in 2002 and 2004 as well as the Big East Coaching Staff of the Year in 2002, 2004, and 2011. She has seen 11 Notre Dame players earn NFCA All-American honors; Andrea Loman (2002-03) and Megan Ciolli (2004-05) were two-time All-Americans. The Irish have collected 41 NFCA all-region citations, 4 Big East Player of the Year awards, 4 Big East Pitcher of the Year awards, and 74 All-Big East honors.

Kris Herman has been head softball coach at Williams College since 2004. In May 2010 she became the 26th Division III coach to reach the 500-win milestone in NCAA history. She has led the Ephs to three straight New England Small College Athletic Conference (NESCAC) championships, advancing to the NCAA College World Series twice. She has a career record of 521-290-5 (.642), and from 1997 to 2006, Herman coached her teams to nine consecutive conference championships. She was named NESCAC Coach of the Year four times and earned New England COTY honors in 2001, 2005, and 2006. In her nearly 25 seasons as a coach, Herman has coached 8 All-Americans and 27 first-team All-New England players.

Herman began her coaching career at her alma mater, Tufts, in 1988. She coached the Jumbos for 16 seasons and compiled a record of 339-164-3 (.679), winning five NESCAC titles and guiding her team to an NCAA tournament appearance in her last seven seasons at the school. Tufts also made its first NCAA World Series appearance under Herman. In May 2011 Herman was promoted to senior women's administrator at Williams.

Head coach **Kyla Holas** has been with the University of Houston softball program since 1999. She has led the team to 11 consecutive winning seasons, 5 NCAA regional appearances (2004, 2007, 2008, 2011, and 2012), and 2 NCAA super regional appearances (2008 and 2011). At the beginning of the 2013 season, Holas held the most wins (434) in Conference USA history. The Cougars are three-time regular-season champions (2007, 2008, 2011) and were the Conference USA tournament champions in 2007. They became only the second team in conference history to sweep both titles in a season.

Holas came to the Cougars program from the University of Florida, where she was responsible for developing the pitchers and catchers for three seasons. Before going to Florida, Holas spent two seasons as an assistant coach at Northern Illinois University. Under her guidance the team reached the NCAA regionals. As an athlete, she led Southwestern Louisiana to a third-place finish at the 1993 NCAA Women's College World Series. She is a three-time NCAA All-American pitcher, received WCWS all-tournament team honors, and was a two-time finalist for the Honda Broderick Cup. Her .839 (104-20) winning percentage is still in the top 15 in NCAA record books.

Kelly Inouye-Perez has served as head coach for the UCLA Bruins since 2007, amassing a record of 255-88 (.743) between the beginning of her UCLA career and 2013. Under her guidance, in 2010 the team had their 12th national title and 11th NCAA championship. After the season, Inouye-Perez and her staff were honored as the NFCA National Coaching Staff of the Year. Over Inouye-Perez's six seasons, Bruins players have earned 16 All-American awards, 25 all-region honors, and 46 All-Pac-10 or All-Pac-12 accolades.

No stranger to the Bruins dugout, Inouye-Perez started her 25th season with the program in 2013. She is a link to four decades of Bruins softball success, joining the UCLA softball program as a freshman and spending 13 years as an assistant coach. As a player and assistant, she attended seven NCAA championships and earned eight Pac-10 titles. Over Inouye-Perez's seasons as an assistant coach, UCLA was 617-150-1; in 2004 she was part of the staff that was named the National Coaching Staff of the Year by the National Fastpitch Coaches Association (NFCA).

Rachel Lawson began her sixth season as the head coach of the Kentucky softball program in 2013. Kentucky made its fourth consecutive appearance in the NCAA tournament in 2012. In 2011 Lawson directed the Wildcats to their first NCAA super regional appearance and finished the season ranked 12th in the country. Before joining the staff at Kentucky, Lawson spent three seasons at Western Kentucky. She served as an assistant coach at Maryland from 1996 to 2002, where she was named part of the National Fastpitch Coaches Association Mid-Atlantic Coaching Staff of the Year. She also served as the associate head coach of the Philadelphia Force professional team in 2006.

Lawson was a two-time all-conference player at Massachusetts, where she was part of a program that advanced to the 1992 Women's College World Series. She was part of squads that advanced to the NCAA tournament her freshman season, won three Atlantic 10 tournament titles, and claimed the league regular-season championship four straight years. Lawson was named an all-conference and All-Atlantic 10 tournament performer and was named to the A-10 academic all-conference squad after each of her final two seasons.

Bob Ligouri is the Des Moines Area Community College softball coach. He joined the program in 2011 and built it from scratch. In his first year of coaching at the collegiate level, he compiled a 42-21 record and led his team to Region 11 and District F championships. His team has also appeared in the NJCAA College World Series. In his second year, the team ranked 12th preseason in the nation for teams entering their second year of existence. Ligouri has overseen 16 academic all-region team members in his time with DMACC.

Before coming to DMACC, Ligouri coached softball at West Des Moines Dowling Catholic and Des Moines East High School. While with the two high schools, he compiled a 636-136 record. His teams won two state championships and were state runners-up twice, making 10 state tournament appearances. For his work with his high school teams, Ligouri was honored with 10 Coach of the Year awards. He oversaw 11 top 10 teams in his 16 years of coaching, and 44 of his players went on to play college softball, including 19 at the Division I level.

Sandy Montgomery is the longest tenured head coach for Southern Illinois University Edwardsville. The 2013 season marked her 25th year as the head coach of the Cougars softball team. At the start of the 2013 season, her career coaching record stood at 849-428-2. She led the Cougars to a Division II national championship in 2007 and five Great Lakes Valley Conference tournament championships. Her teams have played in the NCAA Division II national tournament 11 times and the national finals twice. Additionally, SIUE finished fourth during its first run through the Ohio Valley Conference, qualifying for the 2011 OVC tournament in its first year of eligibility.

Montgomery has coached 11 All-Americans and 52 players with all-region status. She has been inducted into the SIUE Athletics Hall of Fame and Illinois Amateur Softball Association's Hall of Fame. She has received the Great Lakes Valley Conference's Coach of the Year honor four times, the NFCA Regional Coaching Staff of the Year award three times, and the National Staff of the Year honor in 2007. As a player Montgomery was one of the most successful pitchers in SIUE's history, hurling 42 shutouts, being named a Central Region All-American, and being voted Most Valuable Player her senior year.

Teena Murray has been the director of sport performance at the University of Louisville since 2004, where she oversees athlete development and performance for the Cardinals' 21 Olympic sports. She is also the lead performance specialist for women's softball and basketball. Outside the collegiate realm, Murray is the owner of Athlete Construction, LLC. From 2006 to 2010 Murray was the strength and conditioning coach for the U.S. women's national and Olympic ice hockey teams, winning two world championships and a silver medal at the Olympic Games in Vancouver in 2010.

In 16 years in the sport performance industry, Murray has worked at Cornell, UConn, and Louisville. She has also worked as a consultant with USA Hockey, the International Ice Hockey Federation, the NHL's Florida Panthers and Anaheim Ducks, and the AHL's Hartford Wolfpack. Teena holds a master's degree is exercise physiology from the University of North Carolina at Greensboro. She is a master coach with the Collegiate Strength and Conditioning Coaches' Association and is certified by the National Strength and Conditioning Association, United States Weightlifting, Functional Movement Systems, and Precision Nutrition. In 2012 Teena was awarded the Guiding Woman in Sport Award by the National Association of Girls and Women in Sport (NAGWS).

Stacey Nuveman Deniz entered her fifth season at San Diego State in 2013, serving as the recruiting coordinator and the hitting instructor. She has helped SDSU to four straight NCAA regional bids and a combined 133-81 (.621) record in her four seasons on the Mesa. She has assisted the team in breaking many school records, including slugging percentage (.466), doubles (79), home runs (58), RBIs (237), and total bases (692). In addition to coaching, Nuveman Deniz has provided commentary for ESPN, CSTV, and Fox Sports and has served as a studio analyst for ESPN during NCAA tournament action. In the spring of 2010 Nuveman Deniz served as an assistant coach for the women's national team selection camp.

A three-time U.S. Olympian, Nuveman Deniz earned two gold medals (2000 and 2004) and a silver medal (2008) and was inducted into the U.S. Olympic Hall of Fame for her work with the 2004 team. She helped the U.S. national team to a World Cup championship in 2006, two world championships, and two Pan American gold medals. As a collegiate player at UCLA, she set four NCAA records—90 home runs, .945 slugging percentage (both of which rank her first in the NCAA), 240 walks, and 81 intentional walks. She was a four-time first-team NFCA All-American and a three-time Pac-10 Player of the Year, and she helped lead the Bruins to a national championship. For her efforts in the national title run, Nuveman Deniz was named to the All-Women's College World Series team. She was inducted into the UCLA Hall of Fame in 2012.

Donna Papa has been head softball coach at the University of North Carolina since 1986. Papa has led Carolina to the NCAA tournament 10 times, the 2001 Atlantic Coast Conference championship, and 5 regular-season titles, and her teams appeared in the title game on three other occasions. One of the 20 winningest coaches in NCAA history, Papa has compiled an impressive 1,051-569-5 record and is among only 11 NCAA Division I coaches to achieve 1,000 victories. She has been named ACC Coach of the Year five times and has coached 11 All-America players and 56 All-Southeast Region players.

Before arriving in Chapel Hill, Papa spent two seasons as head softball and volleyball coach at Susquehanna University, two seasons as assistant softball coach at St. John's University, and one year as an assistant coach at UNC Greensboro. She played four seasons of softball for the University of Connecticut and was cocaptain in her junior and senior seasons. Her playing career also encompassed stints with two ASA Major Fast Pitch teams. Papa has served on the NFCA All-America Committee and NCAA All-Region Committee and represented the ACC on the NFCA Top 25 Selection Committee twice. She was inducted into the NFCA Hall of Fame in November 2012.

Jeanne Scarpello began her 14th season as the head coach at the University of Nebraska at Omaha in 2013. She led the Mavericks to a Division II national championship in 2001 and is now leading the program in the Division I Summit League. Scarpello is UNO's all-time winningest coach, entering the 2013 season with a 563-181-1 career record. She has led the Mavs to three 50-win seasons and nine 40-win seasons in her 13 years at UNO, including the program's first national title in 2001.

Scarpello has averaged more than 43 wins per season, and her resume includes 12 trips to the NCAA Division II tournament, five conference tournament titles, and one national championship. In 2001 she and her staff were named the NFCA Division II National Coaching Staff of the Year. Scarpello was named the 2001 North Central Conference Coach of the Year after guiding UNO to its second consecutive NCC title. She has coached 8 All-Americans, 2 CoSida Academic All-Americans, 22 All-MIAA selections, 52 All-North Central Conference selections, and 10 Academic All-North Central Conference selections.

In 2013 **Elaine Sortino** completed her 34th season at Massachusetts, where she compiled a 1,267-483-6 (.705) record. She led the Minutewomen to 21 NCAA tournament appearances and three trips to the Women's College World Series. In 2013, Sortino was the third winningest active NCAA Division I coach and never had a losing season at UMass. She won 23 Atlantic 10 regular-season titles and 23 tournament championships.

Sortino posted a 218-134-1 record as the UMass volleyball coach from 1979 to 1986. A native of Yonkers, New York, and a 1971 graduate of Oneonta State University in New York, she earned her master's degree from the University of Bridgeport in 1973. Sortino was inducted into the NFCA Hall of Fame in 2004. Sortino was coach of a Honda Award winner, an Olympic gold medalist, 20 All-America selections, 15 A-10 Players of the Year, 18 A-10 Pitchers of the Year, 9 A-10 Rookies of the Year, and 129 all-conference selections.

Elaine Sortino passed away on Sunday, August 18, 2013, following a lengthy battle with cancer. She will be missed greatly by the softball community, and her legacy will always be remembered.

Bonnie Tholl began her 20th season as a member of the University of Michigan softball coaching staff in 2013, marking her 11th season as associate head coach. Tholl provided guidance for the 2005 Michigan team that shattered school records in nearly every offensive category en route to the program's first-ever national championship. Working closely with outfield players, she has overseen the development of 6 All-Americans, 27 All-Big Ten Conference selections, and a Big Ten Player of the Year. She has been a member of a Speedline/NFCA National Coaching Staff of the Year and is an eight-time recipient of the Great Lakes Region Coaching Staff of the Year.

As a collegiate player, Tholl started four seasons as shortstop at Michigan, becoming the only player in the conference history to earn All-Big Ten first-team honors four times. She was selected to the All-Mideast Regional team three times and was named to the Big Ten All-Decade (1982-92) softball team. Tholl also participated in the 1993 Olympic Sports Festival and played with numerous Amateur Softball Association squads. She was a member of the U.S. Pan American Games qualifying team that advanced to the 1995 Pan American Games and was named to the ASA All-America second team in 1992.

Beth Torina began her second season at the helm of the Louisiana State University softball program in 2013. In her inaugural campaign, she earned a 2012 Women's College World Series berth. The trip to the 2012 WCWS was the program's third overall appearance. That same year, her pitching stuff held a stifling 1.58 staff ERA, tied for second lowest in the SEC. She and her players also excel in community service, regularly visiting hospitals and schools in the Baton Rouge area and participating in the annual Strikeout Ovarian Cancer event.

Torina also serves as the head coach of the USSSA Florida Pride of the National Pro Fastpitch (NPF) League. Their roster features multiple Olympians, including Jessica Mendoza, Caitlin Lowe, and Natasha Watley. The Pride captured the Ringer Cup trophy in 2012 for being the league's regular-season champions, and they won the NPF championship in 2010. Before assuming her duties as head coach, Torina served as an assistant coach for two seasons under Florida head coach Tim Walton. She also coached the Florida International of the Sun Belt Conference for four seasons and is a two-time SBC Coach of the Year.

University of St. Thomas head coach **John Tschida** holds the record for highest win percentage in Division III at .850 (693-121). In nearly 20 years of coaching, he has won three national championships, and every team he has coached has been nationally ranked. Tschida is the only coach in NCAA softball to win national titles at two institutions. Tschida's players have earned 29 NCAA All-American honors, 43 Academic All-American honors, and 86 first-team all-conference awards. He was named Coach of the Year in 2005 and 2004, is a 10-time Minnesota Intercollegiate Athletic Conference Coach of the Year, and is a two-time inductee in the Saint Mary's University Hall of Fame.

As a player, Tschida competed in 17 ISC world tournaments, 18 ASA national tournaments, and 8 NAFA World Series. He was a member of the ISC all-world team in 2002, receiving the ISC world tournament Leading Hitter Award that year. Tschida was a five-time ASA Class A All-American and an ASA men's open All-American in 2006. A two-time NAFA all-world player, he was a member of the 2005 NAFA World Series open championship team. He played baseball for Saint Mary's University as an undergrad and was named an all-conference and all-region baseball player in 1990.

Head coach **Michelle Venturella** entered her fifth season in 2013 at the helm of the University of Illinois at Chicago softball program. In her years with the Flames, she has led the team to a regular-season championship in 2009 and the tournament crown in 2011. She has propelled 8 Flames members on 11 occasions to the all-conference team, and many of her players ranked first in the league for records including batting average, slugging percentage, on-base percentage, and runs scored. For her work with the Flames, Venturella was named the Horizon League Coach of the Year in 2009.

Before arriving at UIC, Venturella spent six seasons as the associate head coach at the University of Iowa, where she assisted the Hawkeyes to a record of 251-116, including five NCAA tournament appearances and a Big Ten regular-season and tournament title in 2003. She also served as an assistant coach at Northern Illinois during the 1996–97 season. As a collegiate athlete, Venturella was catcher for Indiana University, earning All-America honors and being named Big Ten Player of the Year. She also had a six-year stint on the U.S. national team, where she earned four gold medals at the world championships and Olympic Games.

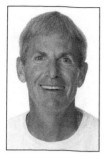

George Wares is the head softball coach at Central College in Iowa. He has the most wins in NCAA Division III history, with a record of 945-313-3 (.750) going into the 2013 season. Under his guidance, the Dutch have competed in 24 NCAA Division III tournaments, and these playoff teams have finished in the national top five 12 times. Wares has piloted the Dutch to four national championships and two national runner-up finishes, and the team has won or shared 11 Iowa Conference titles. He has been named Iowa Conference Coach of the Year 8 times, and he and his staff were named the NFCA Division III Coaching Staff of the Year in 2003 and Regional Staff of the Year in 2001.

Before joining Central College, Wares spent seven years as girls' softball coach at NESCO High School in Zearing, Iowa, posting a 214-94 record and piloting three squads to state tournament berths. He was named all-area Coach of the Year three times. Wares also served as a high school boys' basketball coach for 18 years and spent 4 seasons as an assistant men's basketball coach at Central College. Wares is in his second 3-year term on the NFCA Division III All-America Selection Committee, serving 2 years as chair. In 2007 he was inducted into the NFCA Hall of Fame.

In 2013 **Karen Weekly** entered her 17th season as a collegiate head softball coach and recently became the 58th head coach in NCAA softball history to tally 800 career victories. She is one of just 34 active head coaches in the nation with 800 or more wins. She and cohead coach Ralph Weekly have led the University of Tennessee softball program to five appearances in the Women's College World series in the last eight years, two SEC tournament championships, and the 2007 SEC regular-season championship. She has coached 25 Louisville Slugger/NFCA All-America selections, 39 Louisville Slugger/NFCA all-region players, and 46 All-SEC or All-SEC freshman picks. The UT coaching staff was named NFCA Southeast Region Coaching Staff of the Year in 2010 and 2012.

Before joining the Lady Vols, Weekly compiled a 223-97 record as the University of Tennessee Chattanooga's cohead coach. She played softball at Pacific Lutheran University (where she was an All-American), led NAIA hitters with a .440 batting average, and was named Female Athlete of the Year. She has also worked with USA Softball, most recently serving as a senior national team assistant coach in the summer of 2012.